Cognitive Behavior and Human Computer Interaction Based on Machine Learning Algorithm

Scrivener Publishing
100 Cummings Center, Suite 541J
Beverly, MA 01915-6106

Publishers at Scrivener
Martin Scrivener (martin@scrivenerpublishing.com)
Phillip Carmical (pcarmical@scrivenerpublishing.com)

Cognitive Behavior and Human Computer Interaction Based on Machine Learning Algorithm

Edited by

**Sandeep Kumar, Rohit Raja,
Shrikant Tiwari and Shilpa Rani**

Scrivener
Publishing

WILEY

This edition first published 2022 by John Wiley & Sons, Inc., 111 River Street, Hoboken, NJ 07030, USA and Scrivener Publishing LLC, 100 Cummings Center, Suite 541J, Beverly, MA 01915, USA
© 2022 Scrivener Publishing LLC
For more information about Scrivener publications please visit www.scrivenerpublishing.com.

Wiley Global Headquarters
111 River Street, Hoboken, NJ 07030, USA

For details of our global editorial offices, customer services, and more information about Wiley products visit us at www.wiley.com.

Limit of Liability/Disclaimer of Warranty
While the publisher and authors have used their best efforts in preparing this work, they make no representations or warranties with respect to the accuracy or completeness of the contents of this work and specifically disclaim all warranties, including without limitation any implied warranties of merchantability or fitness for a particular purpose. No warranty may be created or extended by sales representatives, written sales materials, or promotional statements for this work. The fact that an organization, website, or product is referred to in this work as a citation and/or potential source of further information does not mean that the publisher and authors endorse the information or services the organization, website, or product may provide or recommendations it may make. This work is sold with the understanding that the publisher is not engaged in rendering professional services. The advice and strategies contained herein may not be suitable for your situation. You should consult with a specialist where appropriate. Neither the publisher nor authors shall be liable for any loss of profit or any other commercial damages, including but not limited to special, incidental, consequential, or other damages. Further, readers should be aware that websites listed in this work may have changed or disappeared between when this work was written and when it is read.

Library of Congress Cataloging-in-Publication Data

ISBN 978-1-119-79160-7

Cover image: Pixabay.Com
Cover design by Russell Richardson

Contents

Preface

Human-computer interaction (HCI) is the academic discipline, which most of us think of as UI design, that focuses on how human beings and computers interact at ever-increasing levels of both complexity and simplicity. Because of the importance of the subject, this book aims to provide more relevant information that will be useful to students, academics, and researchers in the industry who wish to know more about its real-time application. In addition to providing content on theory, cognition, design, evaluation, and user diversity, this book also explains the underlying causes of the cognitive, social and organizational problems typically devoted to descriptions of rehabilitation methods for specific cognitive processes. Also described are the new modeling algorithms accessible to cognitive scientists from a variety of different areas. Advances in HCI involve interdisciplinary research, the results of which are published in theoretical and applied articles covering a broad spectrum of interactive systems. Therefore, this book is inherently interdisciplinary and publishes original research in computing, engineering, artificial intelligence, psychology, linguistics, and social and system organization as applied to the design, implementation, application, analysis, and evaluation of interactive systems. Since machine learning research has already been carried out for a decade at the international level in various applications, the new learning approach is mainly used in machine learning-based cognitive applications. Since this will direct the future research of scientists and researchers working in neuroscience, neuroimaging, machine learning-based brain mapping and modeling, etc., this book highlights the framework of a novel robust method for advanced cross-industry HCI technologies. These implementation strategies and future research directions will meet the design and application requirements of several modern and real-time applications for a long time to come. Therefore, this book will be a better choice than most available books that were published a long time ago, and hence seldom elaborate on the current advancements necessary for cognitive behavior and HCI algorithms. Included in the book are:

- A review of the state-of-the-art in cognitive behavior and HCI processing models, methods, techniques, etc.
- A review and description of the learning methods in HCI.
- The new techniques and applications in cognitive behavior along with their practical implementation.
- The existing and emerging image challenges and opportunities in the cognitive behavior and HCI field.
- How to promote mutual understanding and networking among researchers in different disciplines.
- The facilitation of future research development and collaborations.
- Real-time applications.

To conclude, we would like to express our appreciation to all of the contributing authors who helped us tremendously with their contributions, time, critical thoughts, and suggestions to put together this peer-reviewed edited volume. The editors are also thankful to Scrivener Publishing and its team members for the opportunity to publish this volume. Lastly, we thank our family members for their love, support, encouragement, and patience during the entire period of this work.

Sandeep Kumar
Rohit Raja
Shrikant Tiwari
Shilpa Rani
October 2021

Cognitive Behavior: Different Human-Computer Interaction Types

S. Venkata Achyuth Rao[1]*, Sandeep Kumar[2]
and GVRK Acharyulu[3]

[1]CSE, SIET, Hyderabad, Telangana, India
[2]Computer Science and Engineering Department, Koneru Lakshmaiah Education
Foundation, Vaddeswaram, Andra Pradesh, India
[3]Operations & Supply Chain, MBA (Healthcare & Hospital Management),
School of Management Studies, University of Hyderabad, Telangana, India

Abstract

Cognitive behavior plays a significant and strategic role in human-computer interaction devices that are deployed nowadays, with artificial intelligence, deep learning, and machine learning computing techniques. User experience is the crucial factor of any successful interacting device between machine and human. The idea of providing a HCUIMS is to create interfaces in terms of the bottom level of any organization as Decision Processing User Interacting Device System (DPUIDS), next at middle level management, Decision Support User Interacting Device Systems (DSUIDS), lastly at executive level, Management Information User Interacting Device System (MIUIDS), where decisions can take at uncertainty at various catastrophic situations. Here are specific gaps demonstrated in the various user's processes in communicating with computers and that cognitive modeling is useful in the inception phase to evolve the design and provide training.

This is provided with the fulfillment of various interactive devices like Individual Intelligences Interactions (I3), Artificial and Individual Intelligences Interaction (AI3), Brain-Computer Interaction (BCI), and Individual Interactions through Computers (I2C) in a playful manner to meet the corporate challenges in all stakeholders of various domains with better user experience.

*Corresponding author: drsvarao@gmail.com

Sandeep Kumar, Rohit Raja, Shrikant Tiwari and Shilpa Rani (eds.) Cognitive Behavior and Human Computer Interaction Based on Machine Learning Algorithm, (1–22) © 2022 Scrivener Publishing LLC

Keywords: Cognitive behavior, user experience, interacting devices, modeling, intelligence

1.1 Introduction: Cognitive Models and Human-Computer User Interface Management Systems

Cognitive models are useful in assessing to make predictions ease at top-level management systems in several aspects or many variables to interact and provide the approximate behavioral aspects observed in various experimental empirical studies. In a real-world lifetime situation, many factors are influenced to produce outcome reports as a behavioral analysis report. This is done neural processing data with the representation of patterns. These models outcome in terms of processes and products interact with various people which are shown in the empirical experiments. These below are necessary tools for psychologists to interact with various designers who care about cognitive models. These models for HCI have an adequate different goal to use necessary interfaces better for users. In general, there are at least three cognitive models in service as a general goal [1].

- Interactive user behavioral predicting systems
- Adaptive interaction observatory changing systems
- Group interaction model building systems

1.1.1 Interactive User Behavior Predicting Systems

Human behavior predicting system interface is designed and deployed as the interaction and communication between users and a machine, an automatic dynamic, versatile system, through a user-machine interface [2]. There are strongly related real-world assumptions, and aspects are there to distinguish the domain of user-machine automatic dynamic, versatile systems, and user-computer interaction. For 50 years onward, the investigations on research in this domain are going on with different interactive human predicting systems that are evolved with the necessary propagated embedded events via a hardware and software interaction built-in displays. The best and emerging ambient designs of user interaction automatic predicting system applications have a right market place and gain values vertically in all the verticals for many products and services in various sectors like medical, transportation, education, games, and entertainment, which are the needs of the industry [3].

1.1.2 Adaptive Interaction Observatory Changing Systems

An adaptive interactive observatory system acquires its psychological aspects to the independent user based on inferences of the user prototype acquisition and reports involving activity in learning, training, inference, or necessary constraints of the decision process. The primary and needful goal of adaptive interaction observatory changing system interfacing adaptation is to consider unique perceptual or physical impairments of individual users; it allowed them to use a dynamic system more flexibly, efficiently, with minimal errors and with less frustration. An adaptive interaction observatory system interface is an embedded software artifact that improves its functionality to interact with an individual user by prototype model, thereby constructing a user model based on partial psychological considerable experience with that user [4].

As there are widespread of www, internet, and gopher services among the population day by day, more sophisticated variety of softwares, emerging technologies involve hardware events, gadgets, widgets, and events that are more and more highly interactive and responsive. Only limited early individual novice people are doing programs on punch cards and submitting late nights and overnight jobs, and subsequently time-sharing systems and debug monitors, text editors have become slower and slower and depend on multiple cores and moving forward to parallel processing. The latest emerging operating systems and real-time operating systems support various interactive software like what you see and what you get. The editor system software is too high for interactive computer games, most efficient and eminent embedded systems, automotive responsive, interactive, and adaptive conservative systems in layered interactive graphical user interfaces, and such subscribers and listeners are the key roles of adaptive interaction observatory changing systems. Such systems have been treated as an essential part of any business and academic lives with a trillion people depend on them to move toward their daily lives. Most academic work on machine learning still focuses on refining techniques and humiliating the steps that may happen at foreseen and after their invocation. Indeed, most investigations, conferences, workshops, and research interests, especially media and entertainment, virtual reality, simulation, modeling, and design, still emphasize differences between broader areas of learning methods. Eventually, evidenced by the decision-tree induction, the design analysis of algorithms, case-based reasoning methods, and statistical and probabilistic schemes often produce very similar results [5].

1.1.3   Group Interaction Model Building Systems

This chapter's main objective is to describe the existing cognitive framework activities on group modeling information systems using synergy responsive dynamics. Such information systems are very few and necessary to be applied in hybrid organizations in order to support to increase in a wide range of business expansion and to take their strategic decisions. In this cognitive group interaction model building theory, the vital methodological dynamics were first located under the individual user interactions and then classified to allow an intensive idea to be given as a requirement analysis report for group activity prototype being a building system consideration [6]. The outcome of this brainstorming dynamics indicates the existing methods to propose a global view of interaction model systems are very rare. Also, three complex issues are needed to discuss: the inception of knowing the users' knowledge, the interaction establishment of a consensus among users, and the main aspects of providing necessary facilitation.

A group interaction model building system is a dynamic system that is characterized by the following:

1. The responsive nature and strong interactions among the actors of the group;
2. An integration exists with necessary interactions, interrelations, and a strong dependency together;
3. An internal abstractive complex cohesiveness is subjected to their feedback; and
4. Fuzziness of the delayed behavioral reactions among the groups to assess or predict.

An organized framework is described here as a generalization of any organized approach, providing inference process and cohesive interactions in the detailed guidelines related to any aspect of group interaction model building. This analysis aims to obtain a broad view of a global vision of investigating the research that applied group interaction modeling systems. Using system dynamics allows drawing keenness to the lack of advanced interactive device management aspects to support the relating behavior aspects.

The group modeling system approach's dynamic behavior is characterized below, emphasizing group interaction model systems.

The modeling process using two types of information systems [7]:

1. Modeling information systems versus group interaction model information systems.
2. Expert modeling systems versus team expert modeling information systems.

1.1.4 Human-Computer User Interface Management Systems

Human-Computer User Interface (HCUI) design mainly emphasizes foreseeing what computer interaction users need to do and approve that the human-computer interface has several elements that are flexible and easy to know, view, navigate, update, manage and modify, and use to provide facilitation in the form of events and widgets. HCUI accomplishes the related features from interpreting, layout design, interaction design, visual design, and information architecture.

A HCUIMS (HCUI Management System) is treated as not as a system but rather an interactive software architecture (an HCUIMS is also called a HCUI Architecture) "in which the design, deployment of various applications' user interface is precise and clearly distinguished from that of other applications' underlying its functionality." Such an eminent division's cohesive objective is to enhance the maintenance ease and adaptability with other softwares. Most of the Modern HCUIMS Architectures are designed with integrated development environments. With the help of abstraction of a user interface from the applications logic, syntax, and semantics, the code generation is better supported for customization. Even these architectures have been proven and useful with a high degree of interaction and had semantic feedback at manipulating interfacing boundaries between applications and HCUIs are difficult or impossible to maintain [8].

1.1.5 Different Types of Human-Computer User Interfaces

1. Interface for Command Line
2. Interface for Menu Driven
3. Interface for Touch-Screen Driven
4. Interface for Graphical User Purpose
5. Interface for Event-Driven Purpose
6. Interface for Sensor-Based Users
7. Interface for Voice-Based Users
8. Interface for Natural Language Users

9. Interface for Form-Based Users
10. Interface for Gesture Driven Users
11. Interface for Mobile Users
12. Interface for Data Base Users
13. Interface for VR Design

1.1.6   The Role of User Interface Management Systems

User interface management system architecture's role is broader than a narrow concern concerning hardware, embedded system software applications, design analysis and algorithms, software procedures, packages, distributed servers, and other programs. The majority of domains with respective disciplines are contributed widely to the discipline of management informative systems, including the following:

1. Traditional ancestor science and technology related disciplines such as functional forms, lambda expressions, predicative calculus, systems theory, operation research, and econometrics;
2. Technology such as electronics, information technology, bioinformatics, nano technology, and computer science;
3. Emerging technologies like security management studies that include cognitive networking, link taping, a man-in-the-middle attack, brute force, cross-site request forgery, and doom-based attack; and
4. Social engineering and behavioral theory of ergonomics, linguistics, etc.

User interface management systems development is exceptionally different because the Information Systems are to be continued adequate modeling and working staff need to serve an efficient role in the enterprise management system organizations [9]. The roles and responsibilities needed to be performed efficiently as given below. Some of them are discussed below.

1. Information system programmers and system analysts need to spare longer to interact with stakeholders individually or group-wise to elicit more useful information to design and

evolve the system interaction meaningful and rapid responsive purpose.

2. Determine what information is useful to take decision-making in uncertain times is a challenging task. For this, information system staff forcing to spare longer time and a great deal to interact with system users.

3. Development and deployment approaches likely building prototyping models are based on either rapid application development model feedback or iterative, incremental feedback from connected users on interaction efficiency concerning their needs.

4. The resultant outcome in the form of Information is visualized as an essential asset by executive information system management people at the top-level directors.

5. The visualized information systems are displayed, not only at the given organizations but also use or deployed in many organizations, as it follows strategically rather than just had an operational role of the given organization.

6. If an uncertain condition, catastrophic, or pandemic environment propagates in uncertainty to take decisions at top-level management, these systems allowed you to give an optional decision-making to be implemented to interactive among connected users.

1.1.7   Basic Cognitive Behavioral Elements of Human-Computer User Interface Management Systems

HCUIMS is more than just the user interface management system interface. There are a gap and significant difference between the user interface and a computer interaction system. As the above discussed, finally, what we consider the HCUIMS to be broad includes any interfaces among users (developers and users) that may require the systems till the life. Hence, operational research scientists, investigators of system development, implementation, acceptance, use, and impact lot in management personnel's decision-making, capture broad HCI issues and concerns. In a nutshell, the broad view of human interaction activities has five components among them: human (users), technology (H/W, S/W, and other related), interaction (communication), task (to accomplish), and context (domain-based).

Finally, from an organizational point of view, there are four essential contexts identified; these are seen in Figure 1.1 [10]:

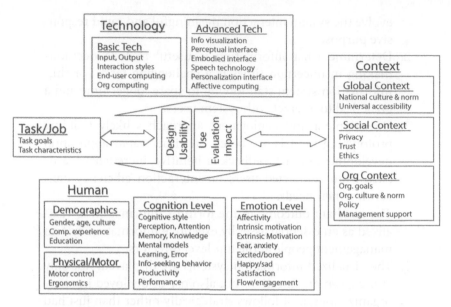

Figure 1.1 Cognitive behavioral elements of broad view of human-computer interface in management [10].

- Organizational context,
- Technology context,
- Social context,
- Global context.

When designing your interface in any one of the above contexts, it should be consistent and predictable in the user choice of interacting elements. Initially, the experts need to train them to use the functionality, operation of various events; if whether they are aware of it or not, users must have to be trained; once they become familiar with elements; if they act in a certain way, they need to adopt those elements when appropriate will help to accomplish with efficiently in utmost satisfaction.

Interface elements include but are not limited to the following:

- Technology and advanced technology: input, output, information, etc.
- Task/job: task goals and task characters
- Human: Demographics, physical/motor, cognitional level, and emotional level

- Context: Organizational context, technology context, social context, and global context.

However, design *usability* is rapidly increasing day by day and refer primarily to the ease with connecting users accomplish their intended tasks and relatively closely associated with the use of evaluation impact calculated with the usability testing. Therefore, many perceive usability as a rather tactical aspect of any human-computer interface management system product design: the global context, social context, technology context, and organizational context. However, usability may not complete with the encompassment of all UI elements relating to ease of use. User interface elements' outcome gives out things like flexibility, adaptability, compatibility and can ease to learn and recognize information in a possible manner and economic affordability also comes into this category [10].

1.2   Cognitive Modeling: Decision Processing User Interacting Device System (DPUIDS)

Cognitive modeling is helpful in the decision processing systems through user interface device systems. Data science and behavioral sciences are viewed as significant parts of any decision making. It gives us a powerful new tool and these are suppressing tedious tasks to make it as simple by analytic indication through behavior changes and represent their consequences day by day and presented to their visuals. Machine learning and data science studies help predict future outcomes by using analytics from widespread large data sets to assess the desired outcomes to accomplish personalized behavioral interventions. This may not be a concern for most businesses' aspects; some of the programs are adequate and applicable to everyday issues. Through cognitive behavior assessment, the investigators and researchers are designed new algorithms to recognize the circumstances around their environments and subsequently change the negative energy to positive energy to bring out more outcomes to meet the predicted outcome. It allows us to quickly do basic arithmetic and read emotional intelligence, body language, postures and gestures, and complete sentences.

1.2.1   Cognitive Modeling Automation of Decision Process Interactive Device Example

For a typical discussion, if anyone of the person, energy is low from any number of tasks or processes or over successive or meetings or engaging intensive concentration, his or her mental energy will be going to be decreased to the point that point the automatic system needs to take over the carry out next task. Where cognitive decision processing user interface device systems are designed and developed with algorithmic prediction, there can begin to identify policymakers' characteristics, factors, and like benefit and appropriately target the interacting people.

The paramedical structure describes the business intelligence user community decision processing system. Data analytics is a process of monitoring, the inception of inspection, cleaning of data like imbalances, identifying skewness, external noise, transforming the data and information through online analytical process and online transaction process, and modeling data to extract useful information through supporting decision-making. Data analysis process has multiple facets and strategic approaches, encompassing diverse techniques under a variety of cubes, names, under a different business, science, and social science domains. Suppose a typical user does not have the expertise or the resources to employ dedicated information technology resources to develop reports, tools, or customization applications. He or she can take the help of software tools, and the visualization of events will help make decisions. In this respect, automatic interactive visualizations are helped on behalf of users.

One aspect of decision processing user interaction device systems is a collection of integrated embodiments of events. Those who respond to a system and collect interactive visualizations methods include receiving a selection of required data through the report processing generation system. Integrated data consists of database storage systems and their active listening interfaces are given between the source senders to the received listener. Those storage databases and respective interfacing devices invoke the necessary methods, automatically generated functional activity then accomplish the user tasks. They are easy to determine an associated visualization for the selected data based on heuristics; it is said that a set of rules is used to determine the associated visualization most appropriately for interacting decision process systems [12].

Decision processing and interacting device systems identify complex data as more accessible, understandable, and usable. These systems are used in the domains like business, organizations, and various endeavors, and massive amounts of data are being collected, processed, and stored. This trend is growing exponentially with the adoption of the internet, intranet, advancing networking technologies, powerful mobile devices, wearable devices, and the like many vast device's interconnectivity. The world makes it into a Global village and most of the devices are connected in the Internet of Things (IoT) and through Sensor Networks. The applications of the

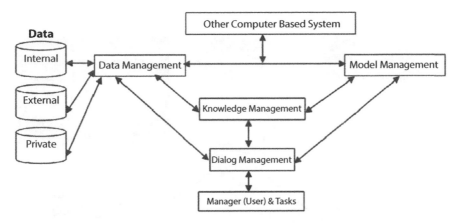

Figure 1.2 Decision processing system user interface device management as external customer [13].

interactive device systems are one of the sets of cognitive-behavioral and neural network-related machine learning, deep learning and type of convolutional networks, and recurrent neural networks that are running an enterprise, such as without limitation, payrolls, inventory, marketing, sales and distribution, vendor management, accounting, supply chain management, and resource planning applications (Figure 1.2) [13].

1.2.2 Cognitive Modeling Process in the Visualization Decision Processing User Interactive Device System

Cognitive models are useful artifacts used to understand a better way to accomplish a real-world object task in our world. In the context of knowledge representation and automated reasoning. The use of visualization tools is used to create useful patterns in the extraction of knowledge.

The important modeling visualization tools are described below with their functionality and objective role of decision processing interaction role in various devices that are shown in the below diagram (Figure 1.3) [15].

The flow chart description is step by step.

1. Views to mental model, thereby computing sensory input devices to visualize data to discover useful information. Understand and justify.
2. A collection of methods, procedures, algorithms, and learning methods on the data preprocessing, interpretation, visualization, storage, analysis, and transformation as compared to desired outcomes.

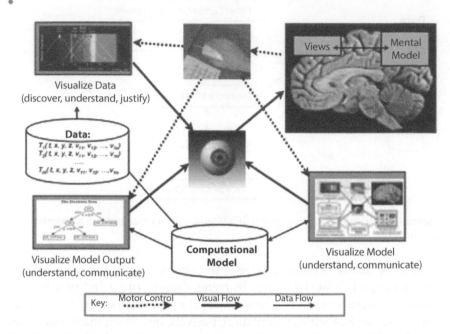

Figure 1.3 Cognitive modeling process in the visualization decision processing user interacting device system [15].

3. Visualize model outputs to understand and communicate the necessary computational models. Finally, the visualization model has been resultant as information.

1.3   Cognitive Modeling: Decision Support User Interactive Device Systems (DSUIDS)

Cognitive models are used to support user interactive device systems in the form of computer programs, applications, algorithms, events, and sensors or devices or components or controls or tools that simulate human performance based on cognitive skills. They are useful through human-computer interaction to assist users in predicting tasks and finding meaningful and useful patterns. If these models are evolved through emerging design methodologies compared with historical interfaces, excellent and strange results are produced with high interactive graphical visualization tools. This strategic approach is abstracted and encapsulated as a yield of the cognitive model decision supported interface device, analogous to and based on a Cognitive Model Decision Support User Interface Management

System (DPUIMS). The following are models and structural representation of interactive management interactive device system. The systems will help exploit the synergy between the branches, and interdisciplinary domain areas have interactions among the users [15].

1.3.1   The Core Artifacts of the Cognitive Modeling of User Interaction

There are various artifacts helped as tools to provide the development of interaction among user interfaces. Some tools can be designed and deployed through a task simulation mechanism in the development of cognitive models. There is no other linkage mechanism that may support and interpret cognitive models to the wide range of interfaces in a large organization's decision support systems (Table 1.1).

For an initial consideration for an Integration purpose, the following is featured process [16]:

1. Creation of computer user interface tools.
2. Task simulation involvement mechanism in a model eye during run-time is necessary interaction as per the model.
3. Need communication mechanism to be passed with information in the cognitive model and simulation of the task.

1.3.2   Supporting Cognitive Model for Interaction Decision Supportive Mechanism

Cognitive decision supportive mechanism implementation is based on essential elements; they are composed with the cognitive architecture via a cognitive modeling tool, and then communication mechanism combined

Table 1.1 The core artifacts provided at the cognitive modeling of user interaction [16].

Artifact	Purpose
Cognitive model	It provides the simulation of the cognitive performance and user's behavior to perform the task.
Task simulation	It provides the task for the cognitive model. Also, the user interface will be used in the model.
Linkage mechanism	It provides the pathway between the model and simulation to communicate for human perception and action. It simulates human perception and action.

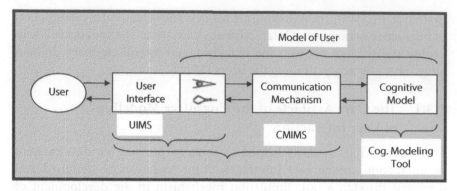

Figure 1.4 Supporting cognitive model for the interaction of decision supportive mechanism [16].

with the hand and eye is implemented, thereby find the respective HCUI to interact with users. This environment model with task simulation tools effectively runs on heterogeneous and homogeneous environments (operating systems, real-time operating systems, various servers and clients, multiple computers, databases, etc.). It is finally integrated with the user interaction management system interface and computer-based management interaction management systems.

Supporting cognitive model (Figure 1.4) for interaction of decision supportive architecture is embodied with the following three necessary steps.

The initial step to provide the model with supporting decision-making capabilities for perception and action among human-computer interaction with the task simulation is to extend the necessary cognitive tools as architecture to become a complete model by adding an eye with a simulated hand.

In the second step of the cognitive model to the simulation, the simulated eye and hand observations are to be recorded, and that information is to pass into the cognitive model for necessary actions.

The model's final step is categorized into two specific parts as simulated eye and hand implemented in that environment as the simulation by using necessary simulation tools, whereas the cognitive model can be separated. Here, there occurs a communication mechanism between two such separated specific parts as in the form of interaction done simulated eye and hand with cognitive modeling [16].

1.3.3 Representational Uses of Cognitive Modeling for Decision Support User Interactive Device Systems

Some of the representations in cognitive modeling topics are described with descriptions in the following diagram [17].

Table 1.2 Representational uses of cognitive modeling for decision support user interactive device systems [17].

Topic	Representational expectations	Comments
Model understand the context	Objectives in the form of sentential statements, to verify the relationship, data discovery, and investigation of data. To high-level requirements for visualization model or architecture. The dominant type of visualization is based on data analysis and exploration.	The ambiguity possible with sentential representations can be an advantage without ambiguity.
Model structure definition	The relationship provided in model supportability through data analysis, visualization of the model, decomposition of the problem, and variable specifications. The dominant type of visualization model may be computed probably with the help of given fullest resources utilization.	The activity usually received total resources what we thought was the significant portion. Visual tools range from "Balloons and Strings" representation of relatedness" to tables of storage format, spreadsheets, and visual framework of activities.
Realization of the model	Identification of solution with the help of a more concrete model as adequate parameter estimation. The dominant visualization type is to be built by continuing the suitable model at various levels of hierarchy.	Supports for the hierarchical problem decomposition into chunks at various levels of visualization.

(Continued)

Table 1.2 Representational uses of cognitive modeling for decision support user interactive device systems [17]. (*Continued*)

Topic	Representational expectations	Comments
Assessment of the model	Provided correctness, feasibility, and acceptability in validation of the model.	The stakeholder target is justified through context given by the right modeler with colleagues, customers, and users.
Implementation of the model	The suitable model is implemented and managed its transmission into active usage.	Completeness of visualization to assist marketing and training. Good speed and benefits concerning turnover in personals the number of new users of the model.

- Understand model context
- Define structural model
- Realization of the model
- Assessment of the model
- Model implementation

1.4   Cognitive Modeling: Management Information User Interactive Device System (MIUIDS)

Today, all industry stakeholders consider the different interfaces since it provides feedback on a new product's effectiveness in real life. However, one must not forget the adoption of interface communication from character user interface data to voice user interface information. The information is a key to the process and storage of any organization. The stakeholder, mainly customer experience, is immediate valuable feedback and product safety and low maintenance are complemented strategically designed with the necessary management user interactive device system. The essential elements of the management user interactive device system are described with the necessary diagram (Figure 1.5).

- Memory
- Encoding
- Storage
- Retrieval

In comparisons of actual with predicted performance, bars for actual performance are always wider. Comments are added to the displays to explain abnormal conditions, explain graphic depictions, reference related displays, and inform pending changes. For example, a display may show that signups may be less than three as forecasted. However, the staff member responsible for the display knows that a down payment from Peru for three aircraft is an end route and adds this information as a comment on the display. Without

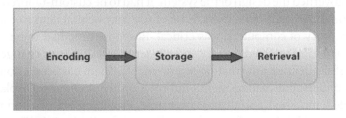

Figure 1.5 Basic elements of management information user interactive device system.

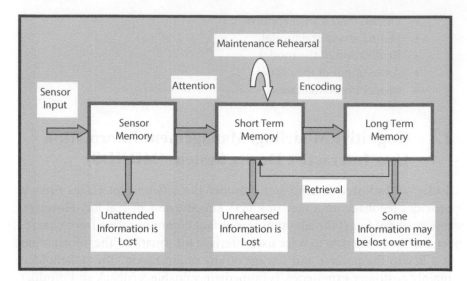

Figure 1.6 Model of memory, information passes through distinct stages in order for it to be stored in long-term memory.

added comments, situations can arise, referred to as "paper tigers", because they appear to require managerial attention though they do not. The MIDS staff believes that "transmitting data is not the same as conveying information" [8]. The displays have been created with the executives' critical success factors in mind. Some of the measures, such as profits and aircrafts sold, are obvious. Other measures, such as employee participation in company-sponsored programs, are less obvious and reflect the MIDS staff's efforts to understand and accommodate the executives' information needs fully.

Keys to the success of MIDS descriptions of successful systems are useful to people responsible for conceptualizing, approving, and developing similar systems. Perhaps even more critical are insights about what makes a system a success. A committed senior executive sponsor wanted a system like MIDS, committed the necessary resources, participated in its creation, and encouraged its use by others. It carefully defined system requirements. Several considerations governed the design of the system. It had to be custom-tailored to meet the information needs of its users. Ease of use, an essential item to executives who were wary of computers, was critical. Response time had to be fast. The displays had to be updated quickly and efficiently as conditions changed. They have carefully defined information requirements. There has been a continuing effort to understand management's information requirements. Displays have been added, modified, and deleted over time. Providing information relevant to management has been of paramount importance (Figure 1.6). The staff that developed the operated and evolved MIDS combines information systems skills and functional area knowledge. The computer analysts are responsible for the system's technical aspects, while the information analysts are responsible for providing the information needed by management. This latter responsibility demands that the information analysts know the business and maintain close contact with information sources and users [18].

The initial version of MIDS successfully addressed the company president's most critical information needs and strengthened his support for the system. There is little doubt that developing a fully integrated system for a full complement of users would have substantial delays and less enthusiasm for the system.

Careful computer hardware and software selection is essential in this model. The decision to proceed with MIDS development was made when the right color terminals at reasonable prices became available. At that time, graphics software was very limited, and it was necessary to develop the software for MIDS in-house. MIDS development could have been postponed until hardware and software with improved performance at reduced cost appeared, but this decision would have delayed providing management with the information needed. Also affecting the hardware selection was the organization's existing hardware and the need to integrate MIDS into the overall computing architecture. While it is believed that excellent hardware and software decisions have been made for MIDS, different circumstances at other firms may lead to different hardware and software configurations. Future plans for MIDS continues to evolve along the lines mentioned previously. Improvements in display graphics are also planned through the use of a video camera with screen digitizing capabilities. Several other enhancements are also projected. A future version of MIDS may automatically present variance reports when actual conditions deviate by more than user-defined levels. Audio output may supplement what is presented by the displays. The system may contain artificial intelligence components. There may be a large screen projection of MIDS displays with better resolution than is currently available. The overriding objective is to provide Lockheed Georgia management with the information they need to effectively and efficiently carry out their job responsibilities.

1.5   Cognitive Modeling: Environment Role With User Interactive Device Systems

Environment plays a crucial role in interacting with various kinds of interactive device systems. Behind this, there are four "E's" that motivate the theories and assumptions of cognition modeling [19]; these are mainly the following:

- Embodied,
- Embedded,
- Extended, and
- Enactive.

So, various interactive devices like Individual Intelligences Interactions (I3), Artificial and Individual Intelligences Interaction (AI3), Brain-Computer Interaction (BCI), and Individual Interactions through Computers (I2C) in a playful manner are provided to meet the corporate challenges in all stakeholders of various domains with better user experience.

1.6   Conclusion and Scope

Cognitive modeling plays a significant and strategic role in human-computer interaction devices deployed these days and in the future, with artificial intelligence, deep learning, and machine learning computing techniques. Data science and data analytics provided an accurate visualization analysis with customer feedback experiences to know the expeditions of the users with their interactions of the above interactive devices. User experience is the crucial factor of any successful interacting device between machine and human because decisions can be uncertain due to various situations. One of the key strengths of the cognitive model interactive device system is its many practical applications. It is used in the field experiment to investigate the effects of cognitive interviewing techniques training on detectives' performance in eyewitness interviews. This means that studies taking the cognitive approach are somewhat scientific and have good internal validity in the long future deterministic decision-making in all the levels of management decisions.

References

1. Ritter, F.E., Baxter, G.D., Gary, R.M., Supporting Cognitive Models as Users. *ACM Trans. Comput.-Hum. Interact.*, 7, 2, 141–173, June 2000.
2. Boden, M.A., *Artificial Intelligence, A Volume in Handbook of Perception and Cognition*, School of Cognitive and Computing Science University of Sussex Brighton, England, Elsevier Inc. Book, 1996.

3. Bernd, Liepert, T., Hahn, A.B., Vasilyeva, A., *An AI PPP A focal point for collaboration on Artificial Intelligence, Data and Robotics, Second Consultation Release, September 2019.*

4. Sanders, N., A Balanced Perspective on Prediction and Inference for Data Science in Industry. *Harv. Data Sci. Rev.*, 1.1, 1–29, Summer 2019, Sep 18, 2019.

5. Rasta, P., *A Planning Guide - Mariana Patra, Information and Communication Technologies in Teacher Education,* The University of Texas at Austin (USA), Division of Higher Education UNESCO 7, place de Fontenay 75352 Paris 07 SP, France, 1998.

6. Pew, R.W. and Mayor, A.S., *Committee on Human-System Design Support for Changing Technology,* National Research Council of the National Academies, The National Academies Press, Washington, D.C., April 1991.

7. Shawn, T., Järvenpää, S., Lee, A.S. (Eds.), Process Models in Information Systems, in: *Information Systems and Qualitative Research,* © Springer Science Business Media Dordrecht, University of Texas at Austin, USA, 1997.

8. Alvarez-Cores, V., Zarate, V., Ramirez Uresis, J.A., Zayas, B.E., Current Challenges and Applications for Adaptive User Interfaces, in: Human–Computer Interaction, I. Maurtua (Ed.), pp. 13–30, IntechOpen, Rijeka, Croatia, 2009.

9. Karim, A.J., the significance of management information systems for enhancing strategic and tactical planning. *J. Inf. Syst. Technol. Manage. (Online)*, 8, 2, 459–470, São Paulo 2011.

10. Zhang, P. and Galleta, D., *Human–Computer Interaction and Management Information Systems: Foundations,* 2006.

11. Samson, A., *an introduction to Behavioral Economics, Guide Behavioral Economics Guide,* Behavioral Science Solutions Ltd and the London School of Economics, 2014.

12. Grosz, A.E., Lai, A.J.F., Schultz, D. et al., Methods and systems for background uploading of media files for improved user experience in production of media-based products, US Patent US 8,799,829 B2, assigned to Interactive Memories, Inc., 2014.

13. Filippos, L. and Mastriano, O., Managerial Decision Support Making in Economic Systems Based on Cognitive Modeling. *Int. J. Eng. Technol.*, 7, 4.3, 588–592, 2018.

14. Berna, I., Stefan, K., Pawed, M. *et al., Building Information Modelling,* Construction Managers' Library, Erasmus, Iceland, Great Britain, 2015.

15. Chen, A., Starke, S.D., Baber, C. *et al.,* A Cognitive Model of How People Make Decisions Through Interaction with Visual Displays School of Psychology. *ACM proceedings of the HCI Conference on human factors in computing systems,* May 2017, pp. 1205–1216.

16. Ritter, F.E., Baxter, G.D. *et al.,* User interface evaluation: How cognitive models can help, in: *Human-computer interaction in the new millennium,* J. Carroll (Ed.), pp. 125–147, Addison-Wesley, Reading, MA, 2001.

17. Paschal, M.F. and Stary, C., The Role of Cognitive Modeling for User Interface Design Representations: An Epistemological Analysis of Knowledge Engineering in the Context of Human-Computer Interaction. *Mind. Mach.*, 8, 203–236, 1998.

18. Houdashelt L, G., Marietta, C.D., Watson, H.J. *et al.*, The Management Information and Decision Support (MIDS) System at Lockheed- Georgia, Executive Information System. *MIS Quart.*, 5, 1–18, March 1998.

19. Ward, D. and Stapleton, M., *Es are good Cognition as enacted, embodied, embedded, affective and extended*, School of Philosophy, Psychology and Language Sciences, University of Edinburgh, Edinburgh, Scotland, United Kingdom, May 2016.

20. Peerce, J., Rogers, Y., Sharp, H., *Interaction design: beyond human- computer interaction*, John Wiley & Sons, Inc, Southern Gate, Chichester, West Sussex, UK, 2002.

21. Bernard, C., Paris-Dauphine *et al.*, Group Model Building Using System Dynamics: An Analysis of Methodological Frameworks, Control Systems, Robotics, And Automation, in: *Human-Machine Interaction*, vol. xxi.

22. Grayed, J.D., Dual Process Theories in Behavioral Economics and Neuro economics: A Critical Review. *Rev. Philos. Psychol.*, 11, 105–136, 2020.

Classification of HCI and Issues and Challenges in Smart Home HCI Implementation

Pramod Vishwakarma[1]*, Vijay Kumar Soni[1], Gaurav Srivastav[1]
and Abhishek Jain[2]

[1]Department of AIT-CSE, Chandigarh University, Mohali (SAS Nagar), India
[2]Department of Computer Science, Roorkee Institute of Technology, Roorkee, India

Abstract

Human-Computer Interaction (HCI) implies an association with humans or individuals with computer or machine. Human-computer cooperation is likewise called as computer-human connection or CHI. HCI is the arranging, planning, and improving human-computer gadgets, predominantly interface of the computer, page, ATM interface, portable interface, etc. The principle point of HCI is to improve the cooperation among utilization and machine or processing association. HCI additionally treated plan and assessed execution of computer screen or other UI. This article manages the part of HCI, its job, and current guidelines. The paper likewise informs us concerning the human gadget cooperation.

Keywords: Human-Computer-Interaction, human cooperation, design, ease of use, ease of use designing, information science, user amicability, MMI, CHI

2.1 Introduction

Computer innovation is persistently advancing. New processors, gadgets, and applications are arising every day. Besides, electronic gadgets, similar

---

Corresponding author: pramod.e9758@cumail.in

Sandeep Kumar, Rohit Raja, Shrikant Tiwari and Shilpa Rani (eds.) Cognitive Behavior and Human Computer Interaction Based on Machine Learning Algorithm, (23–62) © 2022 Scrivener Publishing LLC

to computers, portable telephones, tablets, PDAs, and GPSs, are utilized by more individuals and with new purposes such that they are practically fundamental in our lives. When we talk about computers or then again innovation and how individuals use it, we have unmistakably discussed collaboration. Human-Computer Interaction (HCI) includes the investigation, arranging, and plan of the communication among clients and computers. Communication among clients and computers happens at the UI, which incorporates both programming and equipment. The interface is the space where communication among people and machines happens and the achievement or disappointment of an item depends significantly on its interface. There have been changes in how items work, look, act, and respond to individuals who use them. Through years ago, numerous improvements had occurred here, a large number of them identified with equipment and new gadgets for communication, yet besides in the field of analogies, ideal models, cooperation's styles, guidelines, and so on. Progress in gadget improvement has changed cooperation techniques like mice and consoles to new advancements that allow clients to collaborate in a more available way without extensive learning and transformation. From the old info orders style through direct control or enlarged reality, numerous enhancements had changed how we associate with innovation from the old and hefty monochrome screens to current smart phones. However, this transformation has not been completed at this point. Luckily, there are likewise numerous regions where we can improve to make the association cycle simpler, more agreeable, and better for the last client. All in all, numerous difficulties can be refined in the field of human-computer association. A house is one of the fundamental components of present-day life. Today, the home's customary idea has been advanced to be more brilliant and broadened by present-day data innovation. The smart home was first referenced in the 1990s [38] and as indicated by the Smart Home Association, the Smart Home is "the mix of innovation and administrations through home systems administration for a superior nature of living" [43]. The brilliant home plan depends on dissecting the necessities for present-day living, which incorporate development, comfort, Internet correspondence, advanced gadgets, and mechanized gadgets. The smart home's idea consolidates business items with framework administrations and the executives to help extra prerequisites in the territories of productivity, insight, security, and intuitiveness applied in an eco-accommodating design. These necessities mirror another pattern of assumptions for everyday environments that have advanced with our advanced society's turn of events. Savvy home items have as of late seen an increment in distributed investigations and creatively applied for work on, making the Smart Home a quick creating and well-known region of exploration. Lately, the improvement of the data society and advances in ecological insight have prompted the fast development of framework based applications and administrations, which has brought an assortment of new human-computer cooperation (HCI) measurements play. Astute conditions improve the significance of HCI in the data society because of the presence of new types of uses that can accommodate our everyday needs in a wide range of conditions and application areas. As indicated by a report by the European Commission for Information Society, the idea of ecological insight gives another point of view to underlining a more significant level of easy to understand association, more adequate assistance uphold, more hearty client authority, and expanded help for HCI best practices [43]. In a wise climate, individuals are presented to various types of articles and conditions, in which the climate can distinguish and respond to consistently and straightforwardly. The brilliant home is turning into a significant application field in the cutting edge data society. Numerous new computerized items and administrations are being created on the side of these coordinated and wise registering conditions, thus presenting new difficulties to Smart Home turn of events and the utilization of HCI best practices.

In our cutting-edge society, individuals will, in general, favor straightforwardness. The improvement of the smart home obliges the prerequisites for simplicity of living while at the same time giving another and reformed way of life. Most importantly, the Smart Home can boost family time by streamlining the activity of electronic apparatuses. All-inclusive control cushions can be utilized to work an assortment of brilliant gadgets, for example, TVs, computers, climate control systems, and lights. We can save time by working such gadgets through a savvy home control framework to invest more energy with our loved ones.

Likewise, a Smart Home can be profoundly modified by close to home inclinations. For instance, clients can change the shade of lights or the computerized backdrop's substance at whatever point they need to with just a couple of snaps.

Likewise, we can make specific subjects or styles in various rooms in a brilliant home. At long last, the smart home can deliver a safer climate for the family. With the advances in checking and warning frameworks, we can check our home conditions utilizing cell phones while being ceaselessly from home. Likewise, the smart home can help children or debilitated individuals bolt or open the entryways and windows just as remind the older to kill the oven or then again lights. So, the smart home can essentially improve personal satisfaction.

2.2 Literature Review of Human-Computer Interfaces

"Human-computer collaboration can be seen as two amazing data processors (human and computer) endeavoring to speak with one another through a tight transfer speed, exceptionally obliged interface" [15]. HCI is characterized by [9] as "a control worried about the plan, assessment, and execution of processing frameworks for human use and with the investigation of significant wonders encompassing them" [8]. Another definition is given by [7] that HCI is "the control of planning, assessing and actualizing intelligent computer frameworks for human use, too the investigation of significant wonders encompassing this order"[7]. "HCI includes the planned usage and assessment of intuitive frameworks with regards to the clients' errand and work" [8]. There is disarray what HCI is, a science, a plant science, or a designing order. The definition of science is "HCI is tempered by guess, giving designing style hypotheses and instruments for originators" [3]. HCI is a plan science, "building up an art-based methodology and new exploration strategies to assess existing frameworks. In their expected and assignments setting, utilizing the outcomes to educate originators for the cutting edge regarding frameworks" characterized via Carroll and Campbell [4]. HCI as a designing control, Long and Dowell [5] characterize as "...the plan of people and computers interfacing to perform work adequately" while they deteriorate the order into the plan of people cooperating with computers and plan of computers associating with people. HCI concentrates on how individuals interface with figuring innovation and how a computer framework is planned all the more effectively, more basically, and all the more naturally. These communications have explicit accentuation on the "cooperation at the interface" with the innovation from a more extensive perspective. Today, HCI has pulled in significant consideration by specialists, and "it is perhaps the most basic difficulties confronting software engineering and designing" (IEEE).

While planning UI of these frameworks, clients' psychological cycles with computers should be considered because generally, clients' credits do not match to computer ascribes. Additionally, we should consider that computer frameworks can have non-intellectual consequences for the client, for instance, the client's reaction to virtual universes. Reeves *et al.* [6] indicated that "people have a solid propensity to react to computers in comparable manners as they do to different people" [6]. HCI is an interdisciplinary field that interrelates with numerous controls such as brain research, software engineering, psychological brain science, designing, artificial brainpower, and ergonomics. As of late, other orders contribute to humanism, human sciences, artistry sciences, and so on. Thus, it consolidates the social just as psychological parts of figuring. An essential factor in HCI configuration is the interrelation among Psychology and Computer science, as Carroll *et al.* [14] state:

"Mental hypothesis and techniques ... can give an establishment to better interface plan; however, proportionally, interface configuration gives a rich and point by point good area wherein to evaluate and refine mental hypotheses of complex learning conduct. Maybe the two controls are presently adult enough to consider a genuine relationship." Due to the quick advancement of equipment, programming advances and their diminishing expenses, improvement of new methods like discourse and sound preparing and computer vision, individuals will increasingly utilize computers in their regular day-to-day existences that are from different fields not too acquainted with computers. Likewise, "because of some explanation, a few clients cannot have the option to interface with machines utilizing a mouse and keyboard" [10–12]. This will prompt planning new multimodal human-computer associations that include distinctive info methods like discourse or voice, paper-like composition or pen, and computer vision (enabling the computer to see its environmental factors and decipher them), eye-input innovation, and motion. A multimodal HCI application reacts to enter in more than one correspondence method as it were of sight, contact, hearing, and smell that can contribute to a computer through individual info gadgets. Recently, work area applications have utilized mechanical information strategies through a console, mouse, and visual showcase and utilizing natural WIMP familiar interfaces. Toward the start, there was a solitary client—computer association in the typical HCI applications. Presently, we have a multi-client multimodal association to the computer using new equipment advancements (cameras, haptic sensors, olfactory, receivers, and others) which give "the guarantee for affecting a characteristic instinctive correspondence among human and machine". Jason *et al.* (2005) proposed new age of interfaces that incorporate computer vision, in which HCI a "correspondence among human and a machine". Likewise, Preece *et al.* [7] concur when expressing "Virtual conditions and computer-generated realities regularly offer a feeling of direct actual presence, tangible signals in three measurements, and a characteristic type of collaboration (for instance employing common signals)". This suggests new nature of interfaces of these frameworks, as Faconti *et al.* [13] say: "UIs of numerous application frameworks have started to incorporate various gadgets which can be utilized together to include single articulations.

Such interfaces are normally named multimodal because they utilize various kinds of correspondence channels to get data". As the quantity of the intuitive computer-based frameworks is developing, human exercises are quickly getting interceded by computers. HCI is worried "with the plan, usage, and assessment of those intelligent computer-based frameworks, just as with the multi-disciplinary investigation of different issues influencing this connection" [1], while the principal concern is to guarantee "convenience", operability, discoverability, effortlessness, and learnability also security, utility, viability, effectiveness, availability, and ease of use [1] and adaptability (alludes to varieties in errand consummation techniques upheld by the framework).

• **Human-Computer Interaction**
A decent UI may profit from multiple points of view as it builds profitability and decreases blunders. Very much planned interfaces permit the client to perform well. The three principle modules in HCI are close to home, computers, and connection (communication). All modules are portrayed succinctly.

- Human: The client who utilizes the framework.
- Computer: Hardware on which programming is working.
- Interaction: How client interface, utilizes, or speaks with the framework.

The fundamental HR utilized through HCI incorporates Perception (gaining information utilizing faculties) and Cognition (the way toward downplaying the handling of Information and Physiology). Discernment is textual style classification and size, shading contrast. The thinking asset's correspondences ought to be distinct with reliable reaction decisions for the user [49].

• **HCI: The Interactive Tools**
HCI is the interdisciplinary field fused with software engineering, data science, and brain research. In a general sense, human-computer communication is answerable for implementing new UI with better convenience and intelligence. Likewise, HCI is called man-machine communication now daily; as separated from computer, so many machine associations are managed interfaces. HCI additionally consider as creating distinct and predictive strategies and hypotheses of cooperation. The experts in this field essentially plan and create a site, graphical

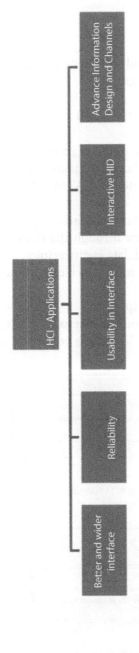

Figure 2.1 The utility of HCI.

interfaces intuitive. HCI is, as of late, increase fame in figuring science because of its more extensive advantage. The current analyst is planning new plan techniques in this field, trying different things with new equipment gadgets (Figure 2.1).

- **Role of HCI:**

The fundamental point and objective of human-computer association (Figure 2.2) is as per the following:

- For planning better UI and computer symbol (graphical interface);
- To make better ease of use of interface;
- Methodologies and cycle for planning interfaces;
- For making computer and ATM UI gorgeous, shaded and intelligent;
- Methods for executing interface;
- For quicker data use through the better data configuration dependent on solid data engineering;
- Advance, first, and solid interface readiness.

- **HCI and Modern Principles**

As indicated by the prestigious ease of use and HCI designing master, it is smarter to follow these standards for a better and elaborate HCI plan.

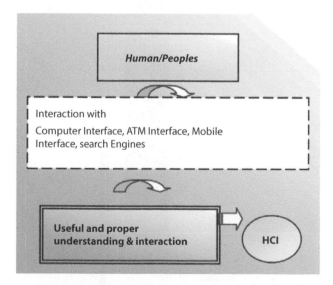

Figure 2.2 The basic of HCI and related spaces.

- Legible Displays: Fundamentally, the showcase decipher-ability ought to be clear and usable;
- According to Christopher, it is fundamental that the sign ought to be clear and usable;
- Top-down preparation is required; fundamentally, the sign ought to be clear and usable;
- It is fundamental to follow the sign in more than once and in numerous elective structures;
- It is vital to eliminate the straightforwardness in the middle of the articles or numbers;
- Fundamentally, the presentation should seem as though the variable that it addresses;
- If moving of subterranean insect part is fundamental, then it is fundamental to follow the move in an example and bear-ing viable with the client's real assumption or mental model;
- There ought to be sufficient significance in the expense of readiness of interfaces;
- It is fundamental to pick the articles which are not difficult to available and time powerful;
- Divided consideration between two data source might be essential for the consummation of one assignment;
- There ought to be conceivable outcomes of access data across different sources;
- A menu agenda and comparative sort of show might be use-ful to the client to number any articles or interface;
- According to Christopher, the standard of prescient sup-porting permit the client to zero in on current conditions, yet besides consider conceivable future condition;
- Another plan or interface ought to be pretty much the same or satisfy the consistency for the client's instance in future use.

- **HCI and HID**

For a better human-computer connection and machine interface, we need reliable and better collaboration gadgets. Both the host and gad-gets should be significantly more helpful and intelligent. The HID convention makes usage of gadgets essential. The host, which implies computer and another machine, ought to be less intricate for better correspondence with the gadgets, including console, mouse, joystick, and others.

The gadget is straightforward to utilize and straightforward because these gadgets will lead all the correspondence. The host needs to recover the HIID descriptor from the gadget and parse it before speaking with the gadget. The principal stream of this is first beginning by input at that point

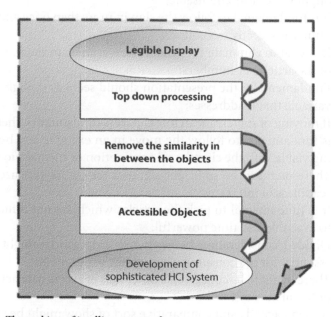

Figure 2.3 The making of intelligent ease of use.

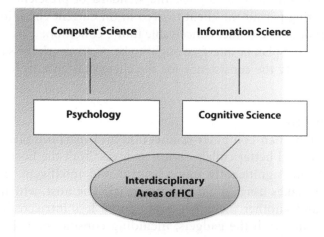

Figure 2.4 The connected fields of HCI and ease of use designing.

yield information streams from the host to the gadget and afterward to the human (Figures 2.3 and 2.4).

- **Primary Issues in HCI**

A few issues are significant in human-computer communication [2] and that we must have as a top priority when planning an interface of a learning climate. The presentation improves with training, and specialists can move past information to the current assignment. At the same time, beginners need painstakingly planned interfaces, investigation, and the variables that facilitate the investigation that has gotten quite possibly the main approaches to become familiar with an interface. The jargon of clients (the orders) increment the utilization of the jargon yet is fixed, although adaptability in the interface is available, it is probably not going to be utilized due to the wide range of various collaboration going on.

2.2.1   Overview of Communication Styles and Interfaces

Collaboration styles allude to the various correspondence methods between a human and a computer dependent on an innovative stage through association strategies, which are "method of utilizing an actual info/yield gadget to play out a conventional errand in a human-computer discourse" [17]. Connection style is clarified "through prototypical components of the interface and how they carry on, for example, order line, pull-down menu, structure fill in, or direct control" [18]. The accompanying essential communication styles and interfaces are utilized.

- **Command-Line Dialects**

This well-known class covers the collaboration among people and computers utilizing the language by composing the orders to a computer, which prompts a message significance prepared to acknowledge input. It gives communication guidelines to the computer straightforwardly, utilizing capacity keys, single characters, truncations, or entire word orders. The order line interfaces are unique in that they offer direct admittance to the framework's usefulness and can be consolidated to apply various devices to similar information. The order line cooperations are disadvantageous because text orders are generally hard to learn and use as obscure catchphrases and exacting related punctuation that a client needs to know before utilizing the framework. This impacts an expansion pace of mistakes. They should be recollected. Mental aides can just be utilized as signals. They are along these lines preferred for master clients over for learners.

- **Menus**

Menus are characterized as a set of alternatives on screen for picking the activity or among choices for information passage. There are three sorts of menus [18]: Pull-down menus, Pop-up menus, and Hierarchical menus. Preece *et al.* [7] proposed a bunch of alternatives showed on the screen where the determination and execution of the choices bring about an adjustment in the interface condition. Not at all like order-driven frameworks, menus have the favorable position that clients do not need to recollect the thing they need, they need to remember it" [7]. The benefit of utilizing menus is that client needs to perceive instead of review objects. The menu alternatives should be gathered legitimately and essential so that the client could perceive the required choice without much stretch. Albeit generally the client clicks with a mouse over the thing to be chosen or utilizing a console, with the new equipment advances built up the client can react through notice orders. There is proof that the number of mistakes declines, time to play out an errand is abbreviate except for complex assignments that need more activities to play out, the route through menus to locate the essential choice requirements additional time.

- **Direct Control**

Direct control interfaces are incredibly famous and influential, particularly with new clients, since they implant controls that are simple to human abilities (pointing, snatching, and moving articles in space), as opposed to prepared practices and "clients have extraordinary power over the presentation and as they select things, the subtleties show up in windows on the slides" [20]. Direct control interfaces "present a bunch of articles on a screen and give the client a collection of controls that can be performed on any of them" [16]. Every procedure on the interface is done straightforwardly and graphically. Composing a program is finished by moving symbols onto the screen and interfacing them together from a programming angle. The "altering assembling-running" cycle is acknowledged by straightforwardly clicking symbols on the screen rather than carefully grammar end orders or activities. There is no compelling reason to recall the sentence structure. This prompts critical punctuation mistakes like the user cannot incorporate non-existing code since it is not on the screen when the user clicks the order symbol and quicker execution of an errand.

As indicated by Shneiderman *et al.* [16], these sorts of controls have a few implications:

1. The nonstop portrayal of the object of interest, and
2. Actual activities or marked catch presses rather than complex grammar.
3. Fast gradual reversible tasks whose sway on the object of interest is quickly noticeable.

As Shneiderman *et al.* [19] numbers the accompanying focal points of direct control to objects:

1. Tenderfoots can learn essential usefulness rapidly, generally through a demon2. Specialists can work incredibly quickly to do a broad scope of assignments.
2. Learned discontinuous clients can hold operational ideas.
3. Blunder messages are seldom required.
4. Clients can see promptly if their activities are promoting their objectives, and if not, they can alter the course of their action.

- **Form Fill-In**
It is "the least difficult style of collaboration that comprises the client being needed to respond to questions or fill in numbers in a fixed arrangement rather like rounding out a structure" [18]. In this structure, the lone sort of client communication is data arrangement, which is valuable for the information section into applications. Additionally, accounting pages are considered as a modern variety of **structure filling.**

- **Natural Language**
The scientists and specialists are more inspired by frameworks that utilize natural language handling as human-computer correspondence, both of discourse and composed info. Based on discourse input, the client should realize which expresses the computer comprehends since computer requires severe directions and clients may get baffled if a lot is standard. The benefit of utilizing this cooperation style is to clients that do not approach consoles or have restricted insight. Simultaneously, ambiguities of the language may cause unforeseen impacts and make it exceptionally hard for a computer to comprehend. A decent viewpoint is that "Regular Language frameworks ought to be stretched out to incorporate non-verbal exchanges" since he contends that "Common" language incorporates motions. Signals can be utilized to frame explicit liquid expressions. Multistring motions can benefit from the capacities of human execution to empower significant ideas to be communicated in a reasonable, fitting, and

"common way" [21]. Regular language cooperations are "a point of view on non-verbal dialogs since they are from numerous points of view, more normal than those dependent on words" [21].

- **Question/Answer and Inquiry discourse**

This is an essential component for contributing to an application in a particular area. The client has posted a progression of inquiries (primarily with yes/no reactions, different decisions, or codes) driven through the cooperation bit by bit. These interfaces are not challenging to learn and utilize yet are restricted in usefulness and force. Inquiry dialects then again are utilized to develop questions to recover data from an information base.

- **WIMP Interface**

Weakling represents windows, symbols, menus, and pointers (in some cases, windows, symbols, mice, and pull-down menus). These interfaces are presumably the most well known and compelling for intelligent conditions. Windows are territories of the screen that carry on as though they were autonomous terminals in their own right. A symbol is a little picture used to address a shut window, record, or another item. The pointer is a significant segment of a WIMP interface since it interfaces the pointing, clicking, squeezing, hauling, and determination of items on the screen which could be moved, altered, investigated, and executed as it better fits the client's vision. Different instruments of computer interface configuration are menus, exchange boxes, checkboxes and radio fastens, etc. These utilize representation strategies and computer illustrations to give a more available interface than order line-based showcases. WIMP plans' crucial objective is to give the client a significant working allegory, for instance, an office or "work area" portrayal instead of the order line interfaces. Its preferences are general application, make capacities express, and give immediate criticism. People are susceptible to pictures and visual data that, on the other hand, can impart a few sorts of data considerably more quickly and viably than some other technique, and as is said, "words generally cannot do a picture justice".

- **Virtual Reality**

"Virtual conditions and computer-generated realities commonly offer a feeling of direct actual presence, tangible prompts in three measurements, and a characteristic type of connection (for instance employing characteristic motions)" [7]. Other than these styles, new collaboration styles have arisen: "discourse input/yield, computer vision-based information (e.g., motions), sound interfaces (e.g., non-discourse sound), material and power criticism, biophysical signals (e.g., retina scanner)" [22–25] which present to us the new age of interfaces that are non-order based with cooperations like eye following interfaces, real counterfeit factors, play-along music backup, and specialists.

2.2.2   Input/Output

The customary info gadgets utilized are console, mouse, and visual showcase utilized in order based communications. New information gadgets are utilized with new equipment innovations like cameras, haptic sensors, olfactory, receivers, and others. The new info advancements utilized are discourse acknowledgment, signal acknowledgment innovations, eye following innovation as non-order based cooperation, strategies for correspondence, and control of multidimensional information; Output gadgets utilized are the customary computer work area, head-mounted showcases, autostereoscopic shows, accessible three-dimensional presentations, the non-discourse sound yield for "imagining" information, and so on, designed for clients with great necessities.

2.2.3   Older Grown-Ups

Society is getting more seasoned. By 2030, the populace level over age 65 will go from 17% to 29% in Asia, North America, and Europe. Individuals live longer, stay more dynamic into a more seasoned age, and remain in their homes longer before finding the requirement for "helped to live" plans. Such an adjustment in socioeconomics carries with it significant changes in the requests for items and administrations. Albeit more seasoned grown-ups are more averse to utilize innovation contrasted with more youthful or moderately aged grown-ups, they additionally utilize a wide assortment of advances [50]. They have numerous assessments about computers, Internet, etc. Albeit some of them discover no issue utilizing them, the degree of dissatisfaction experienced when managing these items is very apparent in different clients. There are various issues they experience when managing innovation: monetary limits, obliviousness about how to utilize it, a sensation of dread to "break" it, and well-being troubles [51–53]. Item guidelines and use data are now and again challenging to grasp, moreover, on account of seniors. Around 25% of the issues they have experienced utilizing innovation might be addressed considering this client's aggregate (for instance, amplifying letter-size or utilizing more exact names) [50]. Now and again, more seasoned grown-ups must choose the option to utilize innovations, for instance, phone voice menu frameworks, cell phones, and air terminal registration booths.

These innovations are probably planned with the assumption that anybody ought to have the option to collaborate with them effectively. However, more seasoned grown-ups report disappointments in their communications because those items have not been intended to oblige the restrictions of this system. The proper use of Universal Design is for a long time or should be viewed in the following year.

Organic, mental, and additionally social issues emerge with age: lack in sensation and discernment, working memory declination, increasingly slow dependable data handling, increasingly slow fruitful obtaining of new techniques, specific consideration issues, development weakness, and relationship challenges. Devices and methods should be offered to relieve these issues. They can be accomplished through the plan of explicitly input/yield gadgets; versatile applications, explicit errand investigation, ease of use, and associations strategies are too systems that could help this objective. Including a delegate test of grown-ups in these assignments could help see some extraordinary attributes of more seasoned grown-up populaces that should be viewed while exploring for them. Medical care innovation is an essential worry for grown-ups of any age, particularly for more established grown-ups (because of their affinity to sickness and ongoing conditions). Exercises, for example, organizing doctor arrangements, making sure to take prescriptions, preparing data about as of late analyzed aliments, checking ongoing conditions are essential for the assignments that would benefit from outside intervention by innovation, which can be improved before very long. At long last, a proper plan of preparing and instructional projects for these clients is a duty regarding appropriate utilization of advancements: explicitly planned training programs are expected to incorporate older folks into a general public where computerized uneducated people have a great danger of social rejection. Versatile preparing, the utilization of reproduction, or the consideration of e-learning strategies are significant rules to consider when planning those projects.

2.2.4   Cognitive Incapacities

Characterizing psychological incapacity is not simple and definitions are generally expansive. It very well may be said that an individual with a psychological handicap has more considerable trouble with at least one sort or mental errands than an average individual. While an individual with significant intellectual incapacities will require help with pretty much every part of the day by day living, somebody with a minor learning handicap might have the option to work satisfactorily despite the inability, even to the degree the incapacity is rarely analyzed. People with psychological impedances can profit by utilizing novel processing advances, social computational frameworks, and setting mindful frameworks and that is only the tip of the iceberg. Innovation might be successful for the analysis, the board and treatment of a few problems like mental imbalance, Down Syndrome, horrible mind injury (TBI), or less intellectual severe conditions like a lack of ability to concentrate clutter (ADD) consistently, dyslexia (trouble perusing), dyscalculia (trouble with math), and learning incapacities all in all. Some rules address how to make web content available to individuals with handicaps, including intellectual ones. Notwithstanding, the usage of these rules does not ensure a complete admittance to the substance. The wide fluctuation among the psychological capacities of an individual with an intellectual handicap convolutes matters a ton. Many web contents cannot be made open to people with significant psychological inabilities, regardless of how enthusiastically the designer attempts. In those circumstances, some substances will consistently be excessively unpredictable for specific crowds. By and by, as a test for the following a very long time, there are still a few things that planners can do to expand the availability of web substance to individuals with less intellectual severe handicaps. Procuring the specialization to create open substance for these clients is a challenge for designers. Experts need to work related to interface creators to share their insight, direct them to grow new strategies for controlling hear-able yield, improving components to recollect arrangements. To finish consecutive activities, lessening the measure of data on a solitary page. To choose fitting designs with no messiness and considering new techniques to pick an alternative among huge informational indexes, giving explicit messages and definitions to abnormal terms. Limiting the psychological burden while surfing, utilizing illustrations to upgrade understanding and just when suitable (never abusing them), creating assistive advancements or programs with worked in versatile highlights, giving reliable orders and highlights along with the site, shortening menus, etc. All these techniques and methods ought to be joined with experimentation and test with genuine clients. The assessment of the existing all-around innovation and the new advancements should likewise be made related to schools and organizations that consider the exceptional clients. What separates intellectually incapacitated from other disabled clients is that the specific issue and its degree is regularly not characterized (not at all like for different clients, for example, outwardly hindered clients), and those experts are presumably the best-qualified ones to guidance during the turn of events and assessment measure.

2.3   Programming: Convenience and Gadget Explicit Substance

- **Software Convenience**

In a perfect world, all products should not be challenging to utilize and open for clients' broad scope. However, unscripted TV dramas that applications and sites, from huge scope organizations to more modest ones, regularly miss the mark regarding the most fundamental ease of use and openness objectives. There are various motivations to legitimize these central obstacles: numerous organizations do not ease using tests. Different organizations do, however, in light of a legitimate concern for speed or decreasing costs they complete tests just toward the start or toward the finish of the advancement cycle or with a diminished number of clients, or thinking about a restricted arrangement of functionalities. Usability testing is not innately troublesome. However, it is time and cash burning-through and challenging to scale when it requires a human perception of the individuals utilizing the product been tried. Robotized convenience tests can help distinguish issues and limits in web-based applications and they can be run with negligible human intercession. It should be noticed that these tests do not supplant other human ease of use tests. However, they supplement them. Another preferred position is that computerized tests can be stumbled into a massive arrangement of site pages an individual would be unrealistic to direct face to face. Notwithstanding the essential difficulties of inconvenience (and openness) testing, there are likewise difficulties in growing great computerized testing systems. Scholastic exploration exists, yet it has restricted admittance and organizations need to decipher the conventional construction of those papers into something that sounds good to them. Many test-computerization devices require their clients to have specialized and programming abilities to compose the tests in different circumstances. Contrasts among the different internet browsers comprise another trouble, or another test, with the test automation programming. Creating devices and structures that would make computerized testing more straightforward and more reasonable for various applications is another test for the following year. Making important summative ease of use test for explicit territories is another test for 2012. Indeed, even exceptionally experienced convenience experts cannot concur on which ease of use issues will affect the ease of use [54]. Computer utilizes different from basic site pages or applications to electronic well-being record frameworks. Unmistakably similar ease of use tests and measurements (even robotized ones) cannot be applied in all conditions. The issue is creating tests that are important across various settings and frameworks or even in creating compelling tests for points of interest regions.

- **Contents Obtained From Various Gadgets**

Today, the quantity of clients getting to the Internet from cell phones is higher than those getting to work area gadgets. Exploration has indicated that a massive level of individuals utilizes the versatile web from their home's solace [55, 56]. New cell phones are grown consistently. Large numbers have more computational abilities and are a lot more modest than the computers we used to utilize not many years back. For instance, the new Galaxy Nexus telephone has a 1,280 × 720 HD screen goal over a gadget with 1 Gb Ram and 32 GB circle, all running in a 1.2 GHZ double center processor. This gadget has functionalities like NFC, gyro, and indicator. However, the qualities of these gadgets (small size, contact connection, etc.) raise the need to put forth extra attempts to guarantee an ideal association experience. Additionally, various applications are utilized either from a cell phone or a work station. With clients perusing the web and utilizing applications from an undeniably different scope of gadgets, stages, and programs, new methods like a reformist upgrade [57] and responsive website composition [58] are fundamental ideas that should be perceived to arrive at the best client experience. It is essential to give clients an undeniable degree of coherence between various settings in certain circumstances, serving one substance to numerous programs and gadgets [59–61]. In different circumstances, individuals merit various substances and administrations relying upon where they are or whether they are fixed or portable (work area/computer or versatile). From now into the foreseeable future, one significant test that ought to be tended to before very long is understanding that interfaces should not be intended for programs/stages/gadgets; however, they should be intended for individuals. Just at that time, programs/stages/gadgets will be genuinely straightforward to clients, failing to remember the "how" and thinking about just the substance.

2.4   Equipment: BCI and Proxemic Associations

2.4.1   Brain-Computer Interfaces

There is solid proof that future human-computer interfaces will empower more normal and natural correspondence among individuals and all sorts of sensor gadgets. Mind computer interfaces are an illustration of this advancement. These interfaces depend on electrical signs delivered by mind movement that can be identified on the scalp, on the cortical surface, or, even, inside the cerebrum. These signs are then converted into yields that permit clients to speak with the computer without the support of fringe nerves and muscles. One of the primary preferences is giving new correspondence and control systems for whom traditional strategies are ineffectual (for instance, quadriplegic or clients with extreme handicaps). There are distinctive account strategies to gauge cerebrum action: intrusive, halfway obtrusive, and non-intrusive techniques. Utilizing intrusive strategies, terminals are embedded straightforwardly into the dark matter of the cerebrum. One of the principal attributes is that they produce the most excellent signals and empower quick acknowledgment of mental states and even accomplish complex cooperations. The burden is that the mind's perplexing response to an embed is still defectively comprehended and may impede long haul execution. These techniques could assist with fixing harmed sight box direct mind inserts and it very well may be conceivable to furnish new usefulness to people with loss of motion. Incompletely intrusive BCI gadgets are embedded inside the skull yet rest outside the cerebrum instead of inside the dark issue. They produce preferred goal signals over non-obtrusive BCIs where the bone tissue of the skull diverts and disfigures flags and have a lower danger of framing scar-tissue in the cerebrum than downright intrusive BCIs. Non-obtrusive techniques use terminals on the outside of the scalp to record the mind's electrical movement. This technique is ideal for people; however, it experiences a diminished spatial goal and expanded commotion because of the separation from mind tissue, the division from it by the covers of the cerebrum, skull, subcutaneous tissue, and scalp. Along these lines, just the synchronized action or enormous quantities of neural components can be distinguished. Perhaps the most common non-intrusive technique is electroencephalography (EEG): it is not difficult to utilize, compact, and has a low set-up expense. The primary drawbacks are the broad preparation needed before clients can work the innovation and require some degree of ability in the individual setting them and intermittent upkeep to guarantee adequately great contact with the skin. Albeit numerous enhancements had occurred in the most recent years, there is a chance to apply these innovations in the connection cycle. Above all else, one serious issue is the need for instruments that can give quick, exact, and dependable control signals.

Noninvasive and obtrusive strategies would make both profits from the improvement of the chronicle techniques. Also, we request examinations to get the importance of signs estimated or, as such, to realize better how the cerebrum functions. Broad utilization of this innovation by people with next to zero handicaps is another test for the future (10). Ongoing improvements in computer equipment give conservative compact frameworks that are incredibly ground-breaking. Activities, for example, "epic"—a 299$ neuro-headset with its SDK (+500$) created by Emotiv—will surely add to speculation and new examination around there. When these difficulties are reached, we could attempt to accomplish higher ones, similar to the improvement of gadgets constrained by musings.

2.4.2   Ubiquitous Figuring—Proxemic Cooperations

Universal registering (ubicomp) is a post-work area model of human-computer communication in which data preparation has been altogether incorporated into ordinary articles and exercises (innovation is all over the place and we use it all the time without contemplating it since it is "undetectable" to the client). The possibility of universal registering as an undetectable calculation was first expressed by Mark Weiser in 1988 at the Computer Science Lab at Xerox PARC. Omnipresent registering environments have various advanced gadgets and administrations that cooperate, and all the while, a considerable lot of them do not know that they are doing as such. Among these gadgets, there are computers associated with the Internet, versatile figuring gadgets, little and modest organized preparing gadgets, advanced sound players, radio recurrence recognizable proof labels, GPS, and intelligent tablets. Universal figuring offers difficulties across software engineering: in frameworks plan and designing, in frameworks demonstrating, in UI plan. A significant topic in ubicomp is investigating novel types of connection between an individual and a gadget, yet also between an individual and their arrangement of gadgets (13). In 1966 anthropologist Edward Hall began the expression "proxemics", a zone of study that recognizes the socially reliant manners by which individuals utilize relational distance to comprehend and intervene in their associations with others [62]. In proxemic collaboration, the conviction is that we can plan frameworks that will let individuals abuse a comparable comprehension of their proxemic relations with their close by advanced gadgets, encouraging more consistent and regular collaborations [63, 64]. Today, there are numerous circumstances where various gadgets stay in a similar room: cell phones, workstations, and tablets. On most occasions, there are particular issues to interconnect these gadgets (the client should have broad information to do it and expects time to design and deal with the correspondence). When the gadgets are associated, there are still issues to perform undertakings among them (for instance, sending a document starting with one gadget then onto the next). It may be said that the presence of one gadget is incognizant in regards to the presence of different gadgets.

Indeed, even these gadgets are oblivious to different perspectives, similar to the number of people in the room or the presence/nonattendance of other non-computerized objects.

This is where proxemics can help: similarly, individuals hope to expand commitment or closeness as they approach others, gadgets should build their network and association prospects as they draw nearer to different gadgets. Greenberg proposes five measurements to quantify nearness: the distance between elements (for instance, one element is or is not in a similar room as another substance), a direction between elements (pitch/move/yaw/pointing toward/reasonably toward/away from the article), personality (exact character/element type), presence of people, movement (speed of movement when an element is pushing toward or away from another element), and area (the actual setting wherein the elements live). Albeit the idea of ubicomp (or even proxemic connections) is notable, some difficulties should be tended to: there is no "official" language to impart these gadgets. It does not exist any guidelines of conduct among them (for instance, would we build up a predominance/administration among various gadgets? How do the proxemic components of the circumstance decide, or sway on, the correspondence of the members?). Another significant viewpoint is to set how the gadgets will respond when they have erroneous or fragmented data of the closeness of different gadgets? At long last, what is anticipated from this communication worldview? There are also different difficulties in planning ubicomp frameworks found in Marquardt and Saul Greenberg's report [65].

2.4.3   Other Gadget-Related Angles

There is no uncertainty about the broad prospects that BCI or ubicomp offer to the universe of human-computer connection. However, there are likewise various difficulties related to gadgets. What is essential to numerous clients is a longing to plan methods of interfacing with computers that fit their natural capacities. To refer to two of them, we can list wearable computers and straightforward gadgets [66–70]. Wearable computers are small electronic gadgets worn by the carrier under, with, or on top of garments. They are accommodating for applications that need more unpredictable computational help than just equipment coded rationales. Straightforward gadgets search for gadgets that do not need an individual's consideration during use: an innovation that is so well fitted to and coordinated with our own lives, natural limits, and activities that they are practically imperceptible being used [71–75]. One year from now, we can stroll in the manner from dark innovation (the one that keeps entangling the client) to square one.

2.5   CHI for Current Smart Homes

2.5.1   Smart Home for Healthcare

As the number of inhabitants in more established grown-ups increments and medical services assets battle to keep pace, mechanical arrangements are essential in improving the older's satisfaction. Numerous researchers accept that the smart home can accomplish its maximum capacity to help individuals out of luck [26–31]. The smart home's essential objective in medical care is to give a checking framework that continually produces subtle information streams that can be utilized to survey the status of one's well-being. Besides, "proportions of physiological signs and personal conduct standards can be converted into precise indicators of well-being hazard, even at a beginning phase, and can be joined with alarm triggering frameworks as a specialized stage to start suitable activity" [32]. Albeit the smart home observing framework is adequate for more seasoned individuals as per the current examination, the apparent incentive from such frameworks is hard to evaluate. These lines are critical to building up a viable input framework for clients related to the well-being related observing information. With successful input, the well-being observing framework can advance better commitment with more seasoned individuals while improving the medical care framework [40].

Other than the shrewd home prerequisites for the old, there has been an expanding number of necessities for highlights that help individuals with inabilities. For example, individuals with dementia (e.g., cognitive decline) may have to live in a savvy climate to make up for their decreased capacities. In any case, when we talk about the smart home or the brilliant climate, the usefulness made using top of the line advances is regularly convoluted for the standard end client to fathom, let alone for individuals with dementia completely [76–78]. It is subsequently fundamental that gadgets are planned to limit immediate, full-included cooperations with end clients. The basic shrewd home ideas center around human-computer collaborations and undertaking finish. Nonetheless, the smart home for individuals with dementia should zero in on recalling clients' practices so that it can assume the part of "update" inhuman consideration. The Smart Home highlights would go about as family individuals, offering types of assistance, for example, turning gadgets on or off dependent on the conditions of the circumstance. These innovations can scarcely supplant human consideration, yet the smart home could alleviate the individuals giving medical care benefits and improve medical services' general nature [41].

2.5.2   Savvy Home for Energy Efficiency

In the previous few years, broad examination and investigation concerning home energy advancements have been led. Today, there is an assortment of approaches to diminish the energy cost in homes by utilizing shrewd projects, for example, proficient energy on the board [36]. For instance, clients' inclinations concerning the living climate can be observed all the more effectively by adding more sensors to improve checking accuracy. Also, some exploration suggests the utilization of a multi-specialist strategy to lessen energy utilization. Improving energy proficiency for the brilliant home and proposing a far-reaching shrewd home framework idea will not just limit current savvy home energy issues, yet additionally improve the odds of making a completely practical Smart Home sooner rather than later [36].

2.5.3   Interface Design and Human-Computer Interaction

With the fast advancement of data innovation, numerous thoughts proposed in the past have become a reality. The utilization of the distributed computing administrations, the accentuation on the interface plan, the hypothesis of human-computer communication, and the improvement of the Internet of Things give fresh out of the plastic new chances to the progression of the brilliant home. To construct a viable distributed computing climate for the Smart Home, we need to beat the real test to oversee and arrange people and items in a brilliant home climate. One arrangement is for fashioners to make powerful savvy home gadgets per client particulars, utilizing a computer-aided plan interface, which is also perceived as a creator situated interface. To improve the proficiency of contact and interchanges among human and the human-made brainpower using Internet foundation and applications, a computer-supported or architect-situated interface is suggested in the production of Smart Home gadgets [33].

Lately, UIs have been viewed as an essential factor in fulfilling individual clients' necessities and inclinations, which bring about UIs that more like an individual UI. To build up individual UI, fashioners should consider setting-driven advancement as a fundamental component in UI production. Setting-driven UIs assume an undeniably significant part in urging clients to adjust to the smart home or the Ambient-Assisted Living climate [43], and a few procedures identified with setting-driven UIs, for example, dynamic methodologies at runtime have likewise been proposed [48]. Ongoing advances and advances have expanded savvy home execution assumptions. Innovations identified with actual settings, for example, sensors and actuators, give a chance to advance the usefulness that is answerable for boosting solace inside the Smart Home, while limiting the utilization of assets [42]. The improvement of sensors and actuators has made it conceivable to screen client conduct. The latest exploration focuses harder on the cooperations among people and the framework; therefore, a smart home outfitted with different touchy administrations gives a decisive stage to meet the majority of the prerequisites for medical care applications [45]. This trendsetting innovation has made brilliant home gadgets more natural and gives a strong establishment to help a motion-based interface. A motion is "any actual development that a computerized framework can detect and react to without the guide of a conventional pointing gadget, for example, a mouse or pointer. A wave, a head gesture, a touch, a toe tap, and even a cocked eyebrow can be a signal" [44]. Motion-based interfaces, for example, camera-based gestural interfaces and movement sensor-based gestural interfaces [39], can be utilized to perceive clients' actual developments without the mediation of conventional gadgets, a console or a mouse [34]. People can collaborate with the general climate in various manners. We can handle various types of gadgets specifically, and we can act and respond in various natural conditions [35]. If the climate can perceive our practices and react to what we do, can we consider it a smart home? It is subsequently imperative to perceive that the latest things have moved toward utilizing more natural UIs. With the advancement of the brilliant climate idea from medical care, data innovations, development catch screens, and viable UIs, the human-computer connection can turn into a reality in our daily lives. A brilliant home furnishes an insightful climate outfitted with different explicit gadgets that can control an encompassing knowledge with a progression of intelligent programmed controls. This astute climate identifies and reacts to human practices and gives an assortment of administrations to occupants [36]. With the advancements of human-computer collaboration and improvement of current culture, the investigation into the Internet of Things has expanded throughout the long term. The fake brain science hypothesis assumes an inexorably fundamental part in the smart home identified with the Internet of Things. The congruity of the smart home has been the focal point of ongoing exploration contemplates. To improve the amicability of human-computer collaboration, enthusiastic acknowledgment of HCI has additionally been directed [37].

2.5.4   A Summary of Status

"Smart Homes are a propelling influx of innovative improvement whose achievement relies upon a combination of the dreams of innovation designers for upgraded usefulness and energy the executives, and the requirements and requests of family units in the mind-boggling places that are homes" [46]. To improve the client experience in the smart home, proficient UI is required. A quality brilliant home framework ought to be assembled upon cutting edge smart gadgets, yet also upon a great HCI plan [47]. As per our contemplates, we accept that the accompanying examination targets ought likewise to be cultivated. Above all else, a focal control framework ought to be set up and an operational cushion is additionally needed to coordinate a wide range of brilliant gadgets. The working frameworks of Smart gadgets ought to be joined together, and norms of correspondence between various gadgets ought to be steady, which can give a fundamental establishment to planning UIs for the Smart Home. What is more, a comprehensive guide tending to how to plan UIs for brilliant gadgets that are focused for use in the Smart Home climate ought to be made. We believe that UIs for various brilliant gadgets are novel. The UI plan ought to be created dependent on principle elements of savvy gadgets and the style of configuration ought to likewise follow the fundamental hypotheses of HCI. Besides, the UI for each individual ought to be shifted depending on the client's availability needs. Client approval and confirmation capacities are essential to help with giving a protected insightful climate. Adaptable interfaces for various clients are additionally essential to improve client experience inside the smart home. Finally, a secure system of data move ought to be worked to guarantee the client's information security. The client's data and conduct are not difficult to record in the Smart Home, and it is fundamental to ensure the client's security.

2.6   Four Approaches to Improve HCI and UX

Confronted with numerous difficulties, the headway of the smart home today stays moderate. Various innovative bottlenecks should be managed before anticipating that the smart home should turn into a far-reaching reality. It is like this to examine targets that can add to the brilliant home's fruitful usage. Accordingly, we propose four ways to deal with improving the plan of the HCI.

2.6.1   Productive General Control Panel

To improve the HCI of the smart home, the overall control board is essential. Today, we have a far off for pretty much every electronic gadget in our home, for example, TV, DVD player, and climate control system, and it is progressively challenging for us to separate these different controllers from one another by superficial appearance. Managing numerous regulators is not an insightful alternative in the brilliant home. In this manner, a widespread regulator ought to be created. An extraordinary client experience relies upon an astounding HCI configuration acknowledged through the widespread control board. There are still a few issues that should be tended to before zeroing in on the control board plan. Above all else, an assembled data correspondence standard ought to be set up. We need our all-inclusive regulator to control a wide range of Smart gadgets simultaneously. It is vital to improve client experience and save time by disentangling the control measures. On the off chance that all the shrewd gadgets can be associated with one control board, the control board's working frameworks ought to likewise be normalized to run distinctive UIs. A viable method to improve the client experience is by synchronizing UIs with the update of brilliant gadgets. For instance, on the off chance that you add another air purifier to a current forced-air system, your regulator's UI should refresh the capacity simultaneously. It is fundamental to build up incorporated correspondence norms for brilliant gadgets before the Smart Home execution; at the end of the day, regardless of what sort of smart gadget clients purchase from Smart Home organizations, the gadget ought to be viable with the control board. A proficient and powerful UI configuration must be created dependent on a developed working framework, and just if an appropriate standard is set up, can a successful Smart Home be figured out. Also, data trade among shrewd gadgets ought to be viable and normalized. Smart home gadgets must be adequately shrewd to speak with one another and the data caught by Smart gadgets just as the records of clients' tasks ought to be divided between brilliant gadgets. To improve the client experience's nature, we need our Smart Home to go about as a benevolent update by telling us what is going on in our home. A warning about the stove will spring up on the TV screen while the broiler is preparing food. When essential, the capacity to advise clients assumes an undeniably significant part in giving a savvy climate, particularly to the individuals who experience difficulty recollecting things just like the individuals who are incapacitated. The data trade among shrewd gadgets gives a critical establishment to a more significant HCI level displayed as a close collaboration with brilliant gadgets. It is likewise fundamental to build up a safe home climate when sharing information caught by different gadgets. To accomplish productive and viable data trade, we could make an information base that uses distributed computing. Data about the client can be recorded by the control board or brilliant gadgets on a day-to-day, regular schedule, and the utilization of distributed computing and capacity in the cloud can give a good coordination point.

2.6.2   Compelling User Interface

A UI is an operational board that can permit the client to control capacities and practices of various types of uses through straightforward developments. The control board can work a wide range of shrewd gadgets in a Smart Home, which raises new difficulties for UI fashioners. A viable UI assumes a critical part in improving the client experience. The UI is broadly utilized by a wide range of essential gadgets, including electronic apparatuses, cell phones, and web-based media sites. The advancement of HCI and its effect on the UI assume an undeniably critical part in building a robust, brilliant home. To plan a productive and viable UI, we propose the accompanying rules. Picture the capacity. A UI for a Smart Home is not quite the same as what we use on telephones or sites. The elements of various shrewd gadgets are vital for clients, and this is the motivation behind why we buy different electronic machines for use in our homes. The Smart gadgets ought to be pictured to improve the client experience for savvy property holders (see Figure 2.5). Above all else, clients need to know which gadgets are being utilized immediately. A virtual impersonation of Smart gadget usefulness on the control board helps clients perceive controls and their related status. For example, when we need to work an oven in our kitchen, a model of the oven ought to be shown encircled by critical capacities, temperature control, clocks, and switches (see Figure 2.5a). It is more productive to separate various gadgets through simultaneous recreation models rather than an assortment of catches. Working full assortments of catches is not natural and can have clients with a negative effect on the general framework. A disentangled re-enactment model is likewise more proper for the old and individuals with inabilities. Pictured models are fundamental in improving the client experience and give more sure encounters to the end clients when contrasted and squeezing catches.

A quality HCI configuration cannot be accomplished without useful criticism. The criticism instrument assumes a significant part in the current HCI plan, and it has been broadly utilized on an assortment of UI

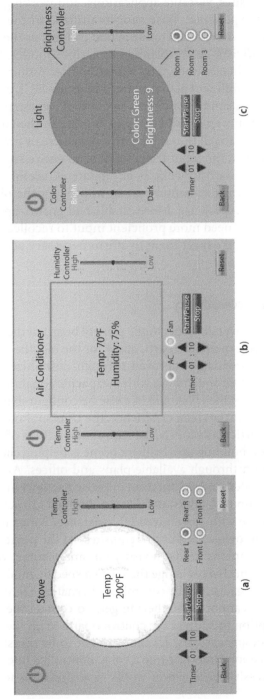

Figure 2.5 Pictured models of smart devices. (a) Model-1 (b) Model-2 (c) Model-3.

types, for example, sites, versatile applications, and working frameworks to improve client experience. Wise gadgets utilized in the smart home should give productive criticism to the actual gadgets or the client's control board. The criticism can be planned in various modes, for example, exchange boxes, lights, sounds, and vibrations. A proficient criticism framework can give different actual signs to upgrade HCI, and this input is fundamental in lessening the client's operational missteps. For example, if the client inputs an invalid number or date in the control board, the framework ought to tell the client with a discourse or proposal before continuing. Moreover, the input framework is an entire segment in permitting the control board to work as an update. A useful input framework also assumes a fundamental part in improving the older and the incapacitated client experience. More established grown-ups or individuals with incapacities need more proficient input to recollect which tasks have been finished and expect them to affirm necessary activities before preparing their orders.

2.6.3   Variable Accessibility

A viable UI gives an overall model to the control board of the smart home. By and by, the client experience, particularly for the old, the incapacitated, and kids, can be essentially improved through customized availability. Above all else, the UI for individuals with incapacities ought to be changed by their capacities, and the UI should likewise be configurable among various clients. To improve the client experience, the UI plan should be as available as expected, particularly for special requirements. One of the principal motivations behind building up a brilliant home is helping clients improve personal satisfaction through available plans and offices. An uncommon UI for the incapacitated can give them an improved activity method and an excellent HCI encounter. Understand that the disabled can achieve a larger part of tasks at home with customized UI assistance. For example, the UI could be changed to oblige various prerequisites. At the point when one of your disabled companions needs to visit your smart home, you ought to have the option to effectively change the UI to a specific mode to permit a wide range of Smart gadgets to be controlled alternately. On the off chance that specific clients cannot move their fingers to contact the screen, they might have the option to address the control board. With the end goal for them to do this, in any case, the UI mode ought to be transformed from an accessible, envisioned interface into a voice-controlled interface. Clients can utilize a successive rundown of words or expressions to control the elements of the shrewd gadgets. For instance, if a client with inability needs to switch on the climate control system (see Figure 2.5b), the person simply needs to say "forced air system", "turn on", "temperature", at that point "up" or "down". It is significant for some clients with actual handicaps to have the option to utilize voice orders that are typically cultivated by contacting the screen to control Smart gadgets.

Furthermore, the approval of shrewd gadget usefulness ought to be variable for various clients. The full usefulness or parts thereof ought to rely upon the client's approval level. The authority of availability gauges the capacity to control savvy gadgets, and a similar gadget may require distinctive authority from various clients. The authority ought to be set up to establish the shrewd home administrations and clients must change this authority with a more significant position authority. It is vital to assemble a safe canny framework by offering various specialists. Above all else, confined admittance to some electronic machines can keep kids from abusing them. Restricting the admittance to gadgets is a successful strategy to help keep youngsters out of peril. Respective apparatuses, for example, ovens, microwaves, and clothes washers, ought to be worked exclusively by grown-ups. When these gadgets are controlled physically, the clients with the appropriate authority should be advised and permitted to initiate activities to assume control over the gadget. It is imperative to rearrange some smart gadgets' usefulness and improve the client experience for youngsters by decreasing the utility of particular gadgets and administrations. It very well might be improper to show each capacity of specific savvy gadgets to clients with a fundamental degree of access authority. To improve client experience, the UI plan should zero in on principle elements of brilliant gadgets. For example, clients with a fundamental degree of power to the TV should have the option to control capacities, force, channels, and volume and they ought not to approach reset the framework back to the industrial facility settings. The diverse approval levels can be set up by giving various scopes of correspondence frequencies permitted. Clients who work different brilliant offices as an overseer ought to approach a wide range of data correspondence frequencies, while the individuals who have fundamental approval to Smart gadgets can just access portions of the correspondence frequencies. This will confine the entrance of clients to some Smart gadgets. Also, we can utilize passwords to set constraints on individual clients concerning a specific shrewd gadget. For example, the secret phrase, a progression of characters or a novel signal can be made by clients with the highest power, and the secret key must be deactivated by the individuals who made it.

2.6.4   Secure Privacy

With the advancement of data innovation, clients should share more close to home data than at any other time to be essential for the cutting edge innovation-driven society. In any case, our information's security scarcely increments and indeed may diminish, with the headway of the innovation. Numerous security should be settled, and coincidental data spills can adversely influence client experience. In a smart home, clients' security concerns an assortment of information and activities, including contact data, online pursuit history, the settings of various Smart gadgets, and clients' way of life. Realize that each activity identified with HCI can be checked and recorded by cutting edge brilliant gadgets, which can be a twofold edged blade. From one perspective, the smart gadgets can rehash a similar activity without the client's info, which permits the client to control Smart gadgets with a straightforward snap or to proceed with an incomplete cycle. It is fundamental for Smart offices to save the client's data from disentangling activities, just as when the gadget or framework is going about as an update. Checking the client's practices likewise assumes a massive part in upgrading the productivity of controlling mart gadgets and adding to the general improvement of HCI. The client's practices are likely recorded and put away in the data set, which can make the client's protection defenseless if the data set is hacked. It is vital to guard the client's data. There might be some business substances that will endeavor to utilize client data to give notices and advancements. Sudden warnings and ads might debase the client experience. Moreover, this sort of undesirable correspondence can disintegrate the client's degree of trust in the HCI. The accompanying components should be set up and stay away from the client experience's interference to build the data security. First, clients ought to have the option to pick on the off chance that they need their shrewd gadgets to record their data or activities by permitting clients to choose their inclinations. There ought to be a check box for clients to choose whether they need their information and practices to be recorded or whether they need to join the improvement program assisting savvy home organizations with gathering the client's information. The understanding identified with terms and conditions ought to be given along the check box. Furthermore, the client's information and conduct records should be put away in a few data sets. The data ought to be circulated among various data sets to diminish data openness when one of the data sets is hacked. Clients ought to likewise have the option to decide to clear the entrance history or records consequently or physically, and clients can decide to get to data sets by entering a secret key or recognizing fingerprints. At last, Smart Home organizations ought to give some safety efforts. For instance, antispy programming and firewalls ought to be introduced in each shrewd office. Clients can conclude whether to purchase these product applications, and if clients buy them, brilliant home organizations should share the obligation when the client's very own data is uncovered. Clients can likewise buy protection for their brilliant gadgets, yet also for the security of their data. Clients and brilliant home organizations should unite to give an agreeable and secure climate.

2.7   Conclusion and Discussion

The hypothesis of the Internet of Things alongside the present status of trendsetting innovation gives a strong establishment to build up and improve the Smart Home. The Smart Home can be utilized to improve the personal satisfaction of individuals with extraordinary necessities. Smart Homes and their utilization of Smart gadgets can likewise lessen the utilization of energy. Moreover, the plan of the HCI assumes an inexorably significant part in improving the smart home. The progression of fundamental advancements, such as sensors, screens, and regulators, gives the apparatuses essential to understand a more compelling and productive client experience. In light of past exploration and examination, just as the essential hypothesis and practice of the Smart Home, we accept that an emphasis on improving the plan of the HCI is significant to upgrade the client experience in the brilliant home. It is fundamental to propose a few methodologies to create proficient and successful HCI plans in the smart home along these lines. We propose four potential methodologies, including proficient general control boards, compelling UIs, variable availability, and secure protection to essentially improve the HCI plan, and, at last, the general client experience. Most importantly, the four methodologies examined in this paper give general direction concerning what ought not out of the ordinary in a smart home. Clients need to get comfortable with control boards and know about the abilities of the UI. The configurability of client admittance to brilliant gadget highlights should likewise be considered because a few clients may require more usefulness than the others. It is likewise vital to ensure kids by building up approval limits. Finally, the four methodologies give some helpful rules that may help planners and engineers who wish to plan and create proficient and successful HCI in the Smart Home. For instance, voice control for the control of savvy gadgets by the disabled. Short-term exploration of the smart home should approve the proposed ideas with the overall population, i.e., clients. Other essential segments of the smart home, such as security-related issues and related diversion points, should likewise be tended to. First and foremost, a reinforcement power source can work autonomously when a power outage happens ought to be set up in a brilliant home for the overall screen and alert framework. Furthermore, there ought to be an auxiliary lock framework consistently in the event of erroneous peruses of the sensors. The electrical radiation should be checked and controlled inside the protected reach, and all electronic apparatuses should be waterproof. Regarding shrewd home amusement, further investigation should be centered around a very much planned modularized structure, making a Smart Home variable without breaking the establishment of the whole structure. Besides, the info and yield ports of all intelligent home machines ought to be indistinguishable or viable. From the utilization of security cameras and temperature screens to distantly controlling TV and forced air system with an application on cell phones, such as an iPhone or an iPad, the ideas of a smart home are getting progressively satisfactory. We accept that the smart home will turn into a need in our lives sooner rather than later. All in all, the improvement of innovation has made extraordinary steps in acknowledging the smart home. A productive and powerful brilliant home cannot be accomplished without the utilization of trend-setting innovation. Nonetheless, the unbounded prerequisites of brilliant home clients will keep on introducing new mechanical difficulties. This is a virtuous cycle. While it is hard to foresee the future bearing of examination and client prerequisites in this field, we wish to introduce some potential difficulties for the future brilliant home. To start with, with the appearance of 3D displaying, the future Smart Home could deliver its brilliant gadgets. Clients could utilize a savvy home 3D printer to create new Smart gadgets or fix harmed offices inside the smart home. Also, a 3D image could be utilized to use a UI used to interface with shrewd gadgets. Besides, a versatile, savvy divider could be utilized to adjust the smart home's design on interest. Smart gadgets, for example, screens, speakers, climate control systems, and lights, could be coordinated into the "Smart divider" to save space.

References

1. Stephanidis, C., *Interfaces for All - Concepts, Methods, and Tools*, pp. 3–17, Lawrence Erlbaum Associates, Mahwah, NJ, 760 pp, 2001.
2. Eisenhauer, M., Hoffman, B., Kretschmer, D., State of the Art Human-Computer Interaction. *GigaMobile/D2.7.1*, September 16, 2002, 2002.

3. Newell, A. and Card, S.K., The Prospects for Psychological Science in human-computer Interaction. *Hum.-Comput. Interact.*, 1, 209–242, 1985.

4. Carroll, J.M. and Campbell, R.L., Artifacts as Psychological Theories: the Case of Human-Computer Interaction. *Behav. Inform. Technol.*, 8, 247–256, 1989.

5. Long, J. and Dowell, J., Conceptions of the Discipline of HCI: Craft, Applied Science, and Engineering, in: *People and Computer V. Proceedings of the Fifth Conference of the British Computer Society Human-Computer Interaction Specialist Group, Univ. of Nottingham*, 5-8 Sept. 1989 CUP, Cambridge, 1989.

6. Reeves, B. and Nass, C., *The Media Equation: how people treat computers, televisions and new media like real people and places*, Cambridge University Press, Cambridge, 1996.

7. Preece, J., *Human-Computer Interaction*, Pearson Education Limited, Essex, England, 1994.

8. Dix, A.J., Finlay, J., Abowd, G., Beale, R., *Human-Computer Interaction*, 2nd edition, Prentice-Hall, Englewood Cliffs, NJ, USA, 1998.

9. ACM SIGCHI, *Curricula for Human-computer Interaction*, ACM Special interest group on computer-human interaction curriculum development group [On-line], New York, U.S.A., 1996, Available: http://www.acm.org/sigchi/cdg/cdg2.html.

10. Jones, A. and O'Shea, T., Barriers to the use of computer-assisted learning. *Br. J. Educ. Technol.*, 3, 13, 207–217, 1982.

11. Rudnicky, A.I., Lee, K.F., Hauptmann, A.G., Survey of current speech technology. *Commun. ACM*, 37, 3, 52–57, 1992.

12. Corso, J.J., *Techniques for Vision-Based Human-Computer Interaction*, A dissertation submitted to The Johns Hopkins University Baltimore, Maryland, August, 2005.

13. Faconti, G.P., Reasoning on Gestural Interfaces through Syndetic Modelling. *ACM SIGCHI Bull.*, 28, 3, July 1996.

14. Carroll, J.M. and Thomas, J.C., Metaphor and the cognitive representation of computing systems. *IEEE Trans. Syst. Man. Cybern.*, 12, 2, 107–115, 1982.

15. Tufte, E.R., *Visual Design of the User Interface*, IBM Corporation, Armonk, N.Y., 1989.

16. Shneiderman, B., Direct Manipulation: A Step Beyond Programming Languages. *IEEE Comput.*, 16, 8, 57–69, 1983.

17. Foley, J.D., van Dam, A., Feiner, S.K., Hughes, J.F., *Computer Graphics: Principles and Practice*, Addison-Wesley, Reading, Mass, 1990, http://lipas.uwasa.fi/~mj/hci/hci11.html.

18. Shneiderman, B., *Designing the User Interface*, Addison-Wesley, New York, U.S.A., 1992.

19. Shneiderman, B., The future of interactive systems and the emergence of direct manipulation. *Behav. Inform. Technol.*, I, 237–256, 1982.

20. Shneiderman, B. and Maes, P., Direct manipulation vs. interface agents interactions. *ACM Digital Library*, 4, 6, 42–61, 1997.

21. Buxton, W., The Natural Language of Interaction: A Perspective on Non-Verbal Dialogues, in: *The Art of Human-Computer Interface Design*, B. Laurel, (Ed.), pp. 405–416, Addison-Wesley, Reading, MA, 1990.
22. Rauterberg, M., Interaction Styles. *ACM Digital Library*, 4, 6, 72–82, 1990.
23. Fetaji, M., Fetaji, B., Ebibi, M., Designing quality e-learning virtual environment for learning Java. To be published in the *CIIT conference proceedings*, Macedonia, Bitola, 21 January 2007.
24. Dumas, J.S. and Redish, J.C., *A practical guide to Usability Testing*, revised edition, pp. 55–62, Pearson Education Limited, New York, U.S.A., 1999.
25. Baeza-Yatez, R. and Ribeiro-Neto, B., Chapter 10, in: *Modern Information Retrieval*, ACM Press, Addison-Wesley, 2001.
26. Anderson, J.R. and Lebiere, C., *The Atomic Components of Thought*, Lawrence Erlbaum Associates, Inc., Mahwah, NJ, 1998.
27. Newell, A., *Unified Theories of Cognition*, Harvard University Press, Cambridge, MA, 1990.
28. Kieras, D.E. and Meyer, D.E., An overview of the EPIC architecture for cognition and performance with application to human-computer interaction. *Hum. Comput. Interact.*, 12, 391–438, 1997.
29. Sutcliffe, A., On the effective use and reuse of HCI knowledge. *ACM Trans. Comput.-Hum. Interact. (TOCHI)*, 7, 2, 2000, Publisher: ACM Press.
30. Shneiderman, B., *Designing the User Interface: Strategies for effective human-computer interaction*, Addison Wesley, Reading, Massachusetts, 1986.
31. Bouchard, K., Bouchard, B., Bouzouane, A., Guidelines to efficient smart home design for rapid AI prototyping: A case study. *Proceedings of the 5th International Conference on Pervasive Technologies Related to Assistive Environments*, Heraklion, Crete, Greece, pp. 1–8, 2012.
32. Chan, M., Campo, E., Estève, D., Fourniols, J., Smart homes - Current features and future perspectives. *Maturitas*, 64, 2, 90–97, 2009.
33. Chen, S., Chang, S., Chang, Y., Exploring a designer-oriented computer-aided design interface for the smart home device. *Comput.-Aided Des. Applic.*, 7, 6, 875–888, 2010.
34. Choi, E., Kwon, S., Lee, D., Lee, H., Chung, M.L., Towards successful user interaction with systems: Focusing on user-derived gestures for smart home systems. *Appl. Ergon.*, 45, 4, 1196–1207, 2014.
35. Davidoff, S., Lee, M.K., Yiu, C., Zimmerman, J., Dey, A.K., Principles of smart home control. *Ubicomp*, 4206, 19–34, 2006.
36. De Silva, L.C., Morikawa, C., Petra, I.M., State of the art of smart homes. *Eng. Appl. Artif. Intell.*, 25, 7, 1313–1321, 2012.
37. Du, K., Wang, Z., Hong, M., Human-machine interactive system on smart home of IoT. *J. China Univ. Posts Telecommun.*, 20, 1, 96–99, 2013.
38. Harper, R., *Inside the smart home*, Springer, London, 2003.
39. Kühnel, C., Westermann, T., Hemmert, F., Kratz, S., Müller, A., Möller, S., I'm home: Defining and evaluating a gesture set for smart-home control. *Int. J. Hum.-Comput. Stud.*, 69, 11, 693–704, 2011.

40. Le, T., Reeder, B., Chung, J., Thompson, H., Demiris, G., Design of smart home sensor visualizations for older adults. *Technol. Health Care*, 22, 4, 657–666, 2014.

41. Orpwood, R., Gibbs, C., Adlam, T., Faulkner, R., Meegahawatte, D., The design of smart homes for people with dementia - user-interface aspects. *Univers. Access Inf. Soc.*, 4, 2, 156–164, 2005.

42. Rashidi, P. and Cook, D.J., Keeping the resident in the loop: Adapting the smart home to the user. *IEEE Trans. Syst. Man Cybern., Part A: Syst. Hum.*, 39, 5, 1–11, 2009.

43. Roe, P.R.W., *Towards an inclusive future*, COST, Brussels, 2007.

44 Saffer, D., *Designing gestural interfaces*, O'Reilly Media, Ottawa, 2009.

45. Vega-Barbas, M., Pau, I., Martin-Ruiz, M.L., Seoane, F., Adaptive software architecture based on confident HCI for the deployment of sensitive services in smart homes. *Sensors*, 15, 4, 7295–7320, 2015.

46. Wilson, C., Hargreaves, T., Hauxwell-Baldwin, R., Smart homes and their users: A systematic analysis and critical challenges. *Pers. Ubiquit. Comput.*, 19, 2, 463–476, 2015.

47. Zhang, B., Rau, P.P., Salvendy, G., Design and evaluation of smart home user interface: Effects of age, tasks and intelligence level. *Behav. Inf. Technol.*, 28, 3, 239–249, 2009.

48. Zimmermann, G., Henka, A., Strobbe, C., Mack, S., Landmesser, A., Towards context-driven user interfaces in smart homes. *Proceedings of the Sixth International Conference on Advances in Human-oriented and Personalized Mechanisms, Technologies, and Services*, Venice, Italy, pp. 98–103, 2013.

49. Patrick, A.S., Chris Long, A., Flinn, S., HCI and security systems. *CHI'03 Extended Abstracts on Human Factors in Computing Systems*, ACM, 2003.

50. Fisk, A.D., y Otros, *Designing for older adults: principles and creative human factors approaches*, 2nd edition, CRC Press, Boca Raton, 2009.

51. WebAIM, WebAIM. Web accessibility in mind, 2020, Online http://webaim.org/articles/cognitive/.

52. The consortium, W3C, *Web Content Accessibility Guides 2.0*, 2021, Online http://www.w3.org/TR/WCAG20/.

53. Harty, J., Finding usability bugs with automated tests. *Commun. ACM*, 54, 2, 44–49, February de 2011.

54. Bailey, B., *Judging the severity of usability issues on web sites: this does not work*, Usability.gov, New York, U.S.A., October 2005, http://www.usability.gov/articles/newsletter/pubs/102005news.html.

55. Wroblewski, L., *When & where are people using mobile devices?*, Lukew Ideation + Design, New York, U.S.A., February 2011, http://www.lukew.com/ff/entry.asp?1263.

56. Samsung Galaxy Nexus specifications, 2011, http://www.google.com/nexus/#/tech-specs.

57. Parker, T., y Otros, *Designing with a progressive enhancement: building the web that works for everyone*, New Riders, New York, U.S.A., 2010.

58. Marcotte, E., *Responsive Web Design*, A-List Apart, New York, U.S.A., May 2010, http://www.alistapart.com/articles/responsive-web-design/.
59. Mcfarland, D.J. and Wolpaw, J.R., Brain-computer interfaces for communication and control. *Commun. ACM*, 54, 5, 60–66, 2001.
60. Dobelle, W.H., Mladejovsky, M.G., Girvin, J.P., Artificial vision for the blind: electrical stimulation of the visual cortex offers hope for a functional prosthesis. *Science*, 183, 440–444, February 1974.
61. Weiser, M., The computer for the 21st century. *Sci. Am.*, 265, 3, 94–100, 1991.
62. Hall, E.T., *The Hidden Dimension*, Doubleday, New York, 1966.
63. Marquardt, N., y Otros, *The Proximity Toolkit: Prototyping Proxemic Interactions in Ubiquitous Computing Ecologies*, October 16–19, ACM, Santa Barbara, CA. The USA, 2011, UIST'2011.
64. Greenberg, S., y Otros, Proxemic Interactions: the new ubicomp? *Interactions*, XVIII, 1, 42–50, January + February 2011, New York: ACM.
65. Marquardt, N. and Greenberg, S., *Informing the design of proxemic interactions*, Department of Computer Science, Calgary, Canada, 2011, Available at: http://dspace.ucalgary.ca/bitstream/1880/48690/1/2011-1006-18.pdf. 2011-1006-18.
66. Bird, J., The unprecedented challenge of designing transparent technologies. *Interactions*, XVIII, 6, 20–23, November 2011, New York: ACM.
67. Sears, A. and Jacko, J.A. (Eds.), *Human-Computer Interaction Handbook*, 2nd Edition, CRC Press, New York, U.S.A., 2007.
68. Jacko, J.A. and Sears, A. (Eds.), *Human-Computer Interaction Handbook*, Lawrence Erlbaum & Associates, Mahwah, USA, 2003.
69. Grudin, J., A moving target: The evolution of human-computer interaction, in: *Human-Computer Interaction Handbook*, 2nd Edition, A. Sears and J.A. Jacko (Eds.), CRC Press, New York, U.S.A., 2007.
70. Myers, B., A brief history of human-computer interaction technology. *Interactions*, 5, 2, 44–54, 1998, ACM Press, http://doi.acm.org/10.1145/274430.274436.
71. Carroll, J.M., *Human-Computer Interaction: History and Status*, Encyclopedia Entry at Interaction-Design.org.
72. Baecker, R.M., Grudin, J., Buxton, W.A.S., Greenberg, S. (Eds.), *Readings in human-computer interaction. Toward the Year 2000*, 2. ed, Morgan Kaufmann, San Francisco, 1995.
73. Paul, P.K., Chatterjee, D., Karn, B., Cloud Computing: emphasizing its possible roles and importance in Information Systems and Centers, in: *IEM/IEEE sponsored international conference proceedings (IEMCON-12)*, [indexed, abstracted in Google Scholar[USA], Cite Ceer, EBSCO], pp. 345–348.
74. Paul, P.K., Chatterjee, D., Karn, B., Cloud Computing: beyond ordinary Information Transfer Cycle. submitted in *National Conference on Computing and Systems*, (Status- Accepted) 15 March, Dept of Computer Science, Burdwan University.

75. Paul, P.K., Sarangi, B.B., Karn, B., Cloud Computing: emphasizing its Facet, Component and Green aspect with special reference to its utilization in the Information Hub, in: *National Conference on Emerging Trends in Computer Application & Management, Faculty of Computer Application and Management*, 24-02-12, 25-02-12, AVIT (AICTE-NBA Accredited Engineering College), Paper published.

76. Choudhary, S., Lakhwani, K., Agrwal, S., An efficient hybrid technique of feature extraction for facial expression recognition using AdaBoost Classifier. *Int. J. Eng. Res. Technol.*, 8, 1, 2012.

77. Kumar, S., Singh, S., Kumar, J., Live Detection of Face Using Machine Learning with Multi-feature Method. *Wireless Pers. Commun.*, 103, 3, 2353–2375, 2018.

78. Kumar, S., Singh, S., Kumar, J., Automatic Live Facial Expression Detection Using Genetic Algorithm with Haar Wavelet Features and SVM. *Wireless Pers. Commun.*, 103, 3, 2435–2453, 2018.

Teaching-Learning Process and Brain-Computer Interaction Using ICT Tools

Rohit Raja[1], Neelam Sahu[2] and Sumati Pathak[3*]

[1]Department of IT, GGV (A Central University) Bilaspur, Chhattisgarh, India
[2]Department of CSE, DRCVRAMAN University Bilaspur, Chhattisgarh, India
[3]Department of CSIT, DRCVRAMAN University Bilaspur, Chhattisgarh, India

Abstract
Teaching is an aid in the process of learning. A teacher is, by default, a learner. A person who is a self-learner turns out to be a teacher, meaning he/she is capable of imparting knowledge to others who are not in a position to spend sufficient time for self-learning. Self-learning is a self-motivated mental exercise to observe, understand, and make a meaningful interpretation of various physical, logical, and philosophical entities. One can accomplish knowledge by self-learning only when one sacrifices the desire to consume time for physical sense-related experiences of pleasure and pain. Self-learning focuses on direct communication between external entities and processes and the brain for cognitive perception and understanding. Teaching should always be viewed as a regenerative feedback system. A brain-computer interface (BCI) provides a pathway for the direct communication between brain and an external device. BCIs provide augmentation, repairing human cognitive and sensory motor functions. Alternatively, "Neuroprosthetics" in neuroscience, which is concerned with neural prostheses of using artificial devices to replace the function of impaired nervous systems or sensory organs. The best examples of neuroprosthetic devices are "cochlear implants", used to restore hearing, and optical neuroprosthetic devices like retinal implants used to restore vision.

Keywords: Brain-computer interface (BCI), artificial intelligence, optical neuroprosthetic devices, retinal implants

---

[*]Corresponding author: sumati.gauraha@gmail.com

Sandeep Kumar, Rohit Raja, Shrikant Tiwari and Shilpa Rani (eds.) Cognitive Behavior and Human Computer Interaction Based on Machine Learning Algorithm, (63–84) © 2022 Scrivener Publishing LLC

3.1 The Concept of Teaching

Teaching should be a formal interactive session. A teacher is expected to have core competence in the subject of his interest, good communication skills, powerful articulation, pleasing manners, admirable body language, and patience [1]. A good teacher always addresses the students with eye-to-eye contact to feel comfortable during the interactive teaching-learning process (TLP). A teacher should prepare for many hours for just 1 hour of delivery in the class. The material to be taught in a class should be organized, and the teacher should use all kinds of visual tools so that the students understand the subject better [4].

Karthikeyan *et al.* [10] developed a hybrid educational data mining model (HEDM) approach which is used for analyzing the performance of the students. Based on distinctive factors, the HGDM approach evaluated the student performances that provided relevant results. Further, this model combined the efficiencies of Naive Baye's classification technique and J48 Classifier for obtaining the results and classifying the student performance in a precise manner [5]. The model was validated with the benchmark education dataset that was available online in the WEKA environment. The results showed that the HEDM outperformed the existing EDM. However, the error rate of HEDM needed to be reduced.

Miguéis *et al.* [15] presented a two-stage model, supported by data mining techniques that used the details available at the end of the first year of students' academic career (path) to predict their overall academic performance. Unlike most literature on educational data mining, academic performance was evaluated from both the average grade achieved and the time taken to conclude the degree. Furthermore, this model developed to segment students based on the dichotomy between failure or high-performance evidence. The segmentation framework allowed the identification of 25 segments of students. The drawback of this model was that sample bias. Despite considering a significant number of students, the conclusions drawn were only valid for the sample considered.

Yadav [25] introduced a hybrid clustering approach for evaluating students' academic performance. The hybrid clustering was based on integrated techniques of subtractive clustering (SC) and fuzzy C-means clustering methods. The evaluation of student academic performance could be considered a clustering problem. The clusters were formed based on the intelligence level of students. In the hybrid clustering model, antecedent and consequent parameters could be readily determined by the SC techniques. SC technique automatically constructed the membership function and fuzzy if-then rule; based on the if-then rule, students' academic performances were evaluated [6].

Mengash [14] presented four academic prediction models based on four well-known data mining techniques: Artificial Neural Network (ANN), Decision Tree, Support Vector Machine (SVM), and Naive Bayes. A dataset of 2,039 students enrolled in Computer Science and Information College of a Saudi public university from 2016 to 2019 was used to validate the suggested methodology. The results demonstrated that applicants' early university performance could be predicted before admission based on specific pre-admission criteria. Results showed that the ANN technique outperformed other techniques with an accuracy rate of 79%, even though ANN performance was not enough for accurate performance evaluation.

Xu *et al.* [24] proposed a machine learning approach for the prediction for the student performance in various degree programs. [5] analyzed undergraduate students' performance using educational data mining. Two aspects of students' performance had been focused upon. First, students' academic achievement at the end of a 4-year study program was predicted. Second, typical progressions were studied, which was combined with the prediction results. Based on this, two important groups of students had been identified: the low and high-achieving students. The results indicated that by focusing on a small number of particularly good or poor performance indicators, it was possible to provide timely warning and support to low achieving students and advice and opportunities to high performing students.

Helal *et al.* [9] created different classification models for predicting student performance, using data collected from an Australian university. The data compromised student information, such as socio-demographic features, university admission basis, and attendance type. An essential objective of the work was the consideration of student heterogeneity in constructing the predictive models. The experiments validated the hypothesis and the experiments revealed that considering both enrolment and course activity features aided in identifying vulnerable students more precisely. Moreover, the experiments cleared that no individual methods provided superior performance in all aspects.

3.2   The Concept of Learning

As per suggestions made by cognitive scientists, a student learns mostly using eyes and ears. The information understood and assimilated by a student is better acquired through the eyes since the human brain's visual cortex is densely connected to the neuronal network compared to the

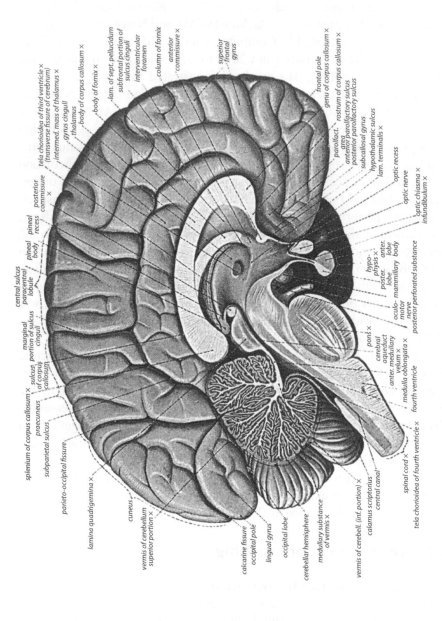

Figure 3.1 Human brain bisected in the sagittal plane.

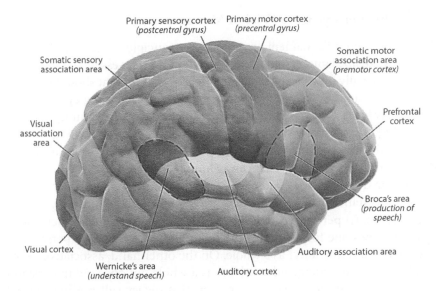

Primary sensory cortex
(postcentral gyrus)

Primary motor cortex
(precentral gyrus)

Somatic motor
association area
(premotor cortex)

Somatic sensory
association area

Prefrontal
cortex

Visual
association
area

Broca's area
(production of
speech)

Visual cortex

Auditory association area

Wernicke's area
(understand speech)

Auditory cortex

Figure 3.2 Functional areas of the human brain.

brain's auditory cortex. Figure 3.1 shows the human brain model bisected in the sagittalplane and Figure 3.2 shows a diagrammatic representation of various portions of the human brain associated with sense organs and their functional areas [2].

Visual information is then stored in the neuronal network for further pattern recognition purposes.

A student in class will benefit a lot from using visual perception, as it will allow that student to understand the subject taught in the class with the help of teaching visual aids [3].

3.2.1   Deficient Visual Perception in a Student

Indeed, any alteration or deficiency in such skills might result in the student's poor academic performance. Various problems at different levels cause deficient visual perception and understanding. In short, a student suffers from a lack of understanding of subjects taught in a classroom because of two primary reasons: (i) partial loss of vision and (ii) lack of concentration. Partial loss of vision is due to defects in the eye lens, retina, and optic nerve that convey visual information to the visual cortex. Lack of concentration is due to a wavering mind, general physical fitness, living conditions, slackness in parental care, depraved friends, media, and inept teachers. There are ways and means for a student to come out of such situations [7, 8].

3.2.2   Proper Eye Care (Vision Management)

A student should fundamentally follow the principle of "early to bed and early to wake up". Uninterrupted sleep for eight hours is essential for general health, especially for a clear-cut vision. Moreover, a student should perform some basic exercises like "Surya Namaskaram" for improving eyesight on a day-to-day basis. One has to consume green vegetables containing vitamins A and D [11]. Mostly, vision is impaired due to either damage in the eye or the pathway or in the visual cortex itself, possibly due to brain injury. Perception using visual mechanism is not well defined because deficiency may occur due to visual agnosia. Visual agnosia makes a student incapable of understanding or recognizing learned objects and entities. Agnosia is of two types: (i) perceptive agnosia and (ii) associative agnosia. Perceptive agnosia allows one to visualize some part of an object, but the person will not understand the object as a whole. On the other hand, associative agnosia allows one to understand an object as a whole but does not understand its object [12]. Students who suffer from this defect will not have visual perception and understanding in the classroom. Some students may suffer from "akinetopsia", which amounts to the inability to see movement. Some of the other defects are "achromatopsia", which means the person would not be able to see colors, "prosopagnosia", which means the person would not be able to recognize already learned objects, and "Alexia", which means the person would not be able to learn along with other students. Certain uncommon defects in visual perception are "chizophrenic hallucinations", which means the person understands distorted visual objects and "Charles-Bonnet Syndrome" means the person would lose vision completely, though the vision system is in order the brain cannot respond to the visual patterns. Visual perception makes students interact with the environment, so it is essential to adopt means and visual management methods [13].

3.2.3   Proper Ear Care (Hearing Management)

Today's students should fundamentally follow the principle of "use mobile phones only when required" and nonstop use of mobile phones would lead to various hearing impairment problems. Figure 3.3 shows the human model and a diagrammatic representation of various portions.

A student is said to have hearing impairment when he is unable to hear sounds properly. Deaf students are either hard of hearing or deaf. Some of the hearing impairment are (i) difficulty in hearing everyday speech, (ii) difficulty in hearing loud speech, (iii) ability to hear some words only when

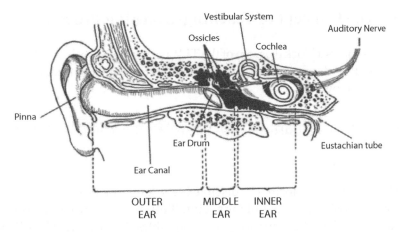

Figure 3.3 Parts of the human ear.

they are shouted in front of the ear, (iv) ability to understand information by lip-reading or using hearing aids, and (v) inability to hear even words that are shouted in front of the ear but understand information only by lip-reading or finger signs. Students having such hearing impairment will not be able to cope up with their studies. Such students need serious medical attention [16].

3.2.4   Proper Mind Care (Psychological Management)

Parents are fundamentally responsible for the onset of good thoughts and practices, including health. Indeed, the environment where a student lives makes a significant impact on the physiological and psychological status. Today's students are cramming machines. They memorize and reproduce in the examinations without any interest or commitment to knowledge transaction [17].

Using "neuropsychological assessment", a mentor may easily measure the cognitive skills of a student. This assessment could be performed on a student using the NEPSY test introduced by Korkman, Kirk, and Kemp. This test allows the mentor to understand how well a student can decode or decipher different rudiments and measure various cognitive resources used by the student to understand and perform as smartly as possible. This test also measures some parameters of visual perception like naming, response time, and processing speed. Hence, vision management, hearing management and psychological management are the essential processes for teaching-learning management. Some necessary details about the TLP are presented in the next section.

3.3   The Concept of Teaching-Learning Process

Figure 3.4 shows a block diagram of the TLP as a regenerative feedback system.

The TLP is clearly defined in a verse of Taitireeya Upanishad, which is presented below [18].

आचार्यःपूर्वरूपम्।अन्तेवास्युत्तररूपम्।विद्यासन्धिः।प्रवचनंसन्धानम्।इत्यधिविद्यम् ।तैत्तिरीयोपनिषद्

Master is the first form; the disciple is the latter form; knowledge is the linking; exposition is the linking's joint. Taitireeya Upanishad consider a word "UNILATERAL" consisting of two syllables. The first syllable is "UNI" and the second syllable is "LATERAL". The meaning of "UNILATERAL" is understood only when these two syllables "UNI" and "LATERAL" are concatenated. So, a teacher is viewed as the first syllable and a student as the second syllable. Just as two syllables' union makes a meaningful word, the teacher's union and the taught make a meaningful output called knowledge generation. This amounts to saying that the TLP is a harmonious activity that leads to knowledge generation. Figure 3.5 shows a conceptual diagram of the TLP [19, 20].

Figure 3.5 shows the conceptual diagram of the TLP introduced in this thesis. The class teacher asks the students, either individually or the entire class students, a question, "Please tell me an example of something that you know that you know". Students answer enthusiastically. Someone says that he knows how to speak English and one more student says that he knows

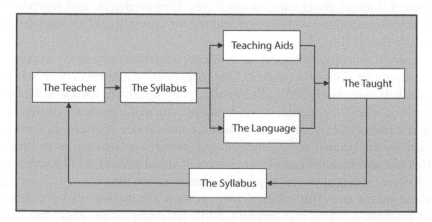

Figure 3.4 Regenerative feedback system of the teaching-learning process.

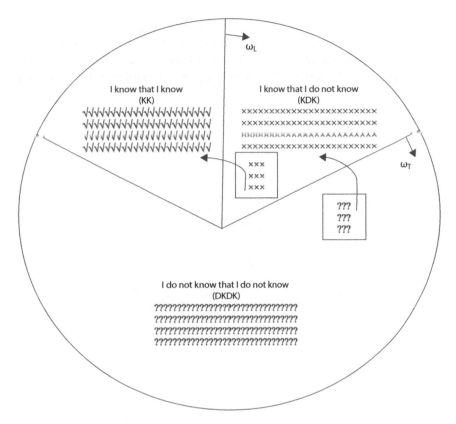

Figure 3.5 Conceptual diagram of the teaching-learning process.

how to drive a car [21]. However, another student says that he knows that he knows the meaning of the word "examination". The teacher is happy to know that all the students respond to his question. He says that he is happy to see the students' responses and he says that he has another question to be asked. He asks them, "Please tell me an example of something that you know that you do not know". Once again, the students responded quickly. One said that he does not know para diving. Another said that he knows that he does not know the Russian language. Many more students responded to the question [22]. Now, the teacher says, "Your responses are wonderful. Now, tell me an example of something that you do not know that you do not know". Students tried but no one could give an example. One cannot give an example of something one does not know that he does not know. The teacher asks the students, "Please tell me the meaning of the English word 'pabulum'". Students blinked. No one knew the very existence of the word "pabulum". Such things that one does not know that he does not know are called "blind spots". Now, concerning Figure 3.6, there are three segments inside the circle (i) region designated as KK region, that is the region containing things that one knows that he knows, (ii) region designated as KDK region, that is the region containing things that one

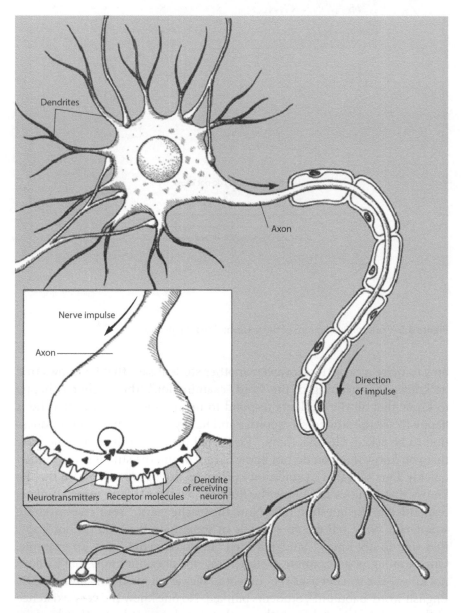

Figure 3.6 Structure of a neuron.

knows he does not know, and (iii) region designated as DKDK region, that is the region containing things that one does not know that he does not know, which are blind spots. Thus, blind spots are things that a student does not know their very existence. The meaning of teaching is that the teacher throws blind spots from the DKDK region to the KDK region. This amounts to saying that the teacher does not spoon-feed students but makes them aware of their blind spots. This is real teaching. The question that arises here is that what would be called real learning. A student has to make efforts to understand the blind spots shown by the teacher by reference and analysis. The fundamental learning is that the student throws the things from his KDK region to KK region and it is real learning. There is a spoke that divides the KK and KDK regions. The student rotates this spoke. There is another spoke that divides the KDK and DKDK regions and the teacher rotates this spoke. The angular velocity with which the teacher rotates his spoke is denoted by ω_T. The velocity with which the student rotates his spoke is denoted by ω_L. Now, the following holds adequate for characterizing the TLP [23].

1. If $\omega_T = \omega_L$, then the TLP is ideal.
2. If $\omega_T < \omega_L$, then the TLP is flawed because of poor teaching.
3. If $\omega_T > \omega_L$, then the TLP is flawed because of poor learning.

An institution with a low TLP score may not produce good students. Hence, efforts should be made to rectify the system. An ideal TLP score is obtained only by the harmonious interaction between the teacher and the taught. There is a detailed description of this kind of superior TLP in Thaitireeya Upanishad.

भृगुर्वै वारुणिः।वरुणंपितरमुपससार।
अधीहिभगवोब्रह्मेति।तस्मांएतत्प्रोवाच।
अन्नंप्राणंचक्षुःश्रोत्रंमनोवाचमिति।
त होंवाच।यतोवाइमानिभूतानिजायंन्ते।
येनजातानिजीवंन्ति।
यत्प्रयंन्त्यभिसंविशन्ति।तद्विजिज्ञासस्व।तद्ब्रह्मेति।
सतपोंऽसतप्यत।सतपंस्तप्वा॥

The sage Bhrugu goes to his father, Varuna, and asks how to know "Brahma", which was a blind spot. The father answers, "Hey Bhrugu!". One should understand "Brahma" only by "Tapasya", that is only by becoming a true seeker (Tapaswi). This was a blind spot for Bhrugu. Varuna made him understand that "Brahma" is perceived only by "Tapasya". Varuna has guided his student (his son). Bhrugu made many efforts to know "Brahma". He identifies various entities.

Like (i) food, (ii) breath, (iii) mind, (iv) external knowledge, and (v) bliss as "Brahma" and analyzed them to find out whether they constitute what is known as "Brahma". First, he thought "Brahma" is food. He does research and finds out that all elements evolve from food, all those evolved sustain in food and finally end in food. Then, he realizes that food cannot be "Brahma" because food has a beginning, sustenance, and ending. Then, he goes to Varuna and tells his findings. Varuna repeats, saying that "Brahma" is understood only by seeking. The verses are given below.

अन्नंब्रह्मेतिव्यंजानात्।अन्नाद्ध्येवखल्विमानि
भुतानिजायन्ते।अन्नेनजातानिजीवन्ति।
अन्नंप्रयन्त्यभिसंविशन्तीति।तद्विज्ञायं।
पुनरेववरुणंपितरमुपंससार।
अधींहिभगवोब्रह्मेति।त होंवाच।
तपंसाब्रह्मविजिंज्ञासस्व।तपोब्रह्मेति।
सतपोंऽतप्यत।सतपंस्तप्वा॥

Then, Bhrugu continues his research and finds out that all elements evolve from the breath (Prana); all those evolved sustain in-breath and finally ended in a breath. Then, he realizes that breath cannot be "Brahma" because the breath has a beginning, sustenance, and ending. Then, he goes to Varuna and tells his findings. Varuna repeats, saying that "Brahma" is understood only by seeking. The verses are given below.

प्राणोब्रह्मेतिव्यंजानात्।प्राणाद्ध्येवखल्विमानि
भूतानिजायन्ते।प्राणेनजातानिजीवन्ति।
प्राणंप्रयन्त्यभिसंविशन्तीति।तद्विज्ञायं।
पुनरेववरुणंपितरमुपंससार।
अधींहिभगवोब्रह्मेति।त होंवाच।
तपंसाब्रह्मविजिंज्ञासस्व।तपोब्रह्मेति।
सतपोंऽतप्यत।सतपंस्तप्वा॥

Once again, Bhrugupurues his research and finds out that all elements evolve from the mind (Manas). All those evolved sustain in mind and finally ended in mind. Then, he realizes that the mind cannot be "Brahma" because the mind has a beginning, sustenance, and ending. Then, he goes to Varuna and tells his findings. Varuna once again repeats, saying that "Brahma" is understood only by seeking. The verses are given below.

मनोब्रह्मेतिव्यंजानात्।मनंसोह्येवखल्विमानि
भूतानिजायंते।मनंसाजातानिजीवंति।
मनःप्रयंत्यभिसंविशन्तीतिं।तद्विज्ञायं।
पुनरेववरुणंपितरंमुपंससार।
अधींहिभगवोब्रह्मेतिं।त होंवाच।
तपंसाब्रह्मविजिज्ञासस्व।तपोब्रह्मेतिं।
सतपोंऽतप्यत।सतपंस्तप्त्वा॥

Bhrugu untiringly continues his research and finds out that all elements evolve from external knowledge (Vignanam), all those evolved sustain in knowledge and finally end in knowledge. Then, he realizes that knowledge cannot be "Brahma" because knowledge has a beginning, sustenance, and ending. Then, he goes to Varuna and explains what he had found. Varuna, as usual, says that "Brahma" is understood only by seeking. The verses are given below.

विज्ञानंब्रह्मेतिव्यंजानात्।विज्ञानाद्ध्येवखल्विमानि
भूतानिजायंते।विज्ञानेनजातानिजीवंति।
विज्ञानंप्रयंत्यभिसंविशन्तीतिं।तद्विज्ञायं।
पुनरेववरुणंपितरंमुपंससार।
अधींहिभगवोब्रह्मेतिं।त होंवाच।
तपंसाब्रह्मविजिज्ञासस्व।तपोब्रह्मेतिं।
सतपोंऽतप्यत।सतपंस्तप्त्वा॥

Bhrugu further extends his research and finds out that all elements evolve from bliss (Anandam), all those evolved sustain in bliss and finally end in bliss. Then, he realizes that bliss cannot be "Brahma" because bliss has a beginning, sustenance, and ending. Then, he goes to Varuna and explains what he had found. Thus, the TLP between Varuna and Bhrugu continued forever. The verses are given below.

आनन्दोब्रह्मेतिव्यंजानात्।आनन्दाध्येवखल्विमानि

भूतानिजायंन्ते।आनन्देनजातानिजीवन्ति।

आनन्दंप्रयंन्त्यभिसंविशन्तीतिं।

सैषाभा गुर्वीवांरुणीविद्या।परमेव्यों मन्प्रतिष्ठिता।

The one who understands this VarunaBhrugu TLP and practices accordingly will become a great person blessed with whatever he wishes. The verses are given below.

सयएवंवेदप्रतितिष्ठति।अन्नंवानन्नादोभंवति।

महान्भवतिप्रजयांपशुभिर्ब्रह्मवर्चसेनं।

महान्कीर्त्या॥

This Varuna-Bhrugu TLP is the ideal TLP and one has to devise methods of appropriate TLP techniques aiming at the ideal TLP. What is suggested in this thesis is that one can use ICT tools to achieve optimum results in the TLP.

3.4   Use of ICT Tools in Teaching-Learning Process

Professional students studying in various higher learning institutions in India are suffering from physiological and psychological problems, which lead to poor academic performance, so the very purpose of having such institutions is almost lost. Reasons for this situation are many. One primary reason is the lack of transparency in the education system. Teachers have become knowledge workers and students study to get degrees to get highly paid jobs. This is true, especially in the wake of an economy-oriented society. People expect great results in a short time. This is the order of the day. Employees expect a high rate of personal economic growth and employers expect a high productivity rate, most of the time much above their employees' capabilities. These expectations have caused a demand for quick teaching and learning in academic institutions. Institutions failing to satisfy these demands face many challenges, including their closures, meaning joblessness for teachers, and deterioration in employable students' availability. In this context, one would look into various possibilities of improving the quality of the TLP [26]. The use of traditional techniques would indeed yield good results with, of course, delayed outcomes. The use of ICT tools and traditional techniques may speed up the process of improving the quality. Some of the ICT tools are discussed in the sequel.

3.4.1 Digital Resources as ICT Tools

Academic institutions should provide universal, equitable, and free access to ICT and ICT-enabled tools and resources to all students and teachers. Given the diversity of India's educational situation, there is a need for a variety of digital content for different subjects in different languages. Unicode fonts could be used to enable universal access and amenability to "transliteration" and "machine translation". The use of interactive ICT tools for an effective TLP like virtual laboratories could be promoted. The development of e-books, animations, lessons, exercises, interactive games, models and simulations, videos, presentation slides, explicit text materials, graphics, or any combinations of the above could be encouraged. Web-based digital repositories containing a variety of digital content will be a boon for students and teachers. Multimedia learning objects could be used in TLP. Teachers and students can jointly develop digital learning resources that contribute to digital repositories. Wikipedia is one such domain where students and teachers can contribute. Groups of specific interests like Artificial Intelligence and Machine Learning could be formed and students and teachers encouraged to participate in discussions. Webinars could be arranged on various subjects, especially during pandemic periods. Media could be encouraged to organize programs for this purpose in addition to their programs of commercial interests. Just like Open Course Wares (OCWs) introduced by MIT Boston, Indian institutes of higher learning can bring out OCWs for the ordinary person [27].

3.4.2 Special ICT Tools for Capacity Building of Students and Teachers

3.4.2.1 CogniFit

VIPER-NAM is a test for improving the cognitive abilities of students and teachers. For example, images of specific objects are shown on the screen for a short time. Then, some letters are shown, only one of which will correspond to the object's name. The observer has to choose the correct answer quickly. This exercise would undoubtedly improve the visual perception of students and teachers.

CogniFit, a software support system, is available in the market, which would help train this ability. CogniFit has a battery of tasks and tests designed to help students and teachers rehabilitate and improve visual perception deficits and other cognitive functions. Using CogniFit, one can strengthen the brain and neural connections similar to strengthening muscle by constant practice. This means that one can improve one's visual perception by using CogniFit. CogniFit has both evaluation tools and a rehabilitation program to help optimize cognitive function. CogniFit is available online and it could be practiced on computers and mobile devices as well. The program is full of fun-filled with exciting brain games, and for every training session, the user will receive a graphical display result that highlights the user's cognitive progress.

3.4.2.2   Brain-Computer Interface

A BCI is a direct communication pathway between a brain and an external device. BCIs are aimed at assisting, augmenting, or repairing human cognitive or sensory-motor functions. Alternatively, "Neuroprosthetics" in neuroscience, which is concerned with neural prostheses of using artificial devices to replace the function of impaired nervous systems or sensory organs. The best examples of neuroprosthetic devices are "cochlear implants", used to restore hearing, and optical neuroprosthetic devices like retinal implants used to restore vision. Some of the advanced BCIs are follows:

1. Biofeedback (BF)
2. Neurofeedback (NF)
3. Brain-Computer Interface (BCI)
4. Adaptive BCI (ABI)
5. Intellectual BCI (IBCI)
6. Brain-to-Brain Interface (BBI)

The brain is mainly the neuronal network. The central part of the brain is the cortex or gray matter. The cortex contains approximately 10^{11} neuronal cells called neurons. Most data processing happens in the cortex. Fundamental to brain function are the nerve cells called neurons. The neurons form various *networks of neurons* that are pathways through which information in the nervous system is transmitted or stored. The brain is an information processing system and computations and symbols best explain information processing, as shown in Figure 3.7. Information processing in the COMPUTER is programs operating on symbols. Information processing in the BRAIN is neural computations involving mental representations as symbols. Mental representations are symbols in the brain that have meaning or encoded information. Brain representations are the activation of the local brain area, accompanied by a specific EEG pattern.

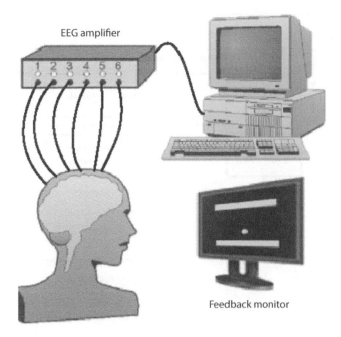

Figure 3.7 Block diagram of a typical neurofeedback system.

Some researchers had already demonstrated that subjects could learn to control their brain activity through intensive training to generate fixed EEG patterns. In fact, "Neurofeedback" is an up-and-coming ICT tool even for some therapies, such as preventing epilepsy seizures. Through the learning process between computers and subjects, the system can understand subjects' mental states by recognizing EEG. Such a learned NF system that can detect different mental states is called Brain-Computer Interface (BCI). Figure 3.8 shows an essential BCI architecture.

BCI translates the EEG signal characteristics into commands, which control devices in the following manner:

- Feature extraction from EEG.
- Feed them a classifier.
- Train classifier with repeated imagination patterns from a given subject.
- After training, BCI relies on the classifier for translating mental imagery.

So, "one mental state" implies "one command"!

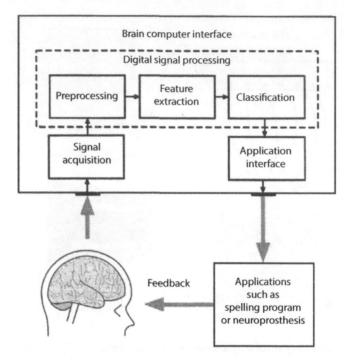

Figure 3.8 BCI architecture.

Training Experiments: operant conditioning (NF Training)

- The computer screen includes three buttons, each identified by their position: left, right, up.
- Subjects learn to associate mental status with each button to enable the BCI system to understand better what they think.
- Five days training every day, half an hour per day.
- Results: the recognition rate is 70% or higher!
- BCI Bypasses the Brain's Normal Pathways of Peripheral Nerves and Muscles.

Hence, one can use a BCI as an ICT tool for improving TLP.

3.5   Conclusion

The quality enhancements of teaching and learning are only possible through information and communication technologies (ICTs) in higher education systems (HES). ICT utilization in the system gives e-learning facilities by maximizing theteaching and learning process in the classroom. Nowadays, teaching and learning methods are converted from traditional forms to online and simulated virtual environments. Many ways can do integrate ICT into the education system. Many private universities and state-level universities are using ICT to enhanced distance learning. With the help of ICT, the teachingcommunity is ready to go to remote areas where people want to study but lack facultiesand facilities. The ICT also helps learners to obtain a qualitative environment of learning from every corner of the world. The trainers and the teachers must learn the new technologies and latest learning styles to benefit the learners. Successful utilization of ICT in any state if India leads to change is to entrust the teachers and backup them to support the students in learning instead of gathering computer skills and establishing softwareand equipment. Integration of ICT and data mining technique allows education to reach the students in the form of information from the stockholder.

References

1. Pathak, S., Raja, R., Sharma, V., Ambala, S., ICT Utilization and Improving Student Performance in Higher Education. *Int. J. Recent Technol. Eng. (IJRTE)*, 8, 2, 5120–5124, July 2019.
2. Pathak, S., Raja, R., Sharma, V., RamyaLaxmi, K., A Framework of ICT Implementation on Higher Educational Institution with Data Mining Approach. *Eur. J. Eng. Res. Sci.*, 4, 5, 2019.
3. Pathak, S., Raja, R., Sharma, V., The Impact of ICT in Higher Education. Published in IJRECE. *IJRECE*, 7, 1, 1650–1656, January-March, 2019.
4. Adekitan, A.I., and Noma-Osaghae, E., Data mining approach to predicting the performance of the first-year student in a university using the admission requirements. *Educ. Inf. Technol.*, 24, 2, 1527–1543, 2019.
5. Asif, R., Merceron, A., Ali, S.A., Haider, N.G., Analyzing undergraduate students' performance using educational data mining. *Comput. Educ.*, 113, 177–194, 2017, 10.1016/j.compedu.2017.05.007.
6. Bharara, S., Sabitha, S., Bansal, S., Application of learning analytics using clustering data Mining for Students' disposition analysis. *Educ. Inf. Technol.*, 23, 2, 957–984, 2018.
7. Francis, K.B. and Babu, S.S., Predicting the academic performance of students using a hybrid data mining approach. *J. Med. Syst.*, 43, 6, 162, 2019.
8. Gabriela, C., Mihai, A., Crivei, L.M., S PRAR: A novel relational association rule mining classification model applied for academic performance prediction. *Proc. Comput. Sci.*, 159, 20–29, 2019, 10.1016/j.procs.2019.09.156.

9. Helal, S., Li, J., Liu, L., Ebrahimie, E., Dawson, S., Murray, D.J., Long, Q., Predicting academic performance by considering student heterogeneity. *Knowledge-Based Syst.*, 161, 134–146, 2018, 10.1016/j.knosys.2018.07.042.

10. Karthikeyan, V.G., Thangaraj, P., Karthik, S., Towards developing hybrid educational data mining model (HEDM) for efficient and accurate student performance evaluation. *Soft Comput.*, 24, 1–11, 2020, 10.1007%2Fs00500-020-05075-4.

11. Khan, A. and Ghosh, S.K., Student performance analysis and prediction in classroom learning: A review of educational data mining studies. *Educ. Inf. Technol.*, 26, 205–240, 2021, 10.1007%2Fs10639-020-10230-3.

12. Khan, A. and Ghosh, S.K., Data mining-based analysis to explore the effect of teaching on student performance. *Educ. Inf. Technol.*, 23, 4, 1677–1697, 2018.

13. Lee, C.S., Wang, M.H., Wang, C.S., Teytaud, O., Liu, J., Lin, S.-W., Hung, P.-H., PSO-based fuzzy markup language for student learning performance evaluation and educational application. *IEEE Trans. Fuzzy Syst.*, 26, 5, 2618–2633, 2018.

14. Mengash, H.A., Using data mining techniques to predict student performance to support decision making in university admission systems. *IEEE Access*, 8, 55462–55470, 2020, 10.1109/ACCESS.2020.2981905.

15. Miguéis, L., Freitas, A., Garcia, Silva, A., Early segmentation of students according to their academic performance: A predictive modeling approach. *Decis. Support Syst.*, 115, 36–51, 2018, 10.1016/j.dss.2018.09.001.

16. Mimis, M., Hajji, M.E., Es-Saady, Y., Guejdi, A.O., Douzi, H., Mammass, D., A framework for smart academic guidance using educational data mining. *Educ. Inf. Technol.*, 24, 2, 1379–1393, 2019.

17. Ouyang, Y., Zeng, Y., Gao, R., Yu, Y., Wang, C., Elective future: The influence factor mining of students' graduation development based on hierarchical attention neural network model with graph. *Appl. Intell.*, 50, 3023–3039, 2020, 10.1007%2Fs10489-020-01692-6.

18. Paloş, R., Maricuţoiu, L.P., Costea, I., Relations between academic performance, student engagement and student burnout: a cross-lagged analysis of a two-wave study. *Stud. Educ. Eval.*, 60, 199–204, 2019, 10.1016/j. stueduc.2019.01.005.

19. Popescu, E. and Leon, F., Predicting academic performance based on learner traces in a social learning environment. *IEEE Access*, 6, 72774–72785, 2018, 10.1109/ACCESS.2018.2882297. hareshvasantdstani.

20. Rao, D.H., Mangalwede, S.R., Deshmukh, V.B., Student performance evaluation model based on scoring rubric tool for network analysis subject using fuzzy logic, in: *2017 International Conference on Electrical, Electronics, Communication, Computer, and Optimization Techniques (ICEECCOT)*, IEEE, pp. 1–5, 2017, 10.1109/ICEECCOT.2017.8284623.

21. Shahiri, A.M. and Husain, W., A review on predicting student's performance using data mining techniques. *Proc. Comput. Sci.*, 72, 414–422, 2015, 10.1016/j.procs.2015.12.157.

22. Tomasevic, N., Gvozdenovic, N., Vranes, S., An overview and comparison of supervised data mining techniques for student exam performance prediction. *Comput. Educ.*, 143, 103676, 2020, 10.1016/j.compedu.2019.103676.

23. Waheed, H., Hassan, S., Aljohani, N.R., Hardman, J., Alelyani, S., Nawaz, R., Predicting the academic performance of students from VLE big data using deep learning models. *Comput. Hum. Behav.*, 104, 106189, 2020, 10.1016/j.chb.2019.106189.

24. Xu, J., Moon, K.H., Van DerSchaar, M., A machine learning approach for tracking and predicting student performance in degree programs. *IEEE J. Sel. Top. Signal Process.*, 11, 5, 742–753, 2017.

25. Yadav, R.S., Application of hybrid clustering methods for student performance evaluation. *Int. J. Inf. Technol.*, 6, 1–8, 2018, 10.1007%2Fs41870-018-0192-2.

26. Yousafzai, B.K., Hayat, M., Afzal, S., Application of machine learning and data mining in predicting the performance of intermediate and secondary education level student. *Educ. Inf. Technol.*, 6, 2, 1–21, 2020, 10.1007%2Fs10639-020-10189-1.

27. Zughoul, O., Momani, F., Almasri, O.H., Zaidan, Zaidan, B.B., Alsalem, M.A., Albahri, Albahri, O.S., Hashim, M., Comprehensive insights into the criteria of student performance in various educational domains. *IEEE Access*, 6, 73245–73264, 2018, 10.1109/ACCESS.2018.2881282.

4

Denoising of Digital Images Using Wavelet-Based Thresholding Techniques: A Comparison

Devanand Bhonsle

SSTC, SSGI, Bhilai, India

Abstract

Noise is an unwanted entity that corrupts the image due to which its quality degrades. This degradation may be suppressing details like edges, ridges, and other fine structures that are important to analyze the details. Hence, removal of noise is essential or at least its effect must be reduced to a certain extent. The process by which an image reduces the noise is called "Image Denoising". It is a filtration technique that suppresses the noise and restores the image. Gaussian noise is one of the noise signals, which corrupts the signals almost in all the frequency band; hence, it is known as white Gaussian noise. Since it is additive, i.e., it is added to all the image's pixel values, Additive White Gaussian Noise. In this chapter, Gaussian noise suppression using various wavelet thresholding has been discussed. Results exhibit the capability of wavelet-based filters to reduce the effect of Gaussian noise to an acceptable extent.

Keywords: Noise, wavelet transform, peak signal to noise ratio, thresholding, mean square error, structural similarity index matrix

4.1 Introduction

Noise may be introduced due to various reasons. Mainly, noise introduces in the images during the acquisition and transmission from source to destination [1]. Environmental condition and quality of sensing elements are the major factors responsible for introducing noise in images while

---

Email: devanandbhonsle@gmail.com

Sandeep Kumar, Rohit Raja, Shrikant Tiwari and Shilpa Rani (eds.) Cognitive Behavior and Human Computer Interaction Based on Machine Learning Algorithm, (85–116) © 2022 Scrivener Publishing LLC

capturing them. Interference in the channel is also responsible for the noise in an image during the transmission process. Lightning and other atmospheric condition may also lead to noise in the images during wireless transmission. Noise introduces during acquisition and transmission [2]. Compression and decompression of the image may also be the reason for introducing noise in the image. The imperfect instruments/sensing elements are the primary sources of noise. For example, dark current noise appears due to the electrons generated due to the thermal effect. It is proportional to the exposure time and temperature of the sensing element. Shot noise is generated due to quantum uncertainty in photoelectron generation [2]. Quantization noise comes into existence during the conversion of some electrons to pixel intensities. In a coherent imaging system, noise is introduced due to the scattering of imaging purposes' signals. Ultrasound imaging system [3–9] is the best example of coherent imaging, which is severely affected by noise, commonly known as speckle [10]. The most common noise is Additive White Gaussian Noise (AWGN) which affects almost all the signals [11]. This chapter aims to eliminate the effect of AWGN from digital images and performance evaluation of techniques. This process is called image filtering or image denoising [12–14]. Noise signals can be broadly divided into three categories, *viz.*, additive noise [11, 15], multiplicative noise [11], and sparse noise [2].

1. **Additive Noise:** If the noise is added up to the pixel values, then it is called additive noise. Let $x(i, j)$ is the two-dimensional image; corrupted by noise $n(i, j)$. If $y(i, j)$ is the noisy image, then $y(i, j) = x(i, j) + n(i, j)$. White Gaussian noise comes under the category of additive noise [11].
2. **Multiplicative Noise:** If the noise multiplies with the pixel values, then it is called multiplicative noise. Noisy image is given as $y(i, j) = x(i, j) \times n(i, j)$. Speckle noise comes under the category of multiplicative noise [11].
3. **Sparse Noise:** Some noise signals corrupt only a few pixels of the image. These types of images are called sparse noise. Although they affect only a few pixels, effect is very severe. It includes salt and pepper noise [2], random valued impulse noise, and vertical and horizontal deadlines.

This chapter will deal with additive noise only, which follows the Gaussian distribution [11]. Since the noise signals fluctuate in the pixel values, they can be categorized as random variables. The Probability Density function (PDF) of any random variable is an equation that links the

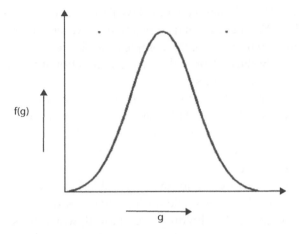

f(g)

g

Figure 4.1 PDF of Gaussian noise.

statistical result's values with its probability of occurrence. Gaussian noise is also called a standard distribution noise model having a bell-shaped PDF curve [10]. It affects both the light and dark areas of an image and additive in nature. Figure 4.1 shows a PDF of Gaussian noise, which is bell-shaped. It equally distributes to the entire frequency band hence called white noise. Gaussian distribution is given as follows:

$$p(z) = \frac{1}{\sigma\sqrt{2\pi}} e^{-\frac{(z-m)^2}{2\sigma^2}} \tag{4.1}$$

where z is the gray level of the pixel, σ is the standard deviation, and m is the image's mean.

4.2   Literature Survey

This part gives the idea about the previous work done for image denoising and many researchers implemented different filters for different noise signals. Noise may be of any type discussed above [11]. It is essential to know the characteristics and their effect on the digital images to implement the filters. The explanation mentioned above-defined various types of noise signals and much literature is available in image denoising. Noise affects the quality of images so that much useful information may either vanish or corrupted. An image has various information, *viz.*, edges, ridges, and fine structure [16, 17]. Below is the description of various techniques proposed in various literature.

Kingsbury [18] implemented a new DWT for image denoising enhancement called DTCWT because; it uses two trees of wavelet filters that provide the real and imaginary parts of the complex wavelet coefficients. It provides less redundancy because it provides suitable directional property. It offers perfect reconstruction and its computational efficiency is very high. These advantages make it an efficient tool for denoising and deblurring for two- and multidimensional signals [18]. Qin et al. [19] developed a denoising technique in which either hard or soft thresholding is applied to shrink wavelet coefficient, and then, the signal is reconstructed [19]. Sveinsson and Benediktsson used Discrete Wavelet Transform (DWT)–based filter bank, which is oversampled and named Double Density Discrete Wavelet Transform (DDDWT). It has single scaling and two wavelet functions which are different. Adaptive thresholding is employed, which uses a non-linear sigmoid function. The thresholding is adaptive for each sub-band [20]. Chen et al. [21] implemented wavelet thresholding method, which incorporates the neighboring coefficients [21] hence called Neigh shrink. It performs better than Wiener Filter (WF) and other conventional wavelet denoising techniques [22]. Fowler [15] developed a technique for the suppression of additive noise using Redundant Discrete Wavelet Transform (RDWT), an expansion of the Undecimated Discrete Wavelet Transform (UDWT) [15]. Eslami and Radha [23] implemented a family of non-redundant geometrical image transforms based on directional filter banks and wavelet transform (WT). It exhibits directional and non-directional basis functions, applied for image denoising and coding [23]. Gu et al. [14] developed 2D fast WT for denoising. Wavelet Packet Analysis (WPA) decomposes low- and high-frequency parts simultaneously. It does local analysis precisely [14]. Borsdorf et al. [12] described denoising method for Computed Tomography (CT) images to preserve its structures. It is a wavelet-based method in which data decompose into two, viz., information and noise signals. It can adapt itself under the noise signal present in the images [12]. Chang et al. [24] proposed a data-driven soft thresholding technique, derived in a Bayesian framework. It performs better than SURE (Stein's Unbiased Risk Estimator) shrink in most cases [24]. Dengwen and Xiaoliu [25] proposed a data-driven Block shrink technique that applies the relevancy of neighbor wavelet coefficients. The drawback of this technique is that it applies thresholding term by term. Thresholding values and block size are the same for all sub-bands, limiting its performance [25]. Miller and Kingsbury [26] implemented AWGN removal technique based on Gaussian Scale Mixture modeling of Neighborhoods of coefficients at adjacent locations and scales. It suppresses the ringing effect and enhances sharpness [26]. Zhang et al. [27] implemented denoising technique based on WT called M-Bayes threshold by combining multiple wavelet representations and Bayes thresholding. Its computational complexity is low [27]. Raj and Venkateswarlu [28] proposed a UDWT with semisoft and stein thresholding operators along with different wavelet families. It removes the blurring and ringing effect efficiently. However, it is slower than DWT because it requires more storage space and more computational cost. As the decomposition level increases, the resolution of UDWT coefficients decreases [28]. Hassan and Saparon [29] implemented Gaussian noise removal technique using DWT. It uses either hard or soft thresholding incorporate with translation-invariant technique. It suppresses the artifact effect. Performance can be improved using adaptive thresholding [29]. Hill *et al.* [30] developed undecimated DTCWT for denoising using bivariate thresholding which is the extension of traditional DTCWT. It improves in lower-scale sub-band localization [30]. Kim *et al.* [31] implemented denoising technique, which uses Haar wavelet in tetrolet domain and locally adaptive thresholding is applied on high-frequency tetrolet coefficients [31]. It preserves the edges. Zhao *et al.* [32] implemented a wavelet denoising technique by applying scanner-dependent threshold estimator and Visu shrink. It outperforms Visu shrink as the decomposition level increases [32].

After studying the various research literature, we may conclude that noise is a common problem in digital images that must be suppressed. Many methods remove the AGWN [11] efficiently, but unfortunately, it suppresses essential features [16]. Wavelet-based thresholding [24, 48] techniques suppress noise signals while preserves the details of the images. The literature survey's basic idea is to get the idea for existing methods, advantages, and limitations. Wavelet-based denoising techniques exhibit better results as compare to other existing techniques. DWT provides good results but suffers from two problems, *viz.*, time variance and less directional selectivity [33]. These two problems have been overcome using DTCWT as it is time invariance and shows good directional selectivity [34]. Wavelet techniques require thresholding by which noisy wavelet coefficient may be either removed entirely or replaced by the calculated values. Many thresholding techniques have been implemented and modifications are still going on. Examples of various thresholding are Neigh shrink [12], SURE shrink, Visu Shrink, Bayes shrink [27], Block shrink [25], bivariate thresholding [35], etc.

4.3   Theoretical Analysis

This part contains the theoretical explanation of WT and various thresholding techniques used for image denoising in this chapter.

4.3.1 Wavelet Transform

It deals with those signals which Fourier or any other transforms cannot represent. Generally, these transforms are sinusoid and extend from (−) to (+) infinity, while wavelets are non-symmetrical and irregular; hence, they can represent the signals containing harmonics oscillation. Wavelets are small waves concentrated in space and time which have finite energy. It is suitable for signal and image processing because it represents the signal without losing information [36]. It provides fair time resolution as well as frequency resolution. It can be broadly categorized into two types:

    (i)   Continuous Wavelet Transform (CWT)
    (ii) Discrete Wavelet Transform (DWT)

4.3.1.1 *Continuous Wavelet Transform*

Wavelets are small waves and they are the family of functions having oscillations and decay quickly. They develop by the construction and expansion of any function [36]. The function is called a mother wavelet, which may be any oscillating function with zero mean and given as follows:

$$\psi_{m,n}(t) = \frac{1}{\sqrt{|m|}} \psi\left(\frac{t-n}{m}\right) \tag{4.2}$$

where $m, n \in R$, $m \neq 0$, m and n represent scaling and translation parameters, respectively.

For any arbitrary signal $x(t)$ at time n and scale m, WT is given as follows:

$$F(M,N) = \int_{-\infty}^{\infty} x(t)\psi_{m,n}(t)dt \tag{4.3}$$

where $F(M, N)$ is the WT of $x(t)$.

By applying Parseval's theorem,

$$F(M,N) = \int_{-\infty}^{\infty} \hat{f}(\omega)\hat{\psi}(\omega)d\omega \tag{4.4}$$

where $\hat{f}(\omega)$ is the spectrum of $\psi_{m,n}(t)$ in time-frequency domain with the energy $\hat{\psi}(\omega)$.

It collects a large amount of data from raw data of the function due to which a large number of coefficients are generated as a result, and large redundant are produced. This is the biggest problem of CWT. This problem can be avoided by using DWT.

4.3.1.2 Discrete Wavelet Transform

It is a discrete form of CWT and it provides two kinds of coefficients with each decomposition level called approximation and detailed coefficients. Mathematically, it can be represented as follows:

$$\psi_{m,n}(t) = \frac{1}{\sqrt{|2^m|}} \psi\left(\frac{t - 2^m n}{2^m}\right) \tag{4.5}$$

where m is scaling and n is translation index, at each level of decomposition.

If an input signal passes through a Low Pass Filter (LPF) followed by a downsampler, then approximation coefficients are generated. If it is passed through a High Pass Filter (HPF) followed by a downsampler, then detail coefficients are generated. Any signal can be decomposed into more than one level. However, resolution deteriorates with the increase of decomposition level. The coefficients obtained from the first level are considered as the input for the next level. DWT has invertible property, i.e., reverse DWT process can also be performed and referred to as Inverse Discrete Wavelet Transform (IDWT). So, if any signal is decomposed using DWT, then it can be reconstructed using IDWT. Below is explaining the decomposition and reconstruction of any signal in the wavelet domain [32, 33].

4.3.1.2.1 Wavelet Decomposition

In this process, an input signal is passed through an LPF followed by the downsampler. As a result, approximation coefficients are generated. If it is passed through an HPF followed by a downsampler, then complex coefficients are generated. Each of these sub-signals is passed through LPF and HPF along with the column data. The resultant is again sampled by Figure 4.2, and it shows the arrangement for one level decomposition process for a digital grayscale image. In this process, the input image splits into four sub-images of size N/2×N/2each.

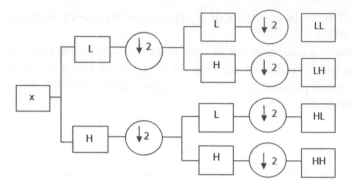

Figure 4.2 Single-level decomposition of 2D image.

Figure 4.3 represents four sub-bands for one level of decomposition using WT. An image can also be decomposed to more levels.

Figure 4.4 represents the three-level decomposition of a digital image where an image is decomposed to three levels which provide approximate and detailed wavelet coefficients.

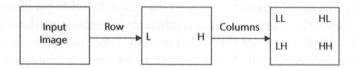

Figure 4.3 Single-level DWT decomposition.

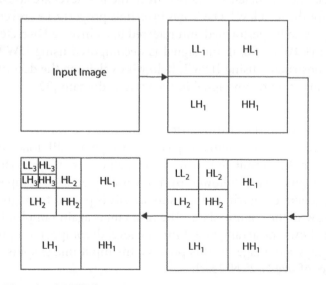

Figure 4.4 Three-level DWT decomposition.

LL sub-band: It is the result of LPF both the rows and columns and contains the rough description of the image hence called "approximation".

HH sub-band: It is the result of HPF in both directions and contains high-frequency components.

LH sub-band: It results from LPF in one direction and contains vertical details corresponds to horizontal edges.

HL sub-band: It results from HPF in another direction and contains details corresponds to vertical edges.

HH, LH, and HL sub-bands are called detail sub-bands as they provide detailed coefficients.

The above discussion shows that a digital image can be decomposed into n^{th} levels until it is decomposed completely or stopped as per requirement.

4.3.1.2.2   Wavelet Reconstruction

It is the reverse process of wavelet decomposition, i.e., the signal can be reconstructed using decomposed wavelet coefficients. All the sub-bands are upsampled and passed through the corresponding inverse filters along with the columns. Both the results are added and upsampled again. Finally, it is filtered using corresponding inverse filters. Astric sign (*) represents inverse filtration. The result of the last stage is added together; thus, the original image is obtained. Figure 4.5 shows the wavelet reconstruction operation.

From the above discussion, it is clear that an image can be decomposed using WT and retrieved back to its original form with no loss of information; thus, an exact image is to be obtained. Hence, DWT is to be used as a useful tool in image processing [1, 36]. Many research papers explain that its better performance than non-wavelet techniques. However, its

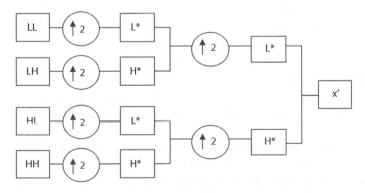

Figure 4.5 Single-level composition step of four sub-images.

performance affects two significant problems, *viz.*, shift variance and low directional selectivity.

(i) Shift Variance
If the small shift in input provides considerable variation in energy distribution between wavelet coefficients at different scales, then this phenomenon is called shift variance. It affects the quality of output badly.

(ii) Poor Directional Selectivity
Since filters are separable and real DWT, they cannot distinguish between the opposing diagonal directions, due to which DWT suffers from the insufficient directional property.

Two properties, *viz.*, shift-invariance and right directional property, are required in image processing applications. Hence, to overcome both the drawbacks, complex wavelet filters have been used. These filters provide shift-invariance and directional both the property simultaneously. However, these filters are difficult to implement hence cannot be used widely.

4.3.1.3 Dual-Tree Complex Wavelet Transform

The deficiencies mentioned above of conventional DWT [18] proposed DTCWT, which exhibits time invariance and provides right directional property [18, 37–40]. It consists of two parallel DWT filter bank trees with respective filters of both trees in approximate quadrature. Due to this structure, it produces wavelet coefficients differently. It generates complex coefficients using a dual-tree of wavelet filters. The filter arrangement decomposes an input image into a pyramid of sub-images with each level; thus, six oriented sub-images are obtained. Amplitude and phase information can be extracted from real and imaginary coefficients. Figure 4.6 shows the filter arrangement for DTCWT. The input is a digital image that is to be decomposed using two sets of filter banks (H_{0a}, H_{1a}) and (H_{0b}, H_{1b}). In the tree, sampling rates can be doubled by eliminating downsampling by two after level 1 filters, H_{0a} and H_{1a}. This process is equivalent to two parallel thoroughly decimated trees, a and b, provided that the delay of H_{0b} and H_{1b} are one sample offset from H_{0a} and H_{1a}. With these modifications, DTCWT has the following properties; which makes it superior to conventional DWT:

(i) **Shift Invariant:** It is approximate shift-invariant, which is desired in image processing.
(ii) **Good Directional Selectivity:** It provides better directional selectivity, as it has twelve directional wavelets (six

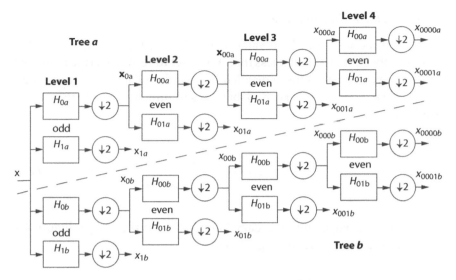

Figure 4.6 Filter arrangement for the dual-tree complex wavelet transform.

for each of imaginary and real trees) oriented at angles in two dimensions.

(iii) **Phase Information:** At any given level, any given sub-band phase can be obtained using its corresponding imaginary and real coefficients.

(iv) **Perfect Reconstruction:** Original signal can be reconstructed completely using all coefficients.

(v) **Less Redundancy:** It provides redundancy of 2^m:1 input signal where m is the signal dimension.

(vi) **Less Computational Complexity:** It is less complicated as compared to the UDWT [41].

4.3.2 Types of Thresholding

Thresholding is a method by which noisy coefficients are removed or suppressed using a specific rule. Wavelet coefficients are generated by applying WT on a noisy image. Among all the coefficients, noisy coefficients are also present. These noisy coefficients are removed or suppressed to a certain extent and finally, inverse WT is applied; a noise-free image is obtained. The efficacy of any method entirely depends upon the thresholding technique. This technique may be divided into, *viz.*, hard thresholding and soft thresholding [42].

4.3.2.1   Hard Thresholding

In this technique, a threshold value λ is to be set. Input is kept as if it is more significant than λ but if less than λ, it is set to zero. This rule is applied only on wavelet coefficients of detailed sub-bands and low-resolution coefficients are kept unaltered. Formidable thresholding operator may be given as follows:

$$W = T_{hard}(X,W) = \begin{cases} X, |X| \geq \lambda \\ 0, |X| < \lambda \end{cases} \tag{4.6}$$

It retains the edge and boundary information of the image. Figure 4.7 illustrates the rigid thresholding scheme.

4.3.2.2   Soft Thresholding

In this technique, coefficients are shrunk toward zero if its magnitude is more significant than the selected thresholding value but set to zero and if it is less than the threshold value [43]. Soft thresholding operator may be given as follows:

$$W = T_{soft}(X,W) = \begin{cases} \text{sgn}\{X\}(|X|-\lambda), |X| \geq \lambda \\ 0 \qquad, |X| < \lambda \end{cases} \tag{4.7}$$

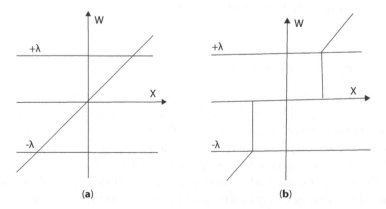

(a)   (b)

Figure 4.7 Hard thresholding scheme: (a) original signal and (b) after hard thresholding.

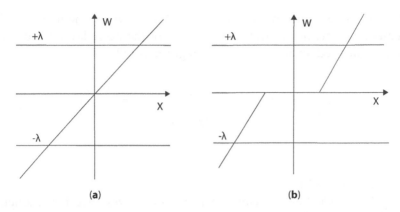

Figure 4.8 Soft thresholding scheme: (a) original signal and (b) after soft thresholding.

Figure 4.8 shows a soft thresholding scheme that outperforms a rigid thresholding scheme.

4.3.2.3   Thresholding Techniques

In this chapter, we have explained various thresholding techniques, *viz.*, SURE shrink, Bayes shrink [27], Neigh shrink [22], Block shrink [25], and Bivariate shrinkage [35, 44]. The description of the thresholding mentioned above schemes is discussed below.

4.3.2.3.1   SURE Shrink
It is given by Donoho and Johnstone, which is based on Stein's Unbiased Risk Estimator (SURE). It combined universal threshold and SURE threshold and abbreviated as SURE shrink. It minimizes Mean Squared Error (MSE) which is given as follows:

$$MSE = \frac{1}{M \times N} \sum_{i=0}^{M-1} \sum_{j=0}^{N-1} [I_1(i,j) - I_2(i,j)]^2 \qquad (4.8)$$

where $I_1(i, j)$ is the original image and $I_2(i, j)$ is a noisy image with size $M \times N$

The SURE Shrink threshold t* is defined as follows:

$$t^* = \min\left(t, \sigma\sqrt{2\log n}\right) \qquad (4.9)$$

t is the value that minimizes SURE, and σ and *n* are the image's noise variance and size, respectively. An estimate of the noise level σ is defined based on the median absolute deviation given as follows:

$$\hat{\sigma} = \frac{median\left(\left\{\left|g_{j-1,k}\right| : k=0,1.......2^{j-1}-1\right\}\right)}{0.6745} \tag{4.10}$$

4.3.2.3.2   Bayes Shrink

Chang, Yu, and Vetterli develop it. Since it minimizes Bayesian risk hence named Bayes shrink. Bayes threshold t_B is given as follows:

$$t_B = \sigma^2/\sigma_s \tag{4.11}$$

where σ_s and σ^2 are signal variances without noise and noise variance, respectively.

Since Gaussian noise is additive and signal and noise both are independent of each other; hence it can be written as follows:

$$\sigma_w^2 = \sigma_s^2 + \sigma^2 \tag{4.12}$$

σ_w^2 can be computed as follows:

$$\sigma_w^2 = \frac{1}{n^2} \sum_{X,Y-1}^{n} w^2(X,Y) \tag{4.13}$$

The signal variance σ_s^2 can be computed as follows:

$$\sigma_w^2 = \sqrt{max\left(\sigma_w^2 - \sigma^2, 0\right)} \tag{4.14}$$

By calculating σ_s^2 and σ^2, Bayes threshold t_B can be calculated. t_B is used to threshold wavelet coefficients at each band [27].

4.3.2.3.3   Neigh Shrink

As we know, significant statistical dependencies between neighbor wavelet coefficients exist; hence, this property is to be exploited to improve the estimation of the noisy coefficient. For an image of size N×N, the most straightforward shrinkage rule is universal threshold given as follows:

$$\lambda = \sqrt{2\sigma^2 \log N^2} \qquad (4.15)$$

λ eliminates more noisy coefficients as N tends to infinity. It is designed in such a manner that; it smoothens the image instead minimizes errors. As the number of pixels is finite in digital images, hence they are not smooth enough. The optimal threshold is $\alpha\lambda$, where α is always much less than value 1 for the natural image. In practice, we get a very similar α value for different types and sizes of images if the soft threshold rule is applied [22].

In the Neigh shrink [22] rule, a neighborhood window $B_{j,k}$ is to be considered around each wavelet coefficient $d_{j,k}$. The window size may be 3 × 3, 5 × 5, etc. Figure 4.9 shows a 3 × 3 neighborhood window centered at the wavelet coefficient to be thresholded.

$$\text{Let } S_{j,k}^2 = \sum_{(i,l)\in B_{j,k}} d_{i,l}^2 \qquad (4.16)$$

Shrinkage is to be done according to the equation:

$$d_{j,k} = d_{j,l}\,\beta_{j,k} \qquad (4.17)$$

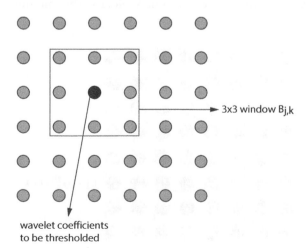

3x3 window B$_{j,k}$

wavelet coefficients
to be thresholded

Figure 4.9 Neighborhood window centered at thresholded wavelet coefficient.

where $\beta_{j,k}$ is the shrinkage function and given as follows:

$$\beta_{j,k} = \left(1 - \lambda^2 \Big/ S_{j,k}^2\right)_+ \tag{4.18}$$

At the end of the formula, the + sign indicates that positive values are kept while negative values are set to zero. It is the modification of the classical soft thresholding scheme. A window size of 3×3 or 5×5 is mostly preferred because if the window size is large, then a large amount of noise will be kept. In general, the larger the window size, the smaller the threshold.

4.3.2.3.4   Block Shrink

It is an example of a thresholding scheme, which is entirely data-driven. It utilizes the relation between the neighboring wavelet coefficients. This approach can decide the optimum size of the block and threshold for every wavelet sub-band by minimizing SURE. It either keeps or kills all coefficients in groups rather than individual coefficients. This property is faster than the conventional thresholding approaches that are applied term by term. It utilizes information about neighbor wavelet coefficients, due to which its estimation precision increases. In the local block thresholding approach, the block size is fixed. The same rule is applied to all resolution levels regardless of wavelet coefficient distribution [25].

Figure 4.10 shows several sub-bands produced when wavelet decomposition of the image is performed by applying WT. For every sub-band, these are divided into numbers of square blocks. This method can choose

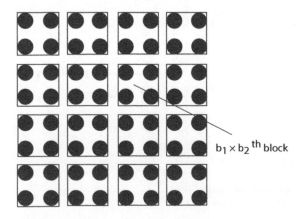

$b_1 \times b_2{}^{th}$ block

Figure 4.10 2 × 2 block partition for a wavelet sub-band.

the optimal block size and threshold for the given sub-band by minimizing Stein's unbiased risk estimate.

4.3.2.3.5   Bivariate Thresholding

It is an adaptive thresholding function proposed by Sendur and Selesnick [35] and it exploits statistical dependencies among wavelet coefficients w_{2k} w_{1k}. An image $x(i, j)$ is affected by a noise signal $n(i, j)$. As a result, a noisy image $y(i, j)$ is obtained. If noise is AWGN, then the noise problem can be given as Equation (4.19).

$$y(i, j) = x(i, j) + n(i, j) \qquad (4.19)$$

In the wavelet domain, the noise problem may be written as follows:

$$y_{1k} = w_{1k} + n_{1k} \qquad (4.20)$$

$$y_{2k} = w_{2k} + n_{2k} \qquad (4.21)$$

By taking into account the statistical dependency between the coefficients and its parents, y_{1k} and y_{2k} are the noisy observations of w_{1k} and w_{2k} and n_{1k} and n_{2k} are noisy sample. We can write

$$y_k = w_k + n_k \quad k = 1\dots \text{ number of wavelet coefficients} \qquad (4.22)$$

where $w_k = (w_{1k}, w_{2k})$ $y_k = (y_{1k}, y_{2k})$ and $n_k = (n_{1k}, n_{2k})$

The standard MAP estimator for w given the corrupted observation y is

$$\hat{w}(y) = \underset{w}{\operatorname{argmax}} \; p_{w|y}(w|y) \qquad (4.23)$$

with some manipulations, Equation (4.23) can become

$$\hat{w}(y) = \underset{w}{\operatorname{argmax}} \; [p_n(y-w).p_w(w)] \qquad (4.24)$$

For coefficients and their parents, a non-Gaussian bivariate PDF is given by

$$p_w(w) = \frac{3}{2\pi\sigma^2}.exp\left(-\frac{\sqrt{3}}{\sigma}\sqrt{w_1^2 + w_2^2}\right) \qquad (4.25)$$

The marginal variance σ^2 depends on the coefficient index$_k$. MAP estimator w_1 has been calculated using these two equations:

$$\hat{w}_1 = \frac{\left(\sqrt{y_1^2 + y_2^2} - \sqrt{3}\,\dfrac{\sigma_n^2}{\sigma}\right)_+}{\sqrt{y_1^2 + y_2^2}} \cdot y_1 \tag{4.26}$$

Equation (4.27) is a bivariate thresholding function where $(g)_+$ is defined.

$$(g)_+ = \begin{cases} 0 & \text{for } g < 0 \\ g & \text{otherwise} \end{cases} \tag{4.27}$$

This estimator requires prior knowledge of noise variance $\left(\sigma_n^2\right)$ and marginal variance (σ^2) for each coefficient σ^2. It can be estimated using neighboring coefficients in the region $N(k)$. It is all coefficients within a square window in which k^{th} the coefficient is located at the center σ_n^2. It can be estimated from noisy coefficients using a robust median estimator.

$$\sigma_n^2 = \frac{median(|\,y_i\,|)}{0.6745}\; y_i \in \text{sub-band HH} \tag{4.28}$$

4.3.3   Performance Evaluation Parameters

It is desirable to know the efficiency of any method. For this purpose, various parameters such as PSNR, MSE, and SSIM are to be calculated. PSNR indicates quantitative while SSIM indicates qualitative performance. Below is the explanation of each parameter below.

4.3.3.1   *Mean Squared Error*

Let two different gray images be $I_1(i, j)$ and $I_2(i, j)$ with the same size of $M \times N$ then MSE between both the images is given as follows:

$$MSE = \frac{1}{M \times N} \sum_{i=0}^{M-1} \sum_{j=0}^{N-1} [I_1(i, j) - I_2(i, j)]^2 \tag{4.29}$$

4.3.3.2   Peak Signal–to-Noise Ratio

Mathematically it is given as follows:

$$PSNR(dB) = 10\log_{10}\frac{255 \times 255}{MSE} \qquad (4.30)$$

If both the images are the same, then MSE is zero and PSNR is infinite [2].

4.3.3.3   Structural Similarity Index Matrix

It measures the image quality obtained from any technique and measures similarity between two images. Its value various from 0 to 1. If it is one, then both the images are the same in all respect. It is calculated between two images both have a standard size. Mathematically it is given as follows:

$$SSIM(I_1,I_2) = \frac{\left(2\mu_{I_1}\mu_{I_2} + C_1\right)\left(2\sigma_{I_1I_2} + C_2\right)}{\left(\mu_{I_1}^2 + \mu_{I_2}^2 + C_1\right)\left(\sigma_{I_1}^2 + \sigma_{I_2}^2 + C_2\right)} \qquad (4.31)$$

μ_{I_1} μ_{I_2}: The mean of image one and image.
$\sigma_{I_1}^2 \sigma_{I_2}^2$: The variance of image one and image two, respectively.

$$\sigma_{xy}$$

$C_1 = (K_1L)^2$ $C_2 = (K_2L)^2$: Two variables used to stabilize division with a weak denominator L are the covariance of two images and the dynamic range of pixel values. The values $K_1 K_2$ are 0.01 and 0.03, respectively.

4.4   Methodology

This part deals with the methodology applied to denoise the digital grayscale images affected by AWGN. Denoising is done in the wavelet domain. We can use conventional DWT for decomposition and IDWT to reconstruct images, but as conventional DWT suffers from the problems mentioned above, DTCWT has been used for better results. As it has less redundancy because it requires less time. Its computational cost is low as compare to

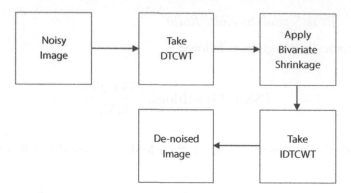

Figure 4.11 Image denoising using DTCWT-based thresholding technique.

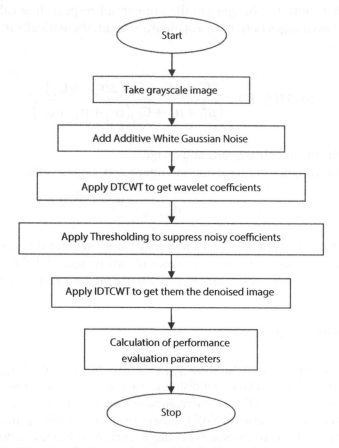

Figure 4.12 Flow chart for the wavelet-based thresholding technique.

UDWT [28]. Figure 4.11 shows a block representation of DTCWT-based image denoising technique. It requires only three simple steps:

(i) Calculate DTCWT to decompose noisy images.
(ii) Modify noisy wavelet coefficients using any thresholding rule.
(iii) Calculate IDTCWT to reconstruct the denoised image.

In the first step, the WT of the noisy image is taken and wavelet coefficients are obtained. Some of the coefficients are noisy hence required to be either removed or replaced.

For this purpose, the thresholding technique is used, which removes or suppresses these noisy coefficients. Reconstruction is required, which is done by inverse WT [45–47] to get the denoised image.

It is desired to calculate some performance evaluation parameters, *viz.*, PSNR, MSE, and SSIM. Figure 4.12 shows the flow diagram, which indicates a step-by-step procedure to know the applied thresholding method.

4.5   Results and Discussion

In this part, the denoising results using techniques mentioned above have been shown in denoised images and performance evaluation parameters obtained from different thresholding techniques. These techniques have been applied to the standard grayscale images of size 512 × 512. These standard images are Lena, barbara, cameraman, and pepper and are shown in Figure 4.13.

A standard image is taken from the database. Now, this image is corrupted by AWGN using MATLAB programming. As a result, a noisy image is obtained. Now various thresholding techniques are to be applied to this noisy image, as discussed in Section 4.4. Now, the amount of noise is to be increased and the procedure repeats. Similarly, the same procedure is applied to other images also. Different denoised images were obtained by applying thresholding techniques, and Figure 4.14 shows the noisy image. From the above figures, it can be concluded that wavelet-based thresholding provides good results. However, its noise removal capability may be more precise by calculating performance evaluation parameters. To validate the performance of various techniques, PSNR and SSIM have been calculated for different noise levels.

Table 4.1 shows PSNR (in dB) and Table 4.2 shows SSIM values for different images under various noise conditions and denoise images obtained from various thresholding techniques. From the tables' observation, it is

Figure 4.13 Standard gray images (512 × 512): (a) lena image; (b) barbara image; (c) cameraman image; (d) pepper image.

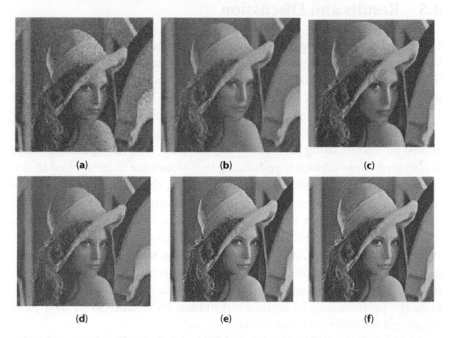

Figure 4.14 (a) Noisy image (noise level = 10); (b) Denoise image (SURE shrink); (c) Denoise image (Neigh shrink); (d) Denoise image (Bayes Shrink); (e) Denoise image (Block shrink); (f) Denoise image (Bivariate shrink).

Table 4.1 PSNR values for grayscale images (512×512) for different values of AWGN.

Test image	Noise level-->	5	10	15	20	25	30
Lena	Noisy	36.323	34.321	28.375	24.389	18.662	14.332
	Denoised (SURE shrink)	38.463	36.883	32.743	27.757	24.854	20.021
	Denoised (Neigh shrink)	38.123	36.385	32.376	28.324	24.334	19.732
	Denoised (Bayes shrink)	38.276	36.455	32.443	27.545	24.002	19.438
	Denoised (Block shrink)	39.456	38.481	35.787	32.764	26.654	24.761
	Denoised (Bivariate shrink)	40.543	39.667	37.721	32.435	26.098	24.405
Barbara	Noisy	35.984	34.562	29.122	24.427	18.549	15.022
	Denoised (SURE shrink)	37.492	36.587	32.142	27.259	24.455	19.023
	Denoised (Neigh shrink)	38.326	36.405	32.381	28.305	24.327	19.722
	Denoised (Bayes shrink)	38.255	36.432	32.419	27.537	23.082	19.419
	Denoised (Block shrink)	39.441	38.457	36.776	32.748	26.635	24.737
	Denoised (Bivariate shrink)	39.913	39.641	36.683	32.421	26.073	24.371

(Continued)

Table 4.1 PSNR values for grayscale images (512×512) for different values of AWGN. (*Continued*)

Test image	Noise level-->	5	10	15	20	25	30
Cameraman	Noisy	35.684	34.652	29.352	24.437	18.565	15.126
	Denoised (SURE shrink)	37.532	36.594	32.203	27.289	24.483	19.124
	Denoised (Neigh shrink)	38.736	36.655	32.781	28.395	24.407	19.932
	Denoised (Bayes shrink)	38.285	36.742	32.529	27.647	23.122	19.391
	Denoised (Block shrink)	39.452	38.476	35.787	32.751	26.732	24.756
	Denoised (Bivariate shrink)	40.001	39.105	37.541	32.545	26.096	24.471
Peppers	Noisy	36.221	34.252	27.644	24.463	19.012	15.726
	Denoised (SURE shrink)	38.222	36.484	32.173	27.259	24.502	19.131
	Denoised (Neigh shrink)	38.741	36.637	32.792	28.382	24.398	19.973
	Denoised (Bayes shrink)	38.297	36.757	32.535	27.662	23.172	19.404
	Denoised (Block shrink)	39.467	38.485	35.799	32.789	26.763	24.781
	Denoised (Bivariate shrink)	40.126	39.117	37.559	32.569	26.102	24.489

Table 4.2 SSIM values for grayscale images (512×512) for different values of AWGN.

Test image	Noise level-->	5	10	15	20	25	30
Lena	Noisy	0.891	0.867	0.752	0.542	0.321	0.139
	Denoised (SURE shrink)	0.927	0.882	0.823	0.734	0.535	0.398
	Denoised (Neigh shrink)	0.903	0.875	0.793	0.721	0.523	0.381
	Denoised (Bayes shrink)	0.911	0.873	0.789	0.735	0.512	0.387
	Denoised (Block shrink)	0.925	0.902	0.891	0.784	0.572	0.402
	Denoised (Bivariate shrink)	0.952	0.935	0.887	0.734	0.583	0.399
Barbara	Noisy	0.873	0.836	0.721	0.476	0.283	0.132
	Denoised (SURE shrink)	0.915	0.873	0.834	0.721	0.514	0.377
	Denoised (Neigh shrink)	0.932	0.876	0.782	0.732	0.513	0.372
	Denoised (Bayes shrink)	0.902	0.867	0.777	0.723	0.512	0.373
	Denoised (Block shrink)	0.939	0.899	0.878	0.772	0.582	0.397
	Denoised (Bivariate shrink)	0.941	0.931	0.891	0.727	0.532	0.399

(Continued)

Table 4.2 SSIM values for grayscale images (512×512) for different values of AWGN. (*Continued*)

Test image	Noise level-->	5	10	15	20	25	30
Cameraman	Noisy	0.888	0.854	0.765	0.545	0.278	0.332
	Denoised (SURE shrink)	0.914	0.875	0.819	0.712	0.523	0.395
	Denoised (Neigh shrink)	0.91	0.872	0.789	0.717	0.518	0.376
	Denoised (Bayes shrink)	0.904	0.869	0.767	0.723	0.511	0.375
	Denoised (Block shrink)	0.921	0.911	0.886	0.779	0.574	0.419
	Denoised (Bivariate shrink)	0.932	0.928	0.886	0.727	0.569	0.365
Peppers	Noisy	0.912	0.892	0.712	0.565	0.391	0.343
	Denoised (SURE shrink)	0.927	0.887	0.834	0.723	0.535	0.389
	Denoised (Neigh shrink)	0.916	0.877	0.792	0.724	0.532	0.388
	Denoised (Bayes shrink)	0.912	0.876	0.782	0.735	0.501	0.387
	Denoised (Block shrink)	0.924	0.911	0.888	0.772	0.569	0.412
	Denoised (Bivariate shrink)	0.934	0.941	0.874	0.739	0.555	0.376

clear that SURE shrink outperforms Neigh shrink and Bayes shrink both the methods. However, its performance does not beat block k shrink and bivariate thresholding technique. The bivariate thresholding technique gives a better response for the image that contains less noise, but if the noise present in the image increases, then block thresholding performs better than the bivariate thresholding most of the time. Figures 4.15 and 4.16 are the bar

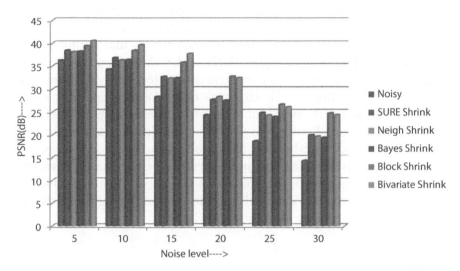

Figure 4.15 PSNR values obtained various thresholding techniques.

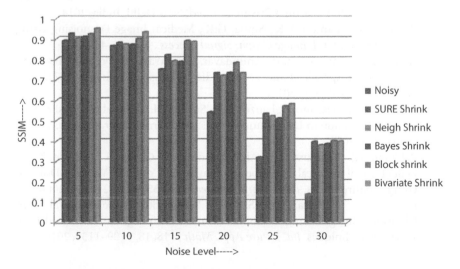

Figure 4.16 SSIM values obtained various thresholding techniques.

graph plotted for noisy and denoised PSNR and SSIM values, respectively, for different noise values present in the Lena image.

4.6   Conclusions

From the above experiments, it is clear that wavelet-based thresholding techniques suppress the noise signals effectively. By visual perception and the calculated performance evaluation parameters, it is clear that thresholding techniques not only remove noise but retains image information as these techniques provide higher PSNR and SSIM values. DTCWT has better results to obtain wavelet coefficients due to its many advantages, as discussed in Section 4.3. SURE shrink outperforms Neigh shrink and Bayes shrink most of the time, not to the block thresholding and Bivariate shrinkage technique. Results also show that the Bivariate technique outperforms the block thresholding technique when the noise level is less however block thresholding technique performs better than the Bivariate shrinkage technique when the noise level is high in the images. Hence, we may conclude that the wavelet-based thresholding technique efficiently removes the AWGN noise from the digital images.

References

1. Sinha, G.R. and Patel, B.C., *Medical Image Processing: Concepts and Applications*, PHI Learning Private Limited, New Delhi, India, 2014.
2. Bhonsle, D., Chandra, V.K., Sinha, G.R., Medical Image De-noising Using Bilateral Filter. *Int. J. Image Graph. Signal Process.*, 4, 6, 36–43, 2012.
3. Amirmazlaghani, M. and Amindavar, H., Wavelet Domain Bayesian Processor for Speckle Removal in Medical Ultrasound Images. *IET Image Process.*, 6, 5, 580–588, 2012.
4. Andria, G., Attivissimo, F., Lanzolla, A., Savino, M., A Suitable Threshold for Speckle Reduction in Ultrasound Images. *IEEE Trans. Instrum. Meas.*, 62, 8, 2270–2279, 2013.
5. Rabbani, H., Vafadust, M., Abolmaesumi, P., Gazor, S., Speckle Noise Reduction of Medical Ultrasound Images in Complex Wavelet Domain Using Mixture Priors. *IEEE Trans. Biomed. Eng.*, 55, 9, 2152–2160, 2008.
6. Bhonsle, D., Chandra, V.K., Sinha, G.R., Speckle Noise Removal from Ultrasound Images Using Combined Bivariate Shrinkage and Enhanced Total Variation Techniques. *Int. J. Pure Appl. Math.*, 118, 18, 1109–1131, 2018.

7. Bhuiyan, M.I.H., Ahmad, M.O., Swamy, M.N.S., Spatially Adaptive Thresholding in Wavelet Domain for Despeckling of Ultrasound Images. *IET Image Proc.*, 3, 3, 147–162, 2009.

8. Farouj, Y., Freyermuth, J.M., Navarro, L., Clausel, M., Delachartre, P., Hyperbolic Wavelet-Fisz De-noising Model Arising in Ultrasound Imaging. *IEEE Trans. Comput. Imaging*, 3, 1, 1–10, 2017.

9. Kongo, R.M., El-Kadmiri, M.L.O., Hassanain, N., Cherkaoui, Md., Dual-Tree Complex Wavelet in Medical Ultrasounds Images Restoration. *IEEE International Conference on Multimedia Computing and Systems*, Tangier, Morocco, pp. 297–303, 2012.

10. Bhonsle, D., Chandra, V.K., Sinha, G.R., Gaussian and Speckle Noise Removal from Ultrasound Images using Bivariate Shrinkage Dual-Tree Complex Wavelet Transform. *i-manager's J. Image Process.*, 2, 2, 1–5, 2015.

11. Bhonsle, D., Chandra, V.K., Sinha, G.R., Additive and Multiplicative Noise Removal From Medical Images Using Bivariate Thresholding by Dual-Tree Complex Wavelet Transform. *1st International Conference on Mathematical Methods and Systems in Science and Engineering*, Tenerife, Spain, pp. 274–280, 2015.

12. Borsdorf, Raupach, R., Flohr, T., Tanaka, J.H., Wavelet-Based Noise Reduction in CT-Images Using Correlation Analysis. *IEEE Trans. Med. Imaging*, 27, 12, 1685–1703, 2008.

13. Chang, S.G., Yu, B., Vetterli, M., Adaptive Wavelet Thresholding for Image De-noising and Compression. *IEEE Trans. Image Process.*, 9, 9, 1532–1546, 2000.

14. Gu, X.F., Shi, J.X., Li, J.P., Huang, Y.Y., Lin, J., Application of Wavelets Analysis in Image De-noising. *International Conference on Apperceiving Computing and Intelligence Analysis*, IEEE, Chengdu, China, pp. 49–52, 2008.

15. Fowler, J.E., The Redundant Discrete Wavelet Transform and Additive Noise. *IEEE Signal Process. Lett.*, 12, 9, 629–632, 2005.

16. Sheikh, H.R. and Bovik, A.C., Image Information and Visual Quality. *IEEE Trans. Image Process.*, 15, 2, 430–444, 2006.

17. Youssef, K., Jarenwattananon, N., Bouchard, L., Feature-Preserving Noise Removal. *IEEE Trans. Med. Imaging*, 34, 9, 1822–1829, 2015.

18. Kingsbury, N., The Dual-Tree Complex Wavelet Transform: A New Technique for Shift Invariance and Directional Filters. *Proceeding of 8th IEEE DSP Workshop*, Bryce Canyon, USA, 1998.

19. Qin, S., Yang, C., Tang, B., Tan, S., The Denoise Based on Translation Invariance Wavelet Transform and its Applications. *Proceeding of a Conference on Structural Dynamics*, pp. 783–787, 2002.

20. Sveinsson, J.R. and Benediktsson, J.A., Double Density Wavelet Transformation for Speckle Reduction of SAR Images. *IEEE International Geoscience and Remote Sensing Symposium*, Toronto, Ontario, Canada, vol. 1, pp. 113–115, 2002.

21. Chen, G.Y., Bui, T.D., Krzyzak, A., Image De-noising using Neighbouring Wavelet Coefficients. *IEEE International Conference on Acoustics, Speech, and Signal Processing*, Montreal, Que., Canada, vol. 2, pp. 917–920, 2004.

22. Chen, G. and Qian, S.E., De-noising of Hyperspectral Imagery Using Principal Component Analysis and Wavelet Shrinkage. *IEEE Trans. Geosci. Remote Sens.*, 49, 3, 973–980, 2011.

23. Eslami, R. and Radha H., A., New Family of Nonredundant Transforms Using Hybrid Wavelets and Directional Filter Banks. *IEEE Trans. Image Process.*, 16, 4, 1152–1167, 2007.

24. Chang, S.G., Yu, B., Vetterli, M., Adaptive Wavelet Thresholding for Image De-noising and Compression. *IEEE Trans. Image Process.*, 9, 9, 1532–1546, 2000.

25. Dengwen, Z. and Xiaoliu, S., Image De-noising Using Block Thresholding. *IEEE Congress on Image and Signal Processing*, Sanya, Hainan, China, pp. 335–338, 2008.

26. Miller, M. and Kingsbury, N., Image De-noising Using Derotated Complex Wavelet Coefficients. *IEEE Trans. Image Process.*, 17, 9, 1500–1511, 2008.

27. Zhang, W., Yu, F., Guo, H.M., Improved Adaptive Wavelet Threshold for Image De-noising. *IEEE Chinese Control and Decision Conference*, Guilin, China, pp. 5958–5963, 2009.

28. Raj, V.N.P. and Venkateswarlu, T., Denoising of Medical Images using Undecimated Wavelet Transform. *IEEE International Conference on Recent Advances in Intelligent Computational Systems*, Trivandrum, India, pp. 483–488, 2011.

29. Hassan, H. and Saparon, A., Still Image De-noising Based on Discrete Wavelet Transform. *IEEE International Conference on System Engineering and Technology*, Shah Alam, Malaysia, vol. 6(2), pp. 188–191, 2011.

30. Hill, P., Achim, A., Bull, D., The Undecimated Dual-Tree Complex Wavelet Transform and Its Application to Bivariate Image De-noising using a Cauchy Model. *19th IEEE International Conference on Image Processing*, Orlando, FL, USA, pp. 1205–1208, 2012.

31. Kim, J.H., Ahn, I.J., Nam, W.H., Ra, J.B., An Effective Post-Filtering Framework for 3-D PET Image De-noising Based on Noise and Sensitivity Characteristics. *IEEE Trans. Nucl. Sci.*, 62, 1, 137–147, 2015.

32. Zhao, J., Lee, J.S., Xu, H., Xu, K., Ren, Z.H., Chen, J.C., Wu, C.H., Scanner-Dependent Threshold Estimation of Wavelet De-noising for Small-Animal PET. *IEEE Trans. Nucl. Sci.*, 64, 1, 705–712, 2017.

33. Ahmad, Alipal, J., Jaafar, N.H., Amira, A., Efficient Analysis of DWT Thresholding Algorithm for Medical Image De-noising. *IEEE International Conference Biomedical Engineering and Sciences*, Langkawi, Malaysia, pp. 772–777, 2012.

34. Sapthagirivasan, V. and Mahadevan, V., De-noising and Fissure Extraction in High-Resolution Isotropic CT Images Using Dual-Tree Complex Wavelet

Transform. *2ⁿᵈ IEEE International Conference on Software Technology and Engineering*, San Juan, PR, USA, vol. 1, pp. 362–366, 2010.

35. Sendur, L. and Selesnick, I.W., Bivariate Shrinkage with Local Variance Estimation. *IEEE Signal Process. Lett.*, 9, 12, 438–441, 2002.

36. Gonzalez, R.C. and Woods, R.E., *Digital Image Processing*, 3ʳᵈ ed., Prentice-Hall, New Jersey, USA, 2009.

37. Kingsbury, N., Shift Invariant Properties of the Dual-Tree Complex Wavelet Transform. *IEEE International Conference on Acoustics, Speech, and Signal Processing*, Phoenix, AZ, USA, vol. 3, pp. 1221–1224, 1999.

38. Kingsbury, N., A Dual-Tree Complex Wavelet Transform with Improved Orthogonality and Symmetry Properties. *IEEE International Conference of Image Processing*, Vancouver, BC, Canada, vol. 2, pp. 375–378, 2000.

39. Kingsbury, N., Complex Wavelets for Shift Invariant Analysis and Filtering of Signals. *Appl. Comput. Harmon. Anal.*, 10, 3, 234–253, 2001.

40. Kingsbury, N., The Dual-Tree Complex Wavelet Transform: A New Efficient Tool for Image Restoration and Enhancement. *9ᵗʰ European Signal Processing Conference*, Rhodes, Greece, pp. 1–4, 1998.

41. Hill, P., Achim, A., Bull, D., The Undecimated Dual-Tree Complex Wavelet Transform and Its Application to Bivariate Image De-noising using a Cauchy Model. *19ᵗʰ IEEE International Conference on Image Processing*, Orlando, FL, USA, pp. 1205–1208, 2012.

42. Bhonsle, D., Chandra, V.K., Sinha, G.R., An Optimized Framework Using Adaptive Wavelet Thresholding and Total Variation Technique for De-noising Medical Images. *J. Adv. Res. Dyn. Control Syst.*, 10, 9, 953–965, 2018.

43. Prakash, O. and Khare, A., Medical Image De-noising Based on Soft Thresholding Using Biorthogonal Multiscale Wavelet Transform. *Int. J. Image Graph.*, 14, 1 & 2, 1–30, 2014.

44. Bhonsle, D., Chandra, V.K., Sinha, G.R., Noise Removal from Medical Images Using Shrinkage Based Enhanced Total Variation Technique. *J. Adv. Res. Dyn. Control Syst.*, 13, 549–560, 2017.

45. Bayram, I. and Selesnick, I.W., On the Dual-Tree Complex Wavelet Packet and M-Band Transforms. *IEEE Trans. Signal Process.*, 56, 6, 2298–2310, 2008.

46. El-Shehaby, A. and Tran, T.D., Implementation and Application of Local Computation of Wavelet Coefficient in the Dual-Tree Complex Wavelets. *16ᵗʰ IEEE International Conference Image Processing*, Cairo, Egypt, pp. 3885–3888, 2009.

47. Ioannidou, S. and Karathanassi, V., Investigation of the Dual-Tree Complex and Shift-Invariant Discrete Wavelet Transform on Quickbird Image Fusion. *IEEE Geosci. Remote Sens. Lett.*, 4, 1, 166–170, 2007.

48. Aravind, N. and Suresh, K.V., An Improved Image De-noising Using Wavelet Transform. *International Conference on Trends in Automation, Communications and Computing Technology*, IEEE, Bangalore, India, pp. 1–5, 2015.

5

Smart Virtual Reality–Based Gaze-Perceptive Common Communication System for Children With Autism Spectrum Disorder

Karunanithi Praveen Kumar[1]* and Perumal Sivanesan[2]

[1]School of Computing, SASTRA University,
Thanjavur, Tamilnadu, India
[2]Department of Information Communication Technology School of Computing,
SASTRA University, Thanjavur, Tamilnadu, India

Abstract

In recent years, advances in computer technology have led to Autism Spectrum Disorders (ASD) interventions. Technology has been used efficiently to provide new avenues that are flexible, adaptable, easily accessible, and cost-effective. It is claimed that personal treatment can be done cheaply. In this proposed scheme, computer-based, primarily virtual reality (VR)–based technology of intelligent adaptation will be implemented as a personal intervention method for analysis of basic social lacks in children and adolescents besides ASD. We will present a research project. Specifically, it uses intelligent techniques to assess emotional states in a computer environment based on eye-catching real-time data (blink rate). In this sense, the studies offered professionals a new generation of smart intervention systems that could adapt and respond to individual risks in children and adolescents with ASD and strengthen specific, long-term intervention targets.

Keywords: Virtual reality (VR), autism spectrum disorder (ASD), pupil diameter (PD), blink rate (BR), fixation duration (FD), pupil radius (PR), blink speed (BS)

*Corresponding author: praveenkumark@sastra.ac.in; praveennhu@gmail.com

Sandeep Kumar, Rohit Raja, Shrikant Tiwari and Shilpa Rani (eds.) Cognitive Behavior and Human Computer Interaction Based on Machine Learning Algorithm, (117–136) © 2022 Scrivener Publishing LLC

5.1   Need for Focus on Advancement of ASD Intervention Systems

As late as 20 years back, Autism Spectrum Disorder (ASD) was believed to be uncommon. Overview gauges show 1 of every 250 youngsters is influenced with ASD in India (http://www.autismsocietyofindia.org/) and 1 out of 88 kids in the USA [19]. The chemical imbalance has been perceived as an inability by India's Government in 1999 (Vaidya, 2009). Notably, there is a developing agreement that serious social and instructive intercession projects can altogether improve short and long-haul results for people with ASD and their families ([21], NRC, 2001). Notwithstanding, with an absence of broadly accessible effective treatment modes for tending to these perplexing abilities later focuses in youth, youthfulness, and early adulthood, it is not amazing that proof proposes the lion's share of people with ASD neglect to accomplish versatile freedom as grown-ups [1]. Along these lines, regardless of the critical need and cultural import of escalated treatment of social and versatile disability at later ages, viable and suitable mediation assets for kids, teenagers, and youthful grown-ups with ASD are missing (Rutter, 2006). Added to this, the expenses of ASD treatment, both roundabout and direct, are believed to be tremendous [32], and an incredible larger part of grown-ups with ASD battle to accomplish practical, versatile freedom [13, 18]. Additionally, given the limit on the accessibility of prepared proficient assets in ASD intercession, almost certainly, arising innovation will assume a significant part in giving more open escalated individualized mediation later on [37].

5.2   Computer and Virtual Reality–Based Intervention Systems

There are various reasons why joining innovation, explicitly PC and virtual reality (VR) frameworks, into mediation practices might be especially important for kids and young people with ASD [3]. The strength of these kinds of innovation for ASD intercession incorporates flexibility, controllability, modifiable tangible incitement, individualized methodology, security, and likely decrease of dangerous parts of the human association during treatment (Strickland, 1997). It is indicated that PC and VR-based intercession may give a rearranged, however, exploratory association climate for youngsters with ASD (Parsons and Mitchell, 2002; Tartaro and Cassell, 2007). Kids with ASD regularly discover human-to-human collaboration as unpredictable and troublesome. In any case, the intricacy of a virtual globe has been controlled with limited interruptions or troubles may consider improved yet epitomized social communication that is less scary for kids with ASD than some mind-boggling social connections (Moore *et al.*, 2000; Tartaro and Cassell, 2007; Standen and Brown, 2005). PC and VR intercession technique additionally can address the considerable troubles with speculation of mastered abilities to this present reality by presenting not just more command over showing fundamental components of complex abilities, yet additionally the capacity to deliberately utilize and strengthen these abilities inside various, controllable, reasonable cooperation conditions (Strickland, 1997; Mitchell *et al.*, 2007).

Further, people with ASD may likewise exhibit improved learning with VR conditions as the PC frameworks, and virtual conditions can undoubtedly convert the credits of, include, or eliminate things in manners that much not be conceivable in a true element yet could be significant to show both concrete and theoretical ideas. Consequently, these profoundly adaptable advances can offer the advantage of representing situations which can be changed to oblige different circumstances that may not be plausible in a given helpful setting as a result of room impediments, asset shortfalls, well-being concerns, and so forth (Strickland, 1997; Parsons and Mitchell, 2002; Parsons *et al.*, 2004). VR has additionally indicated the ability to facilitate the weight, both time and exertion, of prepared advisors in an intercession cycle just as the possibility to permit undeveloped staff (e.g., guardians or friends) to help a member in the mediation (Standen and Brown, 2005). In this way, PC and VR innovation address a medium appropriate for making intuitive intercession ideal models for ability preparing in the center regions of debilitation for kids with ASD.

Nonetheless, current PC and VR innovation as applied to assistive mediation for ASD (Tartaro and Cassell, 2007) are frequently planned in an open-circle style despite the expected focal points. These frameworks might have the option to chain learning by means of parts of execution alone; anyway, they are not equipped for a more serious level of individualization. In particular, they cannot consequently distinguish and fittingly react and adjust support dependent on the youngsters' emotional necessities with ASD [6]. Accordingly, they cannot recognize and anticipate uneasiness just as ideal degrees of feeling the excitement in a way focused on the particular kid. Nonetheless, given the significance of emotional data in ASD mediation practice (Wieder and Greenspan, 2005), a shut circle configuration utilizing this data might be basic for building up an intercession framework that can permit sensible versatile connection to challenge and eagerly advance scaffolded expertise improvement in the specific regions of weakness, for people with ASD.

5.3   Why Eye Physiology and Viewing Pattern Pose Advantage for Affect Recognition of Children With ASD

Youths with ASD regularly have open impedances (the two verbal and nonverbal), especially concerning the articulation of energetic condition, and are depicted by atypical audit plans accomplishing burdens in social data dealing with [2]. They regularly experience conditions of excited or academic squeezing factor surveyed as Autonomic Nervous System origin not including outer articulation (Picard, 2009), testing their inclinations in learning and presenting. These deficiencies portraying the informative impedances place limits on standard observational and conversational systems.

Here is to understand that blessing a PC with a capacity to comprehend certain energetic signs should allow more immense and normal human-PC correspondence. There are two to three modalities, for example, outward appearance, vocal gesture, signs and positions, and eye physiology, that can be used to study people's enthusiastic conditions.

Regardless, as youths with ASD reliably have open impedances, especially concerning the unequivocal articulation of eager states, we intend to pick surmised measures by utilizing the physiological eye signs, for example, pupil diameter (PD) and blink rate (BR) [7]. The physiological signs are dependably open and are not in reality direct affected by the open ineptitudes. Thus, physiological sign procurement may address a system for get-together rich information despite the likely open obstacles of kids with ASD. Also, confirmation that the mind-blowing moves in markers of Autonomic Nervous System action go with change starting with one energetic state then onto the accompanying [15]. For instance, physiological eye records, to be unequivocal, BR and PD, have been considered as solid autonomic degrees of one's critical factor. Studies have announced unconstrained advancement in one's BR (Meyer *et al.*, 1953) and pupillary expanding (Molloy and Simpson, 2007) with stretched-out tension because of an undertaking.

Once more, one's overview design for how a ton and where he/she looks during a social correspondence undertaking can fill in as a colossal marker for understanding one's uneasiness level during an undertaking.

The capacity to get socially important data from faces is a basic limit concerning enabling liquid social correspondence (Trepagnier *et al.*, 2002). Studies have indicated that social phobics show lessened Fixation Duration (FD) while looking toward the excited characters of speakers [15] close by atypical obsession plan while preparing energetic outward appearance (Horley *et al.*, 2003). Here, we picked pressure as the objective energetic state, in light of two major reasons. Regardless, strain acknowledges an enormous part in different human-machine affiliation assignments identified with task execution. Second, restlessness continually co-happens besides ASD and acknowledges a basic part of youngsters' immediate challenges with mental disparity [35].

Providing the attention of energetic data in human-PC correspondence and the enormous effects of the stacked with feeling and cautious elements of kids with ASD on the intercession work on, building up a vigilant design that can change dependent on the eager condition of a kid which is organized from his/her eye physiology and study model may be fundamental [9].

5.4 Potential Advantages of Applying the Proposed Adaptive Response Technology to Autism Intervention

Available technology does not address explicitly how to detect autonomously and efficiently respond to eye physiology and viewing pattern-based affective cues of children besides ASD, including an intervention paradigm to promote complex skill development (Strickland, 1997; Tartaro and Cassell, 2007; Swettenham, 1996; Trepagnier *et al.*, 2006; Parsons *et al.*, 2005; Scassellati, 2005). To represent the core lacks children besides ASD in a competitive skill training, adjustment mechanisms with effective dynamic could be demanded to add multiple factors of willingness like affective cues, intervention goals, and task measures. They can access the power of these cues may permit a smooth, natural, and more productive interaction process.

In effect, such modeling is often what expert therapists and interventionists attempt to do in terms of working with individuals with ASD [10]. Specifically, interventionists try to adeptly infer the affective cues exhibited by the children with ASD to adjust the intervention and reinforcement process to improve learning (Seip, 1996; [29], Wieder and Greenspan, 2005). Therefore, an adaptive technology-based ASD intervention system must also understand and respond to the affective needs, such as these children's anxiety level. Consensus statements from the American Academy of Pediatrics (Myers and Johnson, 2007) and the National Resource Council (NRC, 2001) underscoring the effective intervention for children with ASD include the provision of comprehensive intervention, individual-specific instruction tailored to the nature of the child, promotion of generalization of skills, and incorporation of a high degree of structure/organization. The proposed adaptive response technology for ASD intervention would address all of these essential elements of effective intervention simultaneously, increasing the intervention giver/tool to control and develop intervention-oriented craft systematically.

5.5   Issue

India has been referenced similar to the second biggest on the planet so far as the quantity of people with ASD [25]. Added to this, the lopsided accessibility of fitting instructive, restoration, and different offices intensify the troublesome circumstance the families end up in (Vaidya, 2009). In this manner, the lion's share of people with ASD battle with the center and related versatile disabilities that lamentably frequently, in the end, convert into later neglected requirements for business, lodging, clinical and conduct care, administrations, and supports [13, 18]. Indeed, probably, the best hindrance to advance being developed and execution of intercessions for people with ASD across the life expectancy is simply the heterogeneity of the range. Even though center social correspondence includes and generalized practices are available among all people with ASD, these highlights and techniques are available at different degrees—from nonverbal people with scholarly incapacities requiring continuous concentrated help to people with various knowledgeable qualities fit for versatile autonomy regardless of hindrances identified with their center weaknesses. A reasonable need exists to propel comprehension of the numerous aggregates of ASD to help in our awareness of the actual issue and create focused and customized intercessions.

Notwithstanding, our mediation framework is not fit for determining, in an applied information-driven style, intercessions that will work for every person with ASD [14]. In this regard, collaborative innovation with a physiological and conduct profiling framework equipped for adjusting controlled conditions and fortifying abilities in center spaces slowly yet naturally could demonstrate a powerful device for creating custom-fitted mediations for people with ASD. It might be said, conveying a mainly

mechanical apparatus could make focused on and customized intercession a reality for people with ASD and could be consolidated into complex mediation standards pointed toward improving working and personal
satisfaction for more established kids, youths, and grown-ups with ASD.
Further, such mechanical frameworks might be fit for defeating asset
restrictions by making an intercession device that can be scattered across a
wide assortment of mediation settings [16].

5.6   Global Status

On an international premise, high commonness rates for chemical imbalance recommends distinguishing proof and powerful treatment of ASD
to be frequently portrayed as a general well-being crisis. Examinations
show that 1 of every 88 youngsters in the United States has been recognized to have a mental imbalance [19]. In the United Kingdom, Prof.
Simon Baron-Cohen and his group at Cambridge University found that
for every three kids who analyze mental imbalance, two stay undiscov-
ered officially [8]. Itemized evaluations propose that the commonness
rate among younger students in Cambridge could be as moderate as 1
of every 64 (www.nas.uk.org). The chemical imbalance has been considered the third most regular formative handicap whose occurrence
is more prominent than that of Down Syndrome and Cerebral Palsy
(Vaidya, 2009).

The expenses of ASD, both roundabout and direct, are believed to be
tremendous [32]. At an expected $35–90 billion yearly, the expenses of
ASD to those with the problem, their families, instructive frameworks, and
society are gigantic [32]. Furthermore, there are strong boundaries identified with getting to and actualizing appropriately individualized serious
intercession administrations (e.g., restricted admittance to and accessibility of fittingly prepared experts), absence of accessible information proposing which mediations will turn out better for explicit youngsters, worries
about viability, speculation concerning specific mediations, and extrava-
gant expenses [32, 37].

Confronted with all the troubles, an extraordinary lion's share of
grown-ups with ASD battle to accomplish practical, versatile autonomy
[13, 18]. A wide assortment of potential intercessions has been offered to
address such ground-breaking hindrances and expenses related to ASD
however. Few have been exposed to the afflictions of controlled clinical
preliminaries [17]. Despite the absence of sufficiently controlled treatment examines, a developing assemblage of proof backings the viability

of explicit instructive and conduct intercession techniques, particularly in improving the language, psychological capacities, and less significantly social working in small kids. Generally speaking, it creates the impression that prior and more serious mediations are useful for particular youngsters. However, results change enormously, and this variety is ineffectively perceived ([28], NRC, 2001; Rogers and Vismara, 2008). Further, barely any youngsters treated even inside significantly escalated modalities achieve real abatement of ASD (i.e., utilitarian impedance related with center symptomatology not, at this point present). Longitudinal investigations of ASD demonstrate that the mind greater part of people with ASD (i.e., >70%) neglect to accomplish free status as grown-ups [13, 18]. In light of the developing need to address the challenges looked by the ASD populace, a developing number of studies are examining the uses of cutting-edge intelligent advancements (e.g., PC innovation and computer-generated reality conditions) to social and correspondence linked intercession. People with ASD will, in general, function admirably with PCs, and PCs give an ideal stage to assisting people with ASD to improve their center shortfalls, including social abilities. Different PC programming bundles and VR conditions have been created and applied to address explicit shortages related to mental imbalance, e.g., comprehension of deception consideration, articulation acknowledgment (Silver and Oakes, 2001), critical social thinking [11], and social shows. On a global premise, VR has been generally utilized while planning intercession reads for youngsters with ASD, some of which are as per the following skills.

5.7   VR and Adaptive Skills

In Greece, analysts have planned VR-based conditions for helping the ordinary action ability preparing undertakings (e.g., dress and brushing) among the kids with ASD [20]. In Hungary, specialists utilized VR to instruct the exercises engaged with using public transportation among the members with ASD (Lanyi and Tilinger, 2004). In the UK, agents have led a few pilot reads, including ideal models for encouraging shopping for food, food arrangement, spatial direction, street security, professional preparing, and danger acknowledgment to people with scholarly incapacities (Standen and Brown, 2005). In the USA, a research study exhibited the utilization of VR to prepare road crossing abilities for kids with ASDs [36].

5.8   VR for Empowering Play Skills

In UK, analysts have investigated the utilization of VR to address deficiencies in central emblematic and helpful play in kids with ASDs (Jordan, 2003). In Spain, the research considers utilized VR to help create socialization abilities among the members with ASD while purchasing things from a virtual grocery store (Herrera *et al.*, 2008). In the UK, a novel utilization of virtual programming to affect the advancement of cooperative play was portrayed by Farr *et al.*, who utilized a substantial UI (TUI) implanted into the type of graspable development blocks called "Topobo". With these squares, both average and ASD member gatherings could make and playback enlivened toy activities by programming the toy's developments [30]. Social play with Topobo seemed to demonstrate that by limiting time spent in singular space, the Topobo blocks' idea encouraged more freedoms for social commitment among individuals from the ASD gathering.

5.9   VR for Encouraging Social Skills

The advancement of play abilities is inseparably connected to the more prominent social skills scope for youngsters to create significant associations with others. This movement from play to further developed social cooperations is both liquid and complex and has been suggested by specialists trying to overcome any issues using virtual conditions. In Israel, a group of specialists utilized a straightforward multi-client touchscreen interface [31] to assess the adequacy of a 3-week mediation program called "StoryTable", where kids chosen scenes for a story together and afterward autonomously recorded unconstrained portrayals of the scenes. The mediation's objectives were to share exercises, give consolation and help to the next partaking kids, and improve in arranging social connections with different youngsters [23]. Study results showed massive expansion in support of social practices and more mind-boggling play, just as a decrease of equal play and dull practices. In UK, Parsons *et al.* planned VR-based social ability preparing undertakings among the members with ASD by presenting them to a virtual bistro (Parsons *et al.*, 2004). In the USA, specialists have explored VR-based mediation's utilization while empowering the feeling acknowledgment ability among the members with ASD (LaCava *et al.*, 2007).

Even though these works have made spearheading commitment into innovation helped ASD intercession, at this point, these were planned in an open circle design. In particular, these are execution based (that is, right or off base reactions). They are not fit for anticipating the members' tension level in an individualistic way dependent on the eye physiological and seeing example lists and brilliantly adjust while keeping up the solace level of the member and thus making the way toward acquiring of social abilities pleasurable.

5.10   Public Status

Examination examinations show that 2 to 4 million people have been assessed to have a chemical imbalance in India (Vaidya, 2009). Lamentably, without any vast scope epidemiological examination, such discoveries are theoretical and may under-gauge the quantity of people influenced by chemical imbalance [24]. Because of an absence of mindfulness and data among numerous people, the investigation of chemical imbalance has practically been an unchartered area in India (Vaidya, 2009). Notwithstanding, a chemical imbalance is perceived as an incapacity by the Government of India since 1999.

The onus of profiting suitable determination and giving proper treatment is on the groups of kids determined to have ASD. Added to this is the lopsided accessibility of appropriate instruction, restoration, and different offices, which worsen the challenges these youngsters end up in [26]. As kids with ASD are frequently portrayed with social connection deficiencies and correspondence, nurturing such a kid is regularly testing. Regarding a social construction where similarity is underscored, and contrasts are periodically seen with doubt and antagonism, there are restricted social gap accessible for such families and their youngsters. In any case, in India, talks relating to inability and the obligation of society and state toward its incapacitated residents are making strides, generally by the worldwide accentuation on common liberties, and grass-roots activism and support by willful organizations, self-improvement gatherings, and the relationship of influenced people (Vaidya, 2009).

In India, these families' troublesome social circumstance is deteriorated by the restricted accessibility of prepared proficient assets or unique requirements organizations for these youngsters. Disregarding the expanding work of the non-legislative associations and the effect of the broad communications, familiarity with ASD is as yet kept to chosen metropolitan bags. In Delhi with the huge public and private clinics and all around created and dynamic NGO area has become in a manner of speaking, the "chemical imbalance center point" broad communications effecter India drive significant distances to profit the demonstrative and different office considerable Delhi and discover answers to their inquiries regarding their kids' formative deviances.

The mental imbalance was given acknowledgment as incapacity in its privilege because of the endeavors of handicap related NGOs, and parent uphold associations (Vaidya, 2009). The umbrella association "Parivaar", a National Federation of Parents' Associations for Persons with Mental Retardation, Autism, Cerebral Palsy, and Multiple Disabilities, has assumed a vital part in this unique situation. Almost 200 NGOs and Parents' relationship in India's 30 conditions are incorporated under the "Parivaar" pennant (Vaidya, 2009). The time of the 1990s saw changes in the region of incapacity. Added to the endeavors put in by the NGOs, the Government of India gave a legitimate acknowledgment of chemical imbalance. Three significant Acts of Parliament—The Rehabilitation Council Act of 1992, The Persons with Disabilities Act of 1995, and the National Trust Act of 1999—were declared. The Ministry of Social Justice and Empowerment of India's Government is vested with the duty of running after the financial, social, and instructive turn of events and guaranteeing the government assistance and privileges of the handicapped populace. It has dispatched different projects of study in the field of handicap. From 2004 to 2008, the Ministry presented new courses of study, remembering a Masters for Disability Rehabilitation Administration, MPhil in Special Education, and a bachelor's certificate in Special Education (Mental Retardation) (www. social justice.nic.in).

The help delivered by the Government of India and the significant commitment by the NGOs has rescued mental imbalance once again from the four dividers of the homegrown circle into the public domain and public awareness. Yet, as has been appropriately brought up by Vaidya that, with quick industrialization and a high-speed way of life, the typical examples of help are vanishing inside the metropolitan Indian setting (Vaidya, 2009), and the impediments looked at by the families should be tended to by reasonable other options.

Even though innovation helped ASD mediation progress on an International premise, its impressions are as yet standing by to be acknowledged on a public belief in India.

5.11   Importance

In this hour of need, the innovation-based arrangement can offer a reasonable option for the families to confront the difficulties of driving considerable distances to profit appropriate treatment offices, restricted assets, and the absence of adequately prepared experts. This is the range idea of ASD that calls for individualized treatment, which is hard to accomplish in summed up mediation settings. In any case, this can be tended to by a shrewd versatile VR-based framework proposed here. Likewise, such a framework will assist with understanding the basic psychophysiological profile explicit to a youngster with ASD, and along these lines, this can fill in as a virtual device in possession of the interventionist. As has been called attention to by Bellani, VR, a reenactment of this present reality dependent on PC illustrations, can be valuable as it permits educators and advisors to offer a protected, repeatable and diversifiable climate during versatile expertise mastering [12]. Likewise, VR, which was once viewed as costly and unwieldy, has in the new years gotten simple to utilize and moderately cheap, which can be used in intercession contemplates (Varma *et al.*, 2012).

Our proposed study has numerous reasons. In the first place, we will create VR-based social correspondence situations that would require the members to communicate with their virtual companions (i.e., the symbols). This would be joined by getting information on eye physiology and survey design alongside a clinical onlooker's data sources concerning the member's tension level. These records will be utilized to foresee one's uneasiness level to an assignment. This would help us understand the fundamental psychophysiological component of these kids while they partake in the VR-based social undertaking. Various levels of trouble will likewise be a piece of the undertaking plan.

Consequently, a wise standard represented methodology generator would be utilized to switch errands of changing trouble levels while keeping up the members' low tension level in an individualized way [27]. Finally, we intend to plan a convenience study to test the versatile reaction innovation's viability to improve the social-relational abilities among people with ASD. Survey of mastery accessible with proposed exploring gathering/organization in the subject of the task.

The undertaking proposes to build up a creative, insightful VR-based social correspondence framework that can adjust contingent upon the expectation of one's nervousness level from the ongoing eye physiological and seeing example records. This requires aptitude in versatile frameworks, PC illustrations, full of feeling demonstrating instruments, and psychological science. Our exploration group's ability in these zones would do the trick to achieve this venture.

5.12   Achievability of VR-Based Social Interaction to Cause Variation in Viewing Pattern of Youngsters With ASD

An investigation was done whether cooperation in VR-based social connection errands can change individual survey records for members with

Table 5.1 Viewing pattern indices.

Participant	Mean fixation duration			Object-to-face ratio		
	Trial1(s)	Trial5(s)	%Δ	Trial1	Trial5	%Δ
ASD1	0.285	0.316	14.78	0.314	0.015	95.57
ASD2	0.236	0.578	151.18	0.032	0.000	100.00
ASD3	0.324	0.462	35.32	0.117	0.030	73.72
ASD4	0.452	0.575	32.34	0.091	0.001	97.82

ASD. Such an analysis is significant because kids with ASD will focus less on appearances and more on different items when contrasted with the Typically Developing (TD) youngsters (Jones *et al.*, 2008). In the examination did by the PI, an Arrington Eye Tracker (http://www.arrington research.com/) was utilized. The visual improvement was partitioned into two locales of interest (ROIs): the essence of the symbol and the leftover articles in the VR climate. The errand was as per the following: a sign would portray an individual story for 2–3 minutes. Toward the end of the portrayal, the member was asked to answer a fundamental inquiry on the portrayal's subject. The outcome for four members (ASD1-ASD4) has appeared in Table 5.1. The analysis meets contained five preliminaries. The eye stare of the members was observed progressively.

Two review files, precisely, mean obsession length on the symbol's face district and object-to-confront proportion, were examined because they appeared to demonstrate one's emotional state (Jones *et al.*, 2008). Table 5.1 presents these survey design lists for Trial1 and Trial5. The mean obsession term expanded and object-to-confront proportion diminished somewhere in the range of Trial1 and Trial5 for every member, which suggested that the members focused harder on the face. In this manner, the real outcomes demonstrated that in VR-based social cooperation, the members' survey design shifted. It improved regarding more noteworthy obsession term toward the substance of their virtual communicators with VR-based social errand progress.

5.13 Achievability of VR-Based Social Interaction to Cause Variety in Eye Physiological Indices for Kids With ASD

Here, we present the consequences of an exploration study directed to analyze the adequacy of VR-based frameworks to cause variations in the

Table 5.2 Variation in pupil radius (PR) as a factor of emotion recognition.

	$PR_{MEAN}Neutral$ (mm)	$PR_{MEAN}Happy$ (mm)	%ΔNeutral-to-Happy	$PR_{MEAN}Neutral$ (mm)	$PR_{MEAN}Angry$ (mm)	%ΔNeutral-to-Angry
ASD1	8.035	8.807	9.62	8.035	10.712	33.32
ASD2	6.212	6.271	0.95	6.212	6.395	2.91
ASD3	6.731	6.965	3.52	6.731	7.216	7.23
ASD4	6.744	6.816	1.11	6.740	7.261	7.72
ASD5	7.677	8.031	4.60	7.676	7.710	0.42
ASD6	7.208	7.262	0.76	7.207	7.310	1.41

physiological eye records, to be specific, student distance across (PD) and squint rate (BR) among youngsters with ASD, like other non-VR-based investigations (Partala and Surakka, 2003; Wilbarger *et al.*, 2009). Kids with ASD frequently experience conditions of enthusiastic or intellectual pressure estimated as Autonomic Nervous System initiation without outside articulation (Picard, 2009), testing their inclinations in learning and conveying. Subsequently, perception of outward appearances may not be dependable to realize whether they can perceive others' passionate articulations during social correspondence (McIntosh *et al.*, 2006; Picard, 2009). In this unique situation, eye physiological records could be a significant source to show the cycle of feeling acknowledgment in these kids.

In this investigation, the members saw symbols portraying their encounters while displaying appropriate outward appearances (cheerful, irate, and impartial) during the introduction stage. This was trailed by the communication stage when the members were approached to react to story-related and feeling acknowledgment questions. This was joined by ongoing information procurement of the members' physiological eye lists in a period synchronized way.

As introduced in Tables 5.2 and 5.3, it tends to be seen that both the physiological eye files of the ASD members shifted as a proportion of the feeling acknowledgment applications created in VR. The variety in the eye-physiological records had a pattern like other non-VR–based examinations for all the members (aside from one member who was an exception).

Table 5.3 Variation in blink speed (BS) as a factor of emotion recognition.

	BS_{MEAN} (times/min)		%ΔNeutral-to-Happy	BS_{MEAN} (times/min)		%ΔNeutral-to-Angry
	Neutral	Happy		Neutral	Angry	
ASD1	8.12	13.04	60.17	8.12	23.84	193.21
ASD2	5.41	8.12	50.00	5.41	8.64	59.25
ASD3	7.34	13.15	79.08	7.34	9.88	34.16
ASD4	12.37	14.44	16.35	12.38	15.27	22.67
ASD5	43.33	42.40	−2.15	43.35	71.55	64.94
ASD6	11.31	22.17	96.05	11.31	42.15	273.38

5.14   Possibility of VR-Based Social Interaction to Cause Variations in the Anxiety Level for Youngsters With ASD

In another examination led by Researcher Lahiri, the emotional and physiological variety because of controlled social boundaries (e.g., eye stare and social distance) during social cooperation in VR for both ASD and TD (regularly creating) kids were researched. This investigation included seven sets of kids with ASD and TD (age 13–17 years) coordinated on age and sexual orientation. Social collaborations were planned to utilize Vizard (VR toolbox programming) to project virtual human characters (i.e., symbols) who showed distinctive eye stare designs and remained at various distances while recounting an individual story to the members. We gathered a clinical eyewitness' abstract report on the degrees of feeling state (i.e., tension) for every member who finished two 1.5-hour meetings. The social boundaries of interest, eye stare, and social distance were analyzed in a 4 × 2 plan, introduced in an irregular request dependent on a Latin Squares configuration to represent sequencing and request impacts (Keppel, 1991). Four kinds of eye stare directed the level of time a symbol took a gander at the member. These were labeled as immediate, turned away, typical while talking, and flip of ordinary [4, 22, 33]. Two sorts of social distance, named obtrusive (1.5 ft away) and decency (4.5 ft away), described the distance between the symbol and the member ([5], Hall, 1966; Schneiderman and Ewens, 1971). For example, other social boundaries, outward appearance, and vocal tone were kept as nonpartisan as could be expected. The specialist appraised the members' uneasiness level as they collaborated with the VR-based social correspondence situations.

Investigating the clinical onlooker's abstract rating uncovered that control of social boundaries made emotional changes in the members. The detailed uneasiness bunch means were higher for ASD than for the coordinated TD gathering, which is steady with perceptions of social deficiencies of ASD kids. The standard deviation (SD) for the ASD bunch was higher than that of the TD gathering. This outcome suggested that the ASD bunch was more vulnerable than the TD gathering to control social boundaries in the VR preliminaries. Likewise, the abstract rating scope (nine-point scale) was higher for the ASD bunch than the TD bunch on the revealed uneasiness level. In this way, the outcomes suggested that our VR-based social communication framework was fit for making emotional changes among the members.

Our starter results have exhibited the attainability of creating VR-based look touchy social correspondence frameworks for kids with ASD. That can do (a) establishing functional virtual conditions that can control attributes of social communications in manners that can be identified through physiological eye instruments and estimations of survey design lists of eye stare and (b) making varieties in the full of feeling conditions of the members.

In light of our past work, the following stage is to analyze how this innovation can be applied to social and versatile conduct errands that are touchy to the members' nervousness level anticipated from one's review example and eye-physiological files [38]. Therefore, the VR-based look touchy social correspondence framework should be equipped for adjusting to the members' expected uneasiness level by using a wise guideline administered system generator to cultivate improvement in social undertaking execution while keeping up their solace level. We accept that the proposed examination could start another age of brilliant intercession frameworks that are (a) versatile and receptive to the individual weaknesses of kids and youths with ASD and (b) fit for upgrading explicit mediation objectives pivotal to long haul freedom.

References

1. Welch, K.C., Lahiri, U., Sarkar, N., Warren, Z., Stone, W., Liu, C., Chapter 15 Affect-Sensitive Computing and Autism, IGI Global, Pennsylvania, USA, 2011.
2. Anderson, C.J., Colombo, J., Shaddy, D.J., Visual Scanning and Pupillary Responses in Young Children with Autism Spectrum Disorder. *J. Clin. Exp. Neuropsychol.*, 28, 1238–1256, 2006.
3. APA., *Diagnostic and statistical manual of mental disorders: DSM-IV-TR*, American Psychiatric Association, Washington, DC, 2000.
4. Argyle, M. and Cook, M., *Gaze and Mutual Gaze*, Cambridge Univ. Press, Cambridge, MA, 1976.
5. Argyle, M. and Deal, J., Eye-contact, distance and Affiliation. *Sociometry*, 28, 3, 289–304, 1965.
6. Asha, K., Ajay, K., Naznin, V., George, T., Peter, D., Gesture-based affective computing on motion capture data. *Int. Conf. on Affective Computing and Intelligent Interaction*, 2005.
7. Bancroft, W.J., *Research in Nonverbal Communication and Its Relationship to Pedagogy and Suggestopedia*, ERIC, USA, 1995.
8. Baron-Cohen, S., Scott, F.J., Allison, C., Williams, J., Bolton, P., Matthews, F.E., Brayne, C., Prevalence of autism-spectrum conditions: UK school-based population study. *Br. J. Psychiatry*, 194, 500–509, 2009.

9. Bartlett, M.S., Littlewort, G., Fasel, I., Movellan, J.R., Real-time face detection and facial expression recognition: development and applications to human-computer interaction. *Computer Vision and Pattern Recognition Workshop*, 2003.

10. Ben Shalom, D., Mostofsky, S.H., Hazlett, R.L., Goldberg, M.C., Landa, R.J., Faran, Y., McLeod, D.R., Hoehn-Saric, R., Normal physiological emotions but differences in expression of conscious feelings in children with high-functioning autism. *J. Autism Dev. Disord.*, 36, 3, 395–400, 2006.

11. Bernard-Opitz, V., Sriram, N., Nakhoda-Sapuan, S., Enhancing social problem-solving in children with autism and normal children through computer-assisted instruction. *J. Autism. Dev. Disord.*, 31, 4, 377–384, 2001.

12. Bellani, M., Virtual reality in autism. State of the art. *Epidemiol. Pyschiatr. Sci.*, 3, 235–238, 2011.

13. Billstedt, E., Gillberg, I.C., Gillberg, C., Autism after adolescence: population-based 13-22-year follow-up study of 120 individuals with autism diagnosed in childhood. *J. Autism Dev. Disord.*, Springer, Berlin, Heidelberg, 35, 351–360, 2005.

14. Blocher, K. and Picard, R.W., Affective, social quest: emotion recognition therapy for autistic children, in: *Socially Intelligent Agents: Creating Relationships with Computers and Robots*, K. Dautenhahn, A.H. Bond, L. Canamero, B. Edmonds (Eds.), Kluwer Academic Publishers, Springer, Berlin, Heidelberg, 2002.

15. Bradley, M.M., Emotion and motivation, in: *Handbook of Psychophysiology*, J.T. Cacioppo, L.G. Tassinary, G. Berntson (Eds.), pp. 602–642, Cambridge University Press, New York, 2000.

16. Bradley, M.B., Miccoli, L., Escrig, M.A., Lang, P.J., The pupil as a measure of emotional arousal and autonomic activation. *Psychophysiology*, 45, 4, 602–607, 2008.

17. Brown, R.M., Hall, L.R., Holtzer, R., Brown, S.L., Brown, N.L., Gender and video game performance. *Sex Roles*, 36, 793–812, 1997.

18. Cederlund, M., Hagberg, B., Billstedt, E., Gillberg, I.C., Gillberg, C., Asperger syndrome and autism: a comparative longitudinal follow-up study more than five years after the original diagnosis. *J. Autism Dev. Disord.*, 38, 72–85, 2008.

19. Centers for Disease Control and Prevention (CDC), Prevalence of autism spectrum disorders–autism and developmental disabilities monitoring network, 14 sites, United States, 2008. *Surveill. Summ.*, 61, SS03, 1–19, 2012.

20. Charitos, D., Karadanos, G., Sereti, E., Triantafillou, S., Koukouvinou, S., Martakos, D., Employing virtual reality for aiding the organization of autistic children behavior in everyday tasks, in: *3rd ICDVRAT*, P. Sharkey, A. Cesarani, L. Pugnetti, A. Rizzo (Eds), the University of Reading, Sardinia Italy, pp. 147–152, 2000.

21. Cohen, H., Amerine-Dickens, M., Smith, T., Early intensive behavioral treatment: Replication of the UCLA Model in a community setting. *J. Dev. Behav. Pediatr.*, 27, 2 Suppl, S145–155, 2006.

22. Colburn, A., Drucker, S., Cohen, M., The role of eye-gaze in avatar-mediated conversational interfaces. *SIGGRAPH Sketches and Applications*, New Orleans, Louisiana, USA, 2000.

23. Constantino, J.N., *The Social Responsiveness Scale*, Western Psychological Services, Los Angeles, California, 2002.
24. Daley, T.C., From Symptom Recognition to diagnosis: Children with Autism in urban India. *Soc. Sci. Med.*, 58, 1323–1335, 2004.
25. Daley, T. and Barua, M., Diagnostic Practices and Awareness of Autism Among Indian Pediatricians: A Decade of Data. *International Meeting for Autism Research, IMFAR, 2010*, 2010.
26. Dawson, G. and Osterling, J., Early intervention in autism: Effectiveness and common elements of current approaches, in: *The effectiveness of early intervention: Second generation research*, Guralnick, (Ed.), pp. 307–326, 1997.
27. Dowd, T. and Tierney, J., *Teaching Social Skills to youth*, Boys Town Press, USA, 2005.
28. Eikeseth, S., Outcome of comprehensive psycho-educational interventions for young children with autism. *Res. Dev. Disabil.*, 30, 158–178, 2009.
29. Ernsperger, L., *Keys to Success for Teaching Students with Autism*, Future Horizons, England, 2003.
30. Farr, W., Yuill, N., Raffle, H., Social benefits of a tangible user interface for children with Autistic Spectrum Conditions. *Autism*, 14, 237–252, 2010.
31. Gal, E., Bauminger, N., Goren-Bar, D., Pianesi, F., Stock, O., Zancanaro, M., Weiss, P.L.T., Enhancing Social Communication of Children with High-functioning Autism through a Co-located Interface. *AI Soc.*, 24, 1, 75–84, 2009.
32. Ganz, M.L., The lifetime distribution of the incremental societal costs of autism. *Arch. Pediatr. Adolesc. Med.*, 161, 4, 343–349, 2007.
33. Garau, M., Slater, M., Bee, S., Sasse, M.A., The impact of eye gaze on communication using humanoid avatars. *SIGCHI conference on human factors in computing systems*, pp. 309–316, 2001.
34. Garner, M., Mogg, K., Bradley, B.P., Orienting and maintenance of gaze to facial expressions in social anxiety. *J. Abnorm. Psychol.*, 115, 4, 760–770, 2006.
35. Gillott, A., Furniss, F., Walter, A., Anxiety in high-functioning children with autism. *Autism*, 5, 3, 277–286, 2001.
36. Goldsmith, T., *Using virtual reality enhanced behavioral skills training to teach street-crossing skills to children and adolescents with Autism Spectrum Disorders*, Ph.D. defense, 138 pages, Western Michigan University, Michigan, USA, 2008.
37. Goodwin, M.S., Enhancing and accelerating the pace of Autism Research and Treatment: The promise of developing Innovative Technology. *Focus Autism Other Dev. Disabl.*, Michigan, USA., 23, 125–128, 2008.
38. Green, D., Baird, G., Barnett, A.L., Henderson, L., Huber, J., Henderson, S.E., The severity and nature of motor impairment in Asperger's syndrome: a comparison with Specific Developmental Disorder of Motor Function. *J. Child Psychol. Psychiatry*, 43, 5, 655–668, 2002.

6

Construction and Reconstruction of 3D Facial and Wireframe Model Using Syntactic Pattern Recognition

Shilpa Rani[1]*, Deepika Ghai[2] and Sandeep Kumar[3]

[1]Lovely Professional University, Punjab, India
[2]ECE, Lovely Professional University, Punjab, India
[3]Computer Science and Engineering Department, Koneru Lakshmaiah Education Foundation, Vaddeswaram, Andra Pradesh, India

Abstract

Day by day, the entire world depends on human-computer interactive machines because demands increase in real-time devices being a security concern. The human-computer interactive machine will make human life easy, fast, and more stable. Face recognition is one of the popular applications of image analysis because it has a wide range of law and commercial applications and improved technology after 30 years of continuous research. Human face recognition using machines continuously attracting the researchers and gaining the machine learning–based recognition system gained a certain level of maturity with some limitations. Recognition of face in different illumination and pose variation is still a mostly unsolved problem. 3D face model–based methods are providing the solution to these problems. 3D face models can be designed using image-based methods or laser scan-based methods. Image-based face modeling methods are the more significant reconstruction of the model done through one or more 2D image slices. Our goal is to create an algorithm that can be used for the reconstruction of a 3D model. In this paper, we proposed a novel approach to reconstructing 3D face models using 2D images. First, the facial features are extracted using the syntactic pattern recognition technique. In the second step, dense features are extracted using SIFT technique. In the third step, the shape and shading technique is applied to extract the image's enhanced details. In the fourth step, the Basel face model is applied to create the 3D face image. Our proposed method is efficient because it requires a single image to reconstruct a 3D face model and it is also reconstructs the

Corresponding author: shilpachoudhary2020@gmail.com

Sandeep Kumar, Rohit Raja, Shrikant Tiwari and Shilpa Rani (eds.) Cognitive Behavior and Human Computer Interaction Based on Machine Learning Algorithm, (137–156) © 2022 Scrivener Publishing LLC

wireframe model of the image if the input image is a wireframe model. The proposed methodology's efficiency is verified on publicly available benchmark databases, i.e., Face Warehouse database, USF dataset, and our dataset. The proposed methodology's effectiveness is represented in the result section by comparing the proposed methodology's RMS value with existing methods. The proposed method can design the facial mask for facial burn victims from pre-burn photos.

Keywords: Face recognition, face reconstruction security, human-computer interaction, syntactic

6.1   Introduction

Reconstruction of face model is an excellent research area in computer graphics and computer vision. The face model is used widely in different applications such as image manipulation, face recognition, face reconstruction [1, 2], biometrics [3–5, 39], texture blending [6–8, 40], facial expression, recognition, and face surgery. In the analysis of facial expression, 3D face modeling is used in various visual computation applications, and the recent years, 3D face models gained popularity because of the 3D nature of the human face. Reconstruction of the 3D facial model from 2D images is a fundamental problem in computer vision. This problem's solution is complicated due to some reasons such as occlusion, ambiguities in the image, and loss of information.

In the past 10 years, numerous methods have been proposed for the 3D reconstruction using a single 2D image. Jiang *et al.* [9] proposed an algorithm that reconstructed 3D face images using smooth coarse to adequate optimization. Xiaoguang *et al.* [10] proposed the 2DSAL method (two-dimensional self-supervised learning method), which can construct 3D faces using 2D images. 3D face reconstruction gained more attention in the last three decades since Hu *et al.* [11] reconstructed the 3D image using shape and shading technique. It works on the concept of changing principle. Whenever there is a change in the surface orientation, there is a possibility of a shading change. This method is helpful to recover the character based on the intensity of the pixels in the image. Image formation must be known before applying the shape from the shading method. Queau *et al.* [12] also implemented the shape from the shading technique to reconstruct 3D images. However, these techniques have some drawbacks. These techniques can be applied on the Lambertian surface (LS) because SFS can deal with the face as Lambertian surface. Finding the depth of the image is another difficulty. If the image has a specular surface, then it is impossible to find the depth of the image due to the surface's reflectance behavior. The specular surface will have a mirror-like character; hence, finding the depth is a complicated process and the result would be more worst if dealing with synthetic data. Therefore, it is required to find a method that can work with all type of surfaces.

After the SFS, researchers have introduced a statistical learning-based method for the reconstruction of 3D images. These methods used the learning-based approach. In this direction, Zhang *et al.* [13, 38] proposed a method on temporal-based correspondence. This method has excellent results for high-resolution images. However, this method requires a complex setup, controlled illumination environment, and multiple input images for the reconstruction of 3D images. These methods require rigorous human involvement for finding the features of the face from the image, which makes them computationally expensive. On the other side, some methods [14–16] do not require human interference for tracking facial features. However, these methods required multiple views of the single image and controlled lighting environments. Kemelmacher Shlizerman and Seitz *et al.* [17] proposed 3D face reconstruction using multiple images. This method can produce high-quality 3D face models using photometric stereo. The neural network also follows the learning-based approach and these methods have better performance for regression problems. 3D face reconstruction-based neural network proposed by Blanz and Vetter [18]. This method is a popular parametric face model because of its simplicity and this method is a foundation of other face reconstructed methods. The neural network–based approach requires a massive amount of images for learning purposes and it will be computationally expensive. If a sufficient amount of training dataset is not available, then the neural network does not provide favorable results. Moreover, these methods fail to produce the target face's geometric details due to the limited degree of freedom of low-dimensional data.

6.1.1   Contribution

In this paper, we proposed a novel approach to reconstructing 3D face models using sing 3D image. Our proposed method is efficient because it requires a single image is sufficient to reconstruct a 3D face model. The proposed method takes less time for computation and processing speed is also high, which makes it more useful for real-time systems. The proposed methodology's effectiveness is represented in the result section by comparing the proposed methodology's RMS value with existing methods.

Our proposed method consists of the following steps:

- First, the facial features are extracted from the image using the syntactic pattern recognition technique.

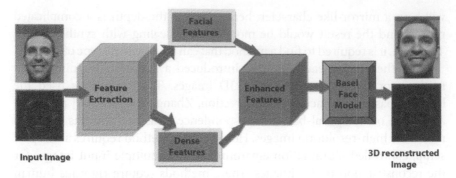

Figure 6.1 Block diagram of the proposed methodology.

- In the second step, dense features are extracted using SIFT technique.
- In the third step, the shape and shading technique is applied to extract the enhanced details from the image.
- In the fourth step, the Basel face model is applied to create the 3D face image.

In the proposed method, facial features are extracted using the syntactic pattern recognition technique. It takes the facial features and extracts the image's depth information, which makes an efficient 3D reconstruction model.

The block diagram of the proposed methodology is represented in Figure 6.1. The rest of the paper is summarized as mentioned as follows: Section 6.2 explains the literature work on this field. Proposed methodology and evaluation parameters are discussed in Sections 6.3 and 6.4. Results are discussed in Section 6.4, and Section 6.5 represents the conclusion.

6.2   Literature Survey

In this section, we performed a brief literature survey on different 3D face reconstruction methods, and these methods can be categorized as optimization-based methods, supervised learning-based methods, and shape and shading-based face reconstruction. A complete comparative study is shown in Table 6.1.

According to the literature survey, many researchers used the supervised learning technique to reconstruct 3D images. These methods required a

Table 6.1 Study of existing methodology.

Sr. no.	Authors & year	Methodology	Database	Remarks
1	Ya-ing Chen et al. [19], 2020	3D Morphable Model Regression	MICC Florence, FRGC2	Error = 2.41 ± 0.62 Error = 5.05 ± 1.44
2	Yangyu Fan et al. [20], 2020	Generative Adversarial Network	WildUV dataset	PSNR = 29.5 SSIM = 0.952
3	Yu-Hsuan Huang et al. [21], 2020	GLADNet	SoF Dataset, CASIA-WebFace	Accuracy Improved by 2.5%
4	H. M. Rehan Afzal et al. [22], 2020	Scale-Invariant Feature Transform (SIFT), Multivariate Gaussian Distribution, Basel face model (BFM)	LFW Database	RMSE = 0.8866 PSNR = 27.27 Error = 1.36 Mean Error = 0.4996 Std. Error = 0.3070 SSIM = 0.9864
5	Qing-Ming Liu et al. [23], 2019	Convolution Neural Network	Helen, CelebA face, CMU+MIT, WHU-SCF datasets	PSNR = 37.496 SSIM = 0.918
6	H. M. Rehan Afzal et al. [24], 2018	Supervised Descent Method (SDM), Multivariate Gaussian Distribution, PCA	LFW Dataset	Perform Better

(Continued)

Table 6.1 Study of existing methodology. (Continued)

Sr. no.	Authors & year	Methodology	Database	Remarks
7	Yudong Guo et al. [25], 2018	Convolution Neural Network (Single-image CoarseNet + Tracking CoarseNet and FineNet)	Self-Dataset	MSE = 0.56 Mean vertex distance = 4.56
8	Luo Jiang et al. [26], 2018	Bilinear Face Model	Face Warehouse, Bosphorus database	3DRMSE = 1.75±0.29 Run-Time CPU = 3min
9	Chen Cao et al. [27], 2014	Active Shape Model, PCA	Face Model Databases	Better Performance
10	Huy Tho Ho et al. [28], 2013	Markov Random Fields, Belief Propagation, Lucas-Kanade (LK) algorithm	FERET, CMU-PIE, Multi-PIE	Recognition Rate = 95.5% on FERET, 98.8% on CMU-PIE, 89.4% on Multi-PIE
11	Mingli Song et al. [29], 2012	Coupled Radial basis Function Network	BU3D database	MSE = 5.60%
12	Jian Lai et al. [30], 2012	Weighted Global Sparse Representation	Extended Yale B and AR database	Recognition Rate = 98.9% and 97.5%

massive amount of data for the training purpose, then only the algorithm gives better results and if any unknown expression is available in the testing dataset, it is not easy to reconstruct the 3D face model. Hence, the proposed methodology is designed to reconstruct any 3D face model without using the supervised machine learning algorithms.

6.3   Proposed Methodology

This section summarizes the proposed methodology. In the proposed method, first, it takes the single image as an input, detects the face in the image, and then performs the following operations (mentioned in Figure 6.1) to reconstruct the 3D face model.

6.3.1   Face Detection

In this step, a single image is taken as an input image. The input image can be simple or it can be the surface of the image. First, the image is scanned for detection of the image. The Viola-Jones method is used for face detection [31]. The results of the technique are mentioned as shown in Figure 6.2.

6.3.2   Feature Extraction

Feature extraction is divided into two steps: First, the facial features are extracted from the image, and then SIFT is applied to extract distinctive features.

6.3.2.1   Facial Feature Extraction

The syntactic pattern recognition approach is used for facial feature extraction from the image in the proposed methodology.

6.3.2.2   Syntactic Pattern Recognition

Syntactic pattern recognition technique is another pattern recognition technique and it comes under structural pattern recognition. To solve the existing problem, syntactic pattern recognition and picture description language used. In this approach, an image can be represented as string grammar and this string grammar can be obtained using the juxtaposition of a string. Juxtaposition can be represented using head and tail positions. PDL can represent simple and intricate patterns. This mechanism can be

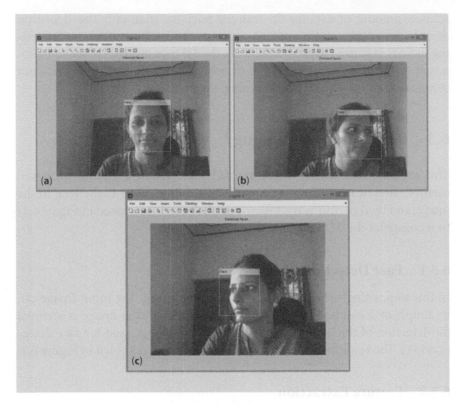

Figure 6.2 (a) Original image. (b) Face detection from the right angle using Viola-Jones method [31]. (c) Face detection from the left angle using Viola-Jones method.

used to represent the contour or wireframe model of the image. As shown in Figure 6.3, the 3D convex polyhedron represents the given image's wireframe, which could be drawn with a minimum of 19 neighborhood pixels. The center cell is 14 and 1, 3, 7, 9, 19, 21, 25, and 27 are corner pixels. These corner pixels represent the given image's wireframe model, which is also called 3D contour or 3D convex polyhedrons. The single 3D image consists of 256 possible 3D convex polyhedrons and all the possible convex polyhedrons are represented in Table 6.2. Figure 6.4 represents the $3 \times 3 \times 3$ size of the voxel array and the smallest possible convex polyhedrons.

In the proposed method, picture description language is used for feature extraction. For tracing the whole image, a $3 \times 3 \times 3$ size voxel is used, as shown in Figure 6.4. The entire face image is traced pixel by pixel, which starts from (1, 1, 1) position and continues in the same direction until the algorithm will not find the first pixel with intensity value one and this first pixel with intensity 1 represents the first component of the face. The proposed methodology can find the entire neighborhood pixel in the preferred

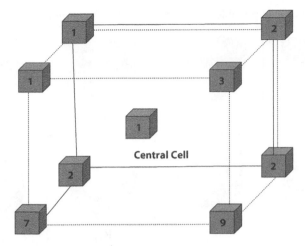

Figure 6.3 3D wireframe concerning central cell 14.

Table 6.2 Sample of possible convex polyhedrons.

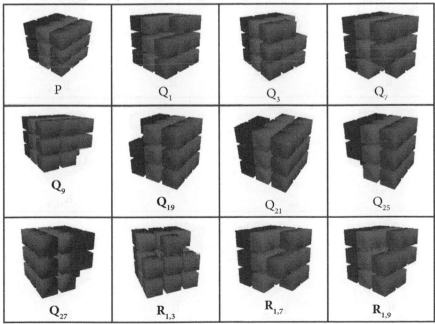

(*Continued*)

Table 6.2 Sample of possible convex polyhedrons. (*Continued*)

$R_{1,19}$	$R_{1,21}$	$R_{1,25}$	$R_{1,27}$
$R_{3,7}$	$R_{3,9}$	$R_{3,19}$	$R_{3,21}$
$R_{3,25}$	$R_{3,27}$	$R_{7,9}$	$R_{7,19}$
$R_{7,21}$	$R_{7,25}$	$R_{7,27}$	$R_{9,19}$
$R_{9,21}$	$R_{9,25}$	$R_{9,27}$	$R_{19,21}$
$R_{19,25}$	$R_{19,27}$	$R_{21,25}$	$R_{21,27}$

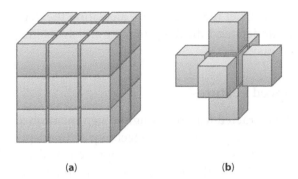

(a)   (b)

Figure 6.4 (a) 3 × 3 × 3 size of voxels array. (b) Smallest possible three-dimensional convex polyhedron.

direction. According to the syntactic pattern recognition technique, in a 2D image, there are nine possible directions where a neighborhood pixel could be present. Similarly, in 3D images, there are 26 possible directions where a neighborhood pixel could be present in all possible planes. The image's tracing will continue until it does not find all the image's possible neighborhood pixels. The same approach will continue for all the possible planes of the 3D image (Central, front, rear). When all the components are traced, they will finally get the knowledge information representing the image. This knowledge vector contains the image's feature and consists of the depth information of the face image, which makes this algorithm novel and unique.

6.3.2.3 Dense Feature Extraction

In this step, SIFT (scale-invariant feature transform) algorithm is applied to get a more distinctive feature from the image. These unique features are helpful in the reconstruction of the 3D face model. The first difference of Gaussian is applied to identify the region of interest and it is invariant to the scale and orientation of the image. In the next step, key points are localized and this is helpful to determine the scale and location of every candidate location. Now, each key point will be assigned to the local image gradient direction. Finally, the gradients of the local image are measured around the key issues.

The benefit of applying SIFT is that it produces the dense feature of the image and the syntactic pattern recognition approach can produce each feature in detail and it also gives the depth inform details of the image, which helps reconstruct the 3D image. Calculating the depth information is necessary to understand the 3D geometry and syntactic pattern recognition makes it easy.

6.3.3   Enhanced Features

In this step, the extracted features using the step mentioned above will be enhanced using the shape and shading technique. The depth of the image, which is calculated using the syntactic approach, will be added to the image, making the image three dimensions. The image can be translated and rotated according to the requirement by adding depth information to the image.

6.3.4   Creation of 3D Model

In this step, we need to align the data with the 3DMM model. In the above step, we retrieved the features from two different methods, and now, these features should be integrated and aligned with the 3DMM model. In this step, a Basel face model is used, which is publically available, and it consists of 100 male and 100 female 3D scans. Now, we need to make a point-to-point correspondence with the Basel face model. The features should be mapped with the face model and sum of the square difference of pixels should be minimum to fit the model. It can be calculated as follows:

$$E = \sum_{x,y} \left\| I_{input}(x,y) - I_{model}(x,y) \right\|^2 \qquad (6.1)$$

This equation is helpful to align the input image on a 3D face model.

6.4   Datasets and Experiment Setup

The proposed algorithm is evaluated on the Face Warehouse database [32], USF dataset, [37] and our dataset. The Face Warehouse dataset contains 150 different subjects with 20 other expressions. Images of varying age groups of people with different facial expressions have been selected to examine the algorithm's performance. USF dataset contains 77 faces that are combination of male and female faces of different ages and races. These face model consists of depth information and texture of real faces. These models have lightning effects which could introduce error in the reconstruction. The proposed methodology is implemented on python using the Anaconda tool. The specification of the system is windows operating system, GPU processor, and 32 GB RAM.

6.5   Results

In the proposed methodology, we evaluated the expression reconstruction results on the Face Warehouse dataset [32]. We applied a rigid transformation to compute the vertex correspondence between the Face Warehouse dataset and the proposed methodology results. This rigid transformation aligns the predicted results and the ground truth results provided by the Face Warehouse dataset. Root mean square error between the corresponding vertices is calculated to compute the performance of the proposed methodology. Table 6.3 represents the mean and standard deviation of the point-to-point root mean square error on the Face Warehouse dataset. The comparative analysis is done with MoFA [33] and 3DMM [34], and it is represented in Figure 6.5. The proposed methodology is also applied on the wireframe of the image, where wireframe model of the image is given as an input and then algorithm can reconstruct the image's wireframe model image. The results of the proposed method are more accurate compared to the existing state of art methods. According to the result analysis, the proposed methodology can generate more identity-specific results. If some unknown expression appears in the image, then MoFA [33] cannot produce accurate results (shown in row 2 Figure 6.5).

Figure 6.6 shows the comparative analysis of error maps for 3D detailed reconstruction with state-of-the-art methods and the result shows that the results of the proposed methodology are more robust than the Sela 17 [35] and Tran18 [36].

Table 6.3 Comparative analysis of mean and standard deviation of point to point RMSE on face warehouse dataset.

Sr. no.	Method	Error
1	MoFA [33]	2.26±0.58
2	3DMM [34]	1.81±0.43
3	Proposed	1.69±0.20

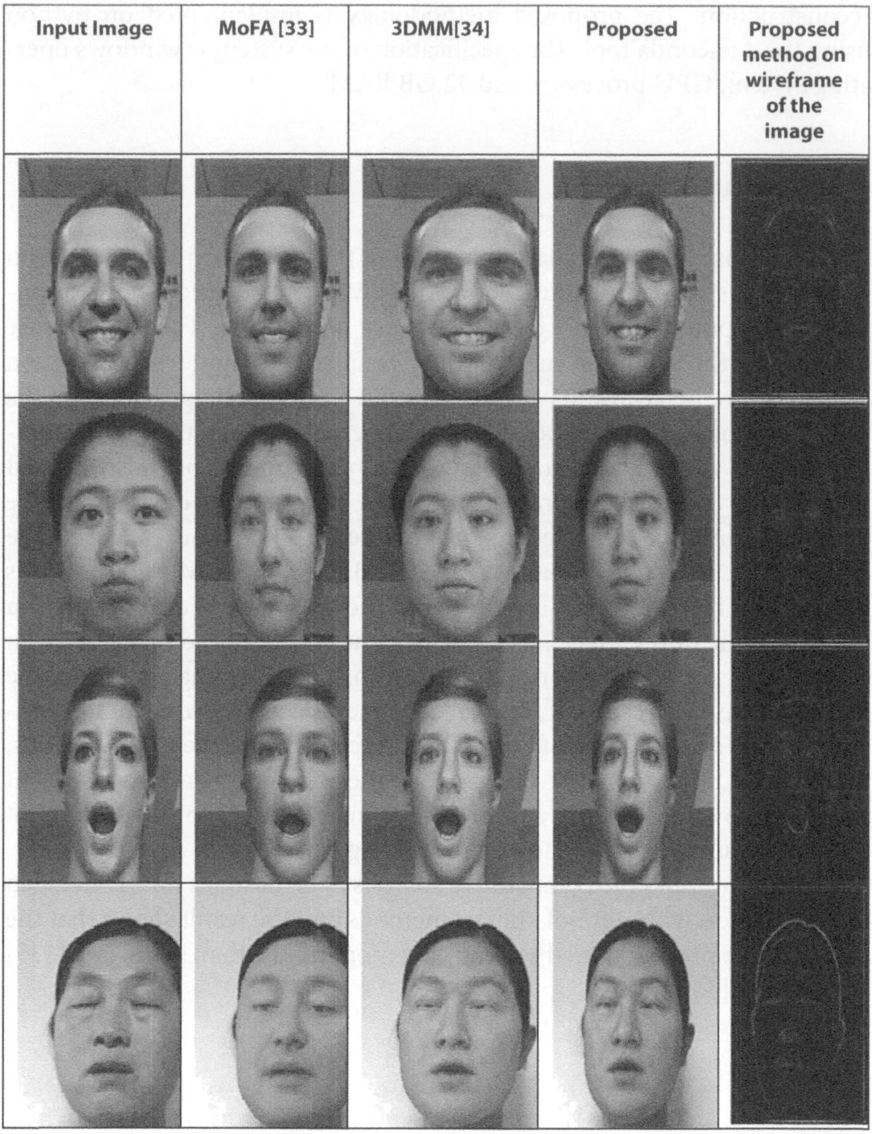

Figure 6.5 Comparative analysis of proposed algorithm with existing technique on face warehouse dataset. (*Continued*)

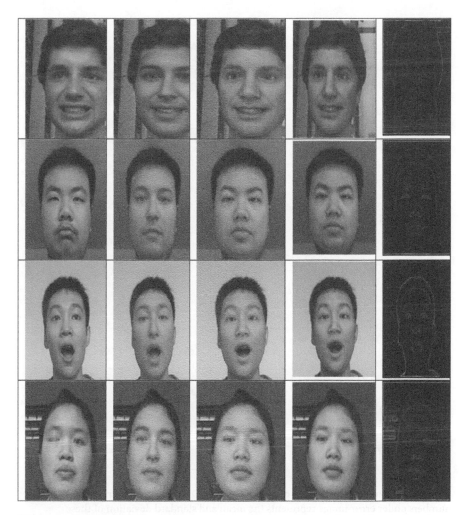

Figure 6.5 (Continued) Comparative analysis of proposed algorithm with existing technique on face warehouse dataset.

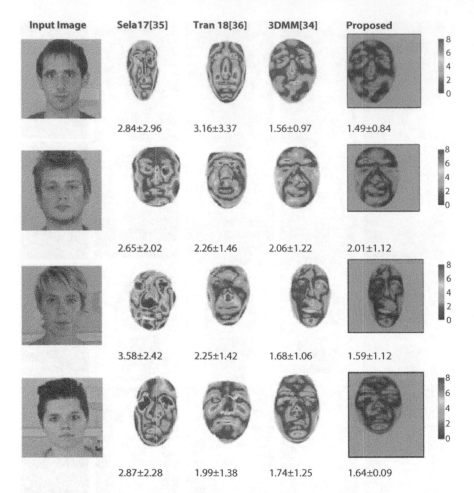

Figure 6.6 Comparative analysis of error maps for 3D detailed reconstruction. The numbers under error image represents the mean and standard deviation of these differences in percentage.

6.6   Conclusion

We proposed a 3D wireframe and face reconstruction model using syntactic pattern recognition. We first extracted the face from the image, and then, the feature is removed using the syntactic pattern recognition technique and SIFT method. In the next step, the feature is enhanced using the shape and shading technique, and finally, the processed data is aligned with the Basel dataset to reconstruct the 3D face model. The proposed methodology results are validated by comparing the results with existing techniques and results are better than the existing state of art methods. The calculation of RMS error represents the efficiency of the proposed method. Syntactic pattern recognition with shape and shading technique makes the algorithm recover the minute details of the image like wrinkles, dimples, and pouts effectively. This method can be used in the real-time system to reconstruct the wireframe and 3D face model and this method can reconstruct the 3D face model with the same facial expression present in the input image. Hence, the proposed methodology can preserve the facial expression in the reconstructed 3D face model. Figure 6.7 represents the reconstruction result of USF dataset. The numbers under error image represents the mean and standard deviation of these differences in percentage.

Input	Reference	Ground truth	Reconstructed Image [17]	Proposed	Reference	Ground Truth	Reconstructed Image	Proposed	GT-Ref	GT-Rec Proposed
									13.8=6.5	3.6=3.0%
									11.8=7.3	4.2=3.5%
									6.7=5.7%	3.0=2.0%

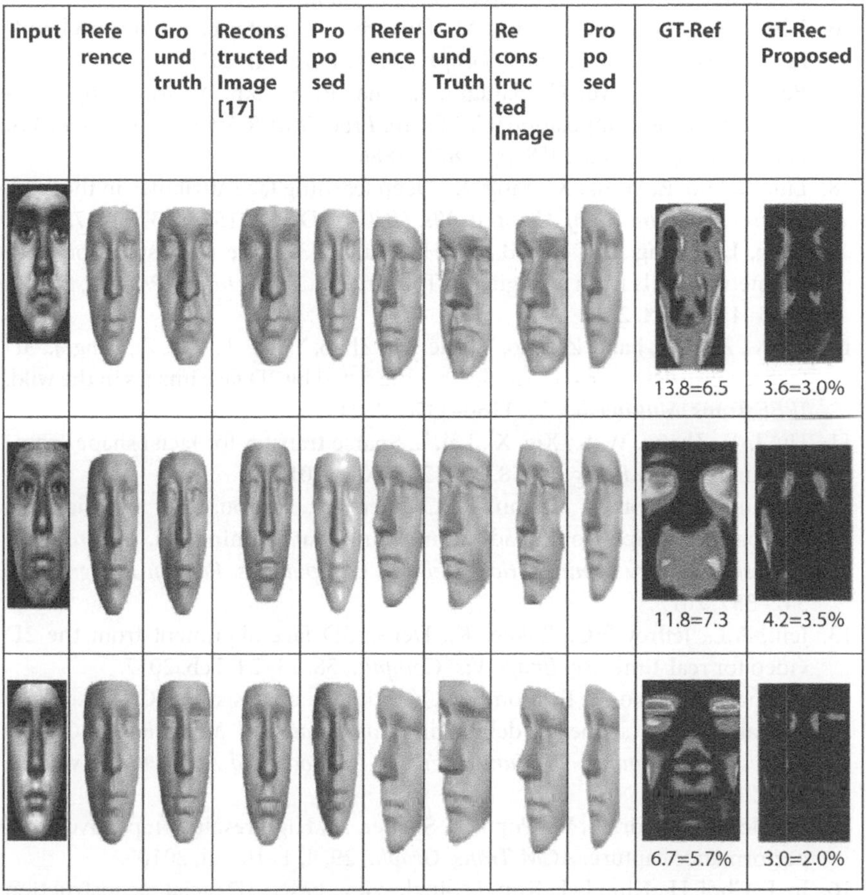

Figure 6.7 Reconstruction result of USF dataset. The numbers under error image represents the mean and standard deviation of these differences in percentage.

References

1. Hu, L., Avatar digitization from a single image for real-time rendering. *ACM Trans. Graph.*, 36, 6, 195, 2017.
2. Sela, M., Richardson, E., Kimmel, R., Unrestricted facial geometry reconstruction using Image-to-Image translation, in: *Proc. IEEE Int. Conf. Comput. Vis. (ICCV)*, Oct. 2017, pp. 1576–1585.
3. Li, T., Bolkart, T., Black, M.J., Li, H., Romero, J., Learning a model of facial shape and expression from 4D scans. *ACM Trans. Graph.*, 36, 6, 1–17, Nov. 2017.
4. Booth, J., Roussos, A., Zafeiriou, S., Ponniah, A., Dunaway, D., A 3D morphable model learnt from 10,000 faces, in: *Proc. IEEE Conf. Comput. Vis. Pattern Recognit. (CVPR)*, Jun. 2016, pp. 5543–5552.
5. Tena, J.R., De la Torre, F., Matthews, I., Interactive region-based linear 3D face models. *ACM Trans. Graph.*, 30, 4, 1–10, Jul. 2011.
6. Ichim, A.E., Bouaziz, S., Pauly, M., Dynamic 3D avatar creation from handheld video input. *ACM Trans. Graph.*, 34, 4, 1–14, Jul. 2015.
7. Bagautdinov, T., Wu, C., Saragih, J., Fua, P., Sheikh, Y., Modeling facial geometry using compositional VAEs, in: *Proc. IEEE/CVF Conf. Comput. Vis. Pattern Recognit*, Jun. 2018, pp. 3877–3886.
8. Liu, Z., Luo, P., Wang, X., Tang, X., Deep learning face attributes in the wild, in: *Proc. IEEE Int. Conf. Comput. Vis. (ICCV)*, Dec. 2015, pp. 3730–3738.
9. Jiang, L., Zhang, J., Deng, B., Li, H., Liu, L., 3D face reconstruction with geometry details from a single imaToll-Free. *E Trans. Image Process.*, 27, 10, 4756–4770, Oct. 2018.
10. Tu, X., Zhao, J., Jiang, Z., Luo, Y., Xie, M., Zhao, Y., He, L., Ma, Z., Feng, J., 3D face reconstruction from a single image assisted by 2D face images in the wild. *IEEE Trans. Multimedia*, 23, 1160–1172, 2021.
11. Hu, J.-F., Zheng, W.-S., Xie, X., Lai, J., Sparse transfer for facial shape-from-shading. *Pattern Recognit.*, 68, 272–285, Aug. 2017.
12. Quéau, Y., Mélou, J., Castan, F., Cremers, D., Durou, J.D., A variational approach to shape-from-shading under natural illumination, in: *Proc. Int. Workshop Energy Minimization Methods Comput. Vis. Pattern Recognit*, pp. 342–357, 2017.
13. Jeni, A.L., Jeffrey, F.C., Takeo, K., Dense 3D face alignment from the 2D video for real-time use. *Image Vis. Comput.*, 58, 13–24, Feb. 2017.
14. Maghari, A., Liao, I., Belaton, B., Quantitative analysis on PCA-based statistical 3D face shape modeling, in: *Computational Modelling of Objects Represented in Images III: Fundamentals, Methods and Applications*, vol. 13, 2012.
15. Bradley, D., Heidrich, W., Popa, T., Sheffer, A., High resolution passive facial performance capture. *ACM Trans. Graph.*, 29, 4, 1–10, Jul. 2010.
16. Jo, J., Choi, H., Kim, I.-J., Kim, J., Single-view-based 3D facial reconstruction method robust against pose variations. *Pattern Recognit.*, 48, 1, 73–85, Jan. 2015.

17. Kemelmacher-Shlizerman, I. and Seitz, S.M., Face reconstruction in the wild, in: *Proc. Int. Conf. Comput. Vis*, Nov. 2011, pp. 1746–1753.
18. Blanz, V. and Vetter, T., A morphable model for the synthesis of 3D faces, in: *Proceedings of the 26th annual conference on Computer graphics and interactive techniques*, pp. 187–194, 1999.
19. Chen, Y., Wu, F., Wang, Z., Song, Y., Ling, Y., Bao, L., Self-supervised learning of detailed 3d face reconstruction. *IEEE Trans. Image Process.*, 29, 8696–87055, 2020.
20. Fan, Y., Liu, Y., Lv, G., Liu, S., Li, G., Huang, Y., Full Face-and-Head 3D Model With Photorealistic Texture. *IEEE Access*, 8, 210709–2107215, 2020.
21. Huang, Y.-H. and Chen, H.H., Face Recognition Under Low Illumination Via Deep Feature Reconstruction Network, in: *2020 IEEE International Conference on Image Processing (ICIP)*, IEEE, pp. 2161–2165, 2020.
22. Rehan Afzal, H.M., Luo, S., Kamran Afzal, M., Chaudhary, G., Khari, M., Kumar, S.A.P., 3D Face Reconstruction From Single 2D Image Using Distinctive Features. *IEEE Access*, 8, 180681–1806895, 2020.
23. Liu, Q.-M., Jia, R.-S., Zhao, C.-Y., Liu, X.-Y., Sun, H.-M., Zhang, X.-L., Face super-resolution reconstruction based on self-attention residual network. *IEEE Access*, 8, 4110–41215, 2019.
24. Rehan Afzal, H.M., Luo, S., Kamran Afzal, M., Reconstruction of 3D facial image using a single 2D image, in: *2018 International Conference on Computing, Mathematics and Engineering Technologies (iCoMET)*, IEEE, pp. 1–5, 2018.
25. Guo, Y., Cai, J., Jiang, B., Zheng, J., Cnn-based real-time dense face reconstruction with inverse-rendered photo-realistic face images. *IEEE Trans. Pattern Anal. Mach. Intell.*, 41, 6, 1294–1307, 2018.
26. Jiang, L., Zhang, J., Deng, B., Li, H., Liu, L., 3D face reconstruction with geometry details from a single image. *IEEE Trans. Image Process.*, 27, 10, 4756–4770, 2018.
27. Cao, C., Weng, Y., Zhou, S., Tong, Y., Zhou, K., Facewarehouse: A 3d facial expression database for visual computing. *IEEE Trans. Visual. Comput. Graphics*, 20, 3, 413–425, 2013.
28. Ho, H.T. and Chellappa, R., Pose-invariant face recognition using markov random fields. *IEEE Trans. Image Process.*, 22, 4, 1573–1584, 2012.
29. Song, M., Tao, D., Huang, X., Chen, C., Bu, J., Three-dimensional face reconstruction from a single image by a coupled RBF network. *IEEE Trans. Image Process.*, 21, 5, 2887–2897, 2012.
30. Lai, J. and Jiang, X., Modular weighted global sparse representation for robust face recognition. *IEEE Signal Process. Lett.*, 19, 9, 571–574, 2012.
31. Wang, Y.Q., An analysis of the Viola-Jones faces detection algorithm. *Image Process. Line*, 4, 128–148, 2014.
32. Cao, C., Weng, Y., Zhou, S., Tong, Y., Zhou, K., FaceWarehouse: A 3D facial expression database for visual computing. *IEEE Trans. Vis. Comput. Graph.*, 20, 3, 413–425, Mar. 2014.

33. Tewari, A. *et al.*, MoFA: Model-based Deep convolutional face autoencoder for unsupervised monocular reconstruction, in: *Proc. IEEE Int. Conf. Comput. Vis. (ICCV)*, Oct. 2017, pp. 1274–128.

34. Chen, Y., Wu, F., Wang, Z., Song, Y., Ling, Y., Bao, L., Self-supervised learning of detailed 3d face reconstruction. *IEEE Trans. Image Process.*, 29, 8696–8705, 2020.

35. Sela, M., Richardson, E., Kimmel, R., Unrestricted facial geometry reconstruction using image-to-image translation, in: *Proc. IEEE Int. Conf. Comput. Vis. (ICCV)*, Oct. 2017, pp. 1576–1585.

36. Tran, A.T., Hassner, T., Masi, I., Paz, E., Nirkin, Y., Medioni, G., Extreme 3D face reconstruction: Seeing through occlusions, in: *Proc. IEEE/CVF Conf. Comput. Vis. Pattern Recognit*, Jun. 2018, pp. 3935–3944.

37. *USF DARPA Human-ID 3D Face Database*, http://www.csee.usf.edu/sarkar, Courtesy of Prof. Sudeep Sarkar, Univ. of South Florida, Tampa, FL, USA, 2010.

38. Raja, R., Sinha, T.S., Patra, R.K., Tiwari, S., Physiological Trait Based Biometrical Authentication of Human-Face Using LGXP and ANN Techniques. *Int. J. Inf. Comput. Secur.*, 10, 2/3, 303–320, 2018.

39. Raja, R., Patra, R.K., Sinha, T.S., Extraction of Features from Dummy face for improving Biometrical Authentication of Human. *Int. J. Lumin. Appl.*, 7, 3–4, 259, 507–512, 2017, Oct-Dec 2017.

40. Raja, R., Sinha, T.S., Dubey, R.P., Orientation Calculation of human Face Using Symbolic techniques and ANFIS. Published *Int. J. Eng. Future Technol.*, 7, 7, 37–50, 2016.

7

Attack Detection Using Deep Learning–Based Multimodal Biometric Authentication System

Nishant Kaushal[1]*, Sukhwinder Singh[1] and Jagdish Kumar[2]

[1]Department of ECE, Punjab Engineering College Chandigarh, Chandigarh, India
[2]Department of EE, Punjab Engineering College Chandigarh, Chandigarh, India

Abstract

Biometrics-based human identity confirmation and management systems have gained popularity in recent years. Biometric traits of an individual ranging from fingerprint, palm print, iris, and face to even gestures have found applications in various devices such as smartphones, and laptops, and even its use has been seen in extensive scale management system, for example, "Aadhaar" in India. As biometrics-based authentication systems have increased, the issue of identity theft has also grown drastically. Biometrics-based authentication systems involve human-computer interaction, as the trait captured via a sensor is processed and then the identity is verified. The most common method used by hackers for identity theft is by using spoofs (presentation attack). Unimodal biometrics-based systems are more vulnerable than multimodal as they involve only one trait than multimodal in which two or more than two traits are used for identity authentication. A multiple expert-based decision-level fused detector has been designed and analyzed for an efficient and secure multimodal biometric-based human identity authentication system.

Keywords: Biometrics, deep learning, multimodal, fingerprint, face, spoof, presentation attack detection

*Corresponding author: kaushalnishantone@gmail.com

Sandeep Kumar, Rohit Raja, Shrikant Tiwari and Shilpa Rani (eds.) Cognitive Behavior and Human Computer Interaction Based on Machine Learning Algorithm, (157–166) © 2022 Scrivener Publishing LLC

7.1   Introduction

Biometrics-based identity authentication devices have grown in usage in the last few decades, ranging from smartphones to even attendance management and recording systems. Biometrics can be understood as a union of two words, i.e., "bios" (lifeform) and "metron" (measure) [1]. Generally, biometric traits are unique to a person, and even two born twins have some biometric traits. Generally, biometrics are classified into two broad types, i.e., behavioral and physiological (Figure 7.1). Behavioral traits comprise measuring an individual's behavior, for example, gestures, voice, and signature. On the other hand, physiological traits comprise measuring physiological characteristics of an individual, for example, fingerprint, palm-print, iris, and DNA [1]. Among these two, physiological-based biometric features are most famous and widely used among the masses, and it can be seen nowadays that most smartphones come with fingerprint-based authentication applications.

However, with an increased dependence on biometrics for identity authentication purposes, identity theft has also been reported. Miscreants, after obtaining the biometric trait of an individual, for example, fingerprint and palm print, try to get illegal access to the individual's private account using synthetic spoofs to present at the sensor and cheat the system. This becomes a big concern when in a democracy like India,

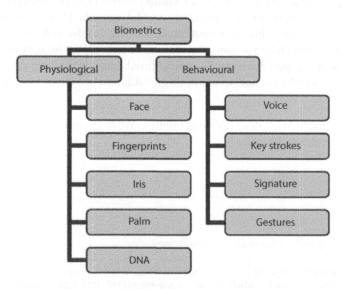

Figure 7.1 Hierarchy of biometric traits [2].

national citizen record management "Aadhaar" used for direct bene-fit transfer (DBT) government schemes is entirely based on biometrics applied authentication system. Some recent breaches show the vulnera-bility of the system.

Researchers have been working actively in this field for the last decade, but still, when unimodal-based (single biometric trait/modality) iden-tity authentication systems are considered, they are highly vulnerable to presentation/spoof attacks. However, when multimodal-based bio-metric authentication systems are considered, they are more resistant against presentation attacks as they provide multi-tier security against spoofs. Multimodal biometrics for identity authentication is not as robust for usage at the device level when unimodal-based techniques are compared.

Some work has been done in the recent past for making biometric-based authentication systems more secure. For example, [3] used fingerprint and iris together with score-level matching for recognition but did not con-sider the evaluation of spoofs. Voice and lip movement-based multimodal techniques have been designed by [4] with data-level fusion. In [5], a CNN (Convolutional Neural Network)–based multimodal biometric authenti-cation system has been designed, employing twin layer fusion. Multiple traits such as signature, face, and palm-print have been used in [6], giving good results and memory size reduction. In [7], a multimodal presentation attack detector has been designed using dynamic fingerprints to employ score level fusion to give good results. A CNN-based spoof resistant sys-tem has been designed in [8] where first, the template matching is done and then spoof is detected via a pre-trained CNN model using palm-vein, fingerprint, and face the biometric traits.

In recent years, deep learning–based CNNs have shown excellent results regarding object detection and image classification. This chapter proposes multiple expert-based presentation attack detection techniques. Our main contributions are as follows:

  i.   Two experts inspired by a lightweight deep neural network
       called MobileNet_v2 [9, 12] have been designed.
  ii. Decision level fusion of these two experts is used for deter-
       mining the impostor.
       a) Analysis based on benchmark datasets such as LivDet
           [10] and IDRND_FASDB [11] has been carried out.

This technique based on multiple experts based on a network like MobileNet_v2 [9] can also be implemented on small devices with relative

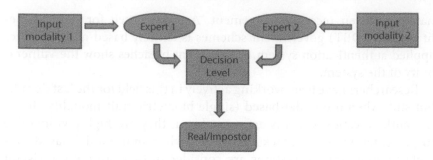

Figure 7.2 Block diagram of the proposed methodology.

ease as compared to other techniques in the literature for a multimodal system–based presentation attack detection. The block diagram for the proposed methodology is as shown in Figure 7.2.

7.2   Proposed Methodology

In this section, the proposed multiple expert-based PA (presentation attack) detector has been discussed. The proposed system can help make multimodal biometric-based identity authentication systems more resistant to malicious attacks that can hamper an individual's privacy. A twin expert–based impostor detector has been proposed based on depth-wise separable convolutions with a bottleneck in which weighted-sums can extract many features in less number of convolutions computational cost becomes 7 to 8 times less. Both the experts are explained in the following sub-sections.

7.2.1   Expert One

In this expert, a network pre-trained on ImageNet [13] and fine-tuned for particular two-class classification of a fake and live fingerprint (using LivDet datasets) is used for calculating the impostor score. A depth-wise detachable CNN with a significantly less computational cost is used. The input image is resized into the range of 128×128 to 244×244 for efficient classification. The impostor probability (in percentage) is calculated for determining the final advice of expert one.

7.2.2   Expert Two

In this expert, also the same as expert one, a network pre-trained on ImageNet [13] and fine-tuned for particular two-class classification of fake

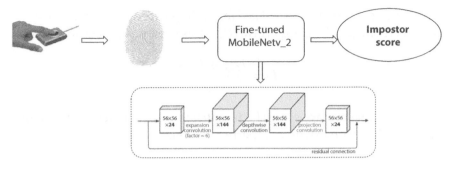

Figure 7.3 Proposed framework for expert one.

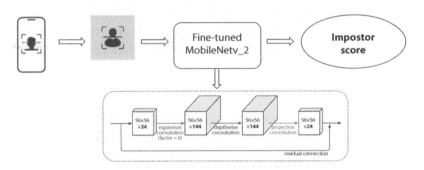

Figure 7.4 Proposed framework for expert two.

and live facial images (using datasets) is used calculating the impostor score. A depth-wise detachable CNN with a significantly less computational cost is used. The input image is resized into the range of 128 × 128 to 244 × 244 for efficient classification. The impostor probability (in percentage) is calculated for determining the final advice of expert one. The proposed framework for expert one and two is as depicted in Figures 7.3 & 7.4 respectively.

7.2.3   Decision Level Fusion

Decision level fusion means a decision from each expert proposed above is fused for a particular set of fingerprint and face image supplied. Extensive iterations/experimentation on various decision level fusion methods, for example, by using "AND" and "OR" logics [14, 15], showed that best fusion could be achieved for least FAR (false acceptance rate; meaning the ratio of impostor permitted to the total number of impostor requests).

When average score (I_A) is calculated for the impostor score from each expert, i.e., expert one (I_{Exp1}) and expert two (I_{Exp2}), as shown in the equation below:

$$I_A = \frac{I_{Exp1} + I_{Exp2}}{2}$$

The resulting average score (I_A) is matched with a predefined threshold, i.e., set as 70% with extensive experimentation.

7.3   Experimental Analysis

In this section, the evaluation of the proposed approach of multiple experts-based attack-resistant multimodal biometric authentication systems has been discussed. Experimentation and evaluation were carried out on different genuine and impostor/fake-based fingerprint and face datasets. Following sections elaborate on the detail of datasets.

7.3.1   Datasets

The proposed multiple expert-based classifiers for genuine/fake detection have been evaluated using various benchmark and open-access datasets available in the research community. Subsequent sub-sections contain the details regarding the datasets used.

    a.   LivDet 2015 [10]
        For expert one, classifying genuine/impostor fingerprint LivDet2015 dataset has been used for evaluation. It is a fingerprint liveness database in which spoofs are made via co-operative methods using ecofelx, gelatin, wood glue, etc., as shown in Table 7.1.
    b.   IDRND_FASDB [11]
        For expert two, an open-access database openly available on Kaggle [11] consisting of 1,596 real images and 7,708 spoof facial images has been used. These images have been acquired using webcams, mobile cameras, and YouTube downloads.

7.3.2   Setup

In the proposed multiple expert-based detectors, the experimentation and analysis have been implemented using Python 3.6 on a system with

Table 7.1 LivDet 2015 dataset details.

Scanner	Model	Resolution (dpi)	Genuine	Impostor
Biometrika	HiScan Pro	1,000	2,000	2,500
Cross-match	L Scan Guardian	200	3,010	2,921
Green Bit	DactyScan26	500	2,000	2,500
Digital Persona	U.are.U 5160	500	2,000	2,502
Total			9,010	10,423

8GB GPU and 64-bit operating system with TensorFlow [16] framework. Rigorous experiments were conducted to evaluate and analyze the experts designed, and the same has been discussed in the following sections.

7.3.3   Results

Fingerprint and face experts were evaluated on the datasets and the results are compared with the other state-of-the-art methods as shown in Table 7.2.

However, when the final decision is evaluated after the decision level fusion, the accuracy comes out to be nearly 100%, whereas, if some spoofs (not seen during the training) are passed, the accuracy decreases below 80%. That means for unknown spoofs, and the system can bypass.

7.4   Conclusion and Future Scope

As the literature suggests that biometrics-based identity authentication systems can be fooled by miscreants using various software and hardware techniques. It becomes quite essential to address this issue as it directly

Table 7.2 LivDet 2015 dataset details.

Expert	Our results (FAR %)	Other techniques	
		FAR %	Ref.
Expert one	4.1	--	--
Expert two	8.9	12	[6]

affects an individual's right to privacy. Multimodal biometrics-based multiple expert detectors have been proposed to address this issue rather than following orthodox methods based on unimodal biometrics. To work effectively even on small devices as it is computationally efficient and evaluated with good results, especially in known spoofs.

This work can be further extended using feature-level fusion for better learning of the CNN for unknown fakes to get better accuracy.

References

1. Jain, A.K., Ross, A.A., Nandakumar, K., *Introduction to Biometrics*, Springer US, USA, 2011.
2. Kaushal, N., Singh, S., Kumar, J., Analysis of Fingerprint Counterfeiting and Liveness Detection Algorithms. *2020 International Conference on Inventive Computation Technologies (ICICT)*, pp. 492–495, 2020.
3. Choras, R.S., Multimodal Biometrics for Person Authentication, in: *Security and Privacy From a Legal, Ethical, and Technical Perspective*, 2019.
4. Wu, L., Yang, J., Zhou, M., Chen, Y., Wang, Q., LVID: A Multimodal Biometric Authentication System on Smartphones. *IEEE Trans. Inf. Forensics Secur.*, 15, 1572–1585, 2020.
5. Xu, H., Qi, M., Lu, Y., Multimodal Biometrics Based on Convolutional Neural Network by Two-Layer Fusion. *2019 12th International Congress on Image and Signal Processing, BioMedical Engineering and Informatics (CISP-BMEI)*, pp. 1–6, 2019.
6. Sujatha, E. and Chilambuchelvan, A., Multimodal Biometric Authentication Algorithm Using Iris, Palm Print, Face and Signature with Encoded DWT. *Wirel. Pers. Commun.*, 99, 1, 23–34, 2018.
7. Bhardwaj, I., Londhe, N.D., Kopparapu, S.K., A spoof resistant multibiometric system based on the physiological and behavioral characteristics of the fingerprint. *Pattern Recognit.*, 62, 214–224, 2017.
8. Sajjad, M., Khan, S., Hussain, T., Muhammad, K., Sangaiah, A.K., Castiglione, A., Esposito, C., Baik, S.W., CNN-based anti-spoofing two-tier multi-factor authentication system. *Pattern Recognit. Lett.*, 126, 123–131, 2019.
9. Sandler, M., Howard, A., Zhu, M., Zhmoginov, A., Chen, L.-C., MobileNetV2: Inverted Residuals and Linear Bottlenecks. In *Proceedings of the IEEE Conference on Computer Vision and Pattern Recognition*, pp. 4510–4520, 2018.
10. Mura, V., Ghiani, L., Marcialis, G.L., Roli, F., Yambay, D.A., Schuckers, S.A., LivDet 2015 fingerprint liveness detection competition 2015. *2015 IEEE 7th International Conference on Biometrics Theory, Applications, and Systems (BTAS)*, pp. 1–6, 2015.
11. spoof_raw.

12. Howard, A., Zhu, M., Chen, B., Kalenichenko, D., Wang, W., Weyand, T., Andreetto, M., Adam, H., MobileNets: Efficient Convolutional Neural Networks for Mobile Vision Applications. *ArXiv*, abs/1704.04861, 1–9, 2017.
13. Deng, J., Dong, W., Socher, R., Li, L., Li, K., Fei-Fei, L., ImageNet: A large-scale hierarchical image database. *2009 IEEE Conference on Computer Vision and Pattern Recognition*, pp. 248–255, 2009.
14. Jain, A.K., Ross, A., Prabhakar, S., An introduction to biometric recognition. *IEEE Trans. Circuits Syst. Video Technol.*, 14, 1, 4–20, 2004.
15. Burr, W., Dodson, D., Polk, W., *Electronic Authentication Guideline*, USA, 2006.
16. Abadi, M., Barham, P., Chen, J., Chen, Z., Davis, A., Dean, J., Devin, M., Ghemawat, S., Irving, G., Isard, M., Kudlur, M., Levenberg, J., Monga, R., Moore, S., Murray, D.G., Steiner, B., Tucker, P., Vasudevan, V., Warden, P., Wicke, M., Yu, Y., Zheng, X., TensorFlow: a system for large-scale machine learning. *Proceedings of the 12th USENIX conference on Operating Systems Design and Implementation*, pp. 265–283, 2016.

8

Feature Optimized Machine Learning Framework for Unbalanced Bioassays

Dinesh Kumar[1]*, Anuj Kumar Sharma[2],
Rohit Bajaj[3] and Lokesh Pawar[3]

[1]Department of CSE, Guru Kashi University, Bathinda, India
[2]Department of CSE, BRCMCET, MD University, Rohtak, India
[3]Department of CSE, Chandigarh University, Chandigarh, India

Abstract

In this research, we have discussed biopsy; the biopsy is a medical procedure done by a surgeon in which a patient is tested for expansion of the disease. We applied specific machine learning espouse on a standard database to get more accurate data. The aim of the paper is found that the precise of a database is increased. Authors collect biopsy databases followed by the surgeon and perform a class balancing process, using tool name that is class balance. Then, we apply four machine learning algorithms that are Multilayer Perceptron, Bagging, Random Committee, and J48. Class Balancer is a straightforward filter to apply that weightage to every instance so that every class instance has the same value in the dataset, such that the sum of all instances in the dataset will remain unchanged. It has been observed from a specific experiment that Multilayer Perception and Bagging algorithm done excellent work, increase accuracy, decrease the error, and increase the TP (true positive rate). This research paper will provide an efficient way to increase the accuracy of the data.

Keywords: Bagging, biopsy, J48, machine learning, multilayer perception, random committee

Corresponding author: kdinesh.gku@gmail.com

Sandeep Kumar, Rohit Raja, Shrikant Tiwari and Shilpa Rani (eds.) Cognitive Behavior and Human Computer Interaction Based on Machine Learning Algorithm, (167–178) © 2022 Scrivener Publishing LLC

8.1   Introduction

The biopsy is a medical test process done by the surgeon so that we come to know about infected tissue. In medical, if there is an issue with particular tissue or fluid, then we remove that part and test in labs to know about the problem. Doctors usually prefer when the initial stage of tissue is not normal. If we want to define biopsy in simple words, then taking tissue from the body is called a biopsy. The biopsy is mainly being for cancer but also helps for other condition. The biopsy is usually for cancer [4, 26], melanoma, and cirrhosis. The biopsy is not a complicated procedure, yet it relies upon the quiet condition; in some situations, it is the evacuation of little tissue, yet it is the organ for testing in labs for some situations. Biopsy guarantees method for the conclusion of the most malignancy. The infected is generally examined using a microscope under a pathologist's guidance when the entire region is removed from the patient, known as an excisional biopsy. An incisional biopsy refers to when a particular region is removed instead of removing the whole part like an excisional biopsy. The incisional biopsy also is known as a core biopsy. When fluid is removed using a needle in such a way, there is no disturbance in the whole structure, and this process is core biopsy [11, 25]. At the point when the disease is suspected, an assortment of biopsy methods can be applied. An excisional biopsy is an endeavor to expel a whole injury. When measuring uninvolved tissue around the injury, the careful edge of the example is analyzed to check whether the illness has spread past the region biopsied. "Clear edges" or "negative edges" imply that no ailment was found at the edges of the biopsy example. "Positive edges" implies that malady was found, and a more extensive extraction might be required, contingent upon the conclusion. Pathologic assessment of a biopsy can decide if a sore is generous or threatening and can help separate between various sorts of malignant growth. As opposed to a biopsy that examples an injury, a more prominent excisional example called a resection may go to a pathologist, commonly from a specialist endeavoring to destroy a known sore from a patient. For instance, a pathologist would inspect a mastectomy example, regardless of whether a past non-excisional bosom biopsy had just settled the finding of bosom disease. Now and again, scratching cells from the surface layer of tissue, for example, from inside the mouth, is sufficient to give an excellent example to assessment. This sort of "scratching biopsy" can be awkward, yet it is not agonizing, so sedative is not required. A cervical screening test is where a spatula, or little brush-like instrument, is utilized to tenderly expel an example of cells from a lady's cervix (the neck of the belly). The cells are then inspected under a magnifying lens for any irregular changes (dysplasia). If the cells show anomalous changes, then it might imply that they are destructive or an improved probability that they will get carcinogenic. At the point when the after effects of your cervical screening test are accessible, your GP will have the option to talk about your treatment alternatives with you or whether further tests are required. How rapidly you get the consequences of your biopsy will rely upon the emergency clinic where you have had the technique and your scenario's desperation. The consequences of routine cervical smear tests ordinarily take between 10 and 14 days to open up, while the after effects of biopsies are done because your primary care physician speculates a genuine condition, for example, disease, might be accessible inside a couple of days. In situations where a biopsy is performed during a medical procedure, an outcome is regularly accessible in practically no time so the correct treatment can be given while the medical procedure is in progress.

8.2   Related Work

A study distributed by researchers says AI calculations useful to biopsy pictures can abbreviate the ideal opportunity to diagnose and treat the sickness that frequently causes changeless physical and psychological harm in kids from devastated territories. The spaces anywhere cleanliness, consumable water, and nourishment are rare. There are soaring paces of youngsters experiencing natural enteric brokenness, an ailment that constrains the gut's capacity to assimilate fundamental supplements and rapid hindered development, weakened mental health, and even passing. The malady influences 20% of kids younger than 5 in low and center pay nations, for example, Bangladesh, Zambia, and Pakistan. However, it additionally influences a few youngsters in the country of Virginia. According to an associate educator, this venture is a case of why she got into medicine. "We are examining an infection to impacts countless kids, and that is by and largely avoidable", she said. So we can use AI in the demonstrative procedure for well-being authorities fighting the sickness. We can also utilize a profound method called "convolutional neural systems" to check many pictures of biopsies. Pathologists would then understand how to further viably monitor patients dependent on anywhere the neural system is searching in support of contrasts and centering its investigation on getting results.

8.3 Proposed Work

Figure 8.1 introduced the unique perspective on the forecast model. The bioassay data, which contains a biopsy dataset with exceptional lopsidedness with some positive and negative cases, is given to the AI structure. In the AI system, first, it parts that information into two sections preparing and testing. The given information is exceptionally imbalanced and has numerous highlights. In this way, for balance, the unequal information Class Balancer [7] calculation is applied. In the subsequent stage, the Multilayer Perception [8] is used to prepare information. This intends to pick the most pleasing subset highlights: valuable, acceptable connection by the objective element. In the wake of choosing significant highlights,

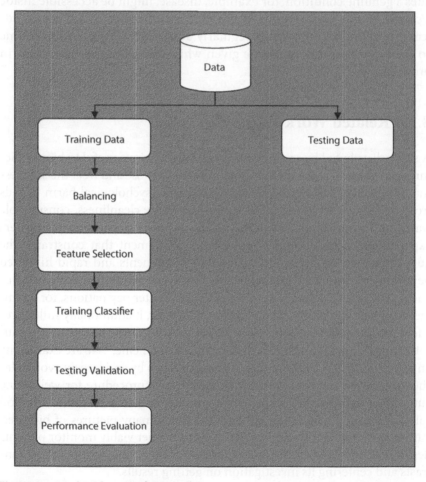

Figure 8.1 Machine learning framework.

it analyzes various classifiers on the preparation information by approving with the test information, and in the last, it confirms the general execution of the model, which classifier gives the best outcome.

8.3.1   Class Balancing Using Class Balancer

Processing implies the arrangement of information before preparing the classifier. The biopsy information is utilized in our dataset, which are imbalanced classes of dynamic and latent mixes. Along these lines, to adjust the dataset, Class Balancer is applied. Class Balancer is a direct channel that doles out example loads so each class of occurrences will have a similar weight and the complete entirety of caseloads in the dataset stays unaltered. When Filtered Classifier is applied to this channel and the base classifier does not actualize Weighted Instances Handler, the loads will again be utilized to frame a likelihood circulation for testing with substitution. This will yield a preparation set where the two classes are (around) adjusted.

8.3.2   Feature Selection

This is on the whole critical pre-processing step that applies before the preparation classifier. This means choosing the subset highlights, which are further significant with a decent connection with the objective. Right now, a multilayer perceptron (MLP) file is applying to the preparation information to choose the best highlights from the profoundly excessive information. We increase with loads and include bias in the perceptron on the off chance you know about the Multilayer Perceptron Algorithm. However, we do this in one layer as it were. We update the weight when we found a blunder in order or miss-arranged. Weight update condition is as follows:

Weight = Weight + Learning_Rate * (Expected – Predicted)*x.

8.3.3   Ensemble Classification

The AI structure is projected to extrapolate both positive and also harmful mixes for bioassay information. So, we have four different model names: Multilayer Perception, Bagging, Random Committee, and J48. Class Balancer applied in research. Bootstrap aggregating is additionally called bagging. This AI group meta-calculation planned to develop the solidness and accuracy of AI calculation utilized in computable characterization and deterioration. This also diminishes modification and assists with abstaining as of overfitting. A MLP is a profound, fake neural system.

It is made out of more than one perceptron and they are made up of an information layer to get the sign. A yield layer settles on a choice about the info, and in the middle of those two, a discretionary number of concealed layers is the genuine computational motor of the MLP. MLPs with one concealed layer are fit for approximating any ceaseless capacity. Preparing includes altering the parameter, or the loads and inclinations, of the model to limit mistakes. Back propagation is utilized to gauge inclination changes relative to the mistake, and this blunder itself can be estimated in an assortment of ways, including by root mean squared mistake (RMSE).

8.4 Experimental

This subheading helps to explain about dataset and training dataset view of the modal.

8.4.1 Dataset Description

There are 81 datasets present in the training database. To retrieve compound for bioassay dataset requires the loss of pre-processing. Some are active and some are inactive; some have more weightage in the database and some have less weightage; we can say that the dataset is highly imbalanced. Sometimes, to find related actives, we need to find them manually. Some problems are related to the bioassay dataset; it has curated data, many false positives, and imbalanced data. In bioassay, data is not curated and is potentially wrong. Nevertheless, publicly available bioassay data is short because most HTS technology is held at private commercial organizations. Finding corresponding confirmatory bioassays is only achieved manually. First, we overcome the imbalanced dataset barrier; we use Class Balancer filter, which uses SMOTE [9] method. What Class Balancer do? Class Balancer first analyzes the weightage of every instance and then gives every instance the same weightage without losing the database uniqueness. After balancing the dataset, we make feature selection [16] to remove an unwanted feature from the database. After removing the useless instances, we get our best 30 instances. For feature selection, we use four algorithms that are Multilayer Perception, Bagging, Random Committee, and J48. Multilayer Perception did excellent work in feature selection; it improves the database accuracy, reducing the error and increasing the TP rate (true positive rate). After that, we supply a training dataset found that everything reflects positively.

8.4.2   Experimental Setting

Different divergent model structure strategies are performed utilizing R language. One of these analysis principal objectives is to figure the precision and create forecasts for a classifier. The dataset is partitioned into the two structures preparing and testing information. In preparing the model, preparing information is to be taken care of to the classifier after processing the information. At that point, it is approved by utilizing test information. To assess the foreseen system's consequences, various assessment measurements, for example, exactness, TP rate, and FP rate, are utilized.

8.5   Result and Discussion

This fragment depicts outcomes, execution, and assessment with an examination of the structure on a standard dataset.

8.5.1   Performance Evaluation

The planned structure exhibition is tried utilizing different metrics [24] like accuracy, TP rate, FP rate, and error, as introduced in Table 8.1.

The table shows the exhibition correlation of enhanced Multilayer Perception by different classifiers. Based on Table 8.1, different charts are plotted to illustrate a similar investigation of various classifiers. In Figure 8.2, an exhibition examination of AI structure is introduced graphically. Figure 8.2a describes the precision of various classifiers. Right now, it has the most elevated exactness among all since it plans to pick.

The most acceptable subset type, which is a significant, is adequate association by goal component. Figure 8.2b describes the error bend,

Table 8.1 Exhibition correlation of enhanced multilayer perception by different classifiers.

Classifier	Multilayer perception	Bagging	Random committee	J48
Accuracy	93.30%	92.4%	84.66%	84.77%
Error	7.79%	7.91%	15.38%	15.38%
TP Rate	0.943%	0.932%	0.816%	0.851%
FP Rate	0.413%	0.460%	0.433%	0.853%

which implies how classifiers perform by and large. On the off chance that they least worth that, it clearly expresses the exactness of the model. Right now, Bagging has the least worth after component choice error decreases suddenly. Figure 8.2c describes the TP rate, which implies an accurately characterized occurrence. Multilayer Perception, Bagging, Random Committee, and J48 perform occurrences. Multilayer Perception, Bagging, Random Committee, and J48 perform great to order the examples accurately. Figure 8.2d describes the FP rate, which implies dishonestly arranged cases. Multilayer Perception, Bagging, and Random Committee execute on a form to erroneously order the occasions with all since this diagram-based

Figure 8.2 Comparison of machine learning structure with classifiers using accuracy, error, TP rate, and FP rate.   (*Continued*)

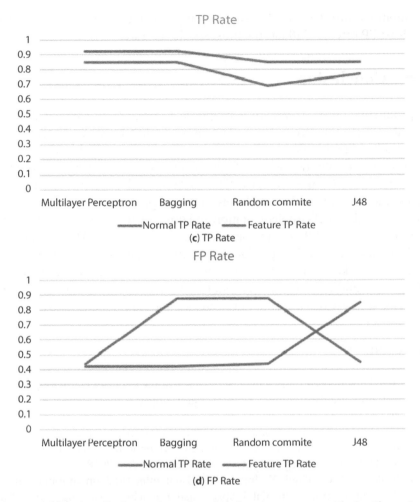

Figure 8.2 (Continued) Comparison of machine learning structure with classifiers using accuracy, error, TP rate, and FP rate.

model utilizes the idea of likelihood conveyance and likelihood hypothesis for forecasts [20]. In any case, J48 has less FP rate before including selection yet after element choice FP is increment. These measurements were performed on various classifiers like Multilayer Perception, Bagging, Random Committee, and J48 [2]. In every one of these classifiers, it very well may be seen that Multilayer Perception gives the highest exactness and Random Committee and J48 have the least, which is 84.61%. On the off chance that we talk about the TP rate, Multilayer Perception and Bagging have the most elevated TP rate, and Random Committee and J48 have the least, which is 0.846. If we talk about FP rate, Multilayer Perception,

Random Committee, and Bagging accomplished great work, which have the least FP rate, yet J48 has the most special FP rate.

8.6   Conclusion

A productive outfit AI system is proposed to prepare an element dimensional and profoundly balance implicit screening bioassay information. One leading famous element determination ranker, mainly the Gini record, is utilized to locate the essential highlights used for preparing the computational model. Furthermore, the Class Balancer calculation is executed to adjust the dynamic and inert classes in the preparation information. With the proposed model's implementation and utilizing the standard dataset, the exactness, TP rate, FP rate, and blunder are seen as 92.30%, 0.923%, 0.423%, and 7.69% separately. This productive structure dependent on group AI calculation can likewise be utilized as a choice framework for the extrapolation of dynamic and idle mixes. Later on, the AI structure will be improved by applying it to various information strategies like Hadoop and Spark.

References

1. Alix-Panabières, C. and Pantel, K., Clinical applications of circulating tumor cells and circulating tumor DNA as liquid biopsy. *Cancer Discov.*, 6, 5, 479–491, May 2016.
2. Hooda, N., Bawa, S., Rana, P.S., B2FSE framework for high dimensional imbalanced data: A case study for toxicity prediction. *Neurocomputing*, 276, 31–41, https://doi.org/10.1016/j.neucom.2017.04.081, 2018.
3. Pankratz, D.G., Choi, Y., Imtiaz, U., Usual interstitial pneumonia can be detected in transbronchial biopsies using machine learning. *Ann. Am. Thorac. Soc.*, 14, 11, 1646–1654, 2017.
4. Ohl, F., Jung, M., Xu, C., Stephan, C., Rabien, A., Gene expression studies in prostate cancer tissue. *J. Mol. Med.*, 83, 1014–1024, 2005.
5. Hooda, N., Bawa, S., Rana, P.S., Optimizing fraudulent firm prediction using ensemble machine-learning: A case study of an external audit. *Appl. Artif. Intell.*, 34, 1, 20–30, https://doi.org/10.1080/08839514.2019.1680182, 2019.
6. Schierz, A.C., Virtual screening of bioassay data. *J. Cheminf.*, 1, 1, 1–21, https://doi.org/10.1186/1758-2946-1-21, 2009.
7. Chakrabarti, P. and Satpathy, B., Class balancing using class balance. *Adv. Comput. Data Sci.*, 1045, 13–21, 2019.
8. Tabari, H. and Talaee, P.H., Multilayer perceptron for reference evapotranspiration estimation in a semiarid region. *Neural Comput. Appl.*, 23, 341–348, 2013.

9. Xu, M. and Wang, J.J., *Smote algorithm with locally linear embedding*, US 2009/0097741 A1, 2009.
10. Ko, J., Baldassano, S.N., Loh, P.L., Kording, K., Machine learning to detect signatures of disease in liquid biopsies - a user's guide. *Lab Chip.*, 18, 395–405, 2018.
11. Kowal, M., Filipczuk, P., Obuchowicz, A., Korbicz, J., Computer-aided diagnosis of breast cancer based on fine needle biopsy microscopic images. *Comput. Biol. Med.*, 43, 10, 1563–1572, 2013.
12. Kuusisto, F., Dutra, I., Nassif, H., Using machine learning to identify benign cases with non-definitive biopsy. *IEEE 15th International Conference on e-Health Networking, Applications and Services*, pp. 283–285, 2013.
13. iGuiu, J.G., iRibé, E.G., iMansilla, E.B., Automatic classification of mammary biopsy images with machine learning techniques, 1999.
14. Wang, Y., Xiao, J., Suzek, T.O., Zhang, J., Wang, J., Zhou, Z.G., Han, L.Y., Karapetyan, K., Dracheva, S., Shoemaker, B.A., Bolton, E., Gindulyte, A., Bryant, S.H., PubChem's BioAssay database. *Nucleic Acids Res.*, 40, D1, D400–D412, https://doi.org/10.1093/nar/gkr1132, 2011.
15. Stork, C., Wagner, J., Friedrich, N.O., de Bruyn Kops, C., Šícho, M., Kirchmair, J., Hit dexter: A machine learning model for the prediction of frequent hitters. *ChemMedChem*, 13, 6, 564–571, https://doi.org/10.1002/cmdc.201700673, 2018.
16. Dash, M. and Liu, H., Feature selection for classification. *Intell. Data Anal.*, 1, 1–4, 131–156, 1997.
17. Agid, R., Sklair-Levy, M., Bloom, A.I., Lieberman, S., CT-guided biopsy with cutting-edge needle for the diagnosis of malign antlymphoma: The experience of 267 biopsies. *Clin. Radiol.*, 58, 2, 143–147, 2003.
18. Snoek, J., Larochelle, H., Adams, R.P., Practical bayesian optimization of machine learning algorithms. *Adv. Neural Inf. Process. Syst.*, 25, 2960–2968, 2012.
19. Dietterich, T.G., Ensemble methods in machine learning. *Multiple Classifier Systems*, pp. 1–15, 2000.
20. Alfaro, E., Gamez, M., Garcia, N., Adabag: An R package for classification with boosting and bagging. *J. Stat. Software*, 54, 2, 1–35, 2013.
21. Bhargava, N., Sharma, G., Bhargava, R., Mathuria, M., Decision tree analysis on j48 algorithm for data mining. *Proc. Int. J. Adv. Res. Comput. Sci. Software Eng.*, 3, 6, 1114–1119, 2013.
22. Baell, J.B. and Holloway, G.A., New substructure filters for removing pan assay interference compounds (PAINS) from screening libraries and their exclusion in bioassays. *J. Med. Chem.*, 53, 7, 2719–2740, 2010.
23. Schierz, A.C., Pubchem bioassay data set, UCI machine learning repository, https://archive.ics.uci.edu/ml/datasets/PubChem+Bioassay+Data, 2009.
24. Jeni, L.A., Cohn, J.F., De La Torre, F., Facing imbalanced data–recommendations for the use of performance metrics, in: *2013 Humaine Association Conference*

on Affective Computing and Intelligent Interaction, pp. 245–251, https://doi. org/10.1109/ACII.2013.47, 2013.

25. Raja, R., Sinha, T.S., Patra, R.K., Tiwari, S., Physiological Trait Based Biometrical Authentication of Human-Face Using LGXP and ANN Techniques. *Int. J. Inform. Comput. Secur.*, 10, 2/3, 303–320, 2018.

26. Raja, R., Patra, R.K., Sinha, T.S., Extraction of Features from Dummy face for improving Biometrical Authentication of Human. *Int. J. Lumin. Appl.*, 7, 3–4, 259, 507–512, 2017.

9

Predictive Model and Theory of Interaction

Raj Kumar Patra*, Srinivas Konda, M. Varaprasad Rao,
Kavitarani Balmuri and G. Madhukar

*Department of Computer Science and Engineering, CMR Technical Campus,
Kandlakoya, Hyderabad, India*

Abstract

The fuse of essential ability structures into instructive frameworks helps recognize how ideas should be introduced to understudies to enhance understudy accomplishment. Numerous abilities have a causal relationship in which one aptitude should be introduced before another, demonstrating a solid expertise relationship. Realizing this relationship can assist with anticipating understudy execution and distinguish essential curves. Ability interactions, be that as it may, are not straightforwardly quantifiable; all things considered, the relationship can be assessed by noticing contrasts of understudy execution across aptitudes. Notwithstanding, such assessment techniques appear to do not have a benchmark model for thinking about their adequacy. On the off chance, two strategies for assessing a relationship's presence yield two distinct qualities: the more precise outcome? In this work, we propose a strategy for contrasting models that endeavor to measure the strength of aptitude interactions. With this technique, we start to distinguish those understudy level covariates that give the most exact models foreseeing the presence of expertise interactions.

Focusing on interactions of execution across abilities, we utilize our technique to build models to foresee the presence of five unequivocally related and five reproduced inadequately related expertise sets. Our strategy can assess a few models that recognize these distinctions with huge precision gains over an invalid model and gives the way to distinguish that interactions of understudy dominance give the main commitments to these increases in our investigation.

Corresponding author: patra.rajkumar@gmail.com

Sandeep Kumar, Rohit Raja, Shrikant Tiwari and Shilpa Rani (eds.) Cognitive Behavior and Human Computer Interaction Based on Machine Learning Algorithm, (179–210) © 2022 Scrivener Publishing LLC

Keywords: Modeling interaction, skill relationship, feature selection, predictive model

9.1   Introduction

Numerous instructive frameworks have actualized an essential structure as a proposed requesting to introduce abilities to understudies. These structures are regularly evolved by area specialists and educators in the field of study and will probably hold ground truth. It is clear, for instance, that interactions can be recognized by noticing abilities at the issue level; by reviewing the means needed for understudies to finish everything, it very well may be realized that any aptitudes needed to finish such issues can be viewed as requirements [1]. For instance, Multiplying Whole Numbers may be essential to Greatest Common Factors, as is utilized in our examination. While causality recommends a solid relationship, it is workable for two abilities to identify with one another. Such interactions are less natural, maybe requiring a comparable point of view or arrangement of steps to settle, regardless of whether the substance of such errands contrasts. Numerous causal ability curves are recognizable by area specialists by noticing content, and however, as depicted, other such interactions might be missed because of their non-instinctive structures. By noticing solid ability interactions distinguished by area specialists, we build a strategy for estimating the generally predictive elements of their reality [2].

We likewise contend that recognizing solid interactions is not sufficient for a technique for the expectation to be viewed as satisfactory. Such a strategy ought to likewise have the option to recognize feeble or non-existent ability Interactions. All things considered, while much consideration and examination are set on organizing essential interactions, a portion of these are bogus positives. An aptitude might be recorded as an essential yet has no evident relationship to its alleged post-imperative ability. In such a case, there are almost no collaborations of execution. Such interactions should likewise be recognized and eliminated or reordered in learning stages to profit the understudies. A lot of examination has taken a gander at estimating the strength of expertise interactions [25, 28] and even the impacts such interactions have on estimating understudy execution [27, 34]. However, without comprehended ground certainties, it is hard to analyze across these strategies. Besides, many of these strategies speak to comparable conceptualizations of execution innately or through varieties of portrayal, for example, collection or focusing. For instance, accomplishment on essential expertise will probably impact accomplishment on a post-imperative ability, yet can be spoken to as the percent of issues addressed accurately authority speed (the number of things expected to finish a task as is usually utilized in keen coaching frameworks), or endless different mixes of highlights. It will be critical to recognize these summed up segments not to fuse that include catching similar conceptualizations into predictive models [3].

This work gives a strategy to assess models that measure the strength of aptitude interactions, and with this model, we endeavor to recognize which highlights best demonstrate a reliable interaction between two abilities. This examination will consolidate a strategy for summing up and recognizing highlights that measure various parts of learning and execution. With this strategy, we look to answer the accompanying two exploration questions:

- What connect level highlights, communicated in this paper as associations of execution between aptitudes are critical in foreseeing the presence or non-presence of expertise interactions?
- Which highlights are the most grounded indicators of aptitude interactions, and does consolidating them make for a more exact predictive model [4]?

The following segment of this paper will talk about a portion of the past exploration performed on ability interactions and essential structures. At that point, we will examine our hypothesis and system to give a pattern model of looking at strategies for estimating ability interactions. Utilizing this model, we, at that point, look at a few ordinarily utilized understudy level highlights and, of the most exact, think about a few unique portrayals of those highlights. At long last, we will examine our discoveries and recommended future works.

9.2   Related Work

The revelation and refinement of essential ability structures have been an important exploration question lately. The effect of this examination on instructive frameworks cannot be overemphasized. Space specialists who plan these structures need information-focused techniques to help their choices; it is crucial to have observational information to help speculate concerning the request in which aptitudes are introduced. It can primarily affect understudy accomplishment and either help or obstruct the learning cycle. Moreover, distinguishing the best essential ability structure will improve understudy demonstrating; knowing an understudy's earlier execution on essential aptitudes can gauge that understudy's presentation on the post-requirements. This can prompt prior mediations for battling understudies, or even assistance rethink dominance maybe understudies who perform very well on an essential requires less practice on a post-imperative or can be given further developed models.

Tatsuoka characterized an information structure called the Q-Matrix, which speaks to the planning of issues to aptitudes: the lines of this framework speak to the issues, and the sections speak to the abilities [33]. Even though the objective of the exploration was to analyze the confusions of understudies, they set various moving examinations that have utilized this information structure as the initial step to discover essential structures [26, 29, 32].

Desmarais and his partners built up a calculation that finds the essential interaction between questions, or things, in understudies' reaction information [30]. They look at sets of things in a test and decide any cooperation existing between each pair. Contingent upon the collaborations and many interaction-related measures, they decide if the two things have an essential interaction between them. Pavlick *et al.* applied this methodology to dissect thing type covariances and propose a various leveled agglomerative grouping technique to refine the labeling of things to aptitudes [31].

Brunskel led a fundamental report in which they utilize understudies' loud information to derive essential structures [28]. Further examination by Scheines *et al.* broadened a causal structure revelation calculation in which a suspicion concerning the immaculateness of things is loose to reflect genuine information and to utilize that to derive essential aptitude structure from information [32].

9.3   Predictive Analytics Process

The predictive examination includes a few stages through which an information investigator can anticipate the future dependent on the current and authentic information. This cycle of predictive investigation is spoken to in Figure 9.1, as given beneath.

9.3.1   Requirement Collection

It should be cleared that what is the point of the forecast to build up a predictive model. Through the expectation, the kind of information which

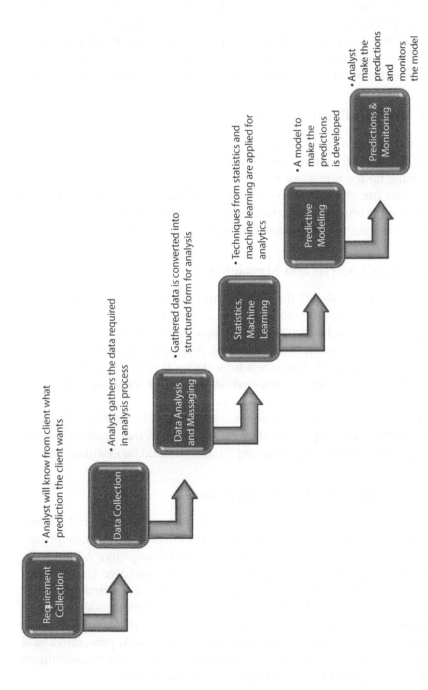

Figure 9.1 Predictive analytics process.

will be picked up should be characterized. For instance, a drug organization needs to know the estimate of a medication's offer in a specific zone to keep away from those meds' expiry. The information investigators sit with the customers to know the necessity of building up the predictive model and how these expectations will profit them. It will be recognized what information about the customer will be needed in building up the model.

9.3.2   Data Collection

In the wake of knowing the necessity of the customer association, the investigator will gather the datasets, which might be from various sources, needed in building up the predictive model. This might be a finished rundown of clients who use or check the results of the organization. This information might be in the organized structure or unstructured structure. The examiner confirms the information gathered from the customers at their site.

9.3.3   Data Analysis and Massaging

Information experts dissect the gathered information and set it up for examination and utilized in the model. The unstructured information is changed over into an organized structure in this progression. When the total information is accessible in the organized structure, its quality is then tried. There are conceivable outcomes that incorrect information is available in the primary dataset or there are many missing qualities against the traits; these all should be tended to. The adequacy of the Predictive model thoroughly relies upon the nature of the information. The investigation stage is here and there alluded to as information munging or kneading the information that implies changing over the crude information into an organization utilized for examination.

9.3.4   Statistics and Machine Learning

The predictive investigation measure utilizes numerous factual and AI procedures. Likelihood hypothesis and relapse examination are the most powerful strategies which are prevalently utilized in the investigation. Additionally, counterfeit neural organizations, choice tree, and uphold vector machines are the devices of AI which are generally utilized in numerous predictive examination undertakings. All the predictive investigation models depend on measurable as well as AI strategies. Consequently, the examiners apply the ideas of insights and AI to create predictive models. AI procedures have a preferred position over traditional measurable methods, yet measurements should be engaged with building up any predictive model.

9.3.5   Predictive Modeling

In this stage, a model is created dependent on measurable and AI procedures and the model dataset. After the turn of events, a piece of primary gathered dataset to check the model's legitimacy and, if fruitful, the model is supposed to be fit. When fitted, the model can make precise forecasts on the new information entered to contribute to the framework. In numerous applications, the multi-model arrangement is decided on an issue.

9.3.6   Prediction and Monitoring

After the practical tests in forecasts, the model is conveyed at the customer's site for regular expectations and decision-making measures. The outcomes and reports are produced by neither the model nor administrative cycle. The model is reliably observed to guarantee whether it gives the right outcomes and makes the exact forecasts. Here, we have seen that predictive examination is certifiably not a solitary advance to make forecasts about what is to come. It is a bit-by-bit measure that includes numerous cycles from necessity assortment to organization and checking for effective use of the framework to settle a dynamic cycle framework.

9.4   Predictive Analytics Opportunities

Even though there is a long history of working with predictive examination and generally applied in numerous spaces for quite a long time, today is the time of predictive investigation because of the headway of advancements and reliance on information [5]. Numerous associations are tending toward predictive investigation to build their primary concern and benefit. There are a few purposes behind this fascination:

- Growth in the volume and kinds of information is motivated to utilize predictive examination to discover experiences from enormous estimated information.
- Faster, less expensive, and easy to understand PCs are accessible for handling.
- An assortment of programming is accessible and more advancements are going on in programming, which is anything but difficult to use for clients.
- The severe climate of developing the association with benefit and the association's monetary states push them to utilize the predictive examination.

The predictive examination is not restricted to the analysts and mathematicians with the advancement of simple to utilize and intuitive programming and its accessibility. It is being utilized in a going all-out by business investigators and administrative choice cycle. Probably, the most widely recognized open doors in the field of predictive can be recorded as follows:

- *Identifying Fraud:* Detection and avoidance of criminal standards of conduct can be improved by joining the numerous examination strategies. The development of network protection is turning into a worry. The conduct examination might be applied to screen the activities of the organization continuously. It might distinguish the irregular exercises that may prompt a cheat. Dangers may likewise be distinguished by applying this idea [35].
- *Decrease of Risk:* Likelihood of default by a purchaser or a customer of assistance might be evaluated ahead of time by the FICO assessment applying the predictive investigation. The predictive model produces the financial assessment utilizing all the information identified with the individual's reliability. This is applied with Mastercard backers and insurance agencies to recognize the fake clients [7].
- *Showcasing Campaign Optimization:* The reaction of clients to acquire an item might be dictated by applying predictive examination. It might likewise be utilized to advance the cross-deal openings. It encourages organizations to draw in and hold the most beneficial clients [8].
- *Activity Improvement:* Forecasting on stock and dealing with the assets can be accomplished by applying the predictive models. Aircraft may utilize predictive examination to set the costs of tickets. Lodgings may utilize predictive models to foresee the number of visitors on a given evening to boost its inhabitance and expanding the income. An association might be empowered to work all the more proficiently by applying the predictive examination [9].
- *Clinical Decision Support System:* Expert frameworks dependent on predictive models might be utilized to conclude a patient. It might likewise be utilized to improve prescriptions for a sickness [10].

9.5   Classes of Predictive Analytics Models

The overall significance of predictive examination is predictive modeling, which implies the scoring of information utilizing predictive models and afterward determining. However, by and large, it is utilized to allude to the controls identified with the investigation. These controls incorporate the cycle of information investigation and are utilized in the business dynamic. These orders can be classified as the accompanying:

- *Predictive Models:* Predictive models demonstrate the inter-action between the presentation of a unit and the traits. This model assesses the probability that the comparative unit in an alternate example is indicating the particular execution. This model is generally applied in advertising where the appropriate responses about client execution are normal. It recreates human conduct to offer responses to a particular inquiry. It ascertains during the exchange by a client to recognize the danger identified with the client or exchange.
- *Descriptive Models:* The expressive model builds up the interaction between the information to distinguish clients or gatherings in a possibility. As predictive models recognize one client or one execution, illustrative models distinguish numerous relations among an item and its clients. Rather than positioning clients on their activities, it sorts clients by their item execution. An enormous number of individual specialists can be reproduced together to make an expectation in spellbinding demonstrating.
- *Decision Models:* The choice models depict the interaction between information, choice, and the after-effect of the conjecture of choice. This relationship is portrayed in the choice model to expect a choice that includes numerous factors. To boost specific results, limit some other results, and enhancement, these models are utilized. It is utilized in creating business rules to deliver the ideal activity for each client or in any condition.

The predictive insightful model is characterized unequivocally as a model that predicts at a nitty-gritty degree of granularity. It creates a predictive score for every person. It is more similar to an innovation that gains for a fact to make expectations about a person's future conduct. This aids in settling on better choices. The exactness of results by the model relies upon the degree of information investigation.

9.6   Predictive Analytics Techniques

All the predictive examination models are assembled into arrangement models and relapse models. Arrangement models foresee the enrollment of qualities to a particular class while the relapse models anticipate a number. We will currently rattle off the effective strategies utilized prominently in building up the predictive models.

9.6.1   Decision Tree

A choice tree is an older model, yet it tends to be utilized in relapse too. It is a tree-like model related to the choices and possible results. The results might be the result of occasions, cost of assets, or utility. In its tree-like structure, each branch speaks to a decision between various other options and all its leaves speak to a choice. In light of the classes of information factors, it parcels information into subsets. It helps the people in the choice investigation. The simplicity of comprehension and translation settle on the choice trees well known to utilize. A standard model of the choice tree is spoken to in Figure 9.2, as given beneath.

A choice tree is spoken to in Figure 9.2 as a tree-like structure. It has the inward hubs named with the inquiries identified with the choice. All the branches coming out from a mode are named with the potential responses to that question. The outer hubs of the tree called the leaves are marked with the issue's choice. This model has the property to deal with the missing information and it is additionally valuable in choosing the fundamental factors. They regularly allude as generative models of acceptance

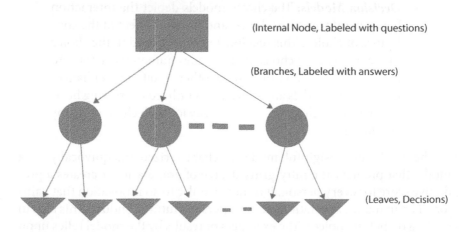

Figure 9.2 Decision tree.

decisions that work on the observational information. It utilizes the more significant part of the information in the dataset and limits the degree of inquiries. Alongside these properties, the choice trees have a few preferred positions and weaknesses. New potential situations can be added to the model, which mirrors the model's adaptability and flexibility. It very well may be coordinated with other choice models according to the prerequisite. They have an impediment to receiving the changes. A little change in the information prompts a massive change in the structure. They linger behind in the exactness of expectation in contrast with other predictive models. The estimation is unpredictable in this model, particularly on the utilization of questionable information.

9.6.2   Regression Model

Relapse is perhaps the most well-known factual strategy which assesses the interaction between factors. It displays the interaction between a reliant variable and at least one autonomous factor. It breaks down how the estimation of ward variable changes in changing the estimations of autonomous factors in the demonstrated interaction [11]. This displayed interaction among reliant and autonomous interaction is spoken to in Figure 9.3, as given beneath.

Regarding the constant information, which is accepted to have an ordinary dispersion, the relapse model finds a vital example in enormous datasets. It is utilized to discover the impact of graphic elements that impact the development of a variable. In relapse, the estimation of a reaction variable

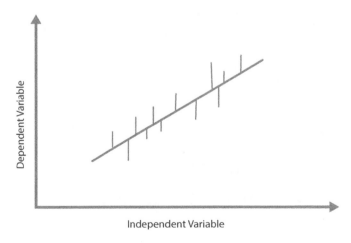

Figure 9.3 Regression model.

is anticipated based on an indicator variable is utilized with all the free factors to plan them with the reliant factors. In this procedure, the reliant variable's variety is described by the relapse work's expectation utilizing likelihood dispersion.

Two kinds of relapse models are utilized in predicting or determining the direct relapse model and the calculated relapse model. The direct relapse model is applied to show straight interaction among needy and free factors. A straight capacity is utilized as relapse work in this model. Then again, the coordinations relapse when there are classifications of ward factors. Through this model, obscure estimations of discrete factors are anticipated based on general estimations of autonomous factors. It can accept a predetermined number of qualities in the forecast.

9.6.3   Artificial Neural Network

The artificial neural organization, an organization of artificial neurons dependent on natural neurons, re-enacts the human sensory system's ability to handle the information flags and create the yields [12]. This is a refined model that is fit for demonstrating very unpredictable relations. The design of a broadly useful fake neural organization is spoken to in Figure 9.4.

Counterfeit neural organizations are utilized in predictive investigation applications as a useful asset for gaining from the model datasets and expecting

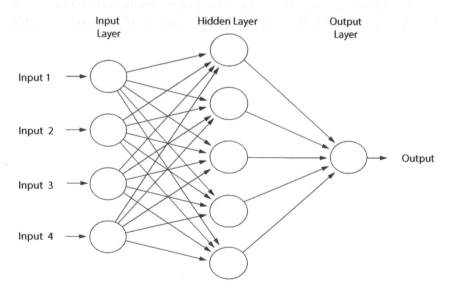

Figure 9.4 Artificial Neural Network.

new information. The organization's info layer is applied for the handling and it is passed to the concealed layer, which a vector of neurons. Different kinds of actuation capacities are utilized at neurons relying on the prerequisite of yield. The yield of one neuron is moved to the neurons of the next layer. At the yield layer, out is gathered that might be the expectation of new information.

There are different models of fake neural organization and each model uses an alternate calculation. Backpropagation is a mainstream calculation that is utilized overwhelmingly in many managed learning issues. Fake neural organizations are utilized in unaided learning issues too. Grouping is the strategy utilized in solo realizing where fake neural organizations are additionally utilized. They can deal with the non-straight interaction in the information. They are likewise utilized in assessing the consequences of relapse models and choice trees. With the capacity of example acknowledgment, these models are utilized in picture acknowledgment issues.

9.6.4 Bayesian Statistics

This procedure has a place with the insights that accept boundaries as irregular factors and utilize the expression "level of conviction" to characterize an occasion's likelihood [13]. The Bayesian measurements depend on Bayes' hypothesis, which terms the occasions prior and posterior. In restrictive likelihood, the methodology is to discover the likelihood of a posteriori occasion given that the priori has happened. Then again, the Bayes' hypothesis finds the likelihood of priori occasion given that the posterior has just happened. It is spoken to in Figure 9.5.

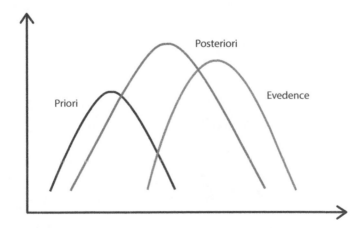

Figure 9.5 Bayesian statistics.

It utilizes a probabilistic graphical model known as the Bayesian organization, which speaks to the irregular factors' restrictive conditions. This idea might be applied to discover the causes with the consequence of those causes close by. For instance, it tends to be applied in finding the sickness dependent on the manifestations [6].

9.6.5   Ensemble Learning

It has a place with the classification of managed learning calculations in the part of AI. These models are created via preparing a few comparative sort models, lastly, consolidating their outcomes on the forecast. Like this, the precision of the model is improved. Improvement in this manner decreases the inclination and diminishes the fluctuation of the model. It helps recognize the best model to be utilized with new information [14]. The example of arrangement utilizing gathering learning is spoken to in Figure 9.6.

9.6.6   Gradient Boost Model

This procedure is utilized in predictive examination as an AI strategy. It is primarily utilized in grouping and relapse-based applications. It resembles a gathering model that groups the expectations of frail predictive models with choice trees [15]. It is a boosting approach that resamples the dataset ordinarily and creates a weighted normal of the resampled datasets. It has the bit of leeway that it is less inclined to overfitting many AI models [16]. The utilization of choice trees in this model aids in fitting the information

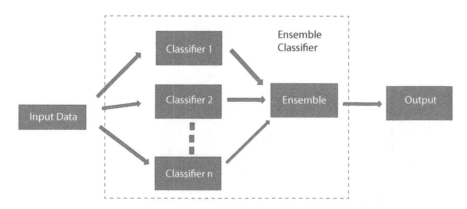

Figure 9.6 Ensemble classifier.

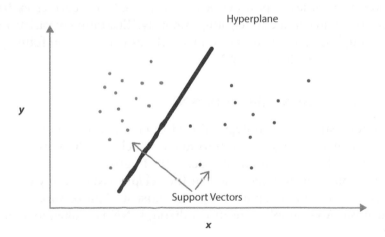

Figure 9.7 Gradient boosting.

decently and the boosting improves the fitting of information. This model is spoken to in Figure 9.7.

9.6.7   Support Vector Machine

It is administered sort of AI strategy prominently utilized in predictive examination. It examines characterization and relapse information [17, 36]. Nonetheless, it is generally utilized in characterization applications. It is a discriminative classifier that is characterized by a hyper-plane to order models into classifications. It is the portrayal of models that are isolated into classifications with an unmistakable hole. The new models are then anticipated to have a place with a class as to which side of the hole they fall. The case of detachment by a help vector machine is spoken to in Figure 9.8.

Figure 9.8 Support Vector Machine.

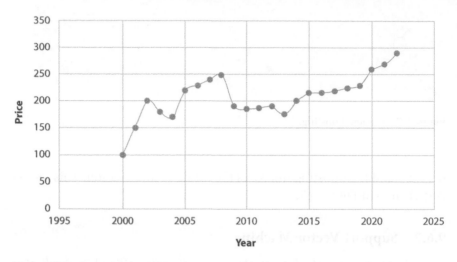

Figure 9.9 Time series analysis.

9.6.8   Time Series Analysis

Time arrangement investigation is a factual method that uses time arrangement information gathered throughout a time frame at a specific span. It consolidates the conventional information mining procedures, what is more, the gauging [18]. The time arrangement investigation is partitioned into two classes, precisely the recurrence space and the time area. It predicts the fate of a variable at future time stretches dependent on the investigation of qualities at past periods. It is utilized in securities exchange expectation and climate anticipating famously. Illustration of variety in the cost throughout the timeframe and its patterns conjecture in future years is spoken as shown in Figure 9.9.

9.6.9   k-Nearest Neighbors (k-NN)

It is a non-parametric strategy utilized in characterization and relapse issues. In this technique, the information includes the k-nearest preparing models in a component space [19]. In grouping issues, the yield is the enrollment of a class, and in the relapse issues, the yield is the property estimation of an item. It is the most straightforward sort of AI calculation. An example of relapse utilizing k-NN is spoken to in Figure 9.10.

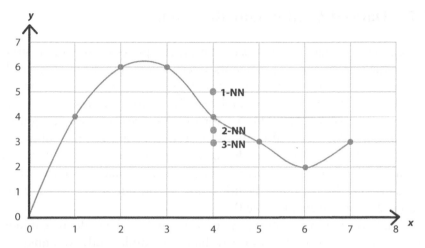

Figure 9.10 Regression utilizing k-NN.

9.6.10   Principle Component Analysis

It is a factual system generally utilized in predictive models for exploratory information investigation. It is firmly identified with the factor investigation, which is utilized in tackling the eigenvectors of a network. It is additionally utilized in portraying the fluctuation in a dataset [20]. The case of guideline segment in a dataset is spoken to in Figure 9.11.

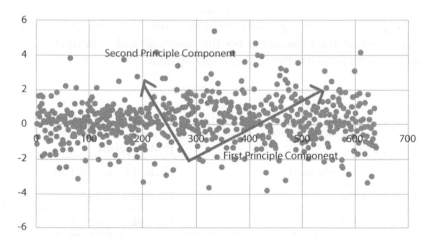

Figure 9.11 Principle component analysis.

9.7   Dataset Used in Our Research

The dataset 1 utilized for this examination comprises correct understudy information from the ASSISTments internet learning stage. The crude information contains understudy issue logs relating to 10 mathematical abilities from the 2018–2019 school year. These 10 aptitudes speak to five ability sets, as recorded in Table 9.1, for which space specialists recognized as having a stable essential relationship. While we are not restricting the use of our proposed pattern model to only essential interactions, these are the most solid to recognize because of the causal impact of substance (if issues in expertise B require the utilization of aptitude A to finish, a stable relationship can be distinguished).

A study containing 24.00 ability sets for which we had adequate understudy information (more noteworthy than 50.00 understudy columns) was directed to 45.00 educators and space specialists who use ASSISTments to distinguish trustworthy ground truth aptitude matches. Each was approached to rate on a size of 1–7, showing the apparent subjective strength of every ability pair's relationship. Five ability sets were chosen to be the most grounded related interactions with the littlest change in assessment scores from the review results. As we are regarding these interactions as truth, we needed to be exceptionally particular of these sets. The subsequent dataset comprises 1,838.00 complete understudy columns from 896.00 one-of-a-kind understudies. This incorporates two columns of information for every understudy for every one of the five ability sets included. The primary line contains data of that understudy's exhibition on the pre- and post-imperative abilities, while the subsequent column contains understudy execution on the essential and a mimicked post-imperative depicted further in the following area.

Table 9.1 The solid ability sets as controlled by area specialists.

Pre-requisite	Post-requisite
Whole No. Multiplication	Highest Common Factor
Integers Subtraction	Operations Order
Whole No. Division	Multiple Digit Division
Rectangle Prism's Volume Without formula	Rectangle Prism's Volume
3D Figure Nets	Rectangle Prism's Surface Area

For every understudy, a component vector was chosen to utilize necessary execution measurements to think about inside our model. This component vector contained eight interaction level highlights speaking to the associations between understudy level essential and post-imperative execution measurements. The created interface level highlights noticed areas depicted underneath:

- **Percent Correct**
  The mean-centered 2 level of right reactions in the essential ability is duplicated by the mean-focused level of right reactions in the post-imperative aptitude.
- **First Problem Correctness (FPC)**
  The principal reaction's paired accuracy in the essential ability increased by the twofold rightness of the primary reaction on the post-imperative expertise.
- **Mastery Speed**
  The mean-focused authority speed of the essential ability is characterized as the number of issues needed for every understudy to accomplish three back-to-back right reactions, duplicated by the mean-focused dominance speed of the post-imperative expertise. Notwithstanding focusing, these qualities were likewise winsorized to make the most immense conceivable worth 10, picked as frequently the most extreme number of day-by-day endeavors permitted inside ASSISTments. All are focusing and winsorizing happened before increasing the two qualities.
- **Z-Scored Percent Correct**
  The z-scored estimation of the mean-focused level of right reactions in the essential aptitude is duplicated by the z-scored estimation of the mean-focused level of right reactions in the post-imperative ability.
- **Binned Mastery Speed (Bin)**
  The numbered container of authority speed as portrayed in [27] of the essential ability is duplicated by the receptacle of dominance speed in the subsequent aptitude. Understudies were set into one of five containers dependent on dominance speed if the task was finished and dependent on percent right if the task was not finished.
- **Z-Scored Mastery Speed**
  The z-scored estimation of mean-focused, winsorized dominance speed in the essential expertise is duplicated by the

z-scored estimation of mean-focused, winsorized authority speed in the post-imperative ability.

- **Receptacle X FPC**
  The binned dominance speed an incentive in the essential aptitude increased by the twofold rightness of the primary reaction in the post-imperative ability.

- **Percent Correct X FPC**
  The mean-focused level of right reactions in the essential aptitude is increased by the double rightness of the primary reaction in the post-imperative ability.

9.8   Methodology

This work's definitive objective is to look at models anticipating the presence or non-presence of expertise Interactions. Our way to deal with this is through the correlation and ID of highlights that most precisely foresee these interactions. Utilizing head segment investigation, we bunch comparative highlights into more summed up conceptualizations to both think about which sorts of highlights matter while anticipating interactions and evading issues of multi-collinearity that may inclination our evaluations. When this standard model is set up, we can build new predictive models from the huge highlights and notice their exactness in anticipating the presence of expertise interactions when contrasted with a necessary invalid or unqualified model.

To look at the use of highlights against a powerless or non-existent relationship, we reproduced another expertise utilizing understudies from the current essential aptitude by producing arbitrary successions of reactions. We haphazardly dole out him/her a likelihood somewhere in the range of 0.50 and 0.90 to make an arbitrary grouping of answers for each current understudy. For instance, an understudy given a likelihood of 0.50 has a half possibility of noting each given issue accurately. We reproduce understudy answers until either dominance is accomplished or the understudy arrives at 10 issues without dominating. An estimation of 10 is picked here; the same number of tasks in ASSISTments is given a day-by-day breaking point of 10 issue endeavors before requesting that the understudy look for help or attempt again on one more day. While we recognize numerous approaches to achieving this re-enactment step, we feel this straightforward strategy adequately makes an aptitude that has no relationship to the first essential as expected. As our proposed strategy is planned to be utilized later on to help recognize unfamiliar pre- or post-essential interactions, we decided to utilize a recreated aptitude instead of arbitrary existing expertise to dodge the chance of arbitrarily choosing an unfamiliar-related ability. Once more, we needed to be exceptionally particular and consider a few such situations as we are endeavoring to make ground truth esteems to make our correlations. We are utilizing these two aptitude sets, one interaction speaking to a solid relationship. In contrast, the other speaking to a non-existent relationship, we can compute an element vector for every understudy in the essential expertise with values from every ability pair. We utilize a paired strategic relapse with a relationship as the needy variable and a few Interaction level covariates to anticipate whether an aptitude relationship exists for every understudy line. The presence of a relationship can be resolved than just by the dominant part administering. However, such estimation is excluded and instead notices precision at the understudy level for a more detailed examination. We start to look at customarily utilized understudy level highlights in this investigation through two levels of examination. The initial step endeavors to analyze highlights' gatherings, summing up various comparative highlights' portrayals into reasonable groupings. Like this, we can see the predictive intensity of what we indicate as starting execution, dominance, and rightness. The subsequent investigation takes a gander at the individual highlights as various portrayals of the general gathering to analyze these indicators at a closer level. We can take each factor of dominance, for instance, and contrast their utilization in a few models to figure out which is the most precise indicator of the presence of ability interactions.

9.8.1   Comparing Link-Level Features

To analyze portrayals of understudy level highlights, we should initially have the option to contrast general conceptualizations of highlights with figure out, giving more clear expectations of the presence of ability Interactions. We need to catch every measurement's genuine portrayals and endeavor to decipher these speculations as sorts of highlights. To achieve this gathering of indicators, we use head segment examination (PCA) to recognize which understudy level highlights connect and illustrate more summed up segments. PCA is principally utilized for dimensionality decrease as we are doing here and enables us to make new factors from the port mappings. The subsequent component arrangement can be found in Figure 9.1. Similar to the case in our investigation and referenced in the past area, we have numerous authority speed measurements, just as a few different highlights. As we can speak to "dominance" in a few different ways, we need to know whether the general idea of authority, as caught by the measurements utilized, is dependably predictive of the presence of aptitude Interactions. Making another arrangement of these groupings' indicators, we can join these into a twofold calculated relapse model to see each predictive intensity. While PCA bunches comparable highlights together depending on their relationships, the review which highlights are assembled can decipher and name each. From this cycle, we found that the vast majority of our highlights fell into three classes for which we have given the names "authority", as this comprises of portrayals of dominance speed, "accuracy", as this comprises of portrayals of the level of right understudy reactions, and "beginning execution", as this comprises of portrayals of understudy execution on the underlying things of every aptitude. Notwithstanding these three classifications, we are additionally left with understudy dominance speed z-scored inside understudy classes as a variable that did not fall under both of the three previously mentioned classifications. In contrast, a determination of authority speed, we accept that this did not associate with the "dominance" class because of the technique for normalization as it is catching this measurement according to understudies' friends. We will readdress this case in our part of the conversation.

When these indicators are recognized and made, we build a twofold strategic relapse model to foresee, for every understudy line, if a relationship exists. This model will give us a centrality worth and coefficient for every indicator in the model, just as a, generally speaking, predictive precision of the model, which will be utilized more for the subsequent investigation.

9.8.2   Comparing Feature Models

After analyzing which summed up gatherings of highlights are critical indicators of aptitude interactions, we can think about the individual student level highlights that fall into every classification by fusing them into discrete models to notice predictive exactness. The preliminary examination investigation is utilized to figure out which classifications are huge in anticipating expertise interactions. Utilizing that data, we can zero in on those groupings with importance to develop models that use factors from each gathering. For instance, the gathering of "dominance", for instance, contains authority speed and binned authority speed, so we can build models utilizing each to look at contrasts in predictive force. To evade issues of collinearity, no single model contains more than one factor from a solitary gathering. This altogether decreases the number of highlights to test contrasted with running this test without first gathering, highlighting, and distinguishing those that are huge as we did in the top try.

Utilizing the critical groupings, we can make 17 models comprising of single sets and trios of highlights. A calculated relapse is run on every one of these models to anticipate the presence of an aptitude relationship. Of the 17 models, 10 produce a factually critical expectation when contrasted with an invalid model. Our invalid model should create a half exactness in a perfect world as there is an equivalent number of excellent and terrible interaction columns in our dataset. This is not generally the situation; nonetheless, as relying upon the component noticed, data might be absent for a specific understudy; dominance speed, for instance, as the number of things endeavored by an understudy before arriving at three back to back right answers, would be absent for any understudy that did not finish the task. Therefore, each model's predictive intensity is depicted as gains in predictive precision, or rather, the exactness of each model less the exactness of the relating invalid model.

9.9   Results

The consequences of the preliminary examination are communicated in Table 9.3. Every one of the three-element groupings of Mastery, Correctness, and Initial Performance made utilizing PCA notwithstanding the Z-Scored Mastery is analyzed inside a similar model, foreseeing the presence of an ability relationship. As these again are interface level highlights portraying collaborations between understudy level execution on essential and post-imperative abilities, it is hard to draw substantial translations from the coefficient esteem, communicated in log-chances units. This coefficient, utilized in the calculated relapse to make the expectations, portrays every part's impact on the reliant variable. For instance, for every unit increment in "authority", the likelihood that the interaction exists diminishes. Once more, as this segment is an accumulation of communication highlights, it is genuinely portraying a collection of contrasts between understudy level highlights, making it hard to make complete cases concerning these qualities alone and was incorporated to show overall pattern segments forecast.

From the table, we can decide the noteworthiness of every segment on the general expectation by surveying the comparing p-values in the third section. Taking a gander at these qualities, we can guarantee that the general gathering of "Rightness" appears to have less of an effect on the model's predictive exactness. As this term is not critical, we can center the rest of our examination on the leftover three parts.

Table 9.2 shows the after-effects of our subsequent examination contrasting the models that we can build with the leftover highlights once the "rightness" gathering has been dismissed. This figure shows the similar

Table 9.2 The after-effects of the PCA examination. All highlights aside from Z-Scored Mastery Speed planned to one of three summed up parts.

	Components		
	1	**2**	**3**
% Correct		0.8210	
FPC			0.8390
Mastery Speed	0.9690		
Z-Score % Correct		0.8650	
Bin	0.9720		
Z-Score Mastery Speed			
FPC X Bin			0.8730
FPC X % Correct		0.6120	

Table 9.3 The coefficients and noteworthiness estimations of the summed up segments examined. From this, we can zero in on models that prohibit highlights contained in the parts with no essentialness.

Components	Coefficient value	Significance
Mastery	−0.2510	<0.0010***
Correctness	0.0150	0.8020
Initial Performance	0.1290	0.0370*
Z-Scored Mastery Speed	−0.1290	<0.0010***

predictive precision of the 10 models that give factually huge forecasts, as found in Table 9.3. Once more, these qualities are communicated as exactness gains, or rather the percent precision increment over the invalid model runs for each predictive model.

9.10   Discussion

This work gives a gauge model of contrasting student-level execution across abilities with measure the strength of an aptitude relationship and analyzes

Table 9.4 The models developed from highlights in the critical summed up parts. Nobody model contains over a solitary element from each summed-up part.

Model	Null accuracy	Model accuracy	Gain in accuracy	Significance
MS (Mastery Speed)	0.630	0.620	0.00	01.000
Z-Scored MS	0.630	0.630	0.00	00.888
FPC	0.500	0.560	0.06	<00.0010***
Bin MS	0.500	0.690	0.19	<00.0010***
Bin X FPC	0.500	0.560	0.06	<00.0010***
Z-Scored MS, Bin	0.500	0.710	0.21	<00.0010***
FPC, MS	0.630	0.620	0.00	01.000
Bin X FPC, MS	0.630	0.620	0.00	01.000
FPC, Bin	0.500	0.690	0.19	<00.0010***
Bin X FPC, Bin	0.500	0.690	0.19	<00.0010***
Z-Scored MS, FPC, MS	0.630	0.630	0.00	00.7540
Z-Scored MS, MS, Bin X FPC	0.630	0.630	0.00	00.9790
Z-Scored MS, Bin, FPC	0.500	0.710	0.20	<00.0010***
Z-Scored MS, Bin, Bin X FPC	0.500	0.710	0.21	<00.0010***
Z-Scored MS, MS	0.630	0.630	0.00	00.8430
Z-Scored MS, FPC	0.500	0.640	0.14	<00.0010***
Z-Scored MS, Bin X FPC	0.500	0.610	0.11	<00.0010***

the precision of the two highlights and models that gauge this worth. Quite a model, in our experience, has not existed preceding this examination. Our technique endeavors to recognize not just the individual highlights that add to better expectations of these interactions, yet additionally moves to sum up comparative highlights into conceptualizations for examination to limit multicollinearity. Our model's foremost segment examination step found that everything except one element planned to one of three parts that we have deciphered as an authority, accuracy, and starting execution. It was discovered the z-scored dominance speed, despite our instinct, did not plan well to gather authority. We can theorize the purpose behind this event by changing our understanding of the element. Authority speed itself is an intriguing measurement as it endeavors to catch two components of execution: a degree of understanding and a pace of learning. Likewise, to repeat an earlier qualification, these measurements are communications of execution across abilities. By z-scoring the measurement, it is catching a relevant impact of every understudy in correlation with different understudies in the class, a qualification that seems to have a considerable impact. Noticing the subsequent model parts from the vital segment investigation in Table 9.2, we could concentrate on those segments with remarkable qualities. Rightness was the lone segment of that model found to have no factual criticalness on the reliant variable. This is positively intriguing, as percent rightness and other such measures are among the most well-known execution measurements. Maybe the cooperation between pre- and post-essential percent right is losing some predictive force from when the measurement is utilized for different execution forecasts.

This perspective outlines one other significant finding that the detailed portrayals of some measurements each contribute distinctively to the predictive precision of the models considered. Models joining dominance speed, for instance, had no substantial exactness gains over an invalid model, while authority speed binning indicated extensive gains as found in Table 9.4. The pattern model of correlation proposed in this investigation gives the way to make that qualification concerning highlights contained inside a similar summed up part gathering. As is found in that figure, highlights outflank any single element, showing a more robust model by catching different execution portrayals.

9.11   Use of Predictive Analytics

There are numerous utilizations of predictive investigation in an assortment of areas. From clinical choice examination to financial exchange expectation where sickness can be anticipated dependent on side effects and profit for a stock, a venture can be assessed individually. We will rattle off here beneath a portion of the famous applications.

9.11.1   Banking and Financial Services

In banking and monetary businesses, there is a massive use of predictive examination. In both, the venture's information and cash are critical, and discovering bits of knowledge from that information and cash development is an unquestionable requirement. The predictive investigation helps in recognizing fake clients and dubious exchanges. It limits the credit hazard on which theories enterprises loan cash to their clients. It helps in strategically pitch and up-sell openings and in holding and drawing in the essential clients. For the monetary enterprises where cash is put resources into stocks or different resources, the predictive examination estimates the profit for ventures and helps in the emotional speculation cycle.

9.11.2   Retail

The predictive examination helps the retail business to recognize the clients and to understand what they need and what they need. By applying this method, they anticipate the conduct of clients toward an item. The organizations may fix costs and set unique proposals on the items to distinguish clients' purchasing conduct. It also helps the retail business anticipate how a specific item will be fruitful in a specific season. They may crusade their items and deal with clients with offers and costs fixed for singular clients. The predictive examination additionally helps the retail enterprises in improving their production network. They distinguish and foresee an item's interest in the particular zone may improve their inventory of items [21].

9.11.3   Well-Being and Insurance

The drug area utilizes predictive examination in medication planning and improving their production network of medications. By utilizing this strategy, these organizations may foresee the expiry of medications in a particular region because of the absence of offer. The protection area utilizes predictive examination models in recognizing and anticipating the misrepresentation claims recorded by the clients. The medical coverage area utilizes this procedure to discover the most dangerous clients of a genuine illness and approach them in selling their protection plans that can be best for their venture [22].

9.11.4 Oil Gas and Utilities

The oil and gas businesses are utilizing predictive examination strategies in gauging the disappointment of gear to limit the danger. They anticipate the prerequisite of assets in the future utilizing these models. Energy-based organizations can anticipate the requirement for upkeep to stay away from any lethal mishap in the future [23].

9.11.5 Government and Public Sector

The public authority organizations utilize massive information-based predictive investigation procedures to distinguish the conceivable crimes in a specific zone. They break down the web-based media information to distinguish the foundation of dubious people and conjecture their future conduct. The legislatures utilize predictive investigation to estimate the populace's future pattern at the national and state levels. In upgrading the network protection, the predictive examination procedures are being utilized going all out [24].

9.12 Conclusion and Future Work

There has been a long history of utilizing predictive models in the undertakings of expectations. Prior, the measurable models were utilized as the predictive models, which depended on the example information of a vast estimated informational index. With the upgrades in software engineering and PC methods' headway, more up-to-date strategies have been created, and better calculations have been presented throughout the timeframe. The improvements in computerized reasoning and AI have changed the universe of calculation where astute calculation methods and calculations are presented. The AI models have a history of being utilized as predictive models. Fake neural organizations got the upheaval in the field of predictive investigation. Given the info boundaries, the yield or eventual fate of any worth can be anticipated. Presently with the progressions in AI and the improvement of profound learning strategies, there is a pattern these days of utilizing profound learning models in predictive examination and they are being applied in a going all out in this errand. This paper opens the extent of the advancement of new models for the assignment of Predictive examination. Likewise, there is an occasion to add extra highlights to the current models to improve their presentation in the errand.

While we have demonstrated that our model can contrast and distinguish highlights that contribute with higher precision in foreseeing the presence of expertise interactions, we likewise need to pressure the significance of this data utilization. The capacity to look at highlights is just the initial step of our model's objective. By distinguishing reliable indicators of ability interactions that we know exist, we can apply it to different aptitudes inside ASSISTments and different frameworks to recognize conceivably new essential curves and all the more likely gauge and foresee extended haul understudy execution learning and maintenance. Having a precise gauge of ability interactions can help rebuild essential structures to give aptitude arrangements in a request that upgrades understudy learning and accomplishment. The work in this paper joined a few aptitudes into a solitary dataset to make expectations. For this situation, we needed to make a strategy that is generalizable somewhat. While our particular range of abilities permits us to make a few cases regarding the exactness of these models' overall aptitudes, it might probably be the situation that expertise interactions are quantifiable in various manners for various abilities. Further examination could rehash the means here on every single one of them gained aptitudes in the dataset. While accuracy was not critical in these outcomes, maybe it is huge while foreseeing particular abilities. Maybe, like our highlights, abilities themselves could be summed up into applied sorts for various investigation types relating to collaborations of execution and their interactions. The element vectors produced for every understudy in our dataset caught many of the most well-known understudy level measurements, however positively, not every one of them. Numerous different viewpoints could be added, including consummation, proportions of the learning rate, time spent on the tasks, hint use, and innumerable different factors. Furthermore, this examination noticed associations communicated as duplications of these terms to depict them as Interaction level highlights. There are different alternative approaches to speak to collaborations or other such changes, including contrasts of qualities, division of qualities, or cross-highlight associations. This was mostly investigated here by taking a gander at Bin Percent Correct X FPC. Such associations model different understudy execution parts and conduct that can be valuable in this kind of relationship forecast.

The system introduced notices models that anticipate abilities as a similar result, while it tends to be adjusted to make examinations on evaluations of relationship qualities as a nonstop result. The technique noticed model exactness at the understudy level for better estimations, yet it is an aptitude level relationship that is being tried. One straightforward expansion of future work could investigate how to consolidate the expectations at an understudy level to make an aptitude level forecast. The strategy would then be able to test interactions on the whole framework expertise structure.

References

1. Elkan, C., *Predictive analytics and data mining*, University of California, San Diego, 2013.
2. Siegel, E., *Predictive Analytics*, John Willey and Sons Ltd, United States, 2016.
3. Nyce, C., *Predictive Analytics White Paper*, American Institute of CPCU/IIA, Irvine, CA, USA, 2007.
4. Eckerson, W., *Extending the Value of Your Data Warehousing Investment*, The Data WarehouseInstitute, United States, 2007.
5. Korn, S., *The Opportunity of Predictive Analytics in Finance*, HPC Wire, United States, 2011.
6. Choudhary, S., Lakhwani, K., Agrwal, S., An efficient hybrid technique of feature extraction for facial expression recognition using AdaBoost Classifier. *Int. J. Eng. Res. Technol.*, 8, 1, 1–7, 2012.
7. Schiff, M., *BI Experts: Why Predictive Analytics Will Continue to Grow*, The Data Warehouse Institute, Renton, USA, 2012.
8. Reichheld, F. and Schefter, P., *The Economics of E-Loyalty*, Harvard Business School Working Knowledge, Retrieved 2018.
9. Dhar, V., Predictions in Financial Markets: The Case of Small Disjuncts. *ACM Trans. Intell. Syst. Technol.*, 2, 3, 2001.
10. Osheroff, J., Teich, J., Middleton, B., Steen, E., Wright, A., Detmer, D., A Roadmap for National Action on Clinical Decision Support. United States, *JAMIA: A Scholarly J. Inf. Health Biomedicine*, 14, 2, 141–145, 2007.
11. Armstrong, J.S., Illusions in regression analysis. *Int. J. Forecasting*, 28, 3, 689–694, 2012.
12. McCulloch, W.S. and Pitts, W., A logical calculus of the ideas immanent in nervous activities. *Bull. Math. Biophys.*, 5, 4, 115–133, 1943.
13. Lee, P.M., *Bayesian Statistics: An Introduction*, 4th Edition, John Willey and Sons Ltd, 2012.
14. Polikar, R., Ensemble based systems in decision making. *IEEE Circ. Syst. Mag.*, 6, 3, 21–45, 2006.
15. Friedman, J.H., Greedy Function Approximation: A Gradient Boosting Machine, Lecture notes, 1999.
16. Kumar, S., Singh, S., Kumar, J., Live Detection of Face Using Machine Learning with Multi-feature Method. *Wireless Pers. Commun.*, 103, 3, 2353–2375, 2018.
17. Hur, B. *et al.*, Support Vector Clustering. *J. Mach. Learn. Res.*, 2, 125137, 2001.
18. Lin, J., Keogh, E., Lonardi, S., Chiu, C., A symbolicrepresentation of time series, with implications forstreaming algorithms. *Proceedings of the 8th*

ACMSIGMOD workshop on research issues in data miningand knowledge discovery, pp. 2–11, 2003.

19. Altman, N.S., An introduction to kernel and nearest-neighbor nonparametric regression. *Am. Stat.*, 46, 3, 175–185, 1992.
20. Abdi, H. and Williams, L.J., Principal componentanalysis. *WIREs: Comput. Stat.*, 2, 4, 433–459, 2010.
21. Das, K. and Vidyashankar, G.S., Competitive advantage in retail through analytics: Developing insights, creating values. *Inf. Manage.*, 2006.
22. Conz, N., *Insurers Shift to Customer-Focused Predictive Analytics Technologies*, Insurance & Technology, 2008.
23. Feblowitz, J., Analytics in Oil and Gas: The Big Deal About Big Data. *Proceeding of SPE Digital Energy Conference*, Texas, USA, 2013.
24. Kim, G.H., Trimi, S., Chung, J.-H., Big-data applications in the government sector. *Commun. ACM*, 57, 3, 78–85, 2014.
25. Adjei, S., Selent, D., Heffernan, N., Pardos, Z., Broaddus, A., Kingston, N., Refining learningmaps with datafitting techniques: Searching forbetter fitting learning maps, in: *Educational DataMining*, 2014.
26. Barnes, T., The q-matrix method: Mining student response data for knowledge, in: *American Association for Artificial Intelligence 2005 Educational Data Mining Workshop*, 2005.
27. Botelho, A., Wan, H., Heffernan, N., The predictionof student first response using prerequisite skills, in: *Learning at Scale*, 2015.
28. Brunskill, E., Estimating prerequisite structure from noisy data, in: *Educational Data Mining*, pp. 217–222, Citeseer, 2011.
29. Chen, Y., Wuillemin, P.-H., Labat, J.-M., Discovering the prerequisite structure of skills throughprobabilistic association rules mining, in: *The 8th International Conference on Educational Data Mining*, pp. 117–124, 2015.
30. Desmarais, M.C., Maluf, A., Liu, J., User-expertisemodeling with empirically derived probabilisticimplication networks. *User Model. User-Adapted Interact.*, 5, 3–4, 283–315, 1995.
31. Pavlik Jr., P.I., Cen, H., Wu, L., Koedinger, K.R., Using item-type performance covariance to improve the skill model of an existing tutor. *Online Submission*, 1–10, 2008.
32. Scheines, R., Silver, E., Goldin, I., Discovering prerequisite relationships among knowledge components, in: *Educational Data Mining*, 2014.
33. Tatsuoka, K.K., Rule space: An approach for dealingwith misconceptions based on item response theory. *J. Educ. Meas.*, 20, 4, 1983.
34. Wan, H. and Beck, J.B., Considering the influence ofprerequisite performance on wheel spinning, in: *Educational Data Mining*, 2015
35. Nigrini, M.J., *Forensic Analytics: Methods and Techniques for Forensic Accounting Investigations*, John Wiley & Sons, Inc., Hoboken, NJ, 2011.
36. Cortes, C., Vapnik, V. Support-vector networks. *Mach. Learn.*, 20, 273–297, 1995. https://doi.org/10.1007/BF00994018 1995

10

Advancement in Augmented and Virtual Reality

Omprakash Dewangan[1]*, Latika Pinjarkar[2], Padma Bonde[3] and Jaspal Bagga[2]

[1]CSE Department, Kalinga University, Atal Nagar, Raipur, CG, India
[2]IT Department, SSTC, SSGI, Bhilai, CG, India
[3]CSE Department, SSTC, SSGI, Bhilai, CG, India

Abstract

Virtual and augmented reality advances are expanding in notoriety. Expanded reality has flourished to date basically on versatile applications, with games like Pokémon Go or the new Google Maps utility as a portion of its ministers. Then again, augmented reality has been promoted principally on account of the computer game industry and less expensive gadgets. Nonetheless, what was at first a disappointment in the mechanical field is re-emerging as of late gratitude to the innovative upgrades in gadgets and handling equipment? In this work, a top-to-bottom investigation of the various fields wherein increased and augmented reality has been utilized has been done. This investigation centers around leading an exhaustive perusing audit zeroed in on these new advancements. The development of every one of them during the most recent years in the primary classes and the nations associated with these advances will be examined. Finally, we will dissect the future pattern of these advances and the territories wherein it is important to research to coordinate these innovations into society.

Keywords: Augmented reality, virtual reality, publications

Corresponding author: omprakash.dewangan@kalingauniversity.ac.in

Sandeep Kumar, Rohit Raja, Shrikant Tiwari and Shilpa Rani (eds.) Cognitive Behavior and Human Computer Interaction Based on Machine Learning Algorithm, (211–240) © 2022 Scrivener Publishing LLC

10.1   Introduction

Increased reality and augmented reality are advancements that have been under exploration for quite a long while [1]. All things being equal, there are a few items that have been created in that line and that are available to the overall population [2, 3]. In any case, because of the general public's requirements and varieties, these advances have deteriorated in specific territories. In this way, it is critical to know the examination advancement they have had as of late and, gratitude to that, to contemplate the latest thing to envision the regions where they will be applied in the coming years.

First, it is helpful to characterize the ideas of expanded reality and augmented reality to all the more likely to comprehend the subject of this work. These terms are essential for the idea of the "virtuality continuum" characterized by Paul Milgram and Fumio Kishino [4]. This term depicts a continuum that goes from reality itself to augmented reality created by a PC. Inside the virtual continuum, we discover the subset of blended reality, characterized as everything between the real world and a virtual climate. In Figure 10.1 we can discover a few meanings of virtual reality (VR), however the most worldwide and comprehensive method of characterizing it is as per the following: "A virtual reality is characterized as a genuine or re-enacted climate in which a perceiver encounters telepresence", composed by Jonathan Steuer [5]. This is the picked definition since it put separated the innovation's suggestions, and like this, there is no compelling reason to indicate any Head-Mounted Displays (HDM) or globes and we can zero in on strategies and applications to attempt to sort out what is the way that the innovation is following. Similarly, we can characterize augmented reality (AR) as a strategy to show additional data over this present reality. With this definition, there is no compelling reason to discuss explicit equipment. However, we can determine strategies and applications and spotlight innovation improvement [6].

Even though the innovations of AR and VR have been a work in progress for quite a while [7], we can say that it has as of late left the research centers, thanks in enormous part to the improvement of the registering limit and the bringing down of the gadgets [8]. These days, increased reality and computer-generated reality can be utilized in a mid-range cell phone [9]. Even though, for more submersion, it would be additionally fascinating to utilize more modern gadgets, albeit somewhat more costly. Nonetheless, this innovation has a little client specialty and a narrow field of use-dependent on games. This work examines these advances' development throughout the most recent years, in which viewpoints have developed more, and

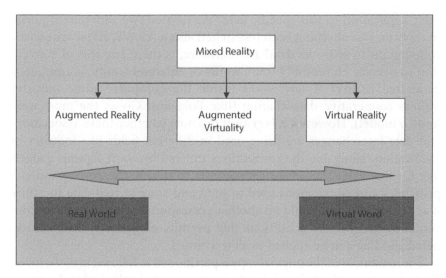

Figure 10.1 Virtual continuum.

the various fields that this advancement has profited. The well-being area has received these vivid innovations to help patients, giving preparing cycles to fears medicines and, in any event, for medical procedure recreations. Likewise, a few logical examinations exhibit that augmented experience helps patients lessen pressure and tension levels notwithstanding torment discernment [10, 11]. They stand apart as exceptionally unique assets for learning and preparing in schooling and industry, accomplishing more productive, intuitive, and participatory learning.

This work's primary objective is to respond to these inquiries: What has been the development of AR and VR not long ago? What is more, what is the pattern that AR and VR will have in the coming years? As said previously, AR and VR have encountered an advancement as of late, yet it is imperative to investigate this development top to bottom. Are AR and VR more famous than previously? These days, lofty organizations are putting resources into these advances.

The most significant works in the most recent years will be broken down and the data got will be utilized to get the decisions about the worldwide advancement of these innovations and the development in the various fields and areas to respond to the main inquiry. For the subsequent inquiry, the distributions throughout the most recent years will be inspected in detail to check these advancements' status (the pinnacle of examination, development, creation, and so forth). Lastly, computer game distributions concerning these innovations will be concentrated to know their application to this specific field. We needed two different inquiries to reply to: Has anything been researched about AR/VR about synergistic cooperation to share its data? Furthermore, is there any sort of convention to oversee community frameworks of enlarged reality or computer-generated reality? A few works inside the computer game industry utilizes cooperative data sharing (like Pokémon Go as the most well-known model). However, it is critical to know whether these associations and data interchanges are being used in different fields like industry or medication, alongside the conventions utilized by some famous gadgets like Oculus Rift. This investigation aims to decide the correspondence principles and conventions used to send and store virtual data to utilize it as an initial step to build up another correspondence and capacity convention for collective conditions that permits all gadgets to be coordinated and that can be applied to all territories.

The remainder of the original copy is partitioned as follows: first, the investigation system is introduced. Next, the outcomes acquired after the examination are point by point and broke down. At last, the ends are uncovered.

10.2   Proposed Methodology

The philosophy utilized in this work relates to the traditional checking survey measure. The preparation steps utilized for this work have appeared in Figure 10.2.

First, we need to dissect the works and compositions of which the data is intriguing for this audit. Like this, we need some fundamental data from these works: title, ISSN (International Standard Serial Number), point, and so forth. At that point, we need to pick the rules utilized for looking through the cycle. Each creator freely utilizes the created manual to look for important data inside the works/compositions from that point onward. Next, all the data got is gathered: the creators trade their original copies, and the looking-through cycle begins once more. This progression is rehashed until each creator surveys all the compositions: in this work, there are three creators, so the aggregate sum of original copies assessed is isolated by three and dispersed over them. Each creator wraps up inspecting all the original copies after three emphases.

Now, all the data is removed from the original copies, put in like manner, and blended. The last survey result will appear in a summing up table. Finally, this information will be broke down to get the data that addresses the inquiries demonstrated in the Introduction segment.

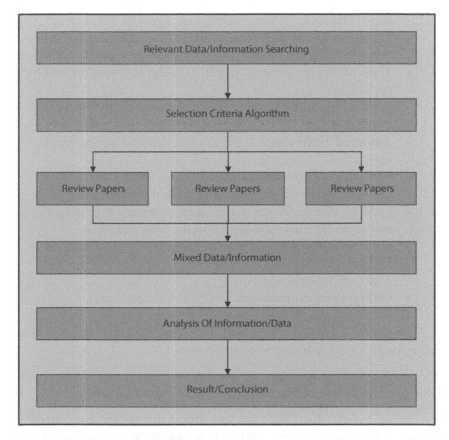

Figure 10.2 Research strategies followed.

10.2.1   Classification of Data/Information Extracted

In this epigraph, the data/information extracted from the inspected original copies is mentioned. This data is necessary to find solutions to the underlying inquiries.

- **Title:** Title of the original copy or work examined.
- **ISBN/ISSN:** Publication's code for a diary original copy or a book part, individually.
- **Keywords:** Words utilized during the pursuit cycle.
- **Information/Data Search:** Criteria used to play out the looking through the cycle.
- **Year of Publication:** Year of distribution of the work looked into.

- **Book/Magazine:** Where the original copy was distributed.
- **Localization:** Country where analysts worked during the examination.
- **Type of Paper:** Type of paper between distribution and application.
- **Type of innovation:** Technology utilized for the exploration, AR or VR.
- **Analyzed Technology:** If the analysts utilized any business innovation.
- **Protocols of Communication:** Name of the convention utilized during the advancement of the work investigated.
- **Field of use:** Field where the work introduced is applied, similar to instruction, industry, well-being, and so on
- **Specialization:** Specialization of paper field.
- **Software:** Is the product accessible?
- **Abstract:** Paper synopsis.
- **Utility:** Extra explanations.

After depicting the most pertinent data required for the examination, the looking-through advance will be itemized.

10.2.2   The Phase of Searching of Data/Information

Just logical papers distributed in worldwide diaries are considered to acquire a lot of good-quality attempts to examine. The principal web crawler utilized in this work is Google Scholar since it coordinates works from a few stages, streamlining this progression. If the data is not finished, Mendeley's information base is utilized to fill it. The watchwords utilized in the looking through cycle are itemized beneath:

- Virtual Reality
- Augmented Reality

Google Scholar is arranged to look through works and licenses from the year 2000, so different refers to books or book sections that are excluded. The data acquired is arranged by significance and just English-composed papers are considered. With this arrangement, the firsts 200 passages are separated and utilized in this work, and it should discuss expanded reality or computer-generated reality (or incorporate some gadget that utilizes one of them).

After the principal search measure, the outcomes acquired are as per the following:

- Virtual reality: 22 papers picked out of 1,490,000 outcomes.
- Augmented reality: 26 papers picked out of 848,000 outcomes.

After investigating the outcomes hastily, the primary pursuit presents one decision: A primary measure of the works got is out of date (numerous papers are obsolete), so a few papers are insufficient for this work. From that point forward, the looking through the cycle is reclassified utilizing an alternate arrangement: the beginning year is changed to 2010 to get later and significant works.

After the subsequent pursuit measure, the outcomes acquired are as per the following:

- Virtual reality: 29 papers picked out of 322,000 outcomes.
- Augmented reality: 54 papers picked out of 132,000 outcomes.

In this event, we get fewer sections than previously; however, we can get more data. Likewise, to get a complete composition information base for this work, two new hunts are finished utilizing expanded catchphrases: collective computer-generated experience and shared increased reality. As definite in the presentation segment, future work must know whether there is sufficient data about collective works that utilize AR or VR.

This last inquiry gets these outcomes:

- Community-oriented augmented simulation: 20 papers picked out of 27,000 outcomes.
- Collaborative expanded reality: 12 papers picked out of 17,100 outcomes.

All the quests get around 1,200 likely papers and we select 189 papers after a first channel. At that point, as nitty-gritty above, we examine global diary works with ISSN, so we take out 26 of them. At long last, we have a data set of 163 papers.

As itemized already, Table 10.1 shows that the top search was made without acceptable measures from 2000; that is why the looking through arrangement changed in the second hunt from 2010.

Table 10.1 Search measure synopsis.

Year	No. of papers selected	Out of results	Keywords searched
2000	22.00	1490000.00	Virtual Reality
2000	26.00	848000.00	Augmented Reality
2010	29.00	322000.00	Virtual Reality
2010	54.00	132000.00	Augmented Reality
2010	20.00	27000.00	Collaborative Virtual Reality
2010	12.00	17100.00	Collaborative Augmented Reality
	Total = 163.00		

10.3 Results

In this segment, the outcomes obtained after examining the works definite beforehand are introduced. To start with, the quantity of distribution advancement is contemplated and introduced. From that point onward, a profound information investigation is finished utilizing the creators' reolocation during the work improvement and the primary subjects on which they are engaged.

10.3.1 Original Copy Publication Evolution

In the wake of gathering the work information base, we dissect the quantity of distributions step by step to advance AR and VR fields. Similarly that this data determination is done, we start this investigation in the year 2000 and we use Google Scholar to get the information. As should be evident in Table 10.2 and Figure 10.3, these days, the notoriety in this field is lower than previously: this is perhaps impacted by the minimal effort of the innovation that made conceivable working with AR in center level cell phones and VR headsets, so these advancements came out from labs to the business and, at last, to the individuals. To make this theory more grounded, we look at Gartner's promotion of cycle [12]; this cycle publicity is known for assessing the arising advancements and when these innovations will be underway. Gartner's promotion cycle speaks to the development of interest

Table 10.2 Evolution of publications houses.

AR number of publications	VR number of publications	Variation in AR	Variation in VR	Year of publication
2300.00	14100.00	--	--	2000
2570.00	15900.00	11.740	12.770	2001
3190.00	17800.00	24.120	11.940	2002
5540.00	19800.00	73.670	11.240	2003
4640.00	23200.00	−16.250	17.170	2004
5160.00	24600.00	11.200	06.030	2005
5820.00	29100.00	12.800	18.290	2006
6670.00	29900.00	14.600	02.750	2007
7410.00	34000.00	11.090	13.710	2008
8070.00	36500.00	08.910	07.350	2009
10800.00	38600.00	33.830	05.750	2010
13400.00	40200.00	24.070	04.140	2011
16900.00	42100.00	26.120	04.730	2012
19700.00	45700.00	16.570	08.550	2013
24400.00	45900.00	23.860	00.440	2014
27600.00	46100.00	13.120	00.440	2015
30500.00	50700.00	10.510	09.980	2016
35400.00	57400.00	16.060	13.210	2017
31100.00	47600.00	−12.050	−17.070	2018
2570.00	27700.00	−79.920	−41.810	2019

in specific advances, characterizing them in five phases during their advantage cycle (in a specific order):

- **Triggered Technology:** innovation is beginning.
- **Expanded Desires Peak:** organizations start to made distributions with progress and disappointments.

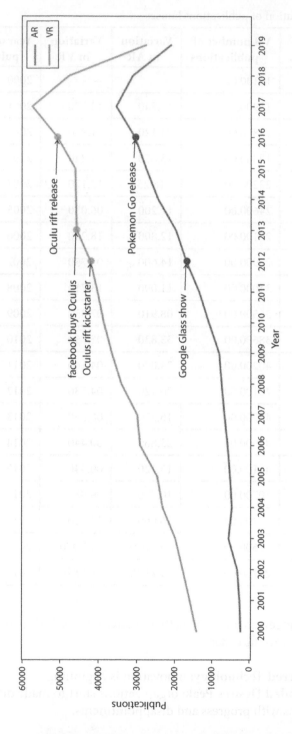

Figure 10.3 Advancement of publications.

- **A Trough of Thwarted Expectation:** the vast majority of the investigations and execution falls flat.
- **Illumination Slope:** second or third ages of the innovation show up.
- **Profitability Plateau:** innovation is standard at this point.

Gartner's promotion cycle advancement for computer-generated reality and expanded reality advances can be seen from the year 2000 as of not long ago in Figure 10.4. In this figure, the "x" hub speaks to the year and the "y" pivot speaks to Gartner's promotion cycle stage where the innovation is put. The situation in this pivot is identified with the significance inside Gartner's promotion cycle.

As shown in Figure 10.4, the primary specter of increased reality in Gartner's publicity cycle is gone back to 2005. This innovation begins in the "Innovation Trigger" segment of the bend until 2010 when it arrives at the part "Pinnacle of swelled desire". The increased reality remains in the segment "Box of disappointment" from 2013 to 2018. At long last, in 2019, it very well may be found again in the "Innovation Trigger" area, however, with the expansion of the expression "Cloud". This advancement demonstrates that, somewhere in the range of 2010 and 2012, it was a famous point and, after those years, its significance decreased. Notwithstanding, this innovation has become fascinating because of the consideration of cloud advances, which give convenience to the end client.

AR advancements show up in various manners inside Gartner's promotion cycle, and all these related terms are considered to show its development in Figure 10.4. To begin with, it very well may be found as "Head-mounted presentation" inside the "Innovation Trigger" area in 2001. Its next event is in 2007 as the expression "Virtual climate/Virtual universes" situated in the "Pinnacle of swelled desire" segment; it remains in this part until 2012. This year, this term changes its part: in the year 2013, it shows up in the "Box of frustration" stage. It is imperative to see that, from 2013 to 2016, and it shows up as the expression "Computer-generated Reality". At long last, in 2016, it comes to the "Slant of edification" stage. AR vanished from the promotion cycle in 2018, so it may be viewed as in the creation stage (this reality will be exhibited after examining the reference).

Summing up this first examination, after the year 2013, the two advancements start a rotting stage until 2019, when both nearly vanish from Gartner's publicity cycle. Notwithstanding, AR is getting another life as an "AR cloud", which is another worldview that utilizations cloud innovations with increased reality works, and it is critical to get center around that as well. With this data, we ought not to expect that augmented simulation will

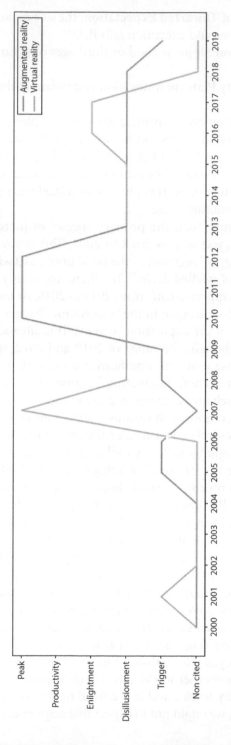

Figure 10.4 Development of AR and VR advancements in the cycle of hype.

build its significance in the following coming years; nonetheless, AR propensity portrays a new beginning with the consideration of cloud advancements, so we ought to anticipate a significant expansion underway and references in this field in the following years.

The mathematical information about the all-out number of distributions in those years (not just the papers chose for this work) appears in Table 10.2.

The information introduced in Table 10.2 is spoken to graphically in Figure 10.3. In the two portrayals, it is essential to notice the propensity identified in Gartner's promotion cycle for AR and VR: the works identified with the two advancements are diminishing over the most recent two years. In Gartner's publicity cycle, its rot stage began in 2013–2014 and its outcomes are seen underway and reference four years after the fact. There is a genuine chance in the following 3–4 years, and there will be an expansion in the number of works and distributions identified with expanded reality because of the expanded significance of AR because of the cloud advances.

These innovations are exceptionally near the game business, so it is imperative to concentrate on this area and study if a similar development can be seen in this field. To do that, a profound looking-through cycle is finished utilizing the most famous stages and gadgets (like Steam or Oculus Rift), searching for games that utilization one of them at any rate. The best way to search for that is by utilizing the steam stage because different stages do not permit to sort by year or search for specific catchphrases. The development of distributions in the game business got is appeared in Figure 10.5.

As can be seen, the created games inclination (see Figure 10.5) is like the composition distributions in computer-generated simulation (see Figure 10.3).

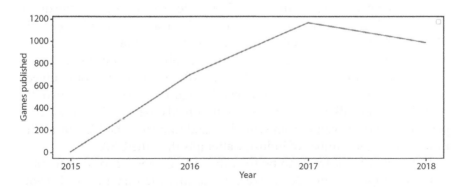

Figure 10.5 Advancement of games published in STEAM.

Game improvement arrived at a top in 2017 and afterward began to diminish. Due to the improvement of computer-generated reality HDM, it is conceivable that this inclination will change and stabilize in a couple of years.

Similar issues are noticed to do this examination in AR: Google Play and Oculus do not permit to sort data by year. Some irregular works here can be noticed (like Pokémon Go), yet a couple of works are acquired. Hence, no inclination can be separated from this data.

10.3.2   General Information/Data Analysis

An overall data study has been done above concerning original copy distributions in the most recent years. Presently, utilizing the technique depicted in the past segment, the composition information base, a subset of 163 compositions, is inspected profoundly to get more itemized data. This examination incorporates the nation where the creators built up the distributions and the field of use.

10.3.2.1   Nations

Initially, an investigation zeroed in on where the distributions come from is completed. After this investigation, the locales that are exploring and creating AR/VR advances will appear.

After breaking down the information base, results are itemized in Figure 10.6 (top). In this figure, it very well may be seen that the outcomes have appeared in a worldwide manner and spotlight on USA and EU (the areas with more distributions in AR and VR). The consequences of the investigation show in Figure 10.6 (top) that the European Union (EU) is the locale that puts more assets in these fields (34.4% of distributions came from this area), the United States of America (USA) follows with 27.3% of the distributions, and Australia can be found in the third spot. As can be seen, the EU and USA take up over 60% of the distributions so that the examination will zero in on these two areas. Presently, we will zero in on the territories to which these districts are contributing. Afterward, the various subjects will be broke down in detail. As shown in Figure 10.6 (base), the two districts have many likenesses in distribution fields. Be that as it may, their principle contrasts came from schooling and industry: the EU put forth a more significant number of industry attempts than the USA.

In Figure 10.7, it tends to be seen that a large portion of the distributions is completed after 2010. We can see that the quantity of distribution of papers diminishes. In any case, this example is not equivalent to

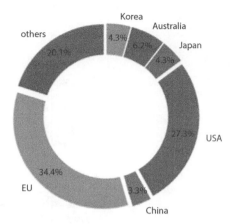

Publications made by country.

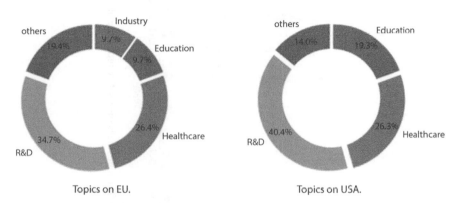

Topics on EU.   Topics on USA.

Figure 10.6 On the top is the level of nations which made an exploration on AR or VR; in the base left is the themes investigated in the EU, and in the base right is the level of subjects investigated in the USA.

found in Figure 10.3: all things considered, the fame diminished in 2017, yet in this event, the pinnacle of ubiquity is in 2010 and, from that point forward, begins diminishing. This reality can result from the reference framework: more established papers have a more significant number of references than more up-to-date ones, so Google Scholar shows first the most referred to works; for this situation, it gives more significance to those works. At last, we analyze the number of distributions of our subset step by step in Figure 10.7. After considering the overall outcomes step by step, they will be isolated in the fundamental points where these advancements are being applied.

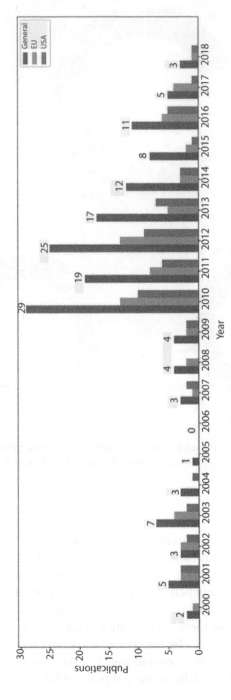

Figure 10.7 Examination of papers picked step by step: The blue line is the relative multitude of papers that year.

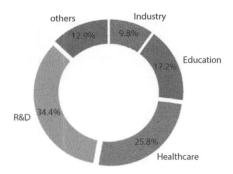

Figure 10.8 Conveyance of developed fields.

10.3.2.2   Themes

The fundamental subjects that have been considered are innovative work (R&D), medical care, instruction, and industry. The circulation of the chose works regarding the chose themes appears in Figure 10.8. In Figure 10.8, it tends to be seen that the most evolved subject is R&D with 34.40% of the works chosen, which is very consistent due to the internet searcher used to choose the works (Google Scholar, which is a stage generally utilized for research works distributions). Be that as it may, 65.60% of the chose works have a place with explicit applications. In this part, three important themes can be noticed: medical care with 25.80%, training with 17.20%, and lastly, industry with 9.80%. We can dissect those outcomes similarly as above, utilizing a year-by-year characterization. These outcomes have appeared in Figure 10.9.

In Figure 10.9, a few subtleties having a place with every point and its development are noticed. Research and development arrive at their pinnacle of prominence in 2010 and 2011. However, it gradually diminishes until 2016, when it arrives at a little pinnacle and diminishes once more. In medical services, it additionally arrives at fame top in 2010 and begins to diminish until 2017. In schooling, the notoriety top is reached in 2012 and 2013. Industry's distributions are practically steady from 2010. In the following subsections, these points are concentrated profoundly to discover more data about them. Additionally, we will contemplate its development in the EU and the USA.

10.3.2.3   R&D Innovative Work

This subject is most referred in the field of different discontinuities that can be acquired. For instance, we can notice works about coordinating VR on cell phones [13], papers about issues in AR [14], works about posture assessment [15, 16], and works about how to utilize P2P (distributed)

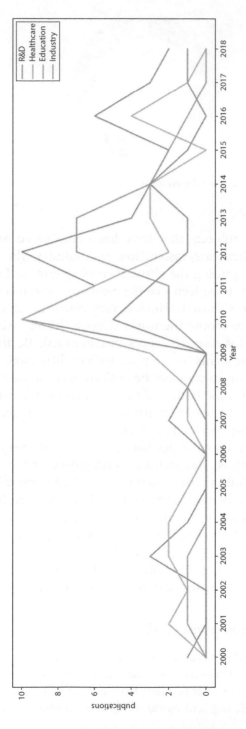

Figure 10.9 Publications development, everything being equal.

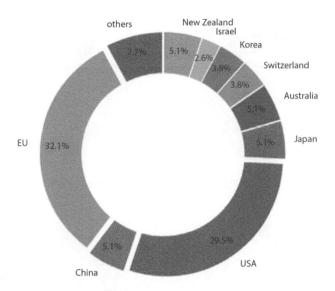

Figure 10.10 Publications in R&D by nations.

organizations to make community-oriented frameworks for AR [17]. The information base utilized in this work, those original copies where the primary point is identified with innovative work are separated in nations, and the outcomes appear in Figure 10.10. Albeit a few nations are spoken to in Figure 10.10, the EU and USA cover 61.60% of the distributions. The excess 38.40% is divided among Asiatic and Oceania nations.

10.3.2.4 *Medical Services*

As we find in 8, medical care is the most well-known field of AR and VR. To start with, we will break down the points considered. In Figure 10.11 (upper left), it tends to be seen that the most pertinent subtopic is a medical procedure, followed intently by brain science and restoration. In the medical procedure field, there are a few works for aiding specialists previously or during a medical procedure [18], preparing for a medical procedure to limit hazards [19], or even a few frameworks to acquaint understudies with this field. In brain research, we discovered papers centered, for instance, on fears [20]. In restoration, most of the works are identified with aiding stroke patients [21, 22].

Concentrating in EU and USA districts [see Figure 10.11 (base)], the broke down information shows that medical procedure and brain research are the most important themes: both cover practically 95.00% of the complete distributions in those locales. In the USA, brain research takes somewhat more interest than a medical procedure and recovery is a significant

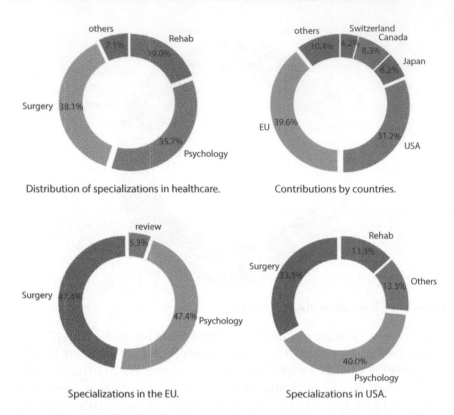

Distribution of specializations in healthcare.

Contributions by countries.

Specializations in the EU.

Specializations in USA.

Figure 10.11 Data about distributions on medical care: The upper left picture is the level of distributions made on medical services. In the upper right is the level of distributions made by nations. In the base left is the distributions made in the EU, and in the correct base is the data of distributions made in the USA.

subject to be considered. This examination is stretched out to all the locales worldwide to look at the outcomes [see Figure 10.11 (upper right)]. True to form, the EU and the USA are the locales with more commitments.

10.3.2.5   *Training and Education*

In this segment, the principal consideration is centered around the subject of training and education. The cycle made for the past subject is accomplished for this one and breaks down the outcomes after that. Those outcomes appear in Figure 10.12. The works identified with these subjects are separated into three classes: first, "Early" stage is identified with works zeroed in on the beginning phases of the training, up to 10 or 11 years of age; "Center" is utilized to mean works for secondary school until they are 18 years of age; lastly, the classification "High" is utilized for works applied

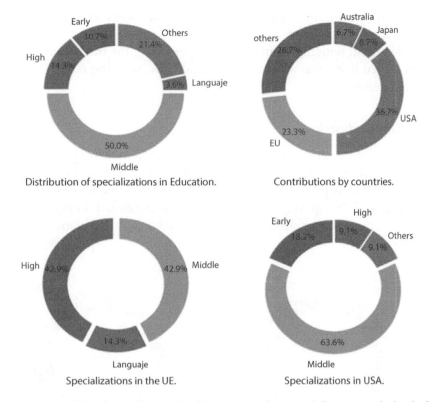

Figure 10.12 Data about educational publications: in the upper left picture is the level of distributions broke down in training. In the upper right is the level of distributions made by nations. In the base left is the distributions made in the EU, and in the correct base is the data of distributions made in the USA.

to college examines. Figure 10.12 (upper left) shows that the most present class is "Center": identified with that, we can discover works zeroed in on assisting understudies with maths [23] or science [24, 25], among others. In the classification "Early", we can discover works zeroed in on showing kids science, too [26]. At last, in the class "High", works are centered around applying complex instructing strategies like joint efforts [27, 28]. We additionally discovered works that utilized AR/VR advances to show dialects [29] in more than one class. The data got from Figure 10.12 shows that half percent of compositions discovered arrangement with working with understudies from center school. Another significant end is that works with more elevated levels look more intriguing than early (more references). In Figure 10.12 (base), it tends to be seen that EU is centered chiefly around the "Center" and "High" levels at the same time, in the USA, the "Center" schooling class covers 63.30% of the works while the "High" classification covers under 10.00%.

At long last, noticing Figure 10.12 (upper right), the fundamental districts zeroed in on this subject are EU and USA, covering 60.00% of the commitments.

10.3.2.6   Industries

At long last, the business point is broken down similarly to the past themes. The summed-up data can be found in Figure 10.13. The data introduced in Figure 10.13 is partitioned into three classes. The first and more well-known one is "Support", covering half of the examined works: in this theme, we can discover strategies to keep up manufacturing plants [30, 31] or airplane.

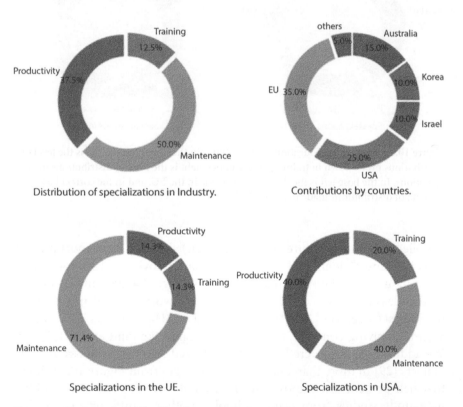

Figure 10.13 Data about distributions on the industry: The upper left picture is the level of distributions examined in the industry. In the upper right is the level of distributions made by nations. In the base left is the distributions made in the EU, and in the correct base is the data of distributions made in the USA.

The subsequent class is "Profitability", which is key in present-day enterprises to acquire better outcomes and more effectiveness in the day by day industry; this should be possible to help laborers work with modern robots or to try and utilize a few applications to make reasonable 3D models and to impart to associates [32–34]. Finally, the classification "Preparing", with 12.50% of the distributions, covers works zeroed in on assisting laborers with figuring out how to utilize their gear [35]. Figure 10.13 (base) presents the investigated data from the USA and the EU. It tends to be seen that 71.00% of the EU's works have a place with the "Support" classification. The "Preparation" and "Efficiency" classifications stay in runner-up in the EU along these lines. On the opposite side, the USA's works inside this theme are centered around efficiency and support. At last, Figure 10.13 (upper right) presents the all-out circulation by nations. As can be seen, the EU and the USA cover 60.00% of the distributions.

10.4 Conclusion

Results have been introduced unexpectedly, centering the data in nations and subjects. Along these lines, it is more evident the future propensity of AR and VR advancements. To start with, all the outcomes are summed up in Table 10.3. After this, the outcomes and their inclination are investigated and portrayed.

Table 10.3 Outline of EU and USA publications by topics.

Regions	Topics	Tendency	Specializations
USA EU	Research and development	Presumably Increases	Web AR, Tracking, Real-time. Mobile, Web AR, Freehand.
USA EU	Medical care	Increment	Psychology, Laparoscopic, Phobias, Surgery. Rehab, Surgery, Stroke.
USA EU	Training & Education	Decrement	Maths, Science, Anatomy, Language.
USA EU	Industries	Stable or not, many publications	Maintenance, Assembly, Aircraft. Procedural assignment, Remote cooperation.

In Table 10.3, the data rundown is investigated for the fundamental themes (D, medical care, instruction, and industry) inside the two most pertinent districts (EU and USA). Be that as it may, significant works zeroed in on different classes or themes have been found in this examination. For instance, we additionally discovered papers about paleohistory [36–38], engineering [39], computer games [40], development [41–43], the travel industry [44–47], geology [17], or extensive information perception.

When the data has been introduced and broke down, it is imperative to re-visit this work's fundamental target. In the presentation, four principle questions were nitty-gritty and, after this work, we can respond to them.

The first was what has been the development of AR and VR recently?
As have been point by point during this work, many works zeroed in on AR and VR fields have been created. A tremendous measure of papers has been distributed, including nations worldwide, yet, we can see that the EU and USA are the principal communities of examination for these innovations. We can likewise observe that the vast majority of the distributions can be assembled in four subjects: innovative work, medical services, schooling, and industry.

The subsequent inquiry introduced was the pattern that AR and VR will have in the coming years?
Utilizing the data acquired from the all-out number of distributions noticed step by step and Gartner's promotion cycle development inclination saw in the distributions, AR and VR advances are losing fame. Investigates in these regions will keep chipping away at them. However, the number of distributions will diminish until they arrive at solidness. In the computer game industry, the propensity noticed is like the one introduced in different fields. One of the most downloaded and messed around (Pokémon Go) depends on AR innovation. However, there are no well-known games that utilization VR innovation, even though there is a small and stable specialty market. AR innovation does not have a well-known apparatus to make computer games. However, it is fundamental to discover it in a few words about a medical procedure, industry, or schooling. We additionally can reason that AR ubiquity will fill in the following years on account of the development of cloud advances and the conceivable outcomes that they can add to AR.

The third inquiry was, has anything been researched about AR/VR about collective connections to share its data?

There are not many much-exploring ventures zeroed in on this subject; however, we can locate some like VirCA (Virtual Collaboration Arena) venture, which is engaged in automated control [48].

The last inquiry was, is there any convention to oversee community-oriented frameworks of increased reality or computer-generated reality? Engineers of VirCA venture use Robotics Technology Middleware (RT-Middleware) to make their situations, and the interconnection is made utilizing a VPN (Virtual Private Network). Aside from this, we did not discover any conventions [49, 50].

In the wake of inquiries introduced toward starting of the work and examining distributions in AR and VR advances. It very well may be presumed that we are as of now in a phase of decay of these advances. Nonetheless, there are certain zones where the pattern is steady or somewhat upward. Moreover, because of the development of cloud innovations, it is entirely conceivable that the inclination will change in the coming years. We can surmise that the interest incline saw in these innovations can change; however, it will require the assistance of new advancements, such as 5G, which will make conceivable lighter and more brilliant gadgets, or AR cloud, which can assist with registering the most perplexing data [51, 52]. Different advancements, as artificial brainpower ideal models or biosensors, are also appropriate to be incorporated with AR and VR applications simultaneously, as can be seen in Gartner's bend, just cloud innovations are connected to the expanded reality field. Additionally, AR applications need ground-breaking equipment frameworks; subsequently, it will be typical that the primary innovation of every one of them that joins AR is the cloud one [53, 54].

About community-oriented conditions, a couple of works are centered on establishing such sorts of conditions. Likewise, there are practically no normalized components to speak to and send data from the virtual climate, which might be one reason why there are no advances in community-oriented conditions. If future works center around creating guidelines like this, then gadgets from various makers and various encoding could be incorporated into a solitary virtual climate [55, 56].

References

1. Pucihar, K.C. and Coulton, P., Exploring the evolution of mobile augmented reality for future entertainment systems. *Comput. Entertain. (CIE)*, 11, 1, 2013.

2. Paavilainen, J., Korhonen, H., Alha, K., Stenros, J., Koskinen, E., Mayra, F., The Pokémon GO experience: A location-based augmented reality mobile game goes mainstream, in: *Proceedings of the 2017 CHI Conference on Human Factors in Computing Systems*, Denver, CO, USA, 6–11 May 2017, pp. 2493–2498.

3. Lv, Z., Halawani, A., Feng, S., Ur Réhman, S., Li, H., Touch-less interactive augmented reality game on the vision-based wearable device. *Pers. Ubiquitous Comput.*, 19, 551–567, 2015.

4. Milgram, P. and Kishino, F., A taxonomy of mixed reality visual displays. *IEICE Trans. Inf. Syst.*, 77, 1321–1329, 1994.

5. Steuer, J., Defining virtual reality: Dimensions determining telepresence. *J. Commun.*, 42, 73–93, 1992.

6. Nincarean, D., Alia, M.B., Halim, N.D.A., Rahman, M.H.A., Mobile Augmented Reality: the potential for education. *Procedia-Soc. Behav. Sci.*, 103, 657–664, 2013.

7. Bajura, M. and Neumann, U., Dynamic registration correction in video-based augmented reality systems. *IEEE Comput. Graph. Appl.*, 15, 52–60, 1995.

8. Yung, R. and Khoo-Lattimore, C., New realities: A systematic literature review on virtual reality and augmented reality in tourism research. *Curr. Issues Tour.*, 22, 2056–2081, 2019.

9. Kimura, Y., Manabe, S., Ikeda, S., Kimura, A., Shibata, F., Can Transparent Virtual Objects Be Represented Realistically on OST-HMDs?, in: *Proceedings of the 2019 IEEE Conference on Virtual Reality and 3D User Interfaces (VR)*, Osaka, Japan, 23–27 March 2019, pp. 1327–1328.

10. Opris, D., Pintea, S., García-Palacios, A., Botella, C., Szamosközi, Ş., David, D., Virtual reality exposure therapy in anxiety disorders: A quantitative meta-analysis. *Depress. Anxiety*, 29, 85–93, 2012.

11. Powers, M.B. and Emmelkamp, P.M., Virtual reality exposure therapy for anxiety disorders: A meta-analysis. *J. Anxiety Disord.*, 22, 561–569, 2008.

12. Gartner's Hype Cycle, accessed on 26 December 2019. Available online: https://www.gartner.com/en/research/methodologies/gartnerhype-cycle.

13. Lai, Z., Hu, Y.C., Cui, Y., Sun, L., Dai, N., Lee, H.S., Furion: Engineering High-Quality Immersive Virtual Reality on Today's Mobile Devices. *IEEE Trans. Mob. Comput.*, 19, 7, 1586–1602, 2019.

14. Kruijff, E., Swan, J.E., Feiner, S., Perceptual issues in augmented reality revisited, in: *Proceedings of the 9th IEEE International Symposium on Mixed and Augmented Reality 2010: Science and Technology*, 13–16 October 2010, ISMAR, Seoul, Korea, 2010.

15. Hagbi, N., Bergig, O., El-Sana, J., Billinghurst, M., Shape recognition and pose estimation for mobile augmented reality. *IEEE Trans. Vis. Comput. Graph.*, 17, 10, 1369–1379, 2011.

16. Murphy-Chutorian, E. and Trivedi, M.M., Head pose estimation and augmented reality tracking: An integrated system and evaluation for monitoring driver awareness. *IEEE Trans. Intell. Transp. Syst.*, 11, 2, 300–311, 2010.

17. Zhihan, L., Yin, T., Han, Y., Chen, Y., Chen, G., WebVR-web virtual reality engine based on the P2P network. *J. Netw.*, 6, 7, 990–998, 2011.
18. Nicolau, S., Soler, L., Mutter, D., Marescaux, J., Augmented reality in laparo-scopic surgical oncology. *Surg. Oncol.*, 20, 3, 189–201, 2011.
19. Vankipuram, M., Kahol, K., McLaren, A., Panchanathan, S., A virtual real-ity simulator for necessary orthopedic skills: A design and validation study. *J. Biomed. Inform.*, 43, 5, 661–8, 2010.
20. Baus, O. and Bouchard, S., Moving from virtual reality exposure-based ther-apy to augmented reality exposure-based therapy: A review. *Front. Hum. Neurosci.*, 4, 8, 112, 2014.
21. Jack, D., Boian, R., Merians, A.S., Tremaine, M., Burdea, G.C., Adamovich, S.V., Recce, M., Poizner, H., Virtual reality-enhanced stroke rehabilitation. *IEEE Trans. Neural Syst. Rehabil. Eng.*, 9, 3, 308–18, 2001.
22. Hondori, H.M., Khademi, M., Dodakian, L., Cramer, S.C., Lopes, C.V., A spatial augmented reality rehab system for post-stroke hand rehabilitation. *Stud. Health Technol. Inform.*, 184, 279–85, 2013.
23. Bujak, K.R., Radu, I., Catrambone, R., MacIntyre, B., Zheng, R., Golubski, G., A psychological perspective on augmented reality in the mathematics classroom. *Comput. Educ.*, 68, 536–544, 2013.
24. Cai, S., Wang, X., Chiang, F.K., A case study of Augmented Reality simu-lation system application in a chemistry course. *Comput. Hum. Behav.*, 37, 31–40, 2014.
25. Bressler, D.M. and Bodzin, A.M., A mixed-methods assessment of students' flow experiences during a mobile augmented reality science game. *J. Comput. Assist. Learn.*, 29, 1–10, 2013.
26. Shelton, B.E. and Hedley, N.R., Using augmented reality for teaching Earth-Sun relationships to undergraduate geography students, in: *Proceedings of the ART 2002—1st IEEE International Augmented Reality Toolkit Workshop*, Darmstadt, Germany, 29–29 September 2002.
27. Monahan, T., McArdle, G., Bertolotto, M., Virtual reality for collaborative e-learning. *Comput. Educ.*, 50, 4, 1339–1353, 2008.
28. Galambos, P., Weidig, C., Baranyi, P., Aurich, J.C., Hamann, B., Kreylos, O., VirCA NET: A case study for collaboration in shared virtual space, in: *Proceedings of the 3rd IEEE International Conference on Cognitive Infocommunications*, 2–5 December 2012, CogInfoCom, Kosice, Slovakia, 2012.
29. Wagner, D. and Barakonyi, I., Augmented reality kanji learning, in: *Proceedings of the 2nd IEEE and ACM International Symposium on Mixed and Augmented Reality*, 10 October 2003, ISMAR, Tokyo, Japan, 2003.
30. Gavish, N., Gutiérrez, T., Webel, S., Rodríguez, J., Peveri, M., Bockholt, U., Tecchia, F., Evaluating virtual reality and augmented reality training for industrial maintenance and assembly tasks. *Interact. Learn. Environ.*, 2 778–798, 2015.

31. Wang, J., Feng, Y., Zeng, C., Li, S., An augmented reality-based system for remote collaborative maintenance instruction of complex products. *IEEE Int. Conf. Autom. Sci. Eng.*, 309–314, 2014.

32. Back, M., Kimber, D., Rieffel, E., Dunnigan, A., Liew, B., Gattepally, S., Foote, J., Shingu, J., Vaughan, J., The virtual chocolate factory: Building a real-world mixed-reality system for industrial collaboration and control, in: *Proceedings of the 2010 IEEE International Conference on Multimedia and Expo*, 19–23 July 2010, ICME, Suntec City, Singapore, 2010.

33. Poppe, E., Brown, R., Johnson, D., Recker, J., A prototype augmented reality collaborative process modeling tool, in: *Proceedings of the CEUR Workshop Proceedings*, 28 August–2 September 2011, Clermont-Ferrand, France.

34. Clark, A. and Dünser, A., An interactive augmented reality coloring book, in: *Proceedings of the 2012 IEEE Symposium on 3D User Interfaces (3DUI)*, Costa Mesa, CA, USA, 4–5 March 2012, pp. 7–10.

35. Matsas, E. and Vosniakos, G.C., Design a virtual reality training system for human-robot collaboration in manufacturing tasks. *Int. J. Interact. Des. Manuf.*, 6, 1–6, 2017.

36. Morgan, C.L., (Re)Building çatalhöyük: Changing virtual reality in archaeology. *Archaeologies*, 11, 139–153, 2009.

37. Vlahakis, V., Ioannidis, M., Karigiannis, J., Tsotros, M., Gounaris, M., Stricker, D., Gleue, T., Daehne, P., Almeida, L., Archeoguide: An augmented reality guide for archaeological sites. *IEEE Comput. Graph. Appl.*, 22, 52–60, 2002.

38. Haugstvedt, A.-C. and Krogstie, J., Mobile augmented reality for cultural heritage: A technology acceptance study, in: *Proceedings of the ISMAR 2012— 11th IEEE International Symposium on Mixed and Augmented Reality*, 5–8 November 2012, Science and Technology Papers, Atlanta, GA, USA, 2012.

39. Whyte, J., Industrial applications of virtual reality in architecture and construction. *Electron. J. Inf. Technol. Constr.*, 8, 43–50, 2003.

40. Thomas, B., Close, B., Donoghue, J., Squires, J., De Bondi, P., Morris, M., Piekarski, W., ARQuake: An outdoor/indoor augmented first-person reality application, in: *Proceedings of the Digest of Papers. Fourth International Symposium on Wearable Computers*, Atlanta, GA, USA, 16–17 October 2000, pp. 139–146.

41. Wang, X., Kim, M.J., Love, P.E., Kang, S.C., Augmented reality in the built environment: Classification and implications for future research. *Autom. Constr.*, 16, 355–368, 2013.

42. Goulding, J., Nadim, W., Petridis, P., Alshawi, M., Construction industry off-site production: A virtual reality interactive training environment prototype. *Adv. Eng. Inform.*, 55, 110–117, 2012.

43. Chi, H.L., Kang, S.C., Wang, X., Research trends and opportunities of augmented reality applications in architecture, engineering, and construction. *Autom. Constr.*, 7, 1, 117–127, 2013.

44. Guttentag, D.A., Virtual reality: Applications and implications for tourism. *Tour. Manage.*, 19, 1, 3–22, 2010.
45. Carrozzino, M. and Bergamasco, M., Beyond virtual museums: Experiencing immersive virtual reality in real museums. *J. Cult. Herit.*, 1, 16–25, 2010.
46. Kounavis, C.D., Kasimati, A.E., Zamani, E.D., Enhancing the tourism experience through mobile augmented reality: Challenges and prospects. *Int. J. Eng. Bus. Manage.*, 2012.
47. Yovcheva, Z., Buhalis, D., Gatzidis, C., 132. Olshannikova, E., Ometov, A., Koucheryavy, Y., Olsson, T., Smartphone augmented reality applications for tourism Visualizing Big Data with augmented and virtual reality: Challenges and research agenda. *E-Rev. Tour. Res. J. Big Data*, 4, 10, 63–66, 2012.
48. Galambos, P. and Baranyi, P., VirCA as intelligent virtual space for RT-middleware, in: *Proceedings of the IEEE/ASME International Conference on Advanced Intelligent Mechatronics*, Budapest, Hungary, 3–7 July 2011.
49. De Crescenzio, F., Fantini, M., Persiani, F., Di Stefano, L., Azzari, P. and Salti, S., 2010. Augmented reality for aircraft maintenance training and operations support. IEEE Computer Graphics and Applications, 31, 1, pp. 96–101.
50. Xiangyu, W., and Dunston, P. S., Comparative effectiveness of mixed reality-based virtual environments in collaborative design. *IEEE Transactions on Systems, Man, and Cybernetics, Part C (Applications and Reviews)*, 41, 3, 284–296, 2011.
51. Xiuquan, Q., Ren, P., Dustdar, S., Liu, L., Ma, H., Chen, J., Web AR: A promising future for mobile augmented reality—State of the art, challenges, and insights. *Proceedings of the IEEE*, 107, 4, 651–666, 2019.
52. Weidong, H., Alem, L., Tecchia, F., Duh, H. B.-L., Augmented 3D hands: a gesture-based mixed reality system for distributed collaboration. *Journal on Multimodal User Interfaces*, 12, 2, 77–89, 2018.
53. Sutcliffe, A. G. and Kaur, K. D., Evaluating the usability of virtual reality user interfaces. *Behaviour & Information Technology*, 19, 6, 415–426, 2000.
54. Comport, A.I., Marchand, É., Chaumette, F., A real-time tracker for markerless augmented reality, in: *Proceedings of the 2nd IEEE and ACM International Symposium on Mixed and Augmented Reality*, 7–10 October 2003, ISMAR, Washington, DC, USA, 2003.
55. Wagner, D., Reitmayr, G., Mulloni, A., Drummond, T., Schmalstieg, D., Real-time detection and tracking for augmented reality on mobile phones. *IEEE Transactions on Visualization and Computer Graphics*, 16, 3, 355–368, 2010.
56. Ejder, B., Bennis, M., Médard, M., Debbah, M., Toward interconnected virtual reality: Opportunities, challenges, and enablers. *IEEE Communications Magazine*, 55, 6, 110–117, 2017.

11

Computer Vision and Image Processing for Precision Agriculture

Narendra Khatri* and Gopal U Shinde

National Agriculture Higher Education Project, Center of Excellence for Digital Farming Solutions for Enhancing Productivity by Robots, Drones and AGVs, Vasantrao Naik Marathwada Krishi Vidyapeeth, Parbhani, India

Abstract

Computer vision is the area through which machines "see". Instead of eyes, it uses cameras to locate, monitor, and quantify the targets for further image processing. In precision agriculture, this technique has been commonly used, playing a crucial role in agricultural automation. This chapter will discuss the numerous computer vision applications in agriculture, *viz.*, detection, plant health monitoring, harvesting, sorting and grading, machine guidance, and field robotics. With high performance and high accuracy, computer vision can improve small-scale farming through agriculture automation to achieve low-cost advantages. The potential implementation of computer vision technology along with deep learning is also briefly addressed. The application of computer vision for agricultural production management based on large-scale datasets is more commonly used to solve agricultural field issues and further improve the agricultural automation system's economics and efficiency.

Keywords: Computer vision, image processing, precision agriculture, agri-drones, robots, AGVs

Corresponding author: narkhatri@gmail.com

Sandeep Kumar, Rohit Raja, Shrikant Tiwari and Shilpa Rani (eds.) Cognitive Behavior and Human Computer Interaction Based on Machine Learning Algorithm, (241–264) © 2022 Scrivener Publishing LLC

11.1   Introduction

The application of computer vision and image processing is noteworthy in precision agriculture and it is increasing continuously due to the affordable cost of the equipment with an increased computational capacity [1]. The incorporation of computer vision and image processing is more advantageous than conventional manual operations. However, there are still some challenges that need to be addressed [2]. Manual operations are tedious and error-prone, while the advanced computer vision and image processing make the process efficient to support agricultural operations. Moreover, integrating these techniques with machine learning enables the analysis of the massive data set accurately and helps implement precision agriculture [3].

This chapter presents a review on the application of computer vision and image processing in precision agriculture, *viz.*, disease detection, fruit type, and plant type. Instead, it outlines studies carried out in various agricultural operations addressing more technological topics, such as vision-based navigation (guidance) systems for autonomous agriculture vehicles and mobile agricultural robots [4]. The following are the key issues explored in particular:

1. Plant/fruit detection
2. Harvesting support, *viz.*, fruit counting, fruit grading, ripeness detection, and yield prediction
3. Plant health monitoring and identification of diseases
4. Vision-based vehicle navigation system for precision agriculture
5. Vision-based mobile robots for agriculture applications

This work is compiled in conjunction with the established review process. The search of the articles was conducted on Google Scholar using the search term "computer vision in precision agriculture", "computer vision and image processing for smart agriculture", "Machine vision in agriculture", and "agriculture robots", etc. There were 54 papers selected for the journal in which the article has covered the depth of the work.

The integration of computer vision and image processing pave the path toward precision agriculture. The addition of machine learning makes the development of the expert system that enhances the workability and efficiency of the system. Deep learning is the advanced version of machine learning. The higher prediction efficiency of deep learning compared to the other machine learning techniques developed the researchers' interest to work and integrate it into the precision agriculture system. Several reviews have been developed and published over the last few years due to the topic's importance.

Barbedo (2013) discussed the image processing applications in the area of agriculture. The disease identification in the plant is performed using digital image processing. Further, the quantification and classification of the images are accomplished to identify the disease [2]. Zareiforoush *et al.* studied and explored the potential of rice quality monitoring through computer vision. The study explored rice production's functional aspects such as shape and size analysis, head rice yield estimation, crack recognition, color analysis, degree of milling, and variety classification [5]. Vithu and Moses studied computer vision applications in food grain production. The computer vision application for the analysis of foreign matter detection is presented [6].

Mousazadeh reviewed navigation systems for off-road vehicles used for agricultural applications [7]. Zhao *et al.* reviewed the past and current research in the vision-based control of the harvesting mobile robots, and the study was focused on analyzing the techniques for identifying the fruit and eye-hand coordination control [8].

The chapter was arranged in mainly six sections: Section 11.1 presents the brief review area and the covered applications. Section 11.2 briefly presents the computer vision and its processing steps. Section 11.3 discusses the machine learning and various machine learning steps for the implementation. Section 11.4 presented various application areas of computer vision in precision agriculture. Section 11.5 concludes the review study.

11.2   Computer Vision

Computer vision is a subarea of computer science engineering in which artificial vision technologies in functional applications are developed. The computer vision system integrates hardware and imaging system to serve the application aspects [9].

- **Image acquisition:** It starts with converting electrical signals from a sensor to numeric representation through the camera. There are two types of image scanning performed in the cameras, *viz.*, area or line. In area scanning, the camera generates an image for each exposer, while inline scanning generates a line of pixels at a time. When a picture is acquired in two dimensions, then the target shifted with the transporter, or the camera moved across a stationary object. The image quality depends upon the illumination during the image acquisition phase. The use of appropriate illumination would boost the system's quality and reliability [10].

- **Image processing:** It is a process of digital image manipulation. Image pre-processing improves the quality of digital images by reducing noise and correcting lightning-related problems. Image analysis is separating the region or the information in the digital image for information retrieval. The image pre-processing is considered low-level image processing, enhancing the digital image quality, such as grayscale adjustment, focus correction, and contrast adjustments to reduce the noise. Meanwhile, middle-level image processing processes include segmentation, definition, and classification of image objects. High-level image processing entails defining and categorizing regions of interest, generally through algorithm classification or ANNs.

11.3   Machine Learning

Machine learning is a branch of artificial intelligence. It is a process of data analysis for automated analytical model building. The idea behind machine learning is to develop a system that can learn from the available data, process it, identify the pattern of the data, and make precise decisions without human intervention. The machine learning algorithms are of mainly three types based on the learning algorithms (i) supervised learning, (ii) unsupervised learning, and (iii) reinforced learning [11]. The programming language for developing the machine learning models in Python, R programming language, Java, and JavaScript. The following are the steps of the machine learning process:

(i)   **Data preparation and acquisition:** The initial step is to collect the required data containing characteristics that could be taken into account in learning. Learning algorithms typically need a significant volume of data that is weighted proportionally. It is necessary to consider matching the need for large volumes of data, ideally without much noise.

(ii) **Selecting characteristics of interest:** Identifying the most appropriate parameter to address the problem is the process of identifying the most appropriate parameter.

(iii) **Algorithm selection:** Selecting the most appropriate and suitable machine learning algorithm to obtain the problems' optimum solution. Many of the times, multiple machine learning algorithms are identified from the literature and the most suitable one is selected after testing it on the current dataset for the given problem.

(iv) **Parameters selection:** Some ML algorithms are customized according to the parameters to be tested.

(v) **Training:** Training in machine learning consists of constructing a computational model with the help of a given collection of inputs, algorithms, and parameters that will be used to predict the responses to new data.

(vi) **Rating:** The developed computational model has to be tested on its accuracy level and rated accordingly to identify the most suitable model.

11.3.1 Support Vector Machine

Support vector machine (SVM) is a well-known technique used for classification applications. It is a non-probabilistic linear classifier that generates a decision threshold with the most significant possible distance between the instances. The classical SVM classifier is capable of classifying the input points into two possible classes. Linear separators can be generated even though they cannot be described linearly in the original space of the inputs [12].

11.3.2 Neural Networks

Artificial neural network (NN) is well-known artificial intelligence technique used for modeling and optimization of complex nonlinear processes. ANN models are data-driven; the ANN models first trained with the training data set composed of input parameter values and output parameter values. Once an ANN-based process model with reasonably good generalization potential is developed, it can effectively optimize its input space to obtain the desired (optimum) process variable's values. Figure 11.1 presents the basic ANN architecture.

11.3.3 Deep Learning

Deep learning networks differ from the standard NNs, *viz.*, the number of nodes in the deep learning is much higher, and the number of layers is more and complex layer interconnection. The development of deep

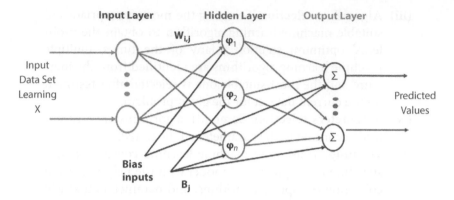

Figure 11.1 Basic ANN architecture.

learning networks needs a massive amount of data set and high computational performance. The four most known deep learning architectures are as follows:

(i)   Unsupervised Pertained Networks,
(ii) Convolutional NNs,
(iii) Recurrent NN,
(iv) Recursive NN.

These deep learning networks are well known and used for solving various problems in the computing domain, *viz.*, sign language, text to speech [13], synthesis and identification of the language [14], signal processing [15], and automatic generation of subtitles [16], among others. Nowadays, deep learning algorithms are used in precision agriculture and high-tech farming. In order to achieve more expressive results, these deep learning algorithms are used in combination.

11.4   Computer Vision and Image Processing in Agriculture

The computer gets vision or "see" through the camera. In the machine, the camera works like eyes to see, locate, monitor, and quantify the targets for further image processing. The camera system can be determined based on the application. These cameras are classified into three categories, namely, RGB, multispectral, and stereovision cameras. Table 11.1 shows a list of cameras used in precision agriculture. The charge-coupled devices

Table 11.1 Cameras used in precision agriculture application.

S. no.	Name of the camera	Application	Pictures	Reference
1	CCD camera	Remote monitoring of the agriculture field		[23]
2	Multispectral camera	Mapping of the crop field		[18]
3	Stereovision camera	3D imagining system of agriculture applications		[24]
4	Real sense camera	Depth and tracking		[20]

(Continued)

Table 11.1 Cameras used in precision agriculture application. (*Continued*)

S. no.	Name of the camera	Application	Pictures	Reference
5	Depth camera	Depth sensing		[20]
6	ZED camera	Depth sensing		[21]
7	Infrared camera	Non-contact temperature measurement		[22]

fall under the category of solid-state semiconductor devices. A monolithic array of closely spaced metal oxide semiconductors forms the photosensitive layer. The light absorbed on the photoconductive substrate and charge accumulates around the isolated "wells" under electrodes' control. Each isolated well presents a pixel. Charges are accumulated for the time it takes to complete a single image scan. The charge build-up is proportional to the intensity of the image. Once the charge is accumulated, the electrode is transferred, line by line, to the registers [17].

Multispectral cameras are the devices which are used for the imaging different wavelength of light. The multispectral camera has five types of imagers; each contains the spectral optical filter, allowing only a particular wavelength to be captured. Multispectral cameras are also deployed for target detection in military applications [18]. Stereovision cameras are a special kind of camera developed to generate images similar to a human binocular vision system. Usually, it contains two or more lenses along with their image sensors. These cameras are used for depth perception [19].

Real sense camera is designed and developed by the Intel corporation; the Intel real sense technology is developed for the depth and tracking of the objects. Similarly, a depth camera and ZED cameras are also used for the depth analysis of the object [20, 21]. Infrared cameras detect the thermal energy emitted by the particular scene which is being captured. It detects the thermal information of the objects under observation. This kind of camera is mostly used for the heat emission analysis of the crops and the plants [22].

This section provides a thorough analysis of the five major fields of computer vision and image recognition and processing in smart agriculture. Vision-based vehicle navigation systems for precision agriculture and vision-based mobile robots for agriculture are the major research areas. This domain is the interdisciplinary domain in which all the mainstream engineering and agriculture engineering branches are working together to develop sustainable autonomous systems.

11.4.1 Plant/Fruit Detection

The fruit and plants are detected from the rest of the background using image segmentation in digital farming solutions. The identification task is the crucial requirement for a further advanced application [25]. Image processing technologies and advanced machine learning techniques can detect objects precisely, quickly, and non-invasively [26]. Table 11.2 presents some of the latest techniques used in plant and fruit detection from the literature.

Table 11.2 Plant and fruit detection techniques.

Method used	Objective	Type	Features	Performance indices	Reference
CNN + SVM + SLIC + PCA	Development of a robust flower identification technique	Apple flower detection	Color and spatial proximity	F measure for apple data set A 93.40%, For B data set 82.20%, and on C data set 79.90%	[27]
ANN + GA	Cluster segmentation for identification of maturity.	Grapes	Color (HSV and L*a*b color spaces)	Percentage accuracy 99.40%	[28]
KNN, ELM, DT, LDA, and Naïve Bayes	NIR hyperspectral imaging system for detection of the mechanical damages induced in Manila mango.	Mango	Spectrum band 700–780 nm, 890–900 nm, and 1,070–1,080 nm	Performance of above 90% except for Naïve Bayes and extraordinary high performance of 97.95% for KNN	[29]
OTSU and multi-layer perceptron (ANN)	The wheat grain species classification	Grains	Color, size, and texture	Accuracy 99.92%	[30]

(Continued)

Table 11.2 Plant and fruit detection techniques. (*Continued*)

Method used	Objective	Type	Features	Performance indices	Reference
Sobel + C-V model	Image segmentation of overlapping of cucumber leaves	Overlapping leaves (cucumber)	Color and shape	Accuracy 95.72%	[31]
PCNN and Immune algorithm	Segmentation of cotton leaves images	Cotton leaves	Color (through histogram analysis and mean gray value)	Accuracy 93.50%	[32]
ANN-HS	Segmentation of various plants at different growth levels in a controlled state	Six different types of plants. Potato and mallow etc.	Color (five features among 126 extracting features of five color species RGB, CMY, HIS, HSV, YIQ, and YCbCr)	Accuracy 99.69%	[33]

11.4.2 Harvesting Support

Harvesting is a vital farming practice required to harvest from the fields of mature crops or fruit. Intensive labor is required for identification and harvesting. A manual sorting process is then carried out based on different aspects, such as height, level of maturity, shape, and extent of the injury. Manual sorting takes time and is susceptible to human mistakes, leading to inconsistency in the overall product consistency [32]. Another very critical activity for harvest assistance is fruit counting. An efficient and automated method of fruit counting may enable farmers to optimize their harvest process. A greater understanding of yield fluctuations across sectors will help farmers make more educated and cost-effective labor allocation, storage, packaging, and transportation decisions [34].

Computer vision has been commonly used to simplify the harvest process, enabling the fruit to be processed and counted more efficiently and reliably without intensive labor. There are several variables, however, that make specific tasks complicated and frustrating. Different lighting conditions may cause the color of the fruit to differ, resulting in misclassification. Overlapping fruits make them difficult to spot and can lead to misclassification and miscounting. Since harvesting is about identifying and selecting the mature crop/fruit, various harvesting chosen approaches from literature are presented in Table 11.3, addressing two suitable approaches to fruit scoring and ripeness detection, while Table 11.4 presents the fruit counting and yield prediction.

11.4.3 Plant Health Monitoring Along With Disease Detection

The health of the plant is monitored using computer vision along with machine learning algorithms. It monitors plants and analyzes the health through the algorithm and identifies the diseases, if any. Detection of the disease is complex and challenging, primarily due to the diseased portion's texture and color variations. The effect of change in the lighting environments may also significantly impact the precision of the disease detection. Table 11.5 enlists some of the published articles for weed and disease identification and features on which the developed method depends.

11.4.4 Vision-Based Vehicle Navigation System for Precision Agriculture

An autonomous vehicle can reduce the human resources requirement, increase efficiency, increase application accuracy, and service protection.

Table 11.3 Fruit grading and ripeness detection approaches.

Method used	Objective	Type	Features	Performance indices	Reference
Binarization + Median filter + Morphological analysis	Geometry based sorting of the mango	Mango	Color and geometrical shape and size	Accuracy of 97.00%	[35]
HOG + Otsu's method + Color thresholding	Detection and sizing calculation of on tree mango	Mango	HOG and CIE L*a*b* c	Fruit detection precision of 100% with R^2 value 0.96 and 0.93 for fruit length and width estimation, respectively	[36]
Backpropagation neural network	Early detection of maturity of tomato	Tomato	Color (HIS Model)	Accuracy of 99.31%	[37]
Morphological + automated thresholding (bimodal statistical analysis)	Estimation of olive diameter and mass	Olive	HSV color space and morphological features	The relative error value is below 2.5%	[38]

Table 11.4 Fruit counting and yield prediction.

Method used	Objective	Fruit/plant type	Features	Performance indices	Reference
Circular Hough transform and HSV color transform	Detection of the flowers and counting	Marigold flower	HSV color space	Mean error value of 5%	[39]
CNN and linear regression	Fruit detection and counting of the fruits	Orange and apple	Image pixel-based	Mean error value of 13.8 and 10.5 for orange and apple, respectively	[40]
Histogram thresholding and watershed segmentation	Detection and counting	Citrus	HSV color space	MAE value of 5.75%	[41]
Otsu and BPNN	Early yield prediction	Apple	Color types RGB and HIS with tree canopy	Correlation parameter value of 0.82 and 0.80 respectively	[42]

Table 11.5 Weed and disease detection.

Method used	Objective/task	Fruit/plant type	Features	Performance indices	Reference
Morphological image analysis	Weed detection	Weed in cauliflower plant fields	HSV color space and morphology	Precision value of 99.04% and recall value 98.91%	[43]
PCA and ANN	Weed detection	Weed in sugar beet field	Wavelet texture features	Accuracy of detection 96.00%	[44]
Deep encoding and decoding	Weed detection	Weed detection in a crop field	Color image (RGB) and plan features	Max precision of 98.16%	[45]
Clustering	*L. botrana* recognition	Insect detection in grapes	Color (gradient and grayscale values)	95.10% Specificity	[46]
Support vector machine	Pest detection in strawberry plant	Strawberry plant	HIS color space and morphology of maximum diameter and min diameter	0.471 MSE	[47]

The life of such automated vehicles used for agriculture applications is longer. When navigation is automatic, autonomously controlled robots can help farmers reduce the need for additional human resources and hours to perform the required task. Even farmers can schedule and execute other high-level activities at the same time [48].

Autonomous navigation is environment-friendly and economical since vehicles do not walk through fields meaninglessly but travel optimally to particular areas of interest by picking the shortest routes. Farmers will then make better use of their capital in terms of time and money [49]. Sophisticated sensors were used by early guiding devices, showing technological feasibility [50]. Navigation is currently closely connected to the location of vehicle details in a global or local coordination framework. Global positioning systems (GPS) are commonly used as sensors for global guidance [51, 52]. The poor accuracy of GPS receivers is the biggest downside of GPS-based navigation, and it is around 50 cm. Further, to increase navigation accuracy, machine vision is used with GPS and sensors [53].

Computer vision has technical features and has tremendous navigation systems to mimic a human operator's eyes [52]. The autonomous mobile agricultural robot navigation system consists of navigation sensors, analytical tools, and navigation techniques [54]. Figure 11.2 represents the vision-based vehicle navigation system used to identify the directive for a vehicle, and image processing methods have been used to crop row images. In [55], images of crop rows are marked using Hough transform.

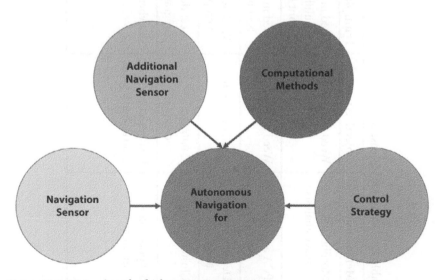

Figure 11.2 Vision-based vehicle navigation system.

The autonomous vehicle's platform uses an E/H steering system, feedforward, and PID steering controller [53, 56]. A computer vision-based row recognition system through Hough transform is intelligently combined to direct an autonomous vehicle around the field [17].

Image pre-processing is done to achieve the image binarization and vertical projection procedure to approximate the image strip crop line's location. The Hough transform determines the identification of crop rows. The autonomous navigation system based on machine vision [57] consists of three stages. Firstly, the camera's tuning is used to obtain the relationship between the coordinates of the image and the earth's coordinates. Then, to achieve a quasi-navigation baseline, pattern recognition, and image processing are used. Finally, via Hough transform, the actual navigation line is extracted from the quasi-navigation baseline.

11.4.5   Vision-Based Mobile Robots for Agriculture Applications

The mobile robots, along with the machine vision, are developed for precision agriculture applications. These mobile robots are designed to serve a specific application for a particular crop. In this series, vision-based mobile robots are mostly used in fruit harvesting. These robots are programmers so that a vision-based system plans the mobile robot path and identifies the matured fruit that needs to be harvested.

Similarly, selective herbicide spraying with mobile robots for weed control. In this, the camera captures the image and it is programmed to identify the weed from the background. The identified plant is spread with the required concentration of the herbicide. The identification of the weed and selective spraying reduces the need for herbicide compared to nap shake spraying. The mobile robot-based system reduces human resources in the agriculture field and reduces the associated cost. Compared to the large implementations suggested for agricultural activities, the narrow line spacing would require thorough treatment and the human operator's fast reaction [55, 58].

Agriculture operations, *viz.*, harvesting, weeding, spraying, transport, agricultural robots, namely, AgroBots, have been introduced. Figures 11.3 and 11.4 show multipurpose agriculture robot and swarm size agriculture robot, respectively. AgroBots can save labor costs, discourage staff from conducting dangerous tasks, and give up-to-date and reliable information to the farmer to support management decisions [61].

Robots are commonly used in the industry for automation, reaching robots in agriculture is relatively uncommon. Compared to agricultural areas, the manufacturing climate is sterile, dry, predictable, and well-lit, while fields have volatile conditions in terms of sun, weather, and terrain

Figure 11.3 The contadino autonomous implement carrier can be used for seeding, weeding, spraying, fertilizing, and monitoring [59].

Figure 11.4 Swarm size agriculture robots [60].

[62, 63]. In comparison, industrial automation requires standardized, essential components that are durable for robotic manipulation, whereas agricultural automation deals with crops that differ in many ways; color, shape, location, and foliage are often covered and handling sensitive. In organized ecosystems and multiple indoor and outdoor agricultural environments, AgroBots have been introduced. In actual field trials, however, only a few vision-guided schemes have been successfully developed and tested.

11.5   Conclusion

In various sectors of agricultural production and industrial food production, computer vision technologies are now commonly used. They can be found in the orange, papaya, almond, potato, citrus, wheat, maize, rice, and soybean grading schemes. Due to the advantages received, its use is justifiable. A straightforward and impartial interpretation of the samples is provided using such systems, providing precise descriptive data. Via these devices, laborious operations may be automated in a non-destructive fashion, generating good results for potential analysis. It was found that current agriculture practices need to be upgraded by the development and utilization of intelligent devices. The final product developed for agriculture automation is integrating computer vision, image processing, and artificial intelligence to automate tasks in the field and incorporate them with agricultural machines and drones. There is a broad scope for exploring advanced computing techniques along with the computer vision for precision agriculture. Expanding GPUs and innovative methods for artificial intelligence are exciting alternatives for future work as well.

References

1. Mahajan, S., Das, A., Sardana, H.K., Image acquisition techniques for assessing legume quality. *Trends Food Sci. Technol.*, 42, 2, 116–133, 2015.
2. Arnal Barbedo, J.G., Digital image processing techniques for detecting, quantifying and classifying plant diseases. *Springerplus*, 2, 1, 1–12, 2013.
3. Mavridou, E., Vrochidou, E., Papakostas, G.A., Pachidis, T., Kaburlasos, V.G., Machine vision systems in precision agriculture for crop farming. *J. Imaging*, 5, (12), 2019.
4. Benson, E.R., Reid, J.F., Zhang, Q., Machine Vision-based Guidance System for Agricultural Grain Harvesters using Cut-edge Detection. *Biosyst. Eng.*, 86, 4, 389–398, 2003.

5. Zareiforoush, H., Minaei, S., Alizadeh, M.R., Banakar, A., Potential Applications of Computer Vision in Quality Inspection of Rice: A Review. *Food Eng. Rev.*, 7, 3, 321–345, 2015.

6. Vithu, P. and Moses, J.A., Machine vision system for food grain quality evaluation: A review. *Trends Food Sci. Technol.*, 56, 13–20, 2016.

7. Mousazadeh, H., A technical review on navigation systems of agricultural autonomous off-road vehicles. *J. Terramechanics*, 50, 3, 211–232, 2013.

8. Zhao, Y., Gong, L., Huang, Y., Liu, C., A review of essential techniques of vision-based control for harvesting robot. *Comput. Electron. Agric.*, 127, 311–323, 2016.

9. Swain, K.C., Zaman, Q.U., Schumann, A.W., Percival, D.C., Bochtis, D.D., Computer vision system for wild blueberry fruit yield mapping. Biosyst. Eng., 106, 4, 389–394, 2010 https://doi.org/10.1016/j.biosystemseng.2010.05.001.

10. Han, L., Haleem, M.S., Taylor, M., A novel computer vision-based approach to automatic detection and severity assessment of crop diseases. *Proc. 2015 Sci. Inf. Conf. SAI 2015*, pp. 638–644, 2015.

11. Marsland, S., *Machine Learning: An Algorithmic Perspective*, Second Edition, Chapman & Hall/CRC, Singapore, Boca Raton, FL, USA, 2014.

12. Liu, M. and Lu, J., Support vector machine—an alternative to artificial neuron network for water quality forecasting in an agricultural nonpoint source polluted river? *Environ. Sci. Pollut. Res.*, 21, 18, 11036–11053, 2014.

13. Li, X., Ma, D., Yin, B., Advance research in agricultural text-to-speech: the word segmentation of analytic language and the deep learning-based end-to-end system. *Comput. Electron. Agric.*, 180, 105908, 2021.

14. Romsdorfer, H. and Pfister, B., Text analysis and language identification for polyglot text-to-speech synthesis. *Speech Commun.*, 49, 9, 697–724, 2007.

15. Yu, J., Zhou, H., Gao, X., Machine learning and signal processing for human pose recovery and behavior analysis. *Signal Process.*, 110, 1–4, 2015.

16. Álvarez, A., Martínez-Hinarejos, C.-D., Arzelus, H., Balenciaga, M., del Pozo, A., Improving the automatic segmentation of subtitles through conditional random field. *Speech Commun.*, 88, 83–95, 2017.

17. Moghaddam, P.A., Arasteh, A.S., Komarizadeh, M.H., Babazadeh, S., Developing a selective thinning algorithm in sugar beet fields using a machine vision system. *Comput. Electron. Agric.*, 122, 133–138, 2016.

18. Parrot Sequoia - The revolutionary multispectral sensor. [Online]. Available: https://www.parrot.com/en/shop/accessories-spare-parts/other-drones/sequoia. [Accessed: 17-Feb-2021].

19. Kim, W.S., Lee, D.H., Kim, Y.J., Kim, T., Lee, W.S., Choi, C.H., Stereo-vision-based crop height estimation for agricultural robots. *Comput. Electron. Agric.*, 181, December 2020, 105937, 2021.

20. Intel® RealSenseTM Technology. [Online]. Available: https://www.intel.in/content/www/in/en/architecture-and-technology/realsense-overview.html. [Accessed: 17-Feb-2021].

21. ZED Stereo Camera | Stereolabs. [Online]. Available: https://www.stereolabs.com/zed/. [Accessed: 17-Feb-2021].

22. Thermal Imaging, Night Vision and Infrared Camera Systems | FLIR Systems. [Online]. Available: https://www.flir.in/. [Accessed: 17-Feb-2021].

23. Digoo 960P Mini Wireless WIFI Home Night Vision Smart Security IP Camera CCD. [Online]. Available: https://www.bihubn.com/index.php?-main_page=product_info&products_id=149800. [Accessed: 17-Feb-2021.

24. Basler ace acA1920-25uc - Area Scan Camera. [Online]. Available: https://www.baslerweb.com/en/products/cameras/area-scan-cameras/ace/aca1920-25uc/. [Accessed: 17-Feb-2021].

25. Malafaia, G., de Araúj, F.G., da Costa Estrela, D., Guimarães, A.T.B., Leandro, W.M., de Lima Rodrigues, A.S., Corn production in soil containing in natura tannery sludge and irrigated with domestic wastewater. *Agric. Water Manage.*, 163, 212–218, 2016.

26. Ji, M., Yang, Y., Zheng, Y., Zhu, Q., Huang, M., Guo, Y., In-field automatic detection of maize tassels using computer vision. *Inf. Process. Agric.*, 8, 1, 87–95, 2021.

27. Dias, P.A., Tabb, A., Medeiros, H., Apple flower detection using deep convolutional networks. *Comput. Ind.*, 99, 17–28, 2018.

28. Behroozi-Khazaei, N. and Maleki, M.R., A robust algorithm based on color features for grape cluster segmentation. *Comput. Electron. Agric.*, 142, 41–49, 2017.

29. Vélez Rivera, N., Gómez-Sanchis, J., Chanona-Pérez, J., Carrasco, J.J., Millán-Giraldo, M., Lorente, D., Cubero, S., Blasco, J., Early detection of mechanical damage in mango using NIR hyperspectral images and machine learning. *Biosyst. Eng.*, 122, 91–98, 2014.

30. Sabanci, K., Kayabasi, A., Toktas, A., Computer vision-based method for classification of wheat grains using artificial neural network. *J. Sci. Food Agric.*, 97, 8, 2588–2593, 2017.

31. Wang, Z., Wang, K., Yang, F., Pan, S., Han, Y., Image segmentation of overlapping leaves based on Chan–Vese model and Sobel operator. *Inf. Process. Agric.*, 5, 1, 1–10, 2018.

32. Zhang, J., Kong, F., Zhai, Z., Wu, J., Han, S., Robust Image Segmentation Method for Cotton Leaf Under Natural Conditions Based on Immune Algorithm and PCNN Algorithm. *Int. J. Pattern Recognit. Artif. Intell.*, 32, 05, 1854011, 2018.

33. Sabzi, S., Abbaspour-Gilandeh, Y., Javadikia, H., Machine vision system for the automatic segmentation of plants under different lighting conditions. *Biosyst. Eng.*, 161, 157–173, 2017.

34. Oppenheim, D., Edan, Y., Shani, G., Detecting tomato flowers in greenhouses using computer vision. *Int. J. Comput. Inf. Eng.*, 11, 1, 104–109, 2017.

35. Momin, M.A., Rahman, M.T., Sultana, M.S., Igathinathane, C., Ziauddin, A.T.M., Grift, T.E., Geometry-based mass grading of mango fruits using image processing. *Inf. Process. Agric.*, 4, 2, 150–160, 2017.

36. Wang, Z., Walsh, K.B., Verma, B., On-tree mango fruit size estimation using RGB-D images. *Sensors (Switzerland)*, 17, 12, 1–15, 2017.

37. Wan, P., Toudeshki, A., Tan, H., Ehsani, R., A methodology for fresh tomato maturity detection using computer vision. *Comput. Electron. Agric.*, 146, February 2017, 43–50, 2018.

38. Ponce, J.M., Aquino, A., Millán, B., Andújar, J.M., Olive-fruit mass and size estimation using image analysis and feature modeling. *Sensors (Switzerland)*, 18, (9), 2018.

39. Sethy, P.K., Routray, B., Behera, S.K., Detection and Counting of Marigold Flower Using Image Processing Technique, in: *Lecture Notes in Networks and Systems*, vol. 41, pp. 87–93, Springer, Singapore, Boca Raton, FL, USA, 2019.

40. Chen, S.W., Shivakumar, S.S., Dcunha, S., Das, J., Okon, E., Qu, C., Taylor, C.J., Kumar, V., Counting Apples and Oranges with Deep Learning: A Data-Driven Approach. *IEEE Robot. Autom. Lett.*, 2, 2, 781–788, 2017.

41. Dorj, U.O., Lee, M., Yun, S.-s., An yield estimation in citrus orchards via fruit detection and counting using image processing. *Comput. Electron. Agric.*, 140, 103–112, 2017.

42. Cheng, H., Damerow, L., Sun, Y., Blanke, M., Early Yield Prediction Using Image Analysis of Apple Fruit and Tree Canopy Features with Neural Networks. *J. Imaging*, 3, 1, 6, 2017.

43. Hamuda, E., Mc Ginley, B., Glavin, M., Jones, E., Automatic crop detection under field conditions using the HSV color space and morphological operations. *Comput. Electron. Agric.*, 133, 97–107, 2017.

44. Bakhshipour, A., Jafari, A., Nassiri, S.M., Zare, D., Weed segmentation using texture features extracted from wavelet sub-images. *Biosyst. Eng.*, 157, 1–12, 2017.

45. Milioto, A., Lottes, P., Stachniss, C., Real-Time Semantic Segmentation of Crop and Weed for Precision Agriculture Robots Leveraging Background Knowledge in CNNs, in: 2018 *IEEE International Conference on Robotics and Automation (ICRA)*, pp. 2229–2235, 2018.

46. García, J., Pope, C., Altimiras, F., A distributed K-means segmentation algorithm applied to Lobesia botrana recognition. *Complexity*, 2017, 1–14, ID 5137317, 2017.

47. Ebrahimi, M.A., Khoshtaghaza, M.H., Minaei, S., Jamshidi, B., Vision-based pest detection based on SVM classification method. *Comput. Electron. Agric.*, 137, 52–58, 2017.

48. Keicher, R. and Seufert, H., Automatic guidance for agricultural vehicles in Europe. *Comput. Electron. Agric.*, 25, 1–2, 169–194, 2000.

49. Radcliffe, J., Cox, J., Bulanon, D.M., Machine vision for orchard navigation. *Comput. Ind.*, 98, 165–171, 2018.

50. Warner, M.G.R. and Harries, G.O., An ultrasonic guidance system for driverless tractors. *J. Agric. Eng. Res.*, 17, 1, 1–9, 1972.

51. *Robotization of Agricultural Vehicles (Part 1): — Component Technologies and Navigation Systems*, Japan International Research Center for Agricultural Sciences | JIRCAS, Japan, 2000.

52. Bell, T., Automatic tractor guidance using carrier-phase differential GPS. *Comput. Electron. Agric.*, 25, 1–2, 53–66, 2000.

53. Han, S., Zhang, Q., Ni, B., Reid, J.F., A guidance directrix approach to vision-based vehicle guidance systems. *Comput. Electron. Agric.*, 43, 3, 179–195, 2004.

54. Wilson, J.N., Guidance of agricultural vehicles - A historical perspective. *Comput. Electron. Agric.*, 25, 1–2, 3–9, 2000.

55. Marchant, J.A., Tracking of row structure in three crops using image analysis. *Comput. Electron. Agric.*, 15, 2, 161–179, 1996.

56. Zhang, Q., Zhang, Q., Reid, J.F., Noguchi, N., Agricultural vehicle navigation using multiple guidance sensors. *Proc. INT. CONF. F. Serv. Robot*, 1999.

57. Jiang, G. and Zhao, C., A vision system based crop rows for agricultural mobile robot. *ICCASM 2010 - 2010 Int. Conf. Comput. Appl. Syst. Model. Proc.*, p. 11, 2010.

58. Muscato, G., Prestifilippo, M., Abbate, N., Rizzuto, I., A prototype of an orange picking robot: Past history, the new robot and experimental results. *Ind. Rob.*, 32, 2, 128–138, 2005.

59. AI, robotics, blockchain make impact, Business | agupdate.com, https://www.agupdate.com/agriview/news/business/ai-robotics-blockchain-make-impact/article_9f70900c-b425-5826-9d42-2a2db2bfcb5f.html.

60. Industry looks to "swarm robots" for sustainable and precise outcomes, FarmingUK News. https://www.farminguk.com/news/industry-looks-to-swarm-robotsfor-sustainable-and-precise-outcomes_51505.html.

61. Ortiz, J.M. and Olivares, M., A vision-based navigation system for an agricultural field robot. *3rd IEEE Lat. Am. Robot. Symp. LARS'06*, pp. 106–114, 2006.

62. Søgaard, H.T. and Lund, I., Application Accuracy of a Machine Vision-controlled Robotic Micro-dosing System. *Biosyst. Eng.*, 96, 3, 315–322, 2007.

63. He, B., Liu, G., Ji, Y., Si, Y., Gao, R., Auto-recognition of navigation path for harvest robot based on machine vision. *IFIP Adv. Inf. Commun. Technol.*, 344 AICT, PART 1, 138–148, 2011.

12

A Novel Approach for Low-Quality Fingerprint Image Enhancement Using Spatial and Frequency Domain Filtering Techniques

Mehak Sood[1]* and Akshay Girdhar[2]

[1]Dept. of Computer Science & Engineering, Chandigarh University, Gharuan, India
[2]Dept. of Information Technology, GNDEC, Ludhiana, India

Abstract

Fingerprints find use in many applications such as law enforcement, health care, and education. Generally, the images of the finger prints are not good quality images because of different input contexts. Most of the existing techniques for enhancing fingerprint images use any one approach: frequency or spatial domain. These techniques are not able to ultimately enhance the complex ridge structure of the images. This chapter proposed a novel algorithm for enhancing the quality of the fingerprint image using frequency and spatial domain both. The frequency and orientation estimations were fed to the Gabor filters bank in the spatial domain to recover the damaged regions and improve the image contrast. The output of the Gabor filter was fed to the frequency domain band-pass filter. The frequency and orientation estimates were done again using the spatial domain–filtered image. The band-pass filter uses these re-estimated estimates to enhance the image further significantly. The results of the proposed algorithm were compared with some of the state-of-the-art techniques over the FVC2004 database. The texture descriptors and minutiae ratios were used to compare the results. Proposed algorithm gives the best texture and achieves a true minutiae ratio (TMR) of 94.82% with a thinning feature extraction technique and a TMR of 90.45% with the mindset feature extraction technique, and low other minutiae ratios as compared to the other state-of-the-art techniques. Moreover, it gives the best results for all the sub-databases of the FVC2004 in comparison with the existing techniques.

*Corresponding author: mehaksood99@gmail.com

Sandeep Kumar, Rohit Raja, Shrikant Tiwari and Shilpa Rani (eds.) *Cognitive Behavior and Human Computer Interaction Based on Machine Learning Algorithm*, (265–300) © 2022 Scrivener Publishing LLC

Keywords: Coherence filtering, fingerprint enhancement, frequency domain filtering, spatial domain filtering, biometrics, fingerprint, image processing

12.1   Introduction

Biometrics is the investigation of consequently perceiving people taking into account their physical and behavioral characteristics. These attributes are also called an individual's biometric characteristics. Biometrics has become an effective person identification tool because of representing a person's intrinsic characteristics. The most crucial decision for a biometric system is to identify an individual [1, 53, 55]. The application's context can be categorized into three systems: identification, verification, and screening [2, 54]. Fingerprints are being used as an identification tool since 300 B.C. The first culture known to have used fingerprints for identification is Chinese [3]. A biometric is judged based on the seven parameters: ubiquity, uniqueness, stability, quantifiability, performance, acceptability, and circumvention. Due to the balance among all parameters, fingerprints are a standout among the most mainstream biometric technologies. They are the most dependable biometric of all. No two persons to date have been found to have similar fingerprints, not even two identical twins. Also, fingerprints are persistent. Even if they get damaged due to some injury or skin disease, they will appear again once the skin is healed because the fingerprint pattern exists far beneath the skin's surface [4].

The two most prominent features of a fingerprint, called minutiae, are as follows:

- Ridge Ending
- Ridge Bifurcation

A ridge ending is a location where a ridge terminates suddenly, and a ridge bifurcation is a location where one ridge gets forked or divided into two or more ridges [5].

The fingerprints images generally are low quality images because different equipment types used to take the print, scars on the skin, dryness or wetness of the skin, the pressure applied on the equipment surface. It is difficult to process these low-quality fingerprints.

Moreover, the earlier manual system which was used to identify fingerprints was too much time-consuming and inefficient. As a result, research work focused on building an efficient Automated Fingerprint Identification System (AFIS). For AFIS to give accurate results, it needs good quality input fingerprint images, which are generally of low-quality for the reasons stated formerly. The process of enhancement of quality of fingerprint images is done by applying various enhancement algorithms.

These algorithms act as a proper pre-processing step in any fingerprint application and do not add any new information to the original fingerprint image; instead, use only the information provided by the original fingerprint image to improve its quality by eliminating noise from the image and highlighting the ROI.

The fingerprint enhancement algorithms are generally two types: the spatial and the frequency domain. The spatial domain methods include Gabor Filters [6, 7], image-scale based filters [8, 9], anisotropic filters [11], directional filters [12, 13], compensation filters [14–16], and residual orientation modeling [17]. Other methods of fingerprints enhancement include frequency-domain methods, such as directional Fourier filters [18], wavelets [20], Log-Gabor filters [19], STFT [21], FFT [22], DCT [23, 24], and so on. Some techniques use both the domains, such as Stationary Wavelet Transform (SWT) and spatial domain filtering [25]. Gabor filters in the frequency domain with histogram equalization and so on.

Spatial domain performs direct manipulation of pixels. Spatial domain techniques involve the convolution of the filter kernel with the fingerprint image, a simple process [26–28]. The spatial domain techniques join the broken ridges, improve contrast, remove noise, and take care of the local fingerprint features because its operation affects individual pixels. However, these techniques produce blurring effect in the image [29, 30].

Frequency domain techniques involve manipulating Fourier transforms of an image and inverse transforms to get the processed image [32–35]. Frequency domain techniques calculate convolution on the complete image rather than individual pixels, making them remove more noise than spatial domain techniques [36–38]. The frequency-domain techniques join the broken ridges, remove the noise, improve the contrast of the image, and sharpen the ridges, making a clear distinction between ridges and valleys. However, as they operate on the complete image, they miss out on the fingerprint image's local information.

As has been observed from the latest fingerprint enhancement trends, the focus has shifted from using either spatial or frequency domain techniques to using both of them [39–43]. The leading cause of this shifting is because each of the categories has its pros and cons.

Although some work has been done to enhance low-quality fingerprint images in different domains, there are still problems like high computational intensity and inefficiency in enhancing the quality of the fingerprint images [44–47].

Therefore, to fill the existing research gaps, a novel fingerprint image enhancement method is proposed in this paper [48, 49]. The proposed algorithm uses techniques from both domains to enhance the quality of fingerprint image.

Fingerprint images are quite different from other grayscale images like facial images, hand geometry images, digital signatures, and hand vein images [50, 51]. The credit for this uniqueness goes to the fingerprint images' unique structure, which includes frequent changes in the ridges' orientation, continuous changes in the gray levels due to adjacent ridges and valleys placement, and so on.

The techniques involved in the proposed algorithm were chosen with the utmost care so that they appropriately take care of the characteristics of the fingerprint images. The highlights of the proposed algorithm are discussed below:

1. The coherence filtering involves optimized rotation invariant anisotropic diffusion filtering, which smooth the image in the ridges' direction. It helps in joining the broken ridges and removing the noise.
2. The ridge filter, which involves a bank of Gabor filters explicitly selected according to the ridge orientation and frequency, is applied to the coherence-enhanced image. Using this step ridges and valleys will be separated. It is helpful to recover the damaged region and also produces the blurring effect of the image.
3. Band-pass filter is applied which used re-estimated ridge orientation and frequency estimation.
4. The proposed algorithm is able to combine the broken ridges, clarifies the ridges and valleys region, and recovers the damaged regions if present, de-noising, contrast enhancement, and smoothes the ridges.

The remaining chapter is designed as follows. The existing related work is discussed in Section 12.2. The detailed design and implementation are discussed in the following Section 12.3. Results are discussed in Section 12.4. Section 12.5 describes the conclusion and future scope.

12.2   Existing Works for the Fingerprint Ehancement

Fingerprint image enhancement techniques are of two types: spatial and frequency domains. Many algorithms have been developed using either spatial domain or frequency domain, or both of them.

12.2.1   Spatial Domain

Spatial domain techniques involve direct manipulation of pixel's gray level values while processing. Spatial domain techniques involve the convolution of the filter kernel with the fingerprint image, a simple process. A smaller kernel is chosen to make the computation more straightforward and more time-efficient. The spatial domain filters work on local regions of the image rather than the whole image, making them remove less noise than frequency-domain techniques.

Hong et al. [5] proposed an algorithm to improve the quality of fingerprint images where the authors first marked the fingerprint image's area into three classes, i.e., well-specified, unrecoverable, and recoverable corrupted region. Firstly, the image is normalized and then the local frequency and region kernel is approximated. These approximations are then fed to the group of perfectly oriented directional Gabor filtering masks to get the ultimately enhanced fingerprint image. The filter used has a unique feature to select the orientation and frequency of the image. Ridges and valley organization is enhanced adaptively by the proposed fast fingerprint enhancement algorithm. Though this algorithm enhances the fingerprint image compared to the original image, it gives some errors in estimating the orientation of the ridges and region mask classification.

Greenberg et al. [10] proposed two methods to enhance fingerprint images in the spatial domain. However, both methods show some improvement in terms of average error, efficiency, and speed compared to the other state-of-the-art techniques. However, the proposed method does not use optimum fingerprint orientation and ridge frequency, which leaves a scope of improvement in the proposed method.

Gottschlichet et al. [6] proposed an algorithm to improve the ridge structure of the fingerprint image by removing the noise. Gottschlich introduced Gabor Filters, which are curved, and these curved filters adapt their shape locally according to the ridges' orientation field in the fingerprint image. A combination of two existing algorithms for estimating orientation, i.e., the line sensor method [26] and the gradient-based method [27], is used to build a more robust method. The idea of this fusion is taken from 2008. The curved regions are constructed using this orientation, which is then used to estimate local ridge frequency. These parameters, i.e., orientation and frequency, are finally used in curved Gabor filters to enhance the low-quality fingerprint images. The proposed combination achieves the lowest Equal Error Rate (EER) of 6.39, 3.45, 1.66, and 1.33 for FVC2004 databases DB1, DB2, DB3, and DB4, respectively, as compared to the other combinations. Though the proposed filter upgrades the images, its running time is very high, limiting its use in time-efficient applications.

More variations of the frequency domain techniques can be found [29, 52].

12.2.2 Frequency Domain

Frequency domain techniques involve manipulating Fourier transforms of an image and inverse transforms to get the processed image. Frequency domain techniques calculate convolution on the complete image rather than individual pixels, making them remove more noise than spatial domain techniques.

Chikkerur et al. [31] proposed two algorithms for fingerprint image enhancement and minutiae extraction. The enhancement algorithm works in the frequency domain and simultaneously calculates the frequency, orientation, and image quality. The mean sensitivity of 79.40% and specificity of 85.29% is produced by proposed algorithm, but damaged regions in enhanced images are not fully recovered.

Chikkerur et al. [21] suggested an enhancement technique based on Short-Time Fourier Transform (STFT) analysis to enhance the poor-quality fingerprint images. The proposed algorithm calculates the frequency image, orientation image, and region kernel in the unified process of STFT. In this, the orientation estimation is probabilistic and accordingly does not experience the ill effects of exceptions. The algorithm made complete use of available contextual information like orientation, frequency, coherence, and reliability. It achieves a 24.6% relative improvement in the FVC2002 database. However, due to complicated input contexts, the non-recoverable damaged regions are not recovered properly by simple STFT analysis and need improvement.

Wang et al. [19] suggested a wavelet domain-based algorithm for improving the ridge clarity and structure of the input image. The first step involves dividing the input image into four sub-bands by a two-dimensional (2D) discrete wavelet transform. Then, based on the referred Gaussian template, the compensation coefficient is adaptively obtained for each sub-band. The algorithm improves ridge continuity and ridge structure, reduces noise, and achieves a more significant singular points (core, delta) identification rate. It achieves better classification accuracy as compared to exiting methods. However, there are overlapping issues in classifying S-type and E-type patterns.

More variations of the frequency domain techniques can be found in Raja *et al.* [52].

12.2.3   Hybrid Approach

The algorithms that come under this category used both the spatial domain and the frequency domain.

Kale *et al.* [25] proposed a low-quality and noisy fingerprint image enhancement algorithm. This algorithm uses a SWT along with morphology functions, mask identification, and spatial domain filtering. Texture descriptors show that the proposed method improves the original fingerprint image's texture, but it cannot recover the more damaged regions of the fingerprint image.

Bartunek *et al.* [34] proposed fingerprint enhancement method, which improves the methods proposed. The authors used a nonlinear dynamic range adjustment method and order statistical filters. Image segmentation is also done to separate the foreground and background data of the enhanced image. Though this algorithm improves contrast, removes false minutiae points, improves EER by a factor of 2 and Area above Curve (AAC) by a factor of 12 as compared to the existing method, the significance of various parameters chosen in the algorithm is not statistically justified. Moreover, the process is computationally very expensive.

Dyre and Sumathi [35] proposed a method to improve fingerprint images' quality using Gaussian band-pass filter and Fast Fourier Transforms (FFT). The method comprises first segmenting and then normalizing the image in spatial domain. After this, FFT is computed and the Gaussian band-pass filter is applied to the FFT of the image. Finally, inverse FFT is applied to get the enhanced image. The proposed method achieves Peak Signal–to-Noise Ratio (PSNR) of 26.4865 dB and a computation time of 0.8644 seconds. It gives better PSNR than other filters such as Butterworth high pass, Butterworth band pass, and Gaussian high pass filter, but it does not take into account essential fingerprint features such as ridge frequency and orientation. Moreover, this method is not efficient in improving very low-quality fingerprint images.

More variations of the hybrid approach techniques can be found in Kocevar *et al.* [36].

12.3   Design and Implementation of the Proposed Algorithm

According to the literature survey, the existing techniques do not always relatively enhance quality of input images. To remove the limitations of the existing techniques, a new and useful method is proposed in this paper. The proposed algorithm uses both the spatial and the frequency domains to enhance the low-quality fingerprint images, as shown in Figure12.1.

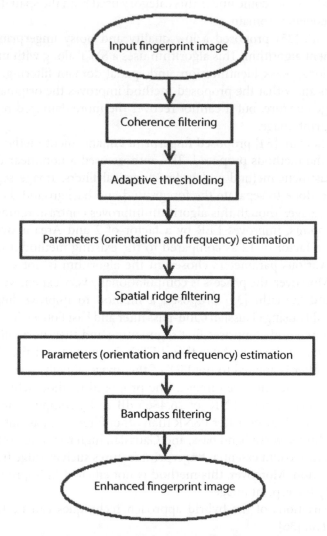

Figure 12.1 Flowchart of proposed algorithm. Workflow diagram.

The algorithm first enhances the input fingerprint image using the coherence filtering in the spatial domain followed by spatial ridge filtering. Band-pass filtering is then used in the frequency domain to enhance the spatial domain–filtered image further. The fingerprint parameters (ridge orientation and ridge frequency) are estimated separately in both domains. The detailed procedure is discussed as follows:

12.3.1   Enhancement in the Spatial Domain

The proposed algorithm involves enhancing the input fingerprint image firstly in the spatial domain. This phase involves first enhancing the image using a scale-space and image-restoration technique called coherence filtering. It makes use of orientation analysis and non-diffusion filtering. This step smoothens the ridges but image has blurring effects. Then, adaptive thresholding was done, which dynamically segments the image. This was followed by orientation and frequency estimation is performed. Finally, these estimates were used in the spatial ridge filter to enhance the fingerprint image. This phase enhances the images keeping ridges orientation and frequency intact but produces an overall blurring effect removed in the proposed algorithm's next phase. The steps involved in this phase are coherence filtering, adaptive thresholding, orientation estimation, frequency estimation, and spatial ridge filtering. These steps are discussed below:

1. *Coherence filtering*: This step was used to smooth the fingerprint ridges using a scale-space–based coherence-enhancing anisotropic diffusion filter with optimized rotation invariance. This technique is especially useful in restoring flow-like textures with line-like structures [37]. It uses a combination of non-linear anisotropic diffusion filtering and orientation analysis using structure tensors. This technique [38] is used to enhance cone-beam CT data [39, 40]. Here, it is proposed to be used to smooth the ridges of the low-quality fingerprint images.

The steps involved in each of the iterations are discussed below:

- The image is smoothened using a Gaussian filter with single dimension Gaussian kernels to calculate the gradients better.
- Find the Gaussian gradients using Scharr's rotation invariant stencil notations. The stencils used are shown in

Equation (12.1). F_x and F_y are first-order derivative filter kernels also called stencils in the x-axis and y-axis, respectively. Gradients in the x-axis and y-axis are represented by u_x and u_y, respectively.

$$F_x = \frac{1}{32}\begin{bmatrix} 3 & 10 & 3 \\ 0 & 0 & 0 \\ -3 & -10 & -3 \end{bmatrix} \text{ and }$$

$$F_y = \frac{1}{32}\begin{bmatrix} 3 & 0 & -3 \\ 10 & 0 & -10 \\ 3 & 0 & -3 \end{bmatrix} \tag{12.1}$$

- Calculate the structure tensor (J_p matrix), also known as scatter matrix, second-order matrix, or Forstner interest operator. It is calculated using Equation (12.2). ∇u is the spatial gradient of image u. Again, Gaussian smoothening is done to smooth the calculated structure tensor.

$$J_p(\nabla u) = \nabla u * \nabla u^T \tag{12.2}$$

- Compute the eigenvalues (v_1, v_2) and eigenvectors (μ_1, μ_2) of the structure tensor. The formulas used to calculate values and vectors are shown in Equations (12.3) to (12.8).

$$v_{2x} = 2 * J_{xy} \tag{12.3}$$

$$v_{2y} = J_{yy} - J_{xx} + \sqrt{(J_{xx} - J_{yy})^2 + 4 * J_{xy}^2} \tag{12.4}$$

$$v_{1x} = -v_{2y} \tag{12.5}$$

$$v_{1y} = v_{2x} \tag{12.6}$$

$$\mu_1 = 0.5 * \left(J_{xx} + J_{yy} + \sqrt{(J_{xx} - J_{yy})^2 + 4 * J_{xy}^2} \right) \tag{12.7}$$

$$\mu_2 = 0.5 * \left(J_{xx} + J_{yy} - \sqrt{(J_{xx} - J_{yy})^2 + 4 * J_{xy}^2} \right) \tag{12.8}$$

where x and y are pixel coordinates, and J_{xx}, J_{yy}, and J_{xy} are elements of J_p matrix calculated in the previous step.

- Construct the edge-preserving diffusion tensors (D). The eigenvalues of D are calculated using Equations (12.9) and (12.10), and these use eigenvectors identical to that of the structure tensor.

$$\lambda_1 = c_1 \tag{12.9}$$

$$\lambda_2 = \begin{cases} c_1 & \text{if } \mu_1 = \mu_2, \\ c_1 + (1 - c_1)e^{\left(\frac{-c_2}{(\mu_1 - \mu_2)^2}\right)} & \text{else,} \end{cases} \tag{12.10}$$

where λ_1 and λ_2 are eigenvalues of D, μ_1 and μ_2 are eigenvectors of the structure tensor, $c_1 \in (0, 1)$, and $c_2 > 0$.

The diffusion tensors (D_{xx}, D_{xy}, D_{yy}) are given by Equations (12.11) to (12.13). v_1 and v_2 are eigenvalues of D, and x and y are pixel coordinates.

$$D_{xx} = \lambda_1 * (v_{1x})^2 + \lambda_2 * (v_{2x})^2 \tag{12.11}$$

$$D_{xy} = \lambda_1 * v_{1x} * v_{1y} + \lambda_2 * v_{2x} * v_{2y} \tag{12.12}$$

$$D_{yy} = \lambda_1 * (v_{1y})^2 + \lambda_2 * (v_{2y})^2 \tag{12.13}$$

- Calculation of flux components (J_1, J_2) using Equations (12.14) and (12.15).

$$J_1 = D_{xx} * u_x + D_{xy} * u_y \tag{12.14}$$

$$J_2 = D_{xy} * u_x + D_{yy} * u_y \tag{12.15}$$

D_{xx}, D_{xy}, and D_{yy} are diffusion tensors, u_x and u_y are image gradients along x and y-direction.

- Use the optimized derivative filters to calculate the value of Equation (12.16).

$$\nabla.(D\nabla u) = \partial_x * J_1 + \partial_x * J_2 \tag{12.16}$$

D is the diffusion tensor, ∂_x and ∂_x are the derivatives in x and y direction, respectively, and J_1 and J_2 are the 2D flux components.
- Explicitly update the value using Equation (12.17).

$$u = u + (\nabla.(D\nabla u)) * \partial t \qquad (12.17)$$

where u is the image, D is the diffusion tensor, ∇u is the image gradient, and t is the diffusion time.

All the above steps are repeated for all the iteration. In the proposed algorithm, the number of iterations is empirically chosen to be 15. This iterative process proved to be quite useful in smoothing the low-quality fingerprint image.

2. *Adaptive thresholding*: This step is useful in thresholding the image dynamically, which reduces intensity variations locally and homogenizes the intensities across the image. Though it does not improve the ridge structure's clarity, this processing step is beneficial for efficiently working on the next processing steps of the proposed work. The global thresholding method can also be used here, but its drawback is that it does not absorb varying image illumination. Instead, the global method brings the image to a particularly mean and variance that is not as efficient as the adaptive thresholding used in the present work.

A window of size 16×16 is used for the purpose. The window size is chosen empirically. The steps [41] involved in the adaptive thresholding are listed below:

- Perform the convolution of the coherence filtered image with the mean.
- Then, subtract the coherence filtered image from the convolved image.
- Perform the thresholding on the output of the above step according to the set threshold. In the proposed algorithm, the threshold is empirically chosen to be 0.01.

The image is divided into a block of 16×16 and a mask is generated according to a threshold value by inverting the threshold image. This mask will be used in the next processing steps.

3. *Orientation estimation*: This step is used to find the orientation of the ridges of the threshold fingerprint image. Orientation

is one of the essential parameters to enhance the fingerprint image correctly. Hence, great precision should be used while performing this step. The technique used in the proposed algorithm is similar to the one used. The orientation is an estimated block wise and each block is assigned orientation according to the most prominent orientation in that block. In this step, the following step is performed on each of the blocks:

- Find the image gradients (G_x, G_y) using the gradient method.
- Then, find each block's orientation using the formulas mentioned in Equations (12.18) to (12.20). Gaussian smoothing of the gradients is performed to estimate the orientation better as it removes the gradient values' ambiguities.

$$G_{xy} = \sum_{u=i-(w/2)}^{i+(w/2)} \sum_{v=j-(w/2)}^{j+(w/2)} 2\, G_x(u,v)G_y(u,v) \qquad (12.18)$$

$$G_{xx} = \sum_{u=i-(w/2)}^{i+(w/2)} \sum_{v=j-(w/2)}^{j+(w/2)} \left(G_x^2(u,v) - G_y^2(u,v)\right) \qquad (12.19)$$

$$O(x,y) = \frac{1}{2} tan^{-1}\left(\frac{G_{xy}}{G_{xx}}\right) \qquad (12.20)$$

where (u, v) are pixel coordinates, G_{xy} and G_{xx} is blocked vertical and horizontal gradients, w is the window size, and $O(x, y)$ is the block orientation.

4. *Frequency estimation*: This step is used to find the ridge frequency, another critical parameter of the fingerprint image after orientation. The image pixel's gray level values can be represented as a sine wave perpendicular to the ridge orientation and this property makes the ridge frequency an essential parameter of the fingerprint image. The threshold image, orientation image, and mask are already evaluated; all these are used to estimate the ridge frequency. Again, the image is divided into blocks of size 36 × 36, and frequency is calculated blockwise. For each block, the following steps are followed:

- As there are noise and corrupted regions in the fingerprint image, the orientation estimates need to be corrected. The new orientation is estimated by finding the mean of the doubled sine and cosine angles to do this. The formula of the new orientation is given in Equations (12.21) to (12.23).

$$G'_{xy} = \mu(\sin(2*O(x,y)))$$ (12.21)

$$G'_{xx} = \mu(\cos(2*O(x,y)))$$ (12.22)

$$O'(x,y) = \frac{1}{2} tan^{-1}\left(\frac{G'_{xy}}{G'_{xx}}\right)$$ (12.23)

G'_{xy} and G'_{xx} are averaged gradient values, $O'(x, y)$ is the new estimated orientation values, and μ represents the mean.
- Find the peaks in the gray level values and then determine the ridges' spatial frequency by dividing the distance between the first and last peaks by one less than the total number of peaks.

5. *Spatial ridge filtering:* This is the actual filtering step where the two essential parameters (orientation and frequency) that are already estimated in the previous steps enhance the spatial domain's fingerprint image. Gabor filters, as used in [5], are used to solve the purpose. These filters have both orientation and frequency-selective properties, making them most suitable to deal with images with curved structures. The general form of Gabor filters is shown in Equations (12.24) to (12.26).

$$h(x,y:O,f) = e\left\{-\frac{1}{2}\left[\frac{x_o^2}{\delta_x^2} + \frac{y_o^2}{\delta_y^2}\right]\right\} \cos 2\pi f x_o$$ (12.24)

$$x_o = x \cos o + y \sin o$$ (12.25)

$$y_o = -x \sin o + y \cos o$$ (12.26)

where o is the orientation of the Gabor filter, f is the frequency of sine wave, and δ_x and δ_y are space constants of Gaussian envelope in the direction of the x-axis and y-axis.

The steps [5] involved in filtering are listed below:

- Find the distinct spatial orientations and frequencies in the fingerprint image using the orientation and frequency estimates.
- Generate the filters for these unique orientations and frequencies.
- Apply the filters to enhance the image.

In the spatial domain processing, although the broken ridges are connected and noise is removed simultaneously, a blurring effect is produced. The spatially filtered image is then passed to the next phase, where using frequency domain techniques, the blurring effect is removed and the image is finally enhanced to remove this effect.

12.3.2   Enhancement in the Frequency Domain

This phase involves enhancing the image using a contextual band-pass filter in the frequency domain. It removes the drawbacks of the spatial domain processing phase and produces sharp ridges with no blurring effect. The processing done is block-wise and the image is divided into blocks of size 16×16 [31]. Firstly, the Fourier transform of the ridge filtered image block is calculated. Then, orientation and frequency are estimated. These estimates are corrected using Gaussian smoothing and then used in the calculation of the coherence image. Finally, band-pass filtering is done using an angular filter. The enhanced image is reconstructed using the inverse Fourier transforms. The steps involved in this phase are FFT, energy map thresholding, orientation estimation, frequency estimation, Gaussian smoothing, coherence image, band-pass filtering, and Inverse Fast Fourier Transform (IFFT). These steps are discussed below:

1. *Fast Fourier Transforms (FFT)*: This step is used to convert the spatial domain image into the frequency domain image using a process called FFT. As the processing is done block-wide in the proposed work, FFT is also calculated blockwise by removing the Direct Current (DC) component.
2. *Energy map thresholding*: This step [31] is used to segment the image. The segmentation is based on the fact that the energy content is shallow in the Fourier spectrum in the regions of noise or where no ridges are present. The expression of the energy image is given in Equation (12.27).

Each value represents the energy value of that block and the fingerprint image is thresholded based on a threshold energy value. Blocks value is less than the threshold value are considered in the background region, while those with a value higher than the threshold value are considered part of the foreground.

$$E = \sum_u \sum_v |F(u,v)|^2 \qquad (12.27)$$

where E denotes the block's energy, $F(u, v)$ is the Fourier spectrum of the block. Then, to obtain a linear scale, the logarithm of the energy map is taken.

3. *Orientation estimation*: This step is used to find the orientation of the fingerprint ridges block-wise. Orientation estimation was also performed in the spatial domain processing phase. Here, it is done again, but this time orientation is estimated using phase one, which helps correct the estimates as ridge structure has improved because of the filtering. The method used to calculate the orientation is similar to the one used. The formulas to calculate the orientation are given in the polar form Equations (12.28) to (12.30).

$$f(r,\varnothing) = \frac{|F(r,\varnothing)|^2}{\int_r^\Box \int_\varnothing^\Box |F(r,\varnothing)|^2 \, d\varnothing dr} \qquad (12.28)$$

$$f(\varnothing) = \int_r^\Box f(r,\varnothing)dr, f(\varnothing) = \int_\varnothing^\Box f(r,\varnothing)d\varnothing, \qquad (12.29)$$

$$E\{\varnothing\} = \int_\varnothing^\Box \varnothing \cdot f(\varnothing) \, d\varnothing \qquad (12.30)$$

$F(r, \varnothing)$ is the Fourier spectrum of the block, $f(r, \varnothing)$ is the probability density function (PDF), $f(\varnothing)$ and $f(r)$ are marginal density functions, $E(\varnothing)$ is the orientation value considering the PDF $f(\varnothing)$, and $\varnothing$ is a random variable.

4. *Frequency estimation*: This step [31] is used to find out the inter-ridge separation, i.e., ridge frequency block-wise. It is one of the essential parameters of a fingerprint image. The frequency estimation is done similarly to the orientation estimation using PDF in Equation (12.29). The frequency value is assumed to be a random variable with PDF(*fr*). The formula for the ridge frequency is given in Equation (12.31).

$$E\{r\} = \int_{\emptyset}^{\square} r \cdot f(r)\, dr \qquad (12.31)$$

$E\{r\}$ is the ridge frequency, $\emptyset$ is rare random variables of PDF, and (*fr*) is the marginal density function.

5. *Gaussian smoothing*: This step is used for smoothening the orientation and frequency estimates using Gaussian smoothing. It helps in correcting the estimates as done. The Gaussian method uses a Gaussian mask of size 5×5 to smoothen the orientation image. The smoothing operation can be performed several times according to the requirement. In the proposed work, orientation smoothing is done three times. A Gaussian mask of size 3×3 and the diffusion process as done to smoothen the frequency image.

6. *Coherence image*: This step is used to find the coherence image, which tells about the central pixel orientation relationship concerning its adjacent pixels in the orientation map. It is associated with the dispersion measure of circular data. The formula to compute the coherence image is given in Equation (12.32).

$$c(x,y) = \frac{\sum_{(i,j)\in W} \left|\cos\big(O(x,y) - O(x_i, y_i)\big)\right|}{W \times W} \qquad (12.32)$$

where $c(x, y)$ is the coherence image, W is the window size, $O(x, y)$ is the central pixel orientation, and $O(x_i, \ )$ Yi is the adjacent pixels' orientation. The coherence is high if adjacent pixels have a similar orientation as the central pixel or other coherence is low. The coherence image is then used in the next step to finding out the bandwidth of the angular filter.

7. *Band-pass filtering*: This is the foremost filtering step in the frequency domain. The filtering is done block-wise by dividing the image into a 16×16 block. Bandwidth is calculated using the coherence image computed in the previous step. It is assumed that f (Ø) is unimodal and centered on E{Ø} and bandwidth is defined as the angular extent where {|Ø − E{Ø}| < Ø$_{BW}$} = 0.5. This lets the angular bandwidth enable itself in the regions of high curvature. The block-wise filtering is done using the formula given in Equations (12.33) and (12.34).

$$H_r(r) = \sqrt{\frac{(rr_{BW})^{2n}}{(rr_{BW})^{2n} + (r^2 - r_{BW}{}^2)^{2n}}} \qquad (12.33)$$

$$H_r(\emptyset) = \begin{cases} \cos^2 \dfrac{\pi(\emptyset - \emptyset_c)}{2\emptyset_{BW}} & \text{if } |\emptyset - \emptyset_c| \leq \emptyset_{BW} \\[2mm] 0, & \text{otherwise} \end{cases} \qquad (12.34)$$

where r_{BW} is the radial bandwidth, $\emptyset_{BW}$ is the angular bandwidth, $\emptyset_c$ is the mean orientation of the block, and r is the random variable of PDF.

The band-pass filter's output is the final enhanced image in the frequency domain and then passed onto the next step to transform it into the spatial domain.

8. *Inverse Fourier Transforms (IFFT)*: This step is used to reconstruct the enhanced image from the Fourier domain processed image using the function given in Equation (12.35).

$$\textit{Enhanced Image} = \text{IFFT }(I) \qquad (12.35)$$

where *I* is the Fourier domain processed image. It brings the enhanced image from the Fourier domain to the spatial domain.

12.4   Results and Discussion

In this section, the proposed work results and the other state-of-the-art techniques are presented and discussed. The public Fingerprint

Verification Competition (FVC) databases (FVC2000, FVC2002, and FVC2004) have been developed as a benchmark to test the performance of the state-of-the-art techniques in fingerprints recognition systems. To compare the results, the images from the most challenging database among these, i.e., FVC2004, are chosen to test the proposed algorithm's efficiency and compare it with the other state-of-the-art techniques [49]. This database is said to be difficult because it contains more low-quality images than the other mentioned databases. FVC2004 set_b database chosen here consists of four sub-databases. Each sub-database consists of 80 fingerprints (i.e., there are 10 persons and each person is all eight fingerprints are included) in 256 gray-scale levels. The images of all these sub-databases are taken using different techniques. The details about which are discussed below:

- The sub-database images, i.e., DB1_B, are taken using optical sensor "V300" with size 640 × 480 pixels at 500 dpi.
- The images of the sub-database, i.e., DB2_B, are taken using the optical sensor "U.are.U 4000" with size 328 × 364 pixels at 500 dpi.
- The sub-database images, i.e., DB3_B, are taken using sweeping thermal sensor "FingerChip FCD4B17CB" with 300 × 3480 pixels 512 dpi.
- The sub-database images, i.e., DB4_B, are taken using synthetic fingerprint generation with size 288 × 384 pixels at 500 dpi (approximately).

The experimental results were conducted on a notebook (Intel Core i5-2410M, 2.30GHZ CPU, and 2.75 GB RAM) having Microsoft Windows 7 Ultimate (32-bit) operating system [52]. The implementation was performed on the MATLAB 2017a platform.

12.4.1 Visual Analysis

First, the original images are of low quality with broken ridges, merged ridges and valleys, noise, less smoothening, low contrast, and damaged regions with missing ridges.

Coherence filtering is smoothing the image well, joining the broken ridges, and removing noise but has limitations for being unable to recover the damaged regions and improve the contrast. Moreover, it produces an additional blurring effect, which makes the distinction between ridges and valleys difficult.

Gabor filtering joins the broken ridges at some places, removes noise, and improves contrast but produces a blurring effect, making the distinction between ridges and valleys difficult. It is unable to recover the ridges in more damaged regions.

Fourier filtering is found to join the broken ridges at some places, improves contrast, removes noise, and sharpens the image but cannot recover the ridges

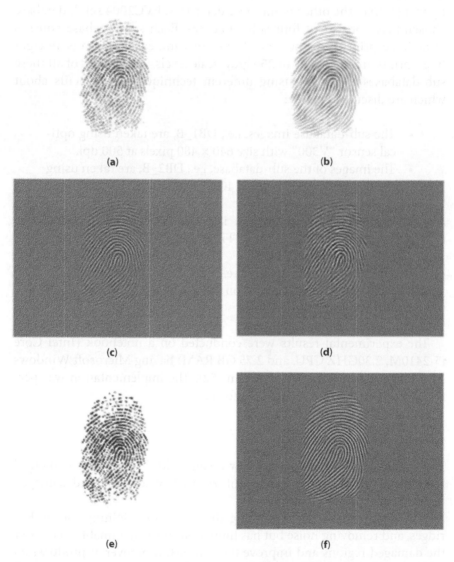

(a)

(b)

(c)

(d)

(e)

(f)

Figure 12.2 (a) Original image (DB1 107_2.tif). (b) Coherence filter. (c) Gabor filter. (d) Fourier analysis. (e) Hybrid approach. (f) Proposed algorithm.

in more damaged regions. Moreover, the image is not adequately smoothed. It can be easily observed that discontinuities still exist in the image.

The hybrid approach improves image contrast but cannot join the broken ridges, remove noise, and distinguish between ridges and valleys. Moreover, smoothing is not done, damaged regions are not recovered.

Finally, in the proposed algorithm, it can be observed that it enhances the images in the best possible way among all the techniques. Broken ridges are correctly joined, damaged areas are recovered, discontinuities are removed, noise is removed, image is very smooth, contrast is improved, and proper distinction can be made between ridges and valleys.

Though in this section, the proposed algorithm is said to be the best by visual analysis. In the following sections, this fact is proved quantitatively with performance metrics such as texture descriptors and minutiae ratios.

12.4.2   Texture Descriptor Analysis

To compare the quality of fingerprint images produced by the proposed algorithm and the other existing techniques, texture descriptors as used were used here. Tables 12.1 to 12.4 show texture descriptor results for images from the four sub-databases of FVC2004.

A good quality input image must have low mean, high standard deviation, high entropy, and high smoothness. On observing the results presented in Tables 12.1 to 12.4, it is quite evident that the proposed algorithm gives the desired values in almost all the cases as compared to the existing methods. Besides being individually better than the other methods, it can be concluded that combining the coherence filtering, Gabor filtering, and Fourier analysis, which is the basic idea of the proposed algorithm, is an optimal choice. This statement is made by keenly observing the texture descriptors' values, which shows that the proposed algorithm outperforms all three constituent schemes. It is also essential to notice that at some places, one or the other method gives the better or almost the same value for some descriptor as compared to the proposed algorithm. However, this observation cannot deny that overall the proposed algorithm gives much better results compared to existing methods.

12.4.3   Minutiae Ratio Analysis

A quantitative assessment of the performance of the proposed enhancement algorithm is done by using ratios as used. Thinning technique is used to extract the fingerprint features. The minutiae ratios are computed

Table 12.1 Texture descriptor results for FVC2004DB1 107_2.tif.

Technique / Descriptor	Original image	Coherence filter [38]	Gabor filter [18]	Fourier analysis [31]	Hybrid approach [35]	Proposed algorithm
Mean	250.6085	250.5816	133.0879	128.2401	246.3166	128.1986
Standard deviation	20.2554	16.9302	13.7880	12.2531	46.2480	25.2929
Entropy	1.0041	1.5069	2.0616	2.0066	0.2173	2.5120
Smoothness	0.9976	0.9965	0.9948	0.9957	0.9995	0.9984

Table 12.2 Texture descriptor results for FVC2004DB2 101_2.tif.

Technique / Descriptor	Original image	Coherence filter [38]	Gabor filter [18]	Fourier analysis [51]	Hybrid approach [35]	Proposed algorithm
Mean	188.3364	188.3175	132.4949	132.1800	76.1997	127.3117
Standard deviation	35.3396	33.4621	29.3635	36.8116	116.7246	43.6397
Entropy	6.2192	6.2130	5.9122	5.9073	0.8798	7.2423
Smoothness	0.9992	0.9991	0.9988	0.9993	0.9999	0.9995

Table 12.3 Texture descriptor results for FVC2004DB3 107_7.tif.

Technique / Descriptor	Original image	Coherence filter [38]	Gabor filter [18]	Fourier analysis [31]	Hybrid approach [35]	Proposed algorithm
Mean	69.5801	69.8131	127.1067	124.3121	79.1279	126.2747
Standard deviation	69.8333	58.8977	35.1768	42.8226	117.9682	43.1717
Entropy	5.4402	7.2846	6.1297	7.0794	0.8935	7.3025
Smoothness	0.9998	0.9997	0.9992	0.9995	0.9999	0.9995

Table 12.4 Texture descriptor results for FVC2004DB4 110_8.tif.

Technique / Descriptor	Original image	Coherence filter [38]	Gabor filter [18]	Fourier analysis [31]	Hybrid approach [35]	Proposed algorithm
Mean	161.2369	161.2330	171.8968	132.0633	184.5471	128.1966
Standard deviation	25.8711	23.4026	32.1160	27.2480	117.0263	44.5906
Entropy	6.5064	6.4072	5.8752	5.7955	0.8503	6.9277
Smoothness	0.9985	0.9982	0.9990	0.9987	0.9999	0.9995

separately for both these feature extraction techniques. The outputs for FVC2004DB1 107_2.tif for both these images are shown in Figure 12.3. Three images are chosen randomly from each of the four sub-databases of FVC2004. Tables 12.5 and 12.6 represents these results.

For a right quality image, the true minutiae ratio (TMR) should be high, and the false minutiae ratio (FMR), dropped minutiae ratio (DMR), and exchanged minutiae ratio (EMR) should be low. It can be seen that the proposed algorithm has the highest TMR ratio (94.82%) among all the methods, while other ratios for it are the least.

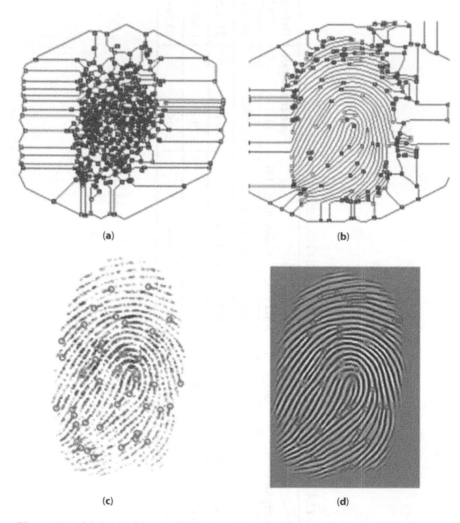

Figure 12.3 (a) Original image. (b) Proposed algorithm using a thinning technique. (c) Original image. (d) Proposed algorithm using mindset technique.

Table 12.5 Minutiae ratio results for the thinning technique.

Ratio / Technique	TMR (%)		FMR (%)		DMR (%)		EMR (%)	
	μ	std	μ	std	μ	std	μ	std
Original image	40.29	17.49	2615.10	2339.76	51.46	20.28	40.53	27.77
Coherence filter [38]	57.21	18.63	1170.66	667.42	42.775	18.62	29.24	13.38
Gabor filter [18]	68.99	12.80	3784.34	1136.49	30.76	13.00	24.75	8.18
Fourier analysis [31]	67.91	15.42	842.53	398.19	32.10	15.42	27.54	4.70
Hybrid approach [35]	61.71	9.69	2869.21	1763.56	38.78	9.47	25.95	9.91
Proposed algorithm	94.82	3.41	479.84	326.42	5.10	3.09	15.11	7.76

Table 12.6 Minutiae ratio results for mindset technique.

Technique	TMR (%) μ	TMR (%) std	FMR (%) μ	FMR (%) std	DMR (%) μ	DMR (%) std	EMR (%) μ	EMR (%) std
Original image	33.12	17.64	31.61	73.39	53.94	25.91	9.35	5.86
Coherence filter [38]	54.78	18.84	30.29	42.19	43.56	19.66	10.63	5.01
Gabor filter [18]	60.07	18.36	17.28	17.23	37.07	18.35	9.675	3.67
Fourier analysis [31]	63.25	17.62	26.29	24.39	35.84	17.53	10.24	3.66
Hybrid approach [35]	41.16	17.28	22.78	39.09	54.91	22.02	8.74	4.97
Proposed algorithm	90.45	5.91	8.51	4.87	50.63	15.48	4.625	2.05

The proposed algorithm has the highest TMR ratio of 90.45%, while all other ratios are less.

12.4.4 Analysis Based on Various Input Modalities

This section compares the proposed work with the other state-of-the-art techniques based on various input modalities such as sweeping optical sensors, sweeping thermal sensors, and synthetic images [46]. FVC2004 set_b databases consist of four sub-databases, each containing images using these four different techniques, respectively. Tables 12.7 and 12.8 represents achieved using images from these different input modalities.

Though the proposed algorithm works best for all the four sub-databases, it gives the best TMR for optical sweeping sensor "U.are.U 4000", best FMR for synthetic fingerprint generation, best DMR, and EMR for thermal sweeping sensor "Finger Chip FCD4B17CB".

Though the proposed algorithm works best for all four sub-databases, it gives the best TMR, FMR, and DMR for synthetic fingerprint generation, best EMR for optical sweeping sensor "V300". Overall, it works best for synthetic fingerprint generation.

12.5   Conclusion and Future Scope

This paper proposes a novel algorithm for low-quality fingerprint image enhancement using both spatial and frequency domain techniques. Some research gaps such as poor performance in regions of high curvature, non-distinction between ridges and valleys, poor performance in recovering highly damaged regions, and so on were found in the existing techniques. The proposed scheme is designed to fill these existing research gaps. The coherence filtering smoothens the broken ridges; the spatial filter removes noise, improves contrast, and recovers the damaged regions. The frequency band-pass filter refines the spatial domain–filtered output results by removing the blurred effect caused by it and further recovers the damaged regions.

Various analyses such as visual analysis, texture descriptor analysis, minutiae ratio analysis, and analysis based on different input modalities show that the proposed algorithm have better performance compared to existing methods. The future work related to this chapter can be using pixel processing instead of block processing, which is expected to improve the computational time.

Table 12.7 Minutiae ratios obtained for the proposed algorithm using the thinning technique.

Ratio / Input modality	TMR (%) μ	TMR (%) Std	FMR (%) μ	FMR (%) std	DMR (%) μ	DMR (%) std	EMR (%) μ	EMR (%) std
Optical sweeping sensor "V300"	92.17	2.73	841.15	370.90	6.78	2.56	18.17	11.71
Optical sweeping sensor "U.are.U 4000"	96.79	1.30	251.73	209.68	3.99	1.38	15.08	11.18
Thermal sweeping sensor "Finger Chip FCD4B17CB"	94.29	5.49	239.42	35.72	5.70	5.49	12.08	4.21
Synthetic fingerprint generation	96.04	2.37	587.07	159.38	3.96	2.37	15.17	4.89

Table 12.8 Minutiae ratios obtained for the proposed algorithm using the mindset technique.

Input modality	TMR (%) μ	Std	FMR (%) μ	std	DMR (%) μ	std	EMR (%) μ	std
Optical sweeping sensor "V300"	81.84	3.19	13.85	6.45	4.54	2.59	3.93	1.42
Optical sweeping sensor "U.are.U 4000"	93.25	3.31	6.72	3.33	4.27	2.09	5.10	2.85
Thermal sweeping sensor "Finger Chip FCD4B17CB"	92.88	4.18	7.33	3.95	9.74	12.80	3.63	1.78
Synthetic finge-print generation	93.84	2.03	6.16	2.03	3.29	0.65	5.83	2.26

References

1. Maltoni, D., Maio, D., Jain, A.K., Prabhakar, *Handbook of Fingerprint Recognition*, 2nd ed., Springer London, London, 2009.
2. Jain, A.K., Ross, A., Pankati, S., Biometrics: A Tool for Information Security. *IEEE Trans. Inf. Forensics Secur.*, 1, 2, 125–173, Jun. 2006.
3. Barnes, J.G., History, in: *The Fingerprint Sourcebook*, pp. 7–24, U.S. Department. Of Justice, Office of Justice Programs, National Institute of Justice, Washington, DC, 2011.
4. Maltoni, D. and Cappelli, R., Fingerprint Recognition, in: *Handbook of Biometrics*, A.K. Jain, P. Flynn, A.A. Ross (Eds.), pp. 23–42, Springer, New York, 2007.
5. Hong, L., Wan, Y., Jain, A.K., Fingerprint image enhancement: algorithms and performance evaluation. *IEEE Trans. Pattern Anal. Mach. Intell.*, 20, 8, 777–789, Aug. 1998.
6. Gottschlich, C., Curved-Region-Based Ridge Frequency Estimation, and Curved Gabor Filters for Fingerprint Image Enhancement. *IEEE Trans. Image Process.*, 21, 4, 2220–2227, 19 Apr. 2012.
7. Yang, J., Liu, L., Jiang, T., Fan, F., A modified Gabor filter design method for fingerprint image enhancement. *Pattern Recognit. Lett.*, 24, 12, 1805–1817, 2003.
8. Almansa, A. and Lindberg, T., Fingerprint enhancement by shape adaptation of scale-space operators with automatic scale-selection. *IEEE Trans. Image Process.*, 9, 12, 2027–2024, Dec. 2000.
9. Cheng, J. and Tian, J., Fingerprint enhancement with dyadic scale-space. *Pattern Recognit. Lett.*, 25, 11, 1273–1284, Aug. 2004.
10. Greenberg, S., Aladjem, M., Kogan, D., Dimitrov, I., Fingerprint image enhancement using filtering techniques, in: *15th International Conference on Pattern Recognition*, Barcelona, 2000.
11. Chen, X., Tian, J., Zhang, Y., Yang, X., Enhancement of Low-Quality Fingerprints Based on Anisotropic Filtering, in: *International Conference, ICB 2006*, Hong Kong, 2006.
12. Fronthaler, H., Kollreider, K., Bigun, J., Local Features for Enhancement and Minutiae Extraction in Fingerprints. *IEEE Trans. Image Process.*, 17, 3, 354–363, Mar. 2008.
13. Chakraborty, S. and Rao, K.R., Fingerprint Enhancement by Directional Filtering, in: *9th International Conference on ECTICON*, Phetchaburi, 2012.
14. Yang, J.C., Park, D.S., Yoon, S., Reference point determination in enhanced fingerprint image, in: *International Symposium on Computational Intelligence and Design*, Wuhan, 2008.
15. Yang, J.C., Park, D.S., Hitchcock, R., effectively enhance low-quality fingerprints with local ridge compensation. *IEICE Electron Expr.*, 5, 23, 1002–1009, 2008.
16. Yang, J., Xiong, N., Vasilako, A.V., Two-Stage Enhancement Scheme for Low-Quality Fingerprint Images by Learning from the Images. *IEEE Trans. Hum.-Mach. Syst.*, 43, 2, 235–248, 15 Mar. 2013.

17. Jirachaweng, S., Hou, Z., Yau, W.Y., Areekul, V., Residual orientation modeling for fingerprint enhancement and singular point detection. *Pattern Recognit.*, 44, 2, 431–442, Feb. 2011.
18. Sherlock, B.G., Monro, D.M., Millard, K., Fingerprint enhancement by directional Fourier filtering. 171, 2, 87–94, 1994.
19. Wang, W.J. and Lee, J.S., Enhanced Ridge Structure for Improving Fingerprint Image Quality Based on a Wavelet Domain. *IEEE Signal Process Lett.*, 22, 4, 390–394, Apr. 2015.
20. Wang, W., Jianwei, L., Huang, F., Feng, H., Design and implementation of Log-Gabor filter in fingerprint image enhancement. *Pattern Recognit. Lett.*, 29, 3, 301–308, Feb. 2008.
21. Chikkerur, S., Cartwright, A.N., Govindaraju, V., Fingerprint Enhancement using STFT Analysis. *Pattern Recognit.*, 40, 1, 198–211, Jan. 2007.
22. Willis, A.J. and Myers, L., A cost-effective fingerprint recognition system for low-quality prints and damaged fingerprint. *Pattern Recognit.*, 34, 2, 255–270, Feb. 2001.
23. Kamei, T. and Mizoguchi, M., Image filter design for fingerprint enhancement, in: *International Symposium on Computer Vision*, Coral Gables, FL, 1995.
24. Jirachaweng, S. and Areekul, V., Fingerprint Enhancement Based on Discrete Cosine Transform, in: *ICB*, Seoul, 2007.
25. Kale, K.V., Manza, R.R., Gornale, S.S., Deshmukh, P.D., Humble, V., SWT based Composite Method for Fingerprint Image Enhancement, in: *International Symposium on Signal Processing and Information Technology*, Vancouver, 2006.
26. Gottschlich, C., Mihailescu, P., Munk, A., Robust orientation field estimation and extrapolation using semilocal line sensors. *IEEE Trans. Inf. Forensics Secur.*, 4, 4, 802–811, Dec. 2009.
27. Bazen, A.M. and Gerez, S.H., Systematic methods for the computation of the directional fields and singular points of fingerprints. *IEEE Trans. Pattern Anal. Mach. Intell.*, 24, 7, 905–919, Jul. 2002.
28. Predd, J.B., Osherson, D.N., Kulkarni, S.R., Poor, H.V., Aggregating probabilistic forecasts from incoherent and abstaining experts. *Decis. Anal.*, 5, 4, 177–189, Dec. 2008.
29. Blotta, E. and Moler, E., Fingerprint Image Enhancement by Differential Hysteresis Processing. *Forensic Sci. Int.*, 171, 2–3, 109–113, May. 2004.
30. Raja, R., Sinha, T.S., Patra, R.K., Tiwari, S., Physiological Trait Based Biometrical Authentication of Human-Face Using LGXP and ANN Techniques. *Int. J. Inf. Comput. Secur.*, 10, 2/3, 303–320, 2018.
31. Chikkerur, S., Wu, C., Govindaraju, V., A Systematic Approach for Feature Extraction in Fingerprint Images, in: *First International Conference*, ICBA, Hong Kong, 2004.
32. Bartunek, J.S., Nilsson, M., Sallberg, B., Claesson, I., Adaptive Fingerprint Image Enhancement with Emphasis on Preprocessing of Data. *IEEE Trans. Image Process.*, 22, 2, 644–656, Feb. 2013.

33. Bartunek, J.S., Nilsson, M., Nordberg, J., Claesson, I., Adaptive fingerprint binarization by frequency domain analysis, in: *Fortieth Asilomar Conference Signals, Systems, and Computers*, Pacific Grove, 2006.

34. Bartunek, J.S., Nilsson, M., Nordberg, J., Claesson, I., Improved adaptive fingerprint binarization, in: *Congress on Image and Signal Processing*, Sanya, 2008.

35. Dyre, S. and Sumathi, C.P., Hybrid Approach to Enhancing Fingerprint Images using filters in the Frequency Domain, in: *IEEE International Conference on Computational Intelligence and Computing Research (ICCIC)*, Coimbatore, 2017.

36. Kocevar, M., Kotnik, B., Chowdhury, A., Kacic, Z., Real-Time Fingerprint Image Enhancement with a Two-Stage Algorithm and Block Local Normalization. *Real-Time Image Process.*, 1–10, 2017.

37. Weickert, J., Multiscale texture enhancement, in: *6th International Conference, CAIP '95*, Prague, 1995.

38. Weickert, J. and Scharr, H., A Scheme for Coherence-Enhancing Diffusion Filtering with Optimized Rotation Invariance. *J. Vis. Commun. Image Represent.*, 13, 1–2, 103–118, Mar. 2002.

39. Kroon, D.J. and Slump, C.H., Coherence Filtering to Enhance the Mandibular Canal in Cone-Beam CT data, in: *Annual Symposium of the IEEE-EMBS Benelux*, Enschede, 2009.

40. Kroon, D., Slump, C.J., Maal, T.J., Optimized Anisotropic Rotational Invariant Diffusion Scheme on Cone-Beam CT, in: *Medical Image Computing and Computer-Assisted Intervention – MICCAI*, Beijing, 2010.

41. Fisher, R., Perkins, S., Walker, A., Wolfart, E., *Adaptive Thresholding*, The University of Edinburgh, 2003, [Online]. Available: http://homepages.inf.ed.ac.uk/rbf/HIPR2/adpthrsh.htm. [Accessed 01 Feb. 2016].

42. Narayan, S.A., Fingerprint Minutiae Extraction, 23 Jun. 2011. [Online]. Available: http://www.mathworks.com/matlabcentral/fileexchange/31926-fingerprint-minutiae-extraction. [Accessed 20 Mar. 2016].

43. Bathla, G. and Khan, G., Energy-efficient Routing Protocol for Homogeneous Wireless Sensor Networks. *Int. J. Cloud Comput.: Serv. Archit. (IJCCSA)*, 1, 1, 12–20, May 2011.

44. Singh, G., Bathla, G., Kaur, S.P., Design of new architecture to detect leukemia cancer from medical images. *Int. J. Appl. Eng. Res.*, 11, 10, 7087–7094, 2016.

45. Bathla, G. and Randhawa, R., Enhancing WSN Lifetime Using TLH: A Routing Scheme, in: *Networking Communication and Data Knowledge Engineering*, pp. 25–35, Springer, Singapore, 2018.

46. Bathla, G., Minimum Spanning Tree-based Protocol for Heterogeneous Wireless Sensor Networks. *I- Manager's J. Wirel. Commun. Netw.*, 1, 4, 12–22, January-March 2013.

47. Bathla, G. and Randhawa, R., Virtual Tier structured Grid-based Dynamic Route Adjustment scheme for mobile sink-based Wireless Sensor Networks (VTGDRA). *Int. J. Appl. Eng. Res.*, 13, 7, 4702–4707, April 2018.

48. Pawar, L., Comparing: Routing Protocols based on sleep mode. *Int. J. Mod. Res., IJMER*, 4, 7, July 2017.

49. Pawar, L., IBEENISH: Improved Balanced Energy Efficient Network Integrated Super Heterogeneous Protocol for Wireless Sensor Networks. *Int. J. Comput. Sci. Netw., IJCSN*, 4, 4, 2015.

50. NIST, *Fingerprint Minutiae Viewer (FpMV)*, 19 Mar. 2017, [Online]. Available: http://www.nist.gov/itl/iad/ig/fpmv.cfm. [Accessed 01 Mar. 2016].

51. Pawar, and Lokesh, Optimized Route Selection based on Discontinuity and Energy Consumption in Delay-Tolerant Networks, in: *Advances in Computer and Computational Sciences*, pp. 439–449, Springer, Singapore, 2017.

52. Raja, R., Patra, R.K., Sinha, T.S., Extraction of Features from Dummyface for improving Biometrical Authentication of Human. *Int. J. Lumin. Appl.*, 3–4, 259, 507–512, 2017.

53. Kumar, S., Singh, S., Kumar, J., Live Detection of Face Using Machine Learning with Multi-feature Method. *Wireless Pers. Commun.*, 103, 3, 2353–2375, 2018.

54. Kumar, S., Singh, S., Kumar, J., Automatic Live Facial Expression Detection Using Genetic Algorithm with Haar Wavelet Features and SVM. *Wireless Pers. Commun.*, 103, 3, 2435–2453, 2018.

55. Choudhary, S., Lakhwani, K., Agrwal, S., An efficient hybrid technique of feature extraction for facial expression recognition using AdaBoost Classifier. *Int. J. Eng. Res. Technol.*, 8, 1, 2012.

13

Elevate Primary Tumor Detection Using Machine Learning

Lokesh Pawar, Pranshul Agrawal*, Gurjot Kaur and Rohit Bajaj

Computer Science and Engineering Department, Chandigarh University,
Mohali, Punjab, India

Abstract

The original site from where the tumor originates is known as the primary tumor. There are three types of tumor in which benign tumor are the most common type of tumor. The further stage of the primary tumor can lead to cancer. In this paper, algorithms are performed on 339 instances of the primary tumor dataset with Weka 3.8 software. The dataset is trained using many machine learning algorithms and the outcomes have been analyzed using the values of accuracy, F-measure, TP rate, FP rate, MCC, and AUC.

Keywords: LogitBoost, machine learning, Weka, IBK

13.1 Introduction

The tumor is the clustering of cells that grow abnormally or metastasize. "Primary" is the first site where the tumor originates and begins to produce cancerous cells [1–3]. The primary tumor is also known as a benign tumor. A primary tumor is generally not life-threatening but, in some cases, it may form cancerous cells, which can lead to a secondary tumor that is deadly. In a primary tumor, the affected cells lose programmed cell death due to which the cell functions get disordered and uncontrollable growth of defected cells starts to form clusters inside the body. The primary tumor is further divided into various types based on the symptoms, which are

---

*Corresponding author: Pranshulagrawal9269@gmail.com

Sandeep Kumar, Rohit Raja, Shrikant Tiwari and Shilpa Rani (eds.) Cognitive Behavior and Human Computer Interaction Based on Machine Learning Algorithm, (301–314) © 2022 Scrivener Publishing LLC

as follows: Adenomas affects epithelial tissue; Fibromas are the fibrous or connective tissue tumor; Hemangiomas develop in blood vessel cells; Lipomas develop from fat cells; Meningiomas grow from membrane which surrounds the brain and spinal cord; Myomas develop from muscle; Nevi affects the skin and produces moles on the skin; Neuromas develop from nerves; Osteochondromas are the painless bumps that appear on joint; Papillomas develop from epithelial tissue and protrude as finger-like overlook. Among these types of tumor, Lipomas, which is generally found in the neck, shoulder, back, or arms, is a common type of tumor in adults, and the primary tumor is not dangerous in the earliest stage. Various machine learning techniques are used to optimize the data in the dataset. The paper will give information about the primary tumor dataset's necessary parameters and show the most abundant factors. The results are extracted and improved data to make it more precise and accurate with some techniques used through the Weka tool. The rest of the paper is written as follows: Section 13.2 shortly explains numerous strategies and connected work. Section 13.3 gives the information about the dataset and also the experimental read of the dataset. Section 13.4 gives a brief explanation of the data and experimental settings. In Section 13.5, the final output has been shown and the dataset is compared. In Section 13.6, the final judgment is mentioned. Finally, Section 13.7 describes the future work.

13.2   Related Works

In this paper, the dataset is classified with various classification techniques [16, 17] and dataset probability is measured to determine the dataset's correctness. With a supervised class balancer's help, the data, which has 339 instances and 17 attributes, is assembled. This paper's primary purpose is to determine age group and gender that are mostly affected by the primary tumor. The previous papers related to the primary tumor dataset [5]. A comprehensive meta-analysis and prospective study are performed to investigate the association between the two [7, 8]. Through that paper, it was studied that right-sided mCRC was common in old cases with multiple sites metastasis, consistent with Yang et al. [11]. The article "dio.org" [12] shows that despite their capacity to disseminate into secondary organs, 4T1 tumor models develop overt metastasis while EMT6- tumor-bearing mice clear DTCs shed from primary tumors as well as those introduced by intravenous (IV) injection. It provides a shred of compelling evidence for the immune-mediated eradication of DTCs following the complete resection of primary tumors. A study was conducted by Sengupta A, et al. [13–15] using feature selection, which is one out of various machine learning techniques. The study's ultimate goal was to demonstrate automated learners' ability to identify viable-tumor and necrotic-tumor regions [9, 10]. This was the first study in osteosarcoma where the necrotic tumor is automatically assessed from WSIs. They have generated digital histology properties based on nuclei features, spatial features, distance-based features, and textural features from the input image tiles for three tissue categories within histology images, viable tumors/necrotic tumors/areas non-tumor.

13.3   Proposed Work

Figure 13.1 shows the diagram of the dataset of machine learning. The dataset is composed of two main parts, which are training and testing, respectively. A class balancer is used to the unbalanced dataset, increasing

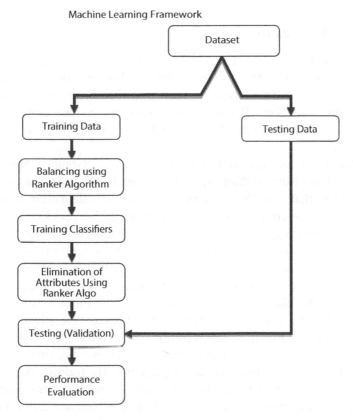

Figure 13.1 Diagrammatical view.

the dataset's features and prediction ratio. After applying the ranker algorithm, specific attributes are eliminated based on the importance of the dataset attributes. The dataset has been tested by taking trails and using each algorithm and classifiers to select the best in the training dataset. The result of the dataset is examined by evaluating the algorithm and gives the best results.

13.3.1   Class Balancing

Initially, the dataset was unbalanced, including essential and unimportant attributes. The unbalanced data is balanced and the prediction ratio is increased using a class balancer. There are many types of filters in Weka in which class balancer is the best and most accurate among them for the primary tumor dataset. It is a type of filter that makes all the instances weigh the same, and the sum of all the instance weights does not change. This property of the class balancer helps the classifiers to give more relevant results.

13.3.2   Classification

The different Weka tools are used to classify and train the dataset for better prediction and better results. Different classifiers that include zero, decision stump, random forest, random tree, IBK, LogitBoost, Bayes Net, logistic, SMO, and Naive Bayes are used to classify the data. For other classification methods, zero provides a baseline as a benchmark. It is dependent on the target class without considering other prediction classes. The Bayes Net classifier represents the Direct Acyclic Graph, whose curve shows the Bayes Net variables [4]. Naive Bayes classifiers are the collection of algorithms that have the same principle for each algorithm. It is based on the Bayes theorem [5]. During the train, the SMO, problems related to quadratic optimization are solved through SMO. A random subset of the attribute is produced for every split in random trees and multiple decision trees make a random forest. It uses more storage in comparison with other classifiers [6]. One level decision tree is a machine learning model, which is known as the decision stump. The value of the single input feature is generally the basis of the predictions made for the dataset. Through the additive model, the logistic loss function is minimized by a meta-estimator, which is called LogitBoost. IBK generally works for each instance on the distance measured to locate k "close" instances present in the training dataset, and it is also known as an instance-based learner. The value of the linear equation is predicted with independent predictors, which are called Logistic functions.

13.3.3   Eliminating Using Ranker Algorithm

Ranker algorithm is one of the machine learning techniques among other different techniques. Many classifiers are used for evaluation, including IBK, whose results were best among all other classifiers. The primary purpose of using IBK for evaluation was to give the best results of prediction after applying ranker algorithm and classification techniques. It gave the highest accuracy among all other classifiers. The ranker algorithm ranks the attributes based on the importance of that attribute in the data. The attributes whose rankings were lowest among the other attributes were eliminated to get better results. IBK classifier uses a distance measure to find k "close" instances in the training dataset and that instances are accustomed to creating a prediction. After elimination and analysis by using the classification technique, the optimized algorithm gave the best results.

13.4   Experimental Investigation

The dataset explanation and experimental perspective of the dataset are discussed in this section.

13.4.1   Dataset Description

1. The taken dataset is the primary tumor dataset in which the dataset is a classified dataset based on various attributes, which include class, age, gender, histologic-type, degree-of-differ, bone, bone marrow, lung, pleura, peritoneum, liver, brain, skin, neck, supraclavicular, axillar, mediastinum, and abdominal.
2. The primary tumor dataset has 339 instances and 17 attributes in the training data. The data is assembled by some oral and written opinion polls using which data is made. The final dataset is made by eliminating the less critical attributes being terminated and the more critical attribute selected and classified using the classification technique.
3. The selected attributes which have more importance in the data are as follows:
   - According to the age dataset, the most affected age group is 30–59, which suffers from a primary tumor.
   - Sex: Females are the principal target of the primary tumor.
   - Histologic type: The primary site for tumor according to the dataset is adeno.

- Degree of difference: According to the dataset, grade 3 is poorly differentiated or undifferentiated tumors. These high-graded tumors are generally very aggressive.

The organs that are mostly affected by the primary tumor are given in the order as follows:
- Abdominal: It is the most affected.
- Bone: It is the second most affected.
- Mediaspinum: It is the third most affected.
- Lung and pleura: These are the fourth most affected.
- Bone marrow: It is the least affected among the selected organs according to the dataset.

13.4.2   Experimental Settings

- Specific classifiers are used to increase the parameters' values and determine the most affected age group and gender for primary tumors. Based on these classifiers, an increment in the correctness of the attributes is recorded.
- This dataset is split into testing and training dataset.
- The training dataset is balanced using a class balancer and different classification techniques applied to train the dataset to make the prediction. Ranker algorithm is applied to the training dataset to evaluate the unnecessary attributes and those unnecessary attributes are eliminated.

13.5   Result and Discussion

The comparison of data, evaluation of performance, and results are discussed in this section.

13.5.1   Performance Evaluation

The data is classified using different algorithms based on specific parameters: TP rate, accuracy, FP rate, error, F-measure, MCC, and AUC, as discussed in Table 13.1 for better prediction and outputs. By analyzing the comparison of applied classifiers, graphs are plotted with the help of Table 13.1. The accuracy of applied algorithms is represented through the graph in Figure 13.2a and IBK attained the highest accuracy among all others. Table 13.2 helps us to understand the performance of optimized algorithm on state of art parameters.

Table 13.1 Comparison of performance of applied classifiers using certain specifications.

Classifier	Decision stump	Random forest	Logistic	Logit boost	IBK	SMO	ZeroR	Naive bayes	Optimized algorithm
Accuracy (%)	69.07	63.56	71.15	72.47	68.17	72.00	48.46	73.52	83.07
Error (%)	30.93	36.43	28.85	27.52	31.83	28.00	51.53	26.47	16.92
TP rate	0.691	0.636	0.712	0.725	0.682	0.72	0.485	0.735	0.831
FP rate	0.309	0.364	0.288	0.275	0.318	0.28	0.515	0.265	0.169
F-measure	0.686	0.631	0.712	0.725	0.679	0.72	0.485	0.735	0.831
MCC	0.393	0.279	0.423	0.45	0.371	0.44	−0.031	0.472	0.663
AUC	0.653	0.65	0.781	0.804	0.723	0.72	0.484	0.792	0.93

Table 13.2 Analytical estimation of selected attributes.

Classifier	Accuracy (%)	Error (%)	TP rate	FP rate	F-measure	MCC	AUC
Random forest	63.56	36.44	0.636	0.364	0.631	0.279	0.65
IBK	68.17	31.83	0.682	0.318	0.679	0.371	0.723
Naïve bayes	73.52	26.47	0.735	0.265	0.735	0.472	0.792
Logit boost	72.47	27.52	0.725	0.275	0.725	0.45	0.804
Optimized algorithm	83.07	16.92	0.831	0.169	0.831	0.663	0.93

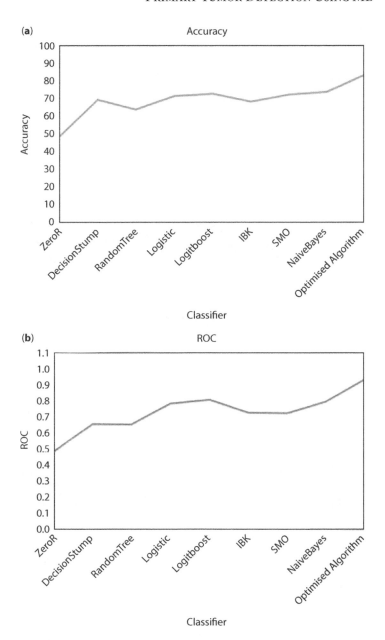

Figure 13.2 (a-d) is Performance evaluation on state of art parameters.   (*Continued*)

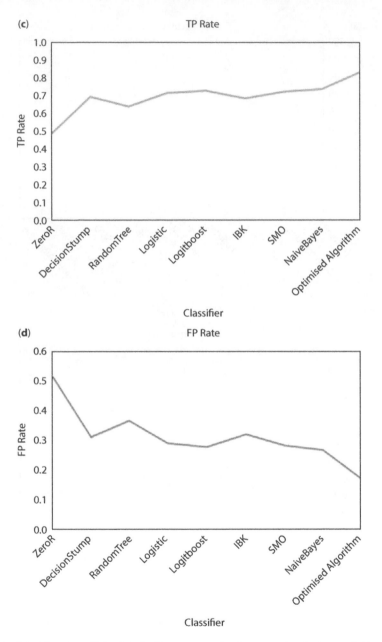

Figure 13.2 (Continued) (a-d) is Performance evaluation on state of art parameters.

The performance of applied algorithms is represented with the help ROC curve graph in Figure 13.2b. The ROC curve is a graph through which the true positive rate and false positive rate are compared and the classifier with the maximum true positive rate is the most appropriate among them, which is IBK. The TP rate gives the information about the accuracy, which is graphically represented in Figure 13.2c. IBK records the maximum TP rate among all of them. The FP rate shows the falsely classified instances, which is given by the graph in Figure 13.2d. IBK has the lowest FP rate. Ranker algorithm is used on applied classifiers and it can be analyzed that IBK is the most accurate and ZeroR is the least accurate in the tested dataset.

13.5.2 Analytical Estimation of Selected Attributes

In this section, the dataset which is taken from the UCI machine learning repository is analyzed. The comparative analysis is done with the past research work on the same dataset using specifications which include F-measure, TP rate, error, FP rate, accuracy, AUC, and MCC of the dataset. The past researchers have classified the data in which Naive Bayes had 73.52% accuracy, LogitBoost had 72.47% accuracy, SMO had 72.00% accuracy, and logistic had 71.15% accuracy. After using various preprocessor techniques such as class balancing and ranker, the algorithm has improved the optimized algorithm's outputs. The improved results are IBK has 83.08% accuracy, random tree has 80.64% accuracy, and random forest has 80.17% accuracy.

13.6 Conclusion

The initial dataset of the primary tumor was unbalanced. The dataset was balanced using a class balancer, which is a subpart of supervised instance algorithms. Then, the data was classified with specific classifiers and certain parameters were noted. After classification, a ranker algorithm was applied to the dataset through which the low ranked attributes were eliminated. Only 10 attributes out of 17 attributes were selected for classification performance. The data's overall performance had an increment: accuracy increased to 83.09%, FP rate decreased to 0.169, TP rate increased to 0.831, MCC increased to 0.663, F-Measure increased to 0.831, and AUC increased to 0.93. This dataset can be enhanced further using better machine learning techniques. The optimized classifier gives the best results among all others, which is shown by experimental results. The result provides information about the most affected gender, which is female and the symptoms from which it can be easily identified.

13.7   Future Work

In the future, new methods and pre-processor techniques can be implemented on the same dataset. The prediction ratio can be increased and the dataset can be classified more precisely with a smaller number of errors. Different techniques such as clustering, ensembling, and many more can increase the dataset's results and tend to give more correctness and less errors. Deep learning and neural network for better outputs and results can also be used. The ranker algorithm can also be used once more on the same dataset and the best attributes can be further selected to increase the rate of preciseness.

References

1. Michalski, R., Mozetic, I., Hong, J., Lavrac, N., The Multi-Purpose Incremental Learning System AQ15 and it is Testing Applications to Three Medical Domains, in: *Proceedings of the Fifth National Conference on Artificial Intelligence*, Morgan Kaufmann, Philadelphia, PA, pp. 1041–1045, 1986.
2. Clark, P. and Niblett, T., Induction in Noisy Domains, in: *Progress in Machine Learning*, I. Bratko and N. Lavrac (Eds.), pp. 11–30, Sigma Press, Wilmslow, UK, 1987.
3. Cestnik, G., Konenenko, I., Bratko, I., Assistant-86: A Knowledge-Elicitation Tool for Sophisticated Users, in: *Progress in Machine Learning*, I. Bratko and N. Lavrac (Eds.), pp. 31–45, Sigma Press, Wilmslow, UK, 1987.
4. www.webmd.com/a-to-z-guides/beningn-tumor-cause-treatments
5. You, X., Wen, C., Xia, Z., Ying, H., Wang, X., Sun, F., Fang, Z., Wang, W., Li,Y., Chen, Q., Zhang, L., Jiang, Y., Primary tumor sidedness predicts bevacizumab benefit in metastatic colorectal cancer patients. *Front. Oncol.*, 9, 723, 1–9, 2019.
6. Ryan, J., Lin, M.-J., Miikkulainen, R., Intrusion Detection With Neural Networks, in: *Advances in Neural Information Processing System*, p. 10, MIT Press, Cambridge, MA, 1998.
7. Pei, J., Upadhayaya, S.J., Farooq, F., Govindaraju, V., Data Mining for Intrusion Detection: Techniques, Applications & Systems, in: *Proceedings of 20th International Conference on Data Engineering*, pp. 877–887, 2004.

8. Zhao, J.-L., Zhao, J.-f., Li, J.-J., Intrusion Detection Based on Clustering Genetic Algorithm, in: *Proceedings of International Conference on Machine Learning & Cybernetics (ICML)*, IEEE Communication Magazine, 2005.

9. Campos, M.M. and Milenora, B.L., Creation & Deployment of Data Mining based Intrusion Detection Systems in Oracle Db 10g, in: *4th International Conference proceedings on Machine Learning & Applications*, 2005.

10. Tavallaee, M., Bagheri, E., Lu, W., Ghorbani, A.A., A detailed analysis of the KDD CUP 99 data set, in: *Proceedings of the Second IEEE international conference on Computational intelligence for security and defense applications*, Ottawa, Ontario, Canada, pp. 53–58, 2009.

11. Yang, J. *et al.*, Characteristics of Differently Located Colorectal Cancers Support Proximal and Distal Classification: A Population-Based Study of 57,847 Patients. *PLoS One*, 11, 12, e0167540, 2016.

12. Https://doi.org/10.1038/s41467-019-09015-1 www.nature.com/naturecommunications.

13. Arunachalam, H.B., Mishra, R., Daescu, O., Cederberg, K., Rakheja, D., Sengupta, A. *et al.*, Viable and necrotic tumor assessment from whole slide images of osteosarcoma using machine learning and deep-learning models. *PLoS One*, 14, 4, e0210706, 2019.

14. Raja, R., Patra, R., Sinha, T.S., Extraction of Features from Dummy face for improving Biometrical Authentication of Human. *Int. J. Lumin. Appl.*, 7, 3-4, Article 259, 507–512, 2017.

15. Raja, R., Sinha, T.S., Dubey, R.P., Orientation Calculation of human Face Using Symbolic techniques and ANFIS. *Published Int. J. Eng. Future Technol.*, 7, 7, 37–50, 2016.

16. Kumar, S., Singh, S., Kumar, J., Automatic Live Facial Expression Detection Using Genetic Algorithm with Haar Wavelet Features and SVM. *Wireless Pers. Commun.*, 103, 3, 2435–2453, 2018.

17. Choudhary, S., Lakhwani, K., Agrwal, S., An efficient hybrid technique of feature extraction for facial expression recognition using AdaBoost Classifier. *Int. J. Eng. Res. Technol.*, 8, 1, 1–7, 2012.

14

Comparative Sentiment Analysis Through Traditional and Machine Learning-Based Approach

Sandeep Singh* and Harjot Kaur

*Department of Computer Science, Guru Nanak Dev University,
Gurdaspur Campus, Punjab, India*

Abstract

People's opinions and sentiments toward products, organizations, and their services can be evaluated through a classification of texts, speeches, and sign-language technologies. Natural Language Processing (NLP) used to perform such subjective tasks is Sentiment Analysis (SA). [1] coined the term SA for the first time finding positive or negative polarities of texts written by people. Nowadays, everybody reads user-review texts for evaluating the sentiments of users before buying any new product. However, it is cumbersome tasks to interpret the exact type of SA, as there are various kinds of SA available, out of which four are essential. These are fine-grained SA, emotion-detection, aspect-based, and intent-analysis SA. The fine-grained SA always gives us precise outcomes regarding text polarity, whereas positive or negative emotions can be obtained through emotion-detection SA. The aspect-based SA is capable of determining sentiments corresponding to different aspects for a single entity. Finally, the fourth significant SA kind provides us more profound concern related to the user's intention. This type of SA is the hardest among all four types. There are multitudes of challenges associated with the process of finding exact sentiments from texts. Sometimes, texts are ironical and contain sarcasm, which is hard for an NLP algorithm to evaluate. Also, there are metaphorical negations that can be difficult to detect. Word ambiguity, multiple polarity, spam detection, co-reference evaluation, and dialectal processing are the key challenges before an analytical system meant for computational linguistics to perform SA. The SA system's real-life applications

---

*Corresponding author: er.ss1989@gmail.com

Sandeep Kumar, Rohit Raja, Shrikant Tiwari and Shilpa Rani (eds.) Cognitive Behavior and Human Computer Interaction Based on Machine Learning Algorithm, (315–338) © 2022 Scrivener Publishing LLC

are analyzing product reviews, monitoring social media texts, evaluating customer support, monitoring brands, managing brand reputation, finding customers' voice, performing market research, and answering community questions automatically, to name a few. SA system applies language deconstruction such as tokenization, lemmatization, parsing, word sense disambiguation, and parts-of-speech tagging before feeding text to machine learning classifier and finally receiving classified text into its correct sentiments. This chapter will cover the basics of SA, its types, followed by the SA system's working, challenges associated with SA systems, and real-life applications of SA, and finally proposes a SA system model using machine learning classifiers.

Keywords: Sentiment analysis, natural language processing, social media text, machine learning, classification, user reviews, polarity, feature extraction

14.1   Introduction to Sentiment Analysis

A field of study that deals with the evaluation of public opinions, attitudes, emotions, and sentiments from social media text using Natural Language Processing (NLP) techniques is termed Sentiment Analysis (SA) [2]. Finding exact SA is NP-hard, where different subjective tasks ranging from SA, opinion extraction, opinion mining, sentiment mining, emotion analysis, and effect analysis to sentiment classification are involved. The term SA is commonly used under the umbrella of SA and opinion mining. In the history of NLP and computational linguistics, the terms opinion mining and SA were used by researchers around 2000 [3, 4]. Significantly less research was done in linguistics and NLP for finding appropriate sentiments and opinions before the year 2000. The last decade has observed active research in this area with a wide range of submissions of research proposals for every SA corner. The commercial aspects of SA render industries flourish in this area by leveraging the latest machine learning techniques to obtain their potential customers' correct sentiments.

14.1.1   Sentiment Definition

Generally, only two types of sentiments are more prominent, *viz.*, positive and negative, associated with each sentence from the author's text. Let us consider an example of text taken from social media platforms, namely, Amazon product reviews [5]. It says, "I bought this mobile one year ago, the camera is amazing, battery life is good, but the only con is its weight, my brother says that it is a bit heavier than other models of the same range."

For the above review, the following observation can be considered for defining sentiment:

This review has two sentiments, both positive and negative, for a mobile phone. If we split this complex sentence into simple pieces delimited by comma, then the second and third part of the sentence is positive about mobile, but the third part expresses adverse concern regarding the phone's weight [6, 7].

Therefore, it is clear from the above observation that sentiment can consist of two essential parts, *viz.*, a target and an opinion, i.e.,

$$Sentiment = (target, opinion)$$

Here, target can be the entity about which the sentiment has been given, and opinion is the variable that can have three values, *viz.*, positive, negative, and neutral.

For instance, the target for the above example is mobile phone and the opinion is optimistic about the camera and battery life, and the opinion about weight is harmful because it is overweight compared to other similar models [8].

Another observation from the above review says that there are different aspects of the target entity about which the opinions are expressed. The three aspects are observed from the above example, camera, battery life, and mobile phone weight. Hence, another tuple to consider for defining sentiment is the aspect, i.e.,

$$Sentiment = (target, aspect, opinion)$$

Hence, the three tuples may represent the sentiment of the review text.

Furthermore, the opinion holder can observe the time observation when an opinion is expressed. This makes the sentiment a personal concern, and the above example shows two opinion holders (me and my brother). Also, the mobile phone was bought 1 year ago. This means that last year (at that time), I was optimistic about the mobile phone and my brother was not all that happy. He was not satisfied with the weight of the mobile phone. The time was also necessary; last year, my brother and I gave opinions about the mobile phone [9]. This year, may our opinion be changed due to the performance of mobile-phone?

Therefore, the sentiment does depend upon time and opinion holder as well. Hence, we amend the definition of sentiment with a various tuple as follows:

$$Sentiment = (target, aspect, opinion, time, opinion-holder)$$

The above definition is precise and may be easy to evaluate a given text's sentiment, especially for the social media texts taken for products, brands, services, etc.

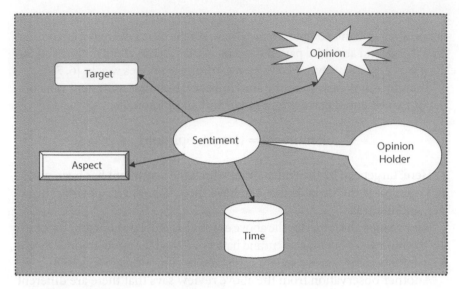

Figure 14.1 Five tuples used to evaluate sentiment.

The above definition stresses the five parts of information in the five-tuple and must correspond to one another [10]. This means the sentiment must correlate to the opinion holder when the opinion was expressed and the target entity's aspect. This way, the above definition is well-formed self-explanatory to describe a sentiment hidden inside any text. Figure 14.1 shows the five components for the evaluation of sentiments formally. However, there are few challenges while evaluating sentiments from the text. The next section will discuss the challenges associated with sentiment evaluation tasks.

14.1.2   Challenges of Sentiment Analysis Tasks

The very first challenge while evaluating correct sentiment from a text is finding a named entity. It is undeniable that all nouns are the named entities to ensure the text's nouns, whether they are correctly identified or not. The process of named-entity-recognition needs to be initiated. Therefore, extraction of entity is a challenging issue in NLP. Sometimes, different spellings of named entities are used, i.e., Samsung may be written as Samy or Sams; similarly, Nokia may be written as Noks as a shorthand. This issue always reduces the accuracy of the named entity's determination from a text [11].

Secondly, each entity's aspect is a concern that reflects the actual word or phrase for the description of that entity. It may indicate the categorical

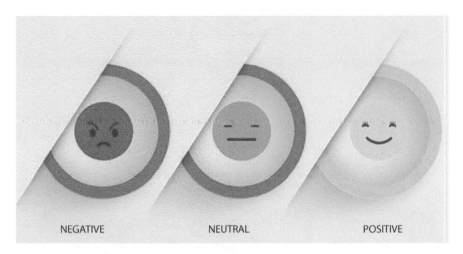

Figure 14.2 Three values of sentiment.

response for some aspects. Hence, the aspect categorization is a crucial challenge while identifying the second tuple of the sentiment. Sometimes, aspect expressions may include nouns, noun-phrases, adjectives, verbs, verb phrases, and adverbs [12, 13]. For example, "This phone is of perfect size and shape, as it fits perfectly in my little hands." This review is explicitly describing the nature of the aspect and is easy to determine for sentiment evaluator. Sometimes, the expression can be of an implicit kind, for example, "This phone is handy and it fits perfectly in my coat's pocket." This expression has a hidden aspect of size since they have not explicitly mentioned the term size and shape. This makes it challenging to evaluate the exact aspect and hence another challenge for sentiment evaluation.

Thirdly, opinion is itself a big challenge because it is a subjective concern. It is challenging for us to limit opinion only to three values, *viz.*, positive, negative, and neutral (refer to Figure 14.2). For example, "This camera is good, but it is a bit overpriced." and "This camera is awesome, even in this little price enhancement." Both of these reviews are positive, but how positive they are is itself an issue. It means from positive texts, identifying the degree of positivity is a big concern and a challenge in sentiment evaluators' hands [14, 15].

14.2   Four Types of Sentiment Analyses

There are four types of opinions, *viz.*, regular, comparative, implicit, and explicit opinion. It depends on how an opinion is expressed inside a text (as shown in the Figure 14.3). The regular opinion is an essential kind of opinion

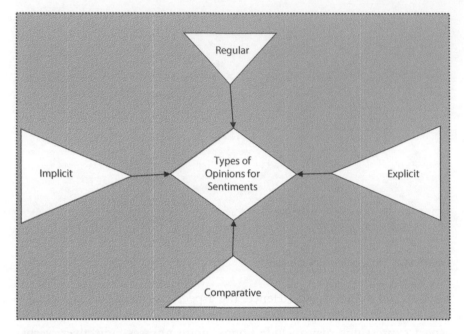

Figure 14.3 Types of sentiments.

where a periodic statement is expressed. For example, "This medicine is an elixir." Here, it is a general opinion of a patient for a medicine. People express these kinds of statements regularly while describing some entities like medicine [16]. However, it may be indirect opinion in regular statements, for example, "This medicine makes my joint-pain worse." Here, the regular opinion is expressed indirectly.

Most of the researchers only considered direct opinion while evaluating sentiments from texts. This may be because indirect opinions are hard to handle. The second type of opinion that gained popularity among the researchers is comparative opinions. The comparisons of similarities and differences between two or more concepts about entities are expressed in comparative opinions. For instance, "My University is better to paymaster than other universities of our region." Generally, the comparative opinions contain comparative degrees of the verb [17, 18].

The third type of opinion is explicit opinions, where personal information is explicitly expressed using either regular opinion or comparative opinion. The exact information about the entity is given for its mentioned aspect here in explicit opinions. Therefore, it is straightforward to evaluate sentiment from the observed statement of this kind. For instance, "I love coffee because it tastes great." and "Milk tastes better than tea." Here, both the statements are subjective and precise, concern about the likings of the opinion holder. Hence, explicit opinions are the easiest to express correct sentiments from the given text [19].

The fourth type of opinion is implicit opinions, where the sentiment information is hidden in text and the concern of the opinion is an objective statement about an entity. Any desirable or undesirable facts are expressed inside implicit statements are hard to evaluate for the sentiment classification. For example, "The camera of this phone takes shiny shots in the daylight." Here in this review, it is tough to say about the opinion's positive or negative polarity because opinion is hidden inside the text. Hence, the implicit opinions are hard to express when it comes to the sentiment evaluation process. Most of the researchers to date have considered explicit opinions for sentiment classification rather than implicit. Others express implicit concerns about syntactic information of any text. The headline of a news story often exudes different sentiments [20, 51].

14.3   Working of SA System

Machine learning methods are used to evaluate sentiment from a given text. Same as a machine learning process, the SA system works in two phases, namely, the training phase and the prediction phase. A machine learning model is trained in the first phase of the process. Generally, a labeled text is provided in this phase for supervised machine learning methods. The machine learning model can associate the given text to some particular feature for deciding its sentiment's polarity [21, 51]. Whereas the unsupervised machine learning systems work for unlabeled data, these methods perform clustering of unlabeled text based on some observed features. Sometimes, the accuracy of sentiment classification for unsupervised machine learning methods is relatively low compared to supervised machine learning methods. The machine learning methods generate feature vectors from given training data; pairs of feature vectors are used to train a model. Later, in the testing or prediction phase, the unseen data is fed to the trained model; based on the training, the prediction results are followed by how well a model is trained. Here, for SA, tags are predicted for unseen data [22]. Figure 14.4 shows the architecture of an SA system. The two phases of the SA system work successively after one another for evaluating sentiments of a text. The only difference between the two phases is that the training phase involves model training, where the tagged training text is inputted into the machine learning model, while in the prediction phase, the untagged text is inputted to the feature extractor, the trained classifier provides the three tags to the text based on the learned features [23, 24].

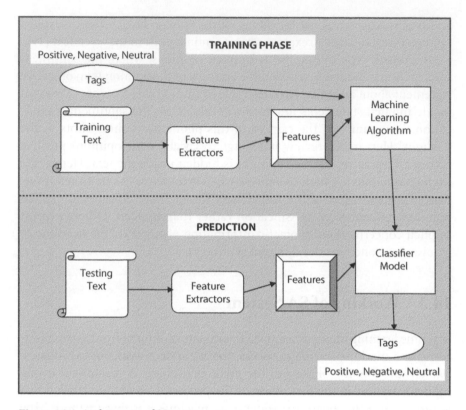

Figure 14.4 Architecture of SA system.

The first step in the training phase is the text vectorization, which is performed by a bag of words or bag of n-grams and their respective frequencies. Some researchers use word embeddings for feature extraction. This type of feature representation makes word vectors of a similar kind with similar representation. Hence, a classifier's classification accuracy may be improved through this new kind of feature extraction [25, 26].

The machine learning methods used to evaluate sentiments, i.e., naïve Bayes, SVM, linear regression, neural networks, and logistic regression, to name a few. Here naïve Bayes is a probabilistic kind of algorithm that uses the Bayes theorem of statistics to predict sentiment tag. Linear regression uses a linear combination of variables X and Y to predict the sentiment along a line segment used for measuring the trend of X in terms of Y. SVM is a non-probability–based classifier that maps distinct regions within a space to separate the dependent variables. SVM creates three regions of positive, negative and neutral features to categorize a piece of text [27].

14.4   Challenges Associated With SA System

There are many challenges associated with the sentiment classification of a text. The challenging task is to classify the sentiment from a text implicitly hidden inside a text. The subjective nature of sentiment is making the problem more complicated. The problematic phase starts when text is more subjective, for example: "my phone stopped working yesterday, it happened after the installation of new updates." This sentence is more subjective and the author of the text is cynical about the mobile phone cannot be evaluated with a simple machine learning classifier [11, 28–31].

The spam from a given social media text is challenging to identify. It is a challenging task to identify a text, whether it is spam or not. Similarly, sarcasm is also a big challenge for machine learning classifiers. For example: "This car is awesome for a long drive as far as mileage is concerned." Looking at this review, one can say that it is a positive review about the car in terms of its mileage. However, when the whole paragraph was read, it was identified that the car was worse at its mileage and hence not preferred for a long drive. Hence, there is a hidden sarcasm present inside the text that can be difficult to identify [22, 26, 32, 33]. Figure 14.5 shows some challenges associated with sentiment classifiers. These are word sense disambiguation, defining sentiment polarity through the algorithm, opinion rating, and sentiment intensity classification, to name a few.

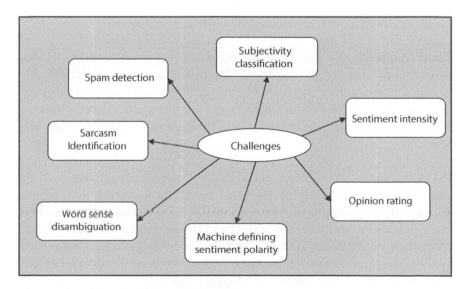

Figure 14.5 Challenges of sentiment classifier.

14.5   Real-Life Applications of SA

There are five major thrust areas where SA is doing wonders. These are business, politics, public action, finance, and language learning [34, 35, 50–52]. All these five areas are mentioned in Figure 14.6, along with their alternative sub-fields where SA is catering to the hour's needs.

14.6   Machine Learning Methods Used for SA

Two types of machine learning methods are commonly used for sentiment classification, namely, supervised and unsupervised machine learning classifiers. The sentiment prediction problem is thought of as a two-class problem where positive and negative reviews are expressed for a given text. If we are talking about online social media reviews, then the reviews with a star rating of 4 are considered a positive review, whereas a review with negative sentiment is expressed with a star rating of 0-, 1-, 2-, and 3-star rating considered as unbiased reviews. A text classification algorithm used for sentiment classification involves many topics ranging from sciences, technologies, sports to politics. Therefore, the words related to respective topics decide the sentiments of the concerned topic. These topic centric words are called features. This feature engineering has been a hot potato among researchers these days. The extraction of critical features for a topic defines the sentiment classifier's accuracy [12, 26, 36–38]. The following are some examples of features used by sentiment classifiers:

Term frequency of a particular word for a topic in a paragraph decides its overall polarity for the sentiment. The individual words are called unigrams, the two-word phrases are bigrams, and the three-word phrases are trigrams, moving the same as the phrases with n words are called n-grams. These features are compelling for the classification of sentiment from the text [39].

Parts of speech: The POS also called parts-of-speech of each word can be vital information for defining the exact sentiment for a text. Sometimes, words with different parts of speech influence the sentiment polarity of a piece of text. For instance, the adjectives influence the sentiment polarity more than simple verbs. Hence, adjectives are treated specially with extra care while defining feature extractors. Researchers have constituted a tree-bank called Penn Treebank for POS tagging [40, 41].

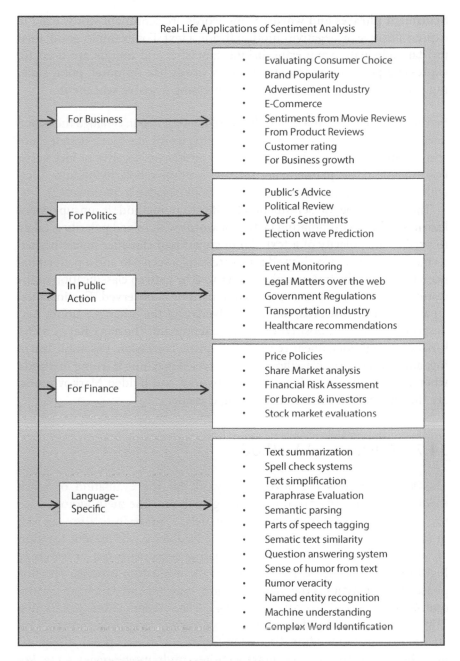

Figure 14.6 Real-life applications of sentiment analysis.

Sentiment phrases and words: Some words are sentiment words used to express positive or negative emotion inside a text. For example, good, love, joy, fair, adequate, wonderful, bright, fantastic, and unique are used for expressing positive sentiments, whereas words like immoral, poor, sucking, terrible, and hatred are used for expressing negative sentiment.

Sentiment shifters: Sometimes, the words or expressions change the orientation of sentiment. For example, the negating words like "not", "do not", "no", and "nothing" can shift the polarity from positive to negative or vice versa. For example, "This phone is not so bad" is positive polarity because "not" with "bad" has been shifting the polarity from negative to positive [42].

The other type of sentiment classification method is unsupervised learning, where a dominating factor for words with mixed polarity is taken to predict the polarity of a text. An unsupervised classifier notes the pattern of consecutive words used for expressing a scenario and a pattern has been learned in the training phase, followed by pattern classification of the testing and validation text if the same pattern is observed. For instance, a pattern with two words, one is an adverb and the other is a noun, may describe a pattern for positive or negative sentiment. The naïve Bayes, SVM, k-nearest neighbors, linear regression, logistic regression, ensemble learning, and decision tree classifiers are supervised machine learning methods, whereas k-means clustering, neural networks, and hidden Markov model are the unsupervised machine learning classifiers.

14.7   A Proposed Method

This section proposes a novel framework for the evaluation of sentiments from text using machine learning analytics. The methodology used for proposing a SA system using an analytics approach is a novice idea in language processing systems. This methodology will present the flow of analytics applications used for evaluating sentiments out of web text. Figure 14.7 shows the steps involved in the evaluation process. The first phase in SA analytics is the data collection; here, textual data from various online sources should be collected using a web scrapping library of Python [23]. We have used bs4 for extracting online text from web sources. Our web sources include online discussion forums, Amazon's product reviews, news headlines from various news websites, imdb movie reviews, etc. For real-time analytics, the data may be massive, it becomes difficult to accommodate this voluminous data using simple extractors, and special data streaming is set using AWS Kinesis for this purpose.

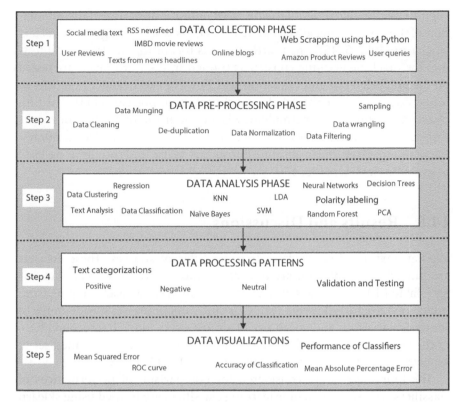

Figure 14.7 Framework for the proposed model.

The second phase in our proposed model is the pre-processing data phase, where data cleaning is performed for missing records, duplicates, inconsistent data, typos, spelling mistakes, dialects, and formatting errors. The processes for performing pre-processing are called data cleaning, data wrangling, munging, data sampling, normalization, and data filtering [43, 44]. The data cleansing takes care of corrupt records that generally include missing values and formatting defects. Simultaneously, data wrangling or munging performs the transformation of data from one format to another. Sometimes, end line delimiters are not appropriately inserted while data extraction due to missing records, the whole format gets disturbed in json format if the tags are not correctly processed.

The third phase is the main phase for processing the collected data. Various algorithms are used for clustering and classification. The training data is made available at this phase for machine learning classifiers. For supervised machine learning algorithms like linear regression, naïve Bayes, support vector machines, decision trees, and random forest, the annotation of the positive, negative, and neutral labels is set through Python's text labeler module [5, 45]. The fourth phase is meant for validation and testing; the machine learning constructs trained in the third phase are tested on the unlabeled test and validation sets. Positive and negative polarities of tested documents are validated against the actual polarities [44]. The fifth phase of the proposed methodology is all about the realization of results through visualizations. Various performance parameters like accuracy, mean square error, mean absolute percentage error, and roc curve are used to evaluate classifiers [46, 47].

14.8   Results and Discussions

We have extracted seven datasets from different sources. These datasets are publicly available and are utilized by most of the researchers of our age. Table 14.1 shows the statistics of seven different datasets ranging from movie reviews to Wikipedia text. Our study encompasses a wide range of sentence variations and vocab size of almost every kind. The second phase of the proposed methodology has refined datasets using a confined set of aspects to enhance classification accuracy [5, 11, 43, 48, 49].

The four metrics are considered for comparison of performances of classifiers. The seven machine learning classifiers are trained using sklearn in Python 3.7 on seven different datasets. The individual classifier's performance is noticed in terms of accuracy, precision, recall, and F-measure. Table 14.2 shows the performance parameters for seven different classifiers for the IMDB dataset. It was observed that neural network classification is

Table 14.1 Dataset statistics.

Dataset domain	# Reviews	# Sentences/ review	# Words/ review	# Vocab
IMDB movie reviews	21,430	6.12	65.23	25,413
Amazon product reviews	34,143	3.21	24.46	12,212
News headlines	29,005	12.33	154.12	9,234
Texts from online blogs	25,312	9.54	78.22	32,541
Wikipedia text	27,415	123.75	245.65	29,607

Table 14.2 Performance comparison of different classifiers for the IMDB dataset (refer Table 14.3). Here, LR is logistic regression, kNN is k-nearest neighbors, NB is naïve Bayes, LDA is latent Dirichlet allocation, SVM is support vector machines, and DT is decision trees.

Classifier	Accuracy (%)	Precision (%)	Recall (%)	F-measure (%)
LR	64.25	82.35	78.45	80.35
kNN	66.23	80.25	83.75	81.96
NB	72.42	78.23	75.24	76.71
LDA	68.25	81.47	74.30	77.72
SVM	69.42	83.15	86.52	84.80
DT	75.12	84.65	89.25	86.89
NN	82.76	86.25	83.78	85.00

Table 14.3 Performance comparison of different classifiers for Amazon product reviews dataset.

Classifier	Accuracy (%)	Precision (%)	Recall (%)	F-measure (%)
LR	44.21	42.55	48.75	45.44
kNN	46.23	60.65	43.15	50.42
NB	42.42	58.13	55.14	56.60
LDA	48.25	41.67	44.50	43.04
SVM	59.42	53.35	56.72	54.98
DT	55.12	54.35	49.85	52.00
NN	62.76	66.75	63.48	65.07

most precise among the seven classifiers with a precision value of 86.25%, whereas the second most precise was decision tree classifier.

It was observed that the neural network classifier is again the most precise among the pool for the Amazon product reviews dataset. However, the precision is relatively lesser than that in the IMDB dataset. The reason is that there is a freedom for Amazon reviews to put arbitrarily about the products. They did democratize the reviewers for writing their reviews and raising their concerns about any products. Sometimes, they deviate a lot

Table 14.4 Performance comparison of different classifiers for news headlines dataset.

Classifier	Accuracy (%)	Precision (%)	Recall (%)	F-measure (%)
LR	64.28	62.51	68.72	65.47
kNN	66.43	50.62	63.11	56.18
NB	82.65	78.15	65.34	71.17
LDA	68.45	61.65	74.23	67.36
SVM	79.23	63.31	56.25	59.57
DT	75.43	64.31	69.65	66.87
NN	72.12	76.71	73.36	75.00

from the subject, and Amazon welcomes all reviewers even if they were abusive the other day, which is why the accuracy and precision have gone down a bit than other confined datasets.

The naïve Bayes classifier with the precision of 78.15% and accuracy of 82.65% has outperformed among the seven classifiers for the news headlines dataset. This dataset contains a wide range of vocabulary. Due to this reason, the NLTK library of Python 3.7 has a wide variety of similar words and synonyms. Table 14.4 shows the performance comparison of seven classifiers for all four metrics of classification.

The online blogs dataset is an open discussion platform, where members engaged in the discussion come from diverse fields and are not limited to a single class (refer Table 14.5). Hence, the text reviews corresponding to open subjects are discussed at a stretch. The trail of reviews sometimes turns into heated debates. People satisfy their ego when the subject of politics and religion come at the turf of discussion. Most of the political and religious discussions spread negative statements more than positive sentiments. The NN has outperformed among the seven classifiers with an accuracy of 62.13% and precision of 66.71%, whereas the lowest classifier in terms of accuracy is the NB classifier.

The most widespread among all the datasets are the Wikipedia dataset; however, the Wikipedia page structure is well defined in terms of hierarchy. We have considered an only introduction, about, and history sections. Most of the time, the texts in these sections are neutral and do not carry positive or negative sentiments. Sometimes, some critical information in the about section carries positive sentiments in terms of the achievements of entities, while the other day, these criticize negative aspects. For this

Table 14.5 Performance comparison of different classifiers for online blogs dataset.

Classifier	Accuracy (%)	Precision (%)	Recall (%)	F-measure (%)
LR	54.22	52.51	58.72	55.44
kNN	56.40	50.62	53.11	51.84
NB	52.61	58.15	55.34	56.71
LDA	58.42	51.65	64.23	57.26
SVM	59.27	53.31	46.25	49.53
DT	65.45	54.31	59.65	56.85
NN	62.13	66.71	63.36	64.99

reason, the DT classifier has the highest accuracy of classification for the Wikipedia dataset. Table 14.6 shows the comparison tables of all four metrics for all seven classifiers.

After individually analyzing all the classifiers, Table 14.7 shows the accuracy of different classifiers. The trend in Figure 14.8 shows that DT and NN classifiers are the topmost performers in terms of accuracy of classification, and the Wikipedia dataset is most appropriate among all the other six datasets. This is because the Wikipedia dataset is most structured and well organized in terms of the topic's context, whereas other datasets are open to embracing the text from off-topic ranges.

Table 14.6 Performance comparison of different classifiers for Wikipedia dataset.

Classifier	Accuracy (%)	Precision (%)	Recall (%)	F-measure (%)
LR	64.22	72.51	78.72	75.49
kNN	66.40	70.62	73.11	71.84
NB	72.61	78.15	75.34	76.72
LDA	78.42	71.65	74.23	72.92
SVM	79.27	83.31	86.25	84.75
DT	85.45	84.31	89.65	86.90
NN	82.13	86.71	83.36	85.00

Table 14.7 Accuracy comparison of different classifiers for different datasets.

Classifier	IMDB movie reviews	Amazon product reviews	News headlines	Texts from online blogs	Wikipedia text
LR	64.25	44.21	64.28	54.22	64.22
kNN	66.23	46.23	66.43	56.4	66.4
NB	72.42	42.42	62.65	52.61	72.61
LDA	68.25	48.25	68.45	58.42	78.42
SVM	69.42	59.42	79.23	59.27	79.27
DT	75.12	55.12	75.43	65.45	85.45
NN	82.76	62.76	72.12	62.13	82.13

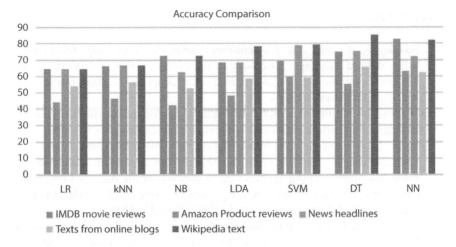

Figure 14.8 Comparison chart of different classifiers for different datasets.

Figure 14.8 shows the comparison chart for all seven datasets and all seven classifiers for four metrics. It clearly shows that DT has outperformed on Wikipedia-text dataset among the seven classifiers, whereas NN has occupied the cliff for the IMDB movie review dataset and NB stood second in terms of accuracy of classification.

14.9 Conclusion

This chapter discusses a detailed definition of sentiment followed by a discussion of a SA system. The second section of this chapter familiarizes the reader with four types of sentiment analyses, followed by the SA system's working in the third section of the chapter. Various challenges associated with the SA system and the SA system's real-world applications are discussed in the fourth and fifth sections. The sixth section of the chapter has thrown light on the usage of machine learning methods for SA. We have also proposed a five-phase model for the classification of sentiments. The results and discussion section make the reader understand how the machine learning classifiers performed to evaluate sentiments from texts. We have gathered seven datasets from publicly available texts from seven different sources. Four performance metrics are used for the evaluation of classifiers. Individually, for all the seven datasets, the performances of classifiers are noted in seven different tables. Finally, the eighth table and comparison chart compare the seven classifiers as per their performances (see Table 14.7) and comparison chart (Figure 14.8).

References

1. Nasukawa, T. and Yi, J., Sentiment analysis: Capturing favorability using natural language processing. *Proceedings of the 2nd International Conference on Knowledge Capture, K-CAP 2003*, pp. 70–77, 2003, https://doi.org/10.1145/945645.945658.

2. Shaikh, M.A.M., Prendinger, H., Ishizuka, M., Sentiment assessment of text by analyzing linguistic features and contextual valence assignment. *Appl. Artif. Intell.*, 22, 6, 558–601, 2008, https://doi.org/10.1080/08839510802226801.

3. Pang, B., Lee, L., Vaithyanathan, S., Thumbs up? Sentiment Classification using Machine Learning Techniques. *Proceedings of the ACL-02 Conference on Empirical Methods in Natural Language Processing - EMNLP '02*, 10(July), pp. 79–86, 2002, https://doi.org/10.3115/1118693.1118704.

4. Turney, P.D., Thumbs Up or Thumbs Down? Semantic Orientation Applied to Unsupervised Classification of Reviews. *Proceedings of the 40th Annual Meeting of the Association for Computational Linguistics (ACL)*, pp. 417–424, 2002, http://www.google.com.

5. Singh, J., Singh, G., Singh, R., Optimization of sentiment analysis using machine learning classifiers. *Hum.-Cent. Comput. Info. Sci.*, 7, 1, 32, 2017, https://doi.org/10.1186/s13673-017-0116-3.

6. Jose, M.R., Co-Extracting Opinions from Online Reviews. *Int. J. Comput. Appl. Technol. Res.*, 5, 2, 95–98, 2016.

7. Choudhary, S., Lakhwani, K., Agrwal, S., An efficient hybrid technique of feature extraction for facial expression recognition using AdaBoost Classifier. *Int. J. Eng. Res. Technol.*, 8, 1, 1–7, 2012.

8. Poria, S., Chaturvedi, I., Cambria, E., Hussain, A., Convolutional MKL based multimodal emotion recognition and sentiment analysis. *Proceedings - IEEE International Conference on Data Mining, ICDM*, pp. 439–448, 2017, https://doi.org/10.1109/ICDM.2016.178.

9. García-Díaz, J.A., Cánovas-García, M., Valencia-García, R., Ontology-driven aspect-based sentiment analysis classification: An infodemiological case study regarding infectious diseases in Latin America. *Future Gener. Comput. Syst.*, 112, 641–657, 2020, https://doi.org/https://doi.org/10.1016/j.future.2020.06.019.

10. Zhang, L. and Liu, B., Sentiment Analysis and Opinion Mining, in: *Encyclopedia of Machine Learning and Data Mining*, pp. 1–10, Morgan & Claypool Publishers, Springer, Bostom, MA, 2016, https://doi.org/10.1007/978-1-4899-7502-7_907-1.

11. Hussein, D. M. E.-D. M., A survey on sentiment analysis challenges. *J. King Saud Univ. - Eng. Sci.*, 133, 9, 7–11, 2016, https://doi.org/10.1016/j.jksues.2016.04.002.

12. Li, S., Wang, Y., Xue, J., Zhao, N., Zhu, T., The impact of a covid-19 epidemic declaration on psychological consequences: A study on active weibo users.

Int. J. Environ. Res. Public Health, 17, 6, 1–9, 2020, https://doi.org/10.3390/ijerph17062032.

13. Spitkovsky, V., II and Jurafsky, D., Punctuation: Making a Point in Unsupervised Dependency Parsing. *Comput. Linguist.*, 15, 19–28, 2011, June, 19–28, https://pdfs.semanticscholar.org/7c34/6777169c60dcf04f24af5b58dc0db1e78901.pdf.

14. Cernian, A., Sgarciu, V., Martin, B., Sentiment analysis from product reviews using SentiWordNet as a lexical resource. *Proceedings of the 2015 7th International Conference on Electronics, Computers and Artificial Intelligence, ECAI 2015*, pp. WE15–WE18, 2015, https://doi.org/10.1109/ECAI.2015.7301224.

15. Dashtipour, K., Poria, S., Hussain, A., Cambria, E., Hawalah, A.Y.A., Gelbukh, A., Zhou, Q., Multilingual Sentiment Analysis: State of the Art and Independent Comparison of Techniques. *Cognit. Comput.*, 8, 4, 757–771, 2016, https://doi.org/10.1007/s12559-016-9415-7.

16. Mueller, M., Wagner, C.L., Annibale, D.J., Hulsey, T.C., Knapp, R.G., Almeida, J.S., Predicting extubation outcome in preterm newborns: A comparison of neural networks with clinical expertise and statistical modeling. *Pediatr. Res.*, 56, 1, 11–18, 2004, https://doi.org/10.1203/01.PDR.0000129658.55746.3C.

17. Vinodhini, G. and Chandrasekaran, R.M., A comparative performance evaluation of a neural network-based approach for sentiment classification of online reviews. *J. King Saud Univ. – Comput. Info. Sci.*, 28, 1, 2–12, 2016, https://doi.org/10.1016/j.jksuci.2014.03.024.

18. Raja, R., Sinha, T.S., Patra, R.K., Tiwari, S., Physiological Trait Based Biometrical Authentication of Human-Face Using LGXP and ANN Techniques. *Int. J. Inf. Comput. Secur.*, 10, 2/3, 303–320, 2018.

19. Grant, M.J. and Booth, A., A typology of reviews: An analysis of 14 review types and associated methodologies. *Health Info. Libr. J.*, 26, 2, 91–108, 2009, https://doi.org/10.1111/j.1471-1842.2009.00848.x.

20. Xingxing, J., Yingkun, C., Kunqing, X., Xiujun, M., Yuxiang, S., Cuo, C., A novel method to integrate spatial data mining and geographic information system. *Geoscience and Remote Sensing Symposium, 2005. IGARSS '05. Proceedings. 2005 IEEE International*, vol. 2(40235056), 4 pp., 2005, https://doi.org/10.1109/IGARSS.2005.1525219.

21. Singh, J., Singh, G., Singh, R., A review of sentiment analysis techniques for opinionated web text. *CSI Trans. ICT*, 4, 2–4, 241–247, 2016, https://doi.org/10.1007/s40012-016-0107-y.

22. Hamdi, A., Shaban, K., Zainal, A., A review on challenging issues in Arabic sentiment analysis. *J. Comput. Sci.*, 12, 9, 471–481, 2016, https://doi.org/10.3844/jcssp.2016.471.481.

23. Ghorbani, M., Bahaghighat, M., Xin, Q., Özen, F., ConvLSTMConv network: a deep learning approach for sentiment analysis in cloud computing. *J. Cloud Comput.*, 9, 1, 1–12, 2020, https://doi.org/10.1186/s13677-020-00162-1.

24. Kim, Y., Convolutional Neural Networks for Sentence Classification. *Proceedings of the 2014 Conference on Empirical Methods in Natural Language Processing (EMNLP)*, pp. 1746–1751, 2014, https://doi.org/10.3115/v1/D14-1181.

25. Grissette, H. and Nfaoui, E.H., Enhancing convolution-based sentiment extractor via dubbed N-gram embedding-related drug vocabulary. *Netw. Model. Anal. Health Inform. Bioinform.*, 9, 1, 1–16, 2020, https://doi.org/10.1007/s13721-020-00248-5.

26. Mehndiratta, P. and Soni, D., Identification of Sarcasm in Textual Data: A Comparative Study. *J. Data Inf. Sci.*, 4, 4, 56–83, 2019, https://doi.org/10.2478/jdis-2019-0021.

27. Xu, Z., Li, P., Wang, Y., Text Classifier Based on an Improved SVM Decision Tree. *Phys. Proc.*, 33, 1986–1991, 2012, https://doi.org/10.1016/j.phpro.2012.05.312.

28. Albayrak, M.D. and Gray-Roncal, W., Data Mining and Sentiment Analysis of Real-Time Twitter Messages for Monitoring and Predicting Events. *2019 9th IEEE Integrated STEM Education Conference, ISEC 2019*, pp. 42–43, 2019, https://doi.org/10.1109/ISECon.2019.8881956.

29. Jin, Z., Yang, Y., Liu, Y., Stock closing price prediction based on sentiment analysis and LSTM. *Neural Comput. Appl.*, 32, 13, 9713–9729, 2019, https://doi.org/10.1007/s00521-019-04504-2.

30. Lin, Y.-F.A., Li, C.-Y.K., Kalinicheva, Y., Huang, M.-C., Lee, C.-H., Wang, H.-C., Chu, H.-H., Case Study of Adapting a Phone-based Support System to Enable Drug-dependent Patients to Develop Coping Skills. *Proceedings of the 2017 CHI Conference Extended Abstracts on Human Factors in Computing Systems - CHI EA '17*, pp. 985–993, 2017, https://doi.org/10.1145/3027063.3053333.

31. Wunnava, S., Qin, X., Kakar, T., Rundensteiner, E.A., Kong, X., Liu, F., Jagannatha, A., Yu, H., Bidirectional LSTM-CRF for Adverse Drug Event Tagging in Electronic Health Records. *Proc. Mach. Learn. Res.*, 90, 48–56, 2018, https://bio-nlp.org/index.php/projects/39-nlp-challenges.

32. Patel, V., Prabhu, G., Kiran, B., *Int. J. Comput. Appl. (0975 – 8887)*, 131, 1, 415–463, 2015.

33. Ren, L., Xu, B., Lin, H., Liu, X., Yang, L., Sarcasm Detection with Sentiment Semantics Enhanced Multi-level Memory Network. *Neurocomputing*, 401, 320–326, 2020, https://doi.org/10.1016/j.neucom.2020.03.081.

34. Lalwani, S., Singhal, S., Kumar, R., Gupta, N., a Comprehensive Survey: Applications of Multi-Objective Particle Swarm Optimization (Mopso) Algorithm. *Trans. Comb.*, 2013, www.combinatorics.ir%5Cnwww.ui.ac.ir.

35. Peters, G., Crespo, F., Lingras, P., Weber, R., Soft clustering - Fuzzy and rough approaches and their extensions and derivatives. *Int. J. Approximate Reasoning*, 54, 2, 307–322, 2013, https://doi.org/10.1016/j.ijar.2012.10.003.

36. King, I., Li, J., Chan, K.T., A brief survey of computational approaches in Social Computing. *2009 International Joint Conference on Neural Networks*, pp. 1625–1632, 2009, https://doi.org/10.1109/IJCNN.2009.5178967.

37. Le, Q.V. and Mikolov, T., Distributed Representations of Sentences and Documents. *Proceedings of the 31 St International Conference on Machine Learning*, Beijing, pp. 1–9, 2014, https://doi.org/10.1145/2740908.2742760.

38. Xia, Y., Cambria, E., Hussain, A., Zhao, H., Word Polarity Disambiguation Using Bayesian Model and Opinion-Level Features. *Cognit. Comput.*, 7, 3, 369–380, 2015, https://doi.org/10.1007/s12559-014-9298-4.

39. Chen, Y.-H. and Li, S.-F., Using latent Dirichlet allocation to improve the text classification performance of support vector machine. *2016 IEEE Congress on Evolutionary Computation (CEC)*, pp. 1280–1286, 2016, https://doi.org/10.1109/CEC.2016.7743935.

40. Kiritchenko, S. and Mohammad, S.M., Sentiment Composition of Words with Opposing Polarities. *Proceedings of NAACL-HLT 2016*, pp. 1102–1108, 2016, https://doi.org/10.18653/v1/N16-1128.

41. Subrahmanian, V.S. and Reforgiato, D., AVA: Adjective-Verb-Adverb Combinations for Sentiment Analysis. *IEEE Intell. Syst.*, 23, 4, 43–50, 2008, https://doi.org/10.1109/MIS.2008.57.

42. Li, S.T., Pham, T.T., Chuang, H.C., Wang, Z.W., Does reliable information matter? Towards a trustworthy co-created recommendation model by mining unboxing reviews. *Inf. Syst. E-Bus. Manage.*, 14, 1, 71–99, 2016, https://doi.org/10.1007/s10257-015-0275-6.

43. Gupta, V. and Lehal, G.S., Automatic text summarization system for the Punjabi language. *J. Emerg. Technol. Web Intell.*, 5, 3, 257–271, 2013, https://doi.org/10.4304/jetwi.5.3.257-271.

44. Singh, J., Singh, G., Singh, R., Singh, P., Morphological evaluation and sentiment analysis of Punjabi text using deep learning classification. *J. King Saud Univ. - Comp. Info. Sci.*, 5, 508–517 April 7, 2018a, https://doi.org/10.1016/j.jksuci.2018.04.003.

45. Singh, J., Singh, G., Singh, R., Singh, P., Optimizing Accuracy of Sentiment Analysis Using Deep Learning Based Classification Technique, in: *CCIS Springer Hiedalberg Germany*, pp. 516–532, Springer, Singapore, 2018b, https://doi.org/10.1007/978-981-10-8527-7_43.

46. Kim, J. and Ahn, I., Weekly ILI patient ratio change prediction using news articles with support vector machine. *BMC Bioinf.*, 20, 1, 1–16, 2019, https://doi.org/10.1186/s12859-019-2894-2.

47. Mihaylov, I., Nisheva, M., Vassilev, D., Application of machine learning models for survival prognosis in breast cancer studies. *Inf. (Switzerland)*, 10, 3, 1–13, 2019, https://doi.org/10.3390/info10030093.

48. Baccouche, A., Garcia-Zapirain, B., Elmaghraby, A., Annotation Technique for Health-Related Tweets Sentiment Analysis. *2018 IEEE International*

Symposium on Signal Processing and Information Technology, ISSPIT 2018, pp. 382–387, 2019, https://doi.org/10.1109/ISSPIT.2018.8642685.

49. Mourad, A. and Darwish, K., Subjectivity and Sentiment Analysis of Modern Standard Arabic and Arabic Microblogs. *Proceedings of the 4th Workshop on Computational Approaches to Subjectivity, Sentiment and Social Media Analysis,* vol. 3, pp. 55–64, 2013, http://en.wikipedia.org/wiki/Varieties_.

50. Li, W., Zhu, L., Shi, Y., Guo, K., Cambria, E., User reviews: Sentiment analysis using lexicon integrated two-channel CNN–LSTM family models. *Appl. Soft Comput. J.,* 94, 1, 1–11, 2020, https://doi.org/10.1016/j.asoc.2020.106435.

51. Kumar, S., Singh, S., Kumar, J., A Study on Face Recognition Techniques with Age and Gender Classification, in: *IEEE International Conference on Computing, Communication and Automation (ICCCA),* May 2017, pp. 1001–1006.

52. Kumar, S., Singh, S., Kumar, J., A Comparative Study on Face Spoofing Attacks, in: *IEEE International Conference on Computing, Communication and Automation (ICCCA),* May 2017, pp. 1104–1108.

15

Application of Artificial Intelligence and Computer Vision to Identify Edible Bird's Nest

Weng Kin Lai[1]*, Mei Yuan Koay[1], Selina Xin Ci Loh[2], Xiu Kai Lim[1] and Kam Meng Goh[1]

[1]Department of Electrical & Electronics Engineering, Faculty of Engineering & Technology, Tunku Abdul Rahman University College, Setapak, Kuala Lumpur, Malaysia
[2]Department of Mechanical Engineering, Faculty of Engineering & Technology, Tunku Abdul Rahman University College, Setapak, Kuala Lumpur, Malaysia

Abstract

Cognitive disability is a common feature associated with a variety of neurological disorders which have increasingly been recognised as major causes of death and disability worldwide. Feigin and Theo in their 2019 study had shown that globally, neurological disorders were the leading cause of disability-adjusted life-years (DALY) and the second leading cause of deaths [1]. There is now evidence that demonstrated neuroinflammation plays an important role in the development of cognitive impairment [2]. However, current available therapies are relatively ineffective in treating or preventing such neurological disorders, thus representing an important, unfulfilled medical need. Hence, developing potential treatment is one of the major areas of research interest.

Edible bird's nests (EBNs) are nests formed from the saliva of swiftlets commonly found in South East Asia. They contain sialic acid which is believed to improve brain function. A recent study by Careena *et al.* using edible birds nest on lipopolysaccharide-induced impairment of learning and memory in Wistar rats revealed that while there is some improvement in cognitive functions,

*Corresponding author: laiwk@tarc.edu.my

Sandeep Kumar, Rohit Raja, Shrikant Tiwari and Shipa Rani (eds.) Cognitive Behavior and Human Computer Interaction Based on Machine Learning Algorithm, (339–360) © 2022 Scrivener Publishing LLC

nevertheless, the effectiveness of the EBNs used are not alike and depend on the source or type of EBNs used [2]. Norhayati, Azman and Wan Nazaimoon have demonstrated that the unprocessed depend EBNs harvested during the rainy seasons gave higher composition of proteins as compared to those collected during the non-rainy seasons [3]. Once they are harvested, the EBNs are graded before they are offered for sale to the public. The conventional way to grade EBNs is carried out manually by trained human operators. However this approach is time consuming, costly, and inefficient with inconsistencies occurring primarily due to human fatigue. To address these issues, a novel and fast multi-features neural fuzzy approach to automatically and accurately identify the grade of EBNs is proposed here. To demonstrate its effectiveness and usefulness, the proposed new approach is compared with several other state-of-the art artificial intelligence (AI) techniques and the results shown. Essentially the main contributions from this investigation are as follows:

1) a novel application of a fuzzy neural approach to accurately identify the grade of EBNs,
2) an automated approach to identify the grade of EBNs based on an intuitive multi-features set,
3) does not need vast amounts of training data that requires human effort and time to compile,
4) fast training and no need for any unique high-performance computing platforms.

Our proposed approach achieved a high accuracy of more than 95% trained on these EBNs images.

Keywords: Image processing, alternative medicine, food supplements, artificial intelligence, edible birds nest

15.1   Introduction

Cognitive disorder is the most common feature associated with different types of neurological disorders, i.e., Alzheimer's, Parkinson's disease, brain injury, and stroke. These disorders are the primary cause of death and different types of disability in human beings. In 2016, neurological disorders affected 276 million lives and caused deaths at 9 million globally [1]. While the disabilities may not be fatal, it is debilitating and contributes to a lower quality of life. No evidence demonstrated neuroinflammation plays a crucial role in cognitive impairment [2] development. The currently available medical treatments and therapies are not useful in preventing or treating such neurological disorders. Hence, developing a potential treatment for these disorders is always an important research area. Edible bird's nests (EBNs) found in South East Asian countries of Malaysia, Indonesia, Thailand, and Vietnam is a multi-billion dollar industry. They are especially popular among some Asian communities due to their high-protein nutrients [5] and sialic acid which is believed to improve brain function.

A recent study by Careena *et al.* using EBNs on lipopolysaccharide-induced impairment of learning and memory in Wistar rats revealed that while there is some improvement in cognitive functions, the effectiveness of the EBNs used is not alike and depends on the source or type of EBNs used. There are two main types of EBNs available on the market today: farmed or those harvested from the wild. *Norhayati*, *Azman*, and *Wan Nazaimoon* have identified that the excellent quality of EBNs was produced during rainy seasons [3]. The unprocessed EBN samples, which are collected during the rainy season, gave a higher amount of protein as compared to the samples which were collected in the non-rainy season. Bird nests can be in any form: raw, cleaned, processed, and graded. The price of EBNss solely depends on the grade. Grade AA nests are the most expensive among the various grades as it is the highest quality, followed by Grade A, B, and C. The grades of EBNss are usually based on their shape, size, color, and impurities level. Conventionally, trained human operators would grade EBNss based on these features. However, the grading results' consistencies can be unreliable as the manual grading process is prone to the human operators' subjectivity [6–8]. Thus, such a tedious grading process leads to production costs, subjectivity in the results, and low efficiency as vast amounts of time are spent on the inspection. Furthermore, hiring and training new operators to inspect the nests is unavoidable for the conventional approach of grading. Notwithstanding the conventional method, with technological advancement in recent decades, some aspects of identifying EBNs have improved dramatically in speed, accuracy, and reliability [4].

This chapter will describe a novel and fast multi-features neural fuzzy approach using a set of unique features to grade EBNs automatically, and the results of the proposed methodology are compared with several state-of-art artificial intelligence (AI) techniques. Our research contributions may be summarized as follow.

1) a novel application of a fuzzy neural approach to accurately grade EBNs,

2) an automated approach to grade EBNs based on an intuitive multi-features set,
3) does not need vast amounts of training data that requires human effort and time to compile,
4) fast training and no need for any unique high-performance computing platforms.

We organized our chapter in the following way: Some prior work is described in Section 15.2, while our proposed approach's methodology is discussed in Section 15.3. Results are then presented in Section 15.4, with conclusions in Section 15.5.

15.2   Prior Work

15.2.1   Low-Dimensional Color Features

Grading of the EBNs that the industry practices are based on size, number of impurities, and overall shape. The grading of EBNs depends on the nest's size nest, and size depends on the number of fingers [7]. The ideal size of the nest is a minimum of three fingers or more extensive than three. These three fingers are the index finger, middle finger and the ring finger of an average adult. Another method to grade the EBNs is based on the number of impurities found in the specimen. These impurities can range from feathers, sand particles, bird droppings, etc. EBNs with lesser impurities will fetch a higher price compared to those with many impurities. Finally, the shape of the harvested nests will have a significant effect on the grade. Deformed EBNs significantly different from their accepted shapes will have a lower commercial value [7]. Lower grades would also have a similar shape as their better counterparts but these will not be even when placed on a horizontal surface, as shown in Figure 15.1.

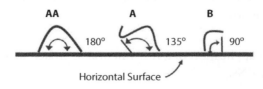

Figure 15.1 Shapes of EBN of grade AA, grade A, and grade B. Adapted from [4].

15.2.2   Image Processing for Automated Grading

Machine vision is always helpful to create an effective automatic grading system. Some researchers have used a computer vision-based system for automatic grading and sorting of agriculture products. Human experts were then used to predict the maturity of mangoes from these images. Gaussian Mixture Model (GMM) based on the set of relevant features of the mangoes was used to predict maturity level. Nandi *et al.* showed that the classification accuracies of the GMM used in their system were as good as those of human experts [8]. Fruits' diseases can be detected through classification and feature extraction methodologies. The fruits tested were apples, palm oil fruits, mangoes, dates, and strawberries. Different variety of fruits has different features for the detection of the disease. The classification technique is applied for disease identification [9]. In this approach, segmentation is applied to differentiate between healthy and infected fruits. According to the percentage of the infection, fruits were graded into different grades.

15.2.3   Automated Classification

Automated classification and grading of agricultural products have been extensively implemented using a variety of different classification techniques [10–12, 40–42]. Moreover, Han Yan et al. developed an adaptive neuro-fuzzy inference system (ANFIS) to classify water quality status of river based on a total of 9 weeks data (845 observations consisting of 3 water quality parameter) collected from 100 monitoring stations in all major river basins in China [44]. B. Ari Kuncoro, and Suharjito investigated ANFIS to classify the texture of crumpled aluminum foil, corduroy, cotton, and orange peel from the Guney and Sarikaya [3–7, 13]. Atashi reported that Alireza *et al.* used ANFIS to detect and diagnose breast cancer based on a set of risk factors [14]. They used ANIFS to identify breast cancer and used 22 features from the standard datasets and then on real data. The results were satisfactory with ANIFS.

15.3   Auto Grading of Edible Birds Nest

The EBNs images were collected from a centralized EBNs processing facility with modern and hygienic facilities. This is a more cost-effective way of processing the EBNs. The EBNs, when harvested, is sent for processing by the individual EBNs farms, which are usually managed on a small scale. They would not provide either the facilities or the human person to process the raw

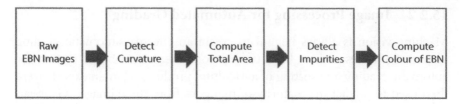

Figure 15.2 Block diagram for feature extraction.

EBNs and grade the EBNs efficiently and consistently. To test the auto grader, we used the EBNs of three different grades: AA, A, and B, which the trained operators had carefully graded. Sixty-three samples were collected and photographs were taken with a standard digital SLR camera fitted with macro-lens.

15.3.1 Feature Extraction

The feature extraction process consists of various image processing techniques and it consists of five different steps, as illustrated in Figure 15.2. Different methods were applied to retrieve the required features from the EBNs images. The features are area, the color of the EBNs curvature, and impurities.

15.3.2 Curvature as a Feature

To model the curvature, a perfect circle will have a value of 1. Therefore, when the shape of the EBNs is a perfect circle, the curvature value will have the maximum value of 1.0, i.e.,

$$curvature = 4 \times \pi \times \frac{area}{perimeter^2} \tag{15.1}$$

If the shape deviates from a perfect circle, then the curvature value will decrease. To compute the curvature of the EBNs, the primary foreground object in each image was segmented and cropped with the background changed to black. The cropped image is then binarized and its edges identified. Random image noise is ignored and the curvature is computed for the larger areas.

15.3.3 Amount of Impurities

HSV (Hue-Saturation-Value) is used to identify the impurities in the EBNs. Figure 15.3 shows the distribution of the intensity of the saturation values for all three grades of EBNs investigated.

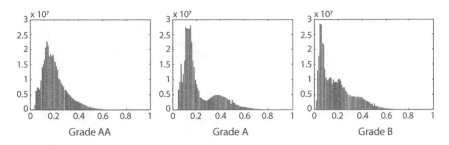

Figure 15.3 Histogram of intensities of saturation layer for various grades.

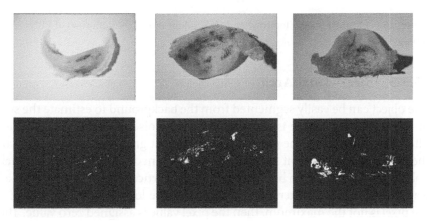

Figure 15.4 Original images (top row) and the impurities detected (bottom row) from EBNs for grade AA, A, and B.

From the histograms of the saturation layer (Figure 15.3) of all three grades, it can be observed that there are significantly more pixels for *saturation* values between the range 0.1 to 0.5, while there are a lesser number of pixels with *saturation* values greater than 0.5. This value is used to correlate with the impurities. The number of pixel values representing impurities is less than the number of the EBNs and background pixels. A higher number of white pixels represent more impurities. Figure 15.4 represents the same.

15.3.4   Color of EBNs

As per the manual inspection of the EBNs image, grade AA is clearer and white and grade B is yellowish or off-white. Impurities like mud or sand will also affect the EBNs color, as shown in Figure 15.5.

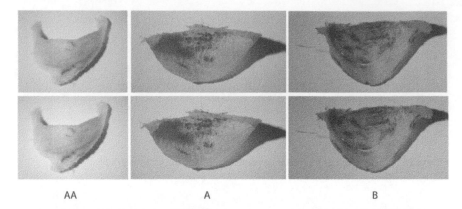

AA   A   B

Figure 15.5 Original image (top row) and HSV colour model (bottom row) of EBNs (grade AA, A, and B).

15.3.5   Size—Total Area

The object can be easily segmented from the background to estimate the size of the EBNs. The image is calculated and for noise removal, the Gaussian filter is used to detect the change in the contrast gradient. The direction of the edge and the gradient for each pixel is obtained using the Sobel kernel. Sobel kernel is applied in both horizontal and vertical directions. Every pixel was then checked to determine whether it is the local maximum or not; if the pixel is not the maximum, then the pixel value is assigned zero value. The threshold value was adjusted with a fudge factor to attain the binary mask that contains the object of the image. The object's area was computed based

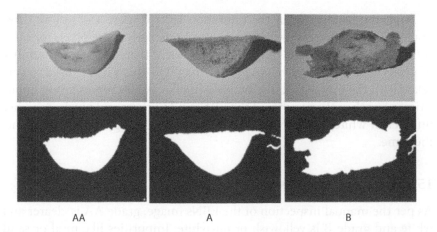

AA   A   B

Figure 15.6 Original images (top row) and the area detected for each image (bottom row).

Table 15.1 Features extracted for various grades.

Grade	Curvature	Size	Impurities	Color
AA	0.3560	5784956	1148060	0.6824
AA	0.7969	2646064	2370178	0.6784
	-	-	-	-
A	0.2403	6333746	133551	0.7608
A	0.4217	5075468	416805	0.7765
	-	-	-	-
B	0.3537	5361693	518880	0.6784
B	0.7216	5084135	4971157	0.6980
	-	-	-	-
	-	-	-	-

on the total number of white pixels from the processed images. Examples of the computed area for each of the three grades are shown in Figure 15.6.

Table 15.1 shows a selection of the four extracted features for each class of EBNs. Notice the different range of values for each feature. Size and estimate of the impurities are in their thousands, whereas curvature and color are less than one.

15.4   Experimental Results

Classification of the EBNs grades has been with ANFIS, and compared with k-Nearest Neighbour (kNN), Naive Bayesian (NB), Support Vector Machines (SVM), as well as Artificial Neural Networks (ANN).

15.4.1   Data Pre-Processing

As the values of the extracted features' values of different ranges, we need to normalize them to the range [0, 1] to avoid the larger numerical values from any of the features dominating the auto-grading process. Hence, we investigated several different data pre-processing methods that converted the raw data into an effective and efficient form before the data were processed.

Linear #1 (Z-score normalization) converts the original input data into zero mean and unit variance. The new value is then normalized into the range of 0 to 1, using the mean, μ and the standard deviation, σ, i.e.,

$$X' = \frac{X - \mu}{\sigma} \tag{15.2}$$

where X is the value to be transformed and X' is the new value.

Linear #2 (decimal scaling) is used to convert the values of the data to the range between 0 and powers of 10, i.e.,

$$X' = \frac{X}{10^j} \tag{15.3}$$

where j is chosen so that 10^j would be equal to or more than the dataset's largest value.

Linear #3 (linearization) is where the data points were mapped to a linear straight line. In this case, the linearization of points was done by dividing each data point by the maximum value for the selected feature so that the new data now lies within the range from 0 to 1:

$$X' = \frac{X}{maximum\ value\ of\ the\ current\ set\ of\ features} \tag{15.4}$$

Linear #4 (min-max normalized value) is a linear scaling algorithm that transforms the original input range into new data ranging from 0 to 1, i.e.,

$$X' = \frac{X - X_{min}}{X_{max} - X_{min}} \tag{15.5}$$

Non-Linear #1 and #2 (sigmoid) is based on the following non-linear transformation:

$$X' = \frac{1}{1 + e^{-x}} \tag{15.6}$$

It is suitable for the datasets which contain a large number of outlier data in which such data are smaller or larger than the median of the mean by three standard deviations. Outlier data smaller than the lower cut-off value will be mapped to 0, while outlier data larger than the higher cut-off value will be mapped to 1. For **Non-Linear #1**, the cut-off was set to just one standard deviation (σ), whereas for **Non-Linear #2**, the threshold is 2σ.

15.4.2 Auto Grading

- **k-Nearest Neighbour (kNN)**

kNN is a popular and simple classifier that requires memory to store the entire training data to be then used to predict the class of the testing data. The kNN classifier searches for k-number of instances or neighbours from a particular query point by considering those closest to that query point [15, 16]. The class of the query point is then determined by the majority voting scheme, where the most frequent class from the k-number of neighbours will be the class for that particular query point. The performance of this classifier was also investigated here. The number of neighbours selected for the kNN classifier can influence the classification accuracy. Recent work by Koay *et al.* [17] has shown that a neighbourhood value of 7 produces the best classification results.

- **Naive Bayesian**

A Naive Bayesian is a probabilistic classifier based on Bayes' theorem (from Bayesian statistics) with strong (naive) independence assumptions. In simple terms, a naive Bayes classifier assumes that the presence (or absence) of a particular feature of a class is unrelated to the presence (or absence) of any other feature. Classifiers built from Naive Bayesian have worked quite well in many different fields, offering useful solutions to complex real-world situations despite the perception of their simplicity. The use of Naive Bayes for defects detection has been promoted by other researchers citing predictive performance and comprehensibility as their significant strengths [18–20]. In agriculture, Thakur and Mehta have investigated the use of Naive Bayesian for mango and apple disease detection [21].

- **Artificial Neural Networks**

The multi-layer perceptron (MLP) feed-forward neural network had been used extensively in many different areas with promising results [22–29]. Our multilayer perceptron neural network (MLP) consists of the usual topology [30], i.e., an input layer, one hidden layer and an output layer. During the training with the back-propagation [31, 32] learning algorithm, the weights are adjusted to minimize the outputs' misclassification error between desired and actual values.

- **Support Vector Machine (SVM)**

SVM developed by V. Vapnik [33] has been known for its effectiveness for various classification problems, especially when only given small datasets. Given a training set of examples (x_i, y_i), i = 1, 2, …, m where input pattern $x_i \in$ Rn and class $y_i \in \{+1, -1\}$, the aim of SVM is to find the optimal hyperplane, which is to classify each pattern. If the patterns are linearly separable, then a hyperplane can be found that separates the data into their respective correct classes. Further details of SVM can easily be found from other published work [34, 35, 43]. In our work, we used an SVM with a linear kernel to perform multiclass classification because of its computational efficiency. Moreover, we implemented one-vs-one coding in SVM where features from different classes are trained using a separate classifier, resulting in N(N − 1)/2 classifiers. This coding suffices to overcome the drawback of imbalanced dataset distribution. Nonetheless, it is more computationally intensive.

- **ANFIS**

ANFIS is a combination of ANN and Fuzzy Inference System (FIS) [13, 44]. The ANIFS architecture can be categorized into five layers and the node in each layer will perform a particular function according to the input signal. Besides, there is a set of parameters (p, q, r) about each node [36], affecting its performance. In case ANIFS has two input values x and y and output is z, then there will be two Takagi and Sugeno Type's fuzzy IF-THEN rules in the rule base, i.e.,

Rule 1: If x is A_1 and y is B_1, then $f_1 = P_1^x + q_1 y + r_1$,

Rule 2: If x is A_2 and y is B_2, then $f_2 = P_2^x + q_2 y + r_2$.

Layer 1: The crisp inputs is assigned with a membership function degree $\left(O_i^1\right)$, indicating how much the input has satisfied the linguistic label (A_i) associated with the input node function, as shown in Equation (15.7). The parameters in Layer 1 is referred as premise parameters.

$$O_i^1 = \mu A_i(x), i = 1, 2 \tag{15.7}$$

Layer 2: The rule nodes calculate the firing strength of a rule by multiplying the corresponding membership degree which are the processed outputs of the incoming signals at Layer 1, as shown in Equation (15.8).

$$w_i = \mu A_i(x) \times \mu B_i(y), _i = 1, 2 \tag{15.8}$$

Layer 3: Here the average nodes calculate the normalization of the firing strength of each rule by dividing each firing strength by the sum of all the rules' firing strength.

$$\overline{w_i} = \frac{w_i}{w_1 + w_2}, i = 1, 2 \tag{15.9}$$

Layer 4: The consequent nodes compute the contribution of each rule toward the overall output, where $\{p_i, q_i, r_i\}$ are the adjustable parameter set, known as consequent parameters.

$$O_i^4 = \overline{w_i} f_i = \overline{w_i}(p_i x + q_i y + r_i) \tag{15.10}$$

Layer 5: Finally, the single output node sums up all the incoming signals from Layer 4 to compute the overall output. Defuzzification will also be carried out to convert the fuzzy result into a crisp output.

$$O_i^5 = overall\ output = \sum_i \overline{w_i} f_i = \frac{\sum_i w_i f_i}{w_i} \tag{15.11}$$

The hybrid learning algorithm then combines the gradient descent method (used in backward pass to propagate the error signal backward to update the premise parameters on Layer 1) and least square method used in the forward pass to update the consequent parameters in Layer 4. The ANFIS classifier was deployed to generate the initial Fuzzy Inference System (FIS) structure and then later to tune the parameters of the classifier using the training data. There are several types of techniques for fuzzy rule extraction in ANFIS namely, grid-partitioning, subtractive clustering and Fuzzy C-Means clustering (FCM). Even though grid partitioning is able to partition the input space for classification but it also faces the curse of dimensionality of input which results in an exponential expansion of the rule base and hence, an increase in computation time and cost [37]. Subtractive clustering and FCM forms clusters in the data space which allows the development of the fuzzy rules (both premise and consequent sections).

- **Subtractive Clustering and Fuzzy C-Means Clustering *(FCM)***
There are two types of clustering method which can be used for fuzzy rule generation. These were investigated to identify which is more suitable for ANFIS in correctly identifying the right EBNs grade. Subtractive clustering is used when the user wants to know the number of clusters as well as the

position of the cluster's centre in the dataset. The cluster estimation and center of the cluster can be found by finding the potential of each data [38]. It is suitable for a higher dimensional dataset to reduce the computational complexity [37]. Table 15.2 shows the result for subtractive clustering for different values of the radius.

It also shows that that the smaller the radius, the larger number the number of rules generated. Unfortunately, this will increase the amount of computation time. Nevertheless, the best performance was obtained when the clustering radius is 0.2, which gives the highest classification accuracy of 82.17% with 44 rules generated. FCM clusters the data where each data point can belong to more than one cluster with different membership

Table 15.2 Classification accuracies for various radii of subtractive clustering.

Radius	Accuracy (%)	Number of rules
1.0	62.13	3
0.9	58.52	4
0.8	66.37	4
0.7	77.46	6
0.6	81.57	8
0.5	81.95	11
0.4	82.11	19
0.3	81.01	28
0.2	82.17	44

Table 15.3 Accuracies for FCM with different clusters.

Number of clusters	Overall accuracy (%)	Number of rules generated
2	74.28	2
3	83.23	3
4	82.45	4
5	69.35	5
6	65.22	6
7	59.68	7

strengths. The objective function is minimized at every iteration so that the cluster centroids and membership strength of each data point can be updated. However, compared with subtractive clustering, FCM is more efficient and effective. Nevertheless, the number of clusters can also be varied, but the classification accuracy is sensitive to the number of clusters assigned. The optimal performance of 83.23% was obtained when used to identify three clusters, as shown in Table 15.3.

15.4.3   Auto Grading of EBNs

The proposed ANIFS was trained with three classes of data with four features (total 63 features) for 100 epochs. The data was separated into different portions of training and testing data. The same strategy was adopted for the other classifiers. In the case of ANFIS, FCM was used to generate the initial FIS structure. It is computationally less expensive and it produced less rules. k-fold cross-validation with 70% for training and the remaining 30% for testing was used to investigate the classifier's performance on the different data pre-processing techniques. Furthermore, all the classifiers were tested for 1,000 iterations to minimize the initial random solutions' sensitivity and the average results recorded.

We tested the neural network on the EBNs from 6 to a maximum of 16 neurons in the hidden layer. The results are summarized in Table 15.4, with the results suggesting that better performance was achieved for 11 hidden neurons in the hidden layer.

ANFIS accurately identified the correct grade, ranging from the lowest at 81.34% with Linear #3 to 94.09% with Non-Linear #2 as summarised in Table 15.5.

The results showed that the classifiers are sensitive to the pre-processing schemes used and performed better on a different scheme. kNN could not match the others' accuracy, managing only 61.54% with Lin_#3. On the other hand, NB was able to match the more modern SVM classifier's

Table 15.4 Sensitivity of the neural net with different number of hidden neurons.

Number of neurons	Classification accuracy (%)
6	88.76
9	88.97
11	89.28
16	88.52

Table 15.5 Auto-grading accuracies (%).

	kNN	NB	ANN	SVM	ANFIS
Lin_#1	59.88	75.93	77.45	84.07	88.62
Lin_#2	54.19	89.70	89.28	89.67	88.53
Lin_#3	61.54	75.93	68.32	84.19	81.34
Lin_#4	60.65	89.70	71.04	89.52	88.83
NL_#1	54.45	72.09	72.82	74.97	93.14
NL_#2	56.06	75.49	74.13	81.97	94.09

Lin, Linear; **NL**, Non-Linear.

accuracy. Besides, if we look at the lowest performance of ANFIS, it still outperforms most of the other classifiers, as illustrated in Table 15.6.

Finally, the Convolutional Neural Network (CNN) was also tested to auto-grade EBNs. MVGG-19 [39], based on the VGG-19 CNN and uses the same number of convolutional layers and max-pooling layers, was chosen. The MVGG-19 used here has 19 layers, with 32 input filters in the first layer. However, the MVGG-19 has a smaller number of parameters than the VGG-19; the MVGG-19 was integrated with Keras library and TensorFlow backend. Moreover, as computationally intensive, the NVIDIA GeForce GTX 1070 GPU was used to speed up the computation. Since the EBNs dataset images have large dimensions, the computation time is much longer. Hence, the dataset images were scaled down before the CNN model can process them. Squashing was adopted to resize the images. Furthermore, as such computation methods thrive on large datasets, data augmentation in the form of random transformations were applied to the existing EBNs dataset, such as horizontal/ vertical flipping, clockwise and

Table 15.6 Maximum and minimum classification accuracies (%).

Classifier	Min	Max
kNN	54.19	61.54
NB	72.09	89.70
ANN	68.32	89.28
SVM	74.97	89.52
ANFIS	81.34	94.09

Table 15.7 Best classification accuracies.

Classifier	Accuracy
kNN	61.54
NB	89.70
ANN	89.28
SVM	89.67
ANFIS	94.09
MVGG-19	88.89

anti-clockwise rotation. Table 15.7 summarizes the best classification accuracy extracted from the various pre-processing schemes.

15.5 Conclusion

Neuroinflammation is crucial in the pathology associated with cognitive impairment, but recent studies have suggested that EBNs can provide some degree of neuroprotection by inhibiting neuroinflammatory and oxidative stress processes [2]. Nevertheless, the quality of the EBNs does play a significant part in its effectiveness in providing neuroprotection. The standard way to identify the quality of EBNs is through human inspection, which can be time-consuming, inefficient with inconsistent results, and labor-intensive.

This chapter presents a new approach to grade EBNs and compares them to human inspection automatically. EBNs images were processed to produce a set of four unique features based on the *curvature*, overall *size*, level of *impurities*, and, finally, *color*. These extracted features were used to differentiate the three different grades (AA, A, and B) of EBNs. As the range of values for these features varies greatly, we have also investigated several normalization techniques. With four features presented to the classifiers, ANFIS performed better than kNN, with the kNN able to only achieve 89% with Linear #2, whereas the ANFIS at 95% with Linear #4. Neural nets, SVM and NB, achieved about 89%, some 6% less accurate than ANFIS. We have also evaluated a non-feature-based approach that does not require any feature extraction as it uses the images. However, as the dataset is relatively small, a significant amount of preparatory work needs to be done before the MVGG-19 CNN learned the various grades and then auto-grades the remaining images not used in training. The CNN was able to produce an average accuracy of 88.89% with this non-features approach.

A significant advantage of our features-based approach is that it is less time-consuming as the system developed here achieved satisfactory results without requiring a vast set of data or any additional computing hardware. In the future, we would like to extend the work to look at EBNss from a different source where the grading may be different and investigate a better imaging system to improve the accuracy of the system further.

Acknowledgments

The authors are grateful to Lim Ed Win and his team at Mobile Harvesters Malaysia Sdn. Bhd.—a state-of-the-art EBNs processing plant with clean-room facilities, for their assistance in this research. The authors are also grateful to Tunku Abdul Rahman University College for financial support and the use of various facilities.

References

1. Feigin, V.L. and Vos, T., Global, regional, and national burden of neurological disorders 1990–2016: a systematic analysis for the Global Burden of Disease Study 2016. *Lancet Neurol.*, 18, 5, 459–480, 2019 May.
2. Careena, S., Sani, D., Tan, S.N., Lim, C.W., Hassan, S., Norhafizah, M., Kirby, B.P., Ideris, A., Stanslas, J., Basri, H.B., Lim, C.T.S., Effect of Edible Bird's Nest Extract on Lipopolysaccharide-Induced Impairment of Learning and Memory in Wistar Rats. Evidence-Based Complementary and Alternative Medicine, 2018, Article ID 9318789, 7 pages, 2018. https://doi.org/10.1155/2018/9318789 [open access]
3. Norhayati, M.K., Azman, O., Wan Nazaimoon, W.M., Preliminary study of the nutritional content of Malaysian edible bird's nest. *Malays. J. Nutr.*, 16, 3, 389–396, 2010.
4. Introduction to Birds Nest, 2018, http://yanwo.saikim.com.my/english/introduction-birds-nest.html, accessed on 28th March 2018.
5. Chua, Y.G., Chan, S.H., Bloodworth, B.C., Li, S.F.Y., Leong, L.P., Identification of edible bird's nest with amino acid and monosaccharide analysis. *J. Agric. Food Chem.*, 63, 1, 279–289, 2014.
6. Goh, K.M., Lai, W.K., Ting, P.H., Koh, D., Wong, J.K.R., Size Characterisation of Edible Bird Nest Impurities: A Preliminary Study. *21ˢᵗ International Conference on Knowledge-Based and Intelligent Information and Engineering Systems* (KES2017), Marseille, France, 6–8 September 2017, pp. 1072–1081, 2017.
7. Tan, K.H., Chia, F.C., Ong, A.H.K., Impact of Swiftlet's Moult Season on the Value of Edible Birds Nests. *International Conference on Intelligent Agriculture*, IPCBEE, vol. 63, IACSIT Press, Singapore, 2014, vol. 63.4.

8. Nandi, C.S., Tudu, B., Koley, C., An automated machine vision-based system for fruit sorting and Grading, in: *Sixth International Conference on Sensing Technology (ICST)*, pp. 195–200, 2012.

9. Solanki, U. and U. K. J. D. G. T., A Survey on Detection of Disease and Fruit Grading. *Int. J. Innov. Emerg. Res. Eng.*, 2, 2, 109–114, 2015.

10. Park, K., Hong, Y.K., Ki, G.H., Lee, J., Classification of apple leaf conditions in hyperspectral images for diagnosis of Marssonina blotch using mRMR and deep neural network. *Comput. Electron. Agric.*, 148, 179–187, 2018.

11. Rumpf, T., Römer, C., Weis, M., Sökefeld, M., Gerhards, R., Plümer, L., Sequential support vector machine classification for small-grain weed species discrimination with particular regard to Cirsium arvense and Galium aparine. *Comput. Electron. Agric.*, 80, 89–96, 2012.

12. Mohapatra, A., Shanmugasundaram, S., Malmathanraj, R., Grading of ripening stages of red banana using dielectric properties changes and image processing approach. *Comput. Electron. Agric.*, 143, 100–110, 2017.

13. Guney, K. and Sarikaya, N., Adaptive Neuro-Fuzzy Inference System for Texture Image Classification. *Int. Conf. Autom. Cogn. Sci. Opt. Micro-Electro-Mechanical Syst. Inf. Technol.*, vol. 19, no. 3, pp. 3–7, 2015.

14. Atashi, A., Nazeri, N., Abbasi, E., Dorri, S., Breast Cancer Risk Assessment Using Adaptive Neuro-Fuzzy Inference System (ANFIS) and Subtractive Clustering Algorithm. *Multidiscip. Cancer Investig.*, 1, 2, 20–26, 2017.

15. Hill, T. and Lewicki, P., *STATISTICS: Methods and Applications*, StatSoft, Tulsa, 2007.

16. Aldayel, M.S., K-Nearest Neighbour classification for glass identification problem. *Proceedings of International Conference on Computer Systems and Industrial Informatics*, pp. 1–5, 2012.

17. Koay, M.Y., Loh, S.X.C., Lai, W.K., Goh, K.M., Feature Selection for Automated Grading of Edible Birds Nest with ANFIS. *Proceedings of the International Conference on Control, Robotics and Informatics (ICCRI2018)*, Kuala Lumpur, Malaysia, April 2018, 2018.

18. Wang, T. and Li, W., Naive Bayes Software Defect Prediction Model. *Proceedings of the 2010 International Conference on Computational Intelligence and Software Engineering*, pp. 1–4, 2010.

19. Sankar, K., Kannan, S., Jennifer, P., Prediction of Code Fault Using Naive Bayes and SVM Classifiers. *Middle-East J. Sci. Res.*, 20, 1, 108–113, 2014.

20. Veni, S. and Srinivasan, A., Defect Classification Using Naïve Bayes Classification. *Int. J. Appl. Eng. Res.*, 12, 220, 12693–12700, 2017.

21. Thakur, R. and Mehta, P., Bayesian Classifier Based Advanced Fruits Disease Detection. *Int. J. Eng. Dev. Res.*, 5, 3, 1237–1241, 2017.

22. Zabidi, A., Lee, Y.K., Mansor, W., Yassin, I.M., Sahak, R., Classification of Infant Cries with Asphyxia Using Multilayer Perceptron Neural Network. *Proceedings of the Second International Conference on Computer Engineering and Applications*, vol. 1, pp. 204–208, 2010.

23. Catalan, J.A., Jin, J.S., Gedeon, T.D., Reducing the Dimensions of Texture Features for Image Retrieval Using Multi-layer Neural Networks. *J. Pattern Anal. Appl.*, 2, 2, 196–203, 1999.

24. Brown, W., Gedeon, T.D., Barnes, R., The Use of a Multilayer Feedforward Neural Network for Mineral Prospectivity Mapping. *Proceedings 6th International Conference Neural Information Processing (ICONIP'99)*, Perth, pp. 160–165, 1999.

25. Sharma, N. and Gedeon, T.D., Artificial Neural Network Classification Models for Stress in Reading. *Proceedings of 19th International Conference on Neural Information Processing 2012 (ICONIP 2012)*, pp. 388–395, 2012.

26. Ali, R., Jiang, B., Man, M., Hussain, A., Luo, B., Classification of Fish Ectoparasite Genus Gyrodactylus SEM Images Using ASM and Complex Network Model. *Proceedings of the 21st International Conference on Neural Information Processing 2014 (ICONIP2014)*, pp. 103–110, 2014.

27. Sharda, R. and Delen, D., Predicting box-office success of motion pictures with neural net-works. *Expert Syst. Appl.*, 30, 2, 243–254, 2006.

28. Eftekharian, E., Khatami, A., Khosravi, A., Nahavandi, S., Data Mining Analysis of an Urban Tunnel Pressure Drop Based on CFD Data. *Proceedings of the 22nd International Conference on Neural Information Processing 2015 (ICONIP2015)*, pp. 128–135, 2015.

29. Azcarraga, A., Talavera, A., Azcarraga, J., Gender-Specific Classifiers in Phoneme Recognition and Academic Emotion Detection. *Proceedings of the 23rd International Conference on Neural Information Processing 2016 (ICONIP 2016)*, pp. 497–504, 2016.

30. Rosenblatt, F., The Perceptron: A Probabilistic Model for Information Storage and Organization In The Brain. *Psychol. Rev.*, 65, 6, 386–408, 1958.

31. Rosenblatt, F., *Principles of Neurodynamics: Perceptrons and the Theory of Brain Mechanisms*, Spartan Books, Washington DC, 1961.

32. Russell, S.J. and Norvig, P., *Artificial Intelligence: A Modern Approach*, Third Edition, Pearson Education, Inc, 20102010.

33. Vapnik, V., *The nature of statistical learning theory*, Second edition, Springer Verlag, New York, 1999.

34. Liantoni, F. and Hermanto, L.A., Adaptive ant colony optimization on Mango classification using K-nearest neighbor and support vector machine. *J. Inf. Syst. Eng. Bus. Intell.*, 3, 2, October 2017, 75–79, 2017.

35. Cristianini, N. and Shawe-Taylor, J., *An introduction to support vector machines*, Cambridge University Press, Cambridge, 2000.

36. Jang, J.S.R., ANFIS Adaptive-Network-Based Fuzzy Inference System. *IEEE Trans. Syst. Man Cybern.*, 23, 3, 665–685, 1993.

37. Rajab, S., A New Approach to ANFIS Modeling using Kernel-based FCM Clustering. *Global J. Comput. Sci. Techol. D Neural Artif. Intell.*, 15, 1, 581–586, 2016.

38. Aziz, D., Ali, M.A.M., Gan, K.B., Saiboon, I., Initialization of adaptive neuro-fuzzy inference system using fuzzy clustering in predicting primary triage

category. *4ᵗʰ Int. Conf. Intell. Adv. Syst. A Conf. World Eng. Sci. Technol. Congr. - Conf. Proc.*, vol. 1, pp. 170–174, 2012.

39. Krizhevsky, A., Sutskever, I., Hinton, G.E., ImageNet classification with deep convolutional neural networks, *Proceedings of the 25th International Conference on Neural Information Processing Systems (NIPS'12)*, vol. (1), December 2012, pp. 1097–1105.

40. Fu, L., Sun, S., Li, R., and Wang, S., Classification of Kiwifruit Grades Based on Fruit Shape Using a Single Camera. Sensors (Basel), 16, 7, 1012, 2016.

41. Pereira, D.R., Papa, J.P., Saraiva, G.F.R., Souza, G.M., Automatic classification of plant electrophysiological responses to environmental stimuli using machine learning and interval arithmetic. *Comput. Electron. Agric.*, 145, 35–42, 2018A.

42. Pereira, L.F.S., Barbon Jr., S., Valous, N.A., Barbin, D.F., Predicting the ripening of papaya fruit with digital imaging and random forests. *Comput. Electron. Agric.*, 145, 76–82, 2018B.

43. Vapnik, V., Universal learning technology: Support Vector Machine, Special Issue on Information Utilizing Technologies for Value Creation. *NEC J. Adv. Technol.*, 2, 2, 137–144, 2005.

44. Yan, H., Zou, Z., Wang, H., Adaptive neuro-fuzzy inference system for classification of water quality status. *J. Environ. Sci.*, 22, 12, 1891–1896, 2010.

16

Enhancement of Satellite and Underwater Image Utilizing Luminance Model by Color Correction Method

Sandeep Kumar[1]*, E. G. Rajan[1] and Shilpa Rani[2]

[1]Computer Science and Engineering Department, Koneru Lakshmaiah Education Foundation, Vaddeswaram, Andra Pradesh, India
[2]Department of CSE, Neil Gogte Institute of Technology, Hyderabad, India

Abstract

The eminence of satellite and the underwater image is meager due to the belongings of water, air, and its contamination. Water and air properties cause attenuation of light travels through the water and air medium, resulting in low contrast, blur, inhomogeneous lighting, and color diminishing of the satellite and underwater images. The work proposes submerging and satellite picture enhancements that merged the iterative wavelet algorithm and the white balance method with the contrast limited adaptive histogram equalization (CLAHE). The biggest problem in overflowing images is the blurring effect due to instability in the water flow, inadequate lighting, and low contrast. The significant issues in satellite images, i.e., glare, blurriness, and low contrast which affect the accuracy. The proposed work solves these problems that can enhance the appearance and obtained better outcomes. Multiple inputs were used, including images corrected by hue and increased by comparison while testing the proposed methodology. Entropy, peak signal–to-noise ratio (PSNR), and deployment time have been considered while performed. Approaches such as Dark Channel Prior (DCP), Opposite Modification (CA), and Discrete Transform Wavelets (DWT)–Dynamic CLAHE (DCLAHE) are used to fit the proposed protocol. Execution results indicate that this approach will increase perceptual efficiency by contrasting it with previous procedures and has a good impact on the submerged picture.

Keywords: Submerged image, satellite images, CLAHE, image enhancement

*Corresponding author: dr.sandeepsahratia@gmail.com

Sandeep Kumar, Rohit Raja, Shrikant Tiwari and Shilpa Rani (eds.) Cognitive Behavior and Human Computer Interaction Based on Machine Learning Algorithm, (361–380) © 2022 Scrivener Publishing LLC

16.1   Introduction

Numerous submerged pictures in the ocean and air planning encounter poor see capacity, which is influenced by low lighting and commotion contamination in submerged and satellite images [1–3]. The light has been debilitated exponentially encountering in the water because of the processing and scrambling. Light's essentialness will liberally fall off while the high light is scoff up by water [2–5]. The degree of upkeep hangs on the distinct frequency of light (RGB), which provokes the concealing cast of lowered photographs [6–9]. Moreover, there are two kinds of dispersing, one forward spreading that prompts clouding and the additional one across dissipating that affects less disease value [10–13]. Getting clear and the great submerged picture is not an easy task since submerged imaging, generally, encounters these properties [14–16]. Thinking about lowered picture development methodologies is crucial for the sea utilization of image vision [17, 54–55].

The rest of the paper has been configured into five parts: Section 16.2 provides information on related work; Section 16.3 describes the proposed work; Section 16.4 analyzes the evaluation of proposed work; finally, Section 16.5 concludes with a summary.

16.2   Related Work

Xi Qiao *et al.* [4] presented a half and half technique utilizing the CLAHE and Wavelet Transform (WT) for submerged IE. This strategy enhances the unpredictability and decreases the uproar of the sea cucumber's lowered picture through and through. Also, the proposed framework prevents the influence of under- and over-redesigned regions in the picture yield. This procedure has interlaced two methodologies; the planning time is a shortcoming [4].

Shu Zhang *et al.* [10] have presented LAB-MSR, excited by the first MSR structure. It frames the lowered photographs in the CIELAB concealing room. Half of the respective three-dimensional channels are associated with the three networks, as shown by every network's characteristics. In like manner, this paper looks at the debasement characteristics of the lowered pictures, which supports the advancement of this system [10].

Wang R *et al.* [5] introduced a novel strategy wherein they utilized the all-out variety technique. In this work, the picture quality is not acceptable after preparing regarding boundaries [5]. Puniani S. *et al.* [3] manage these binary matters. It uses L*a*b* concealing space, which is without a device. Likewise, an edge securing smoothing has been facilitated with fluffy picture updates, so boundaries did not impact and remain spared [3]. Yujie Li Y. *et al.* [2] portrayed a novel method to recover submerged pictures by devignetting and shading amendment. Disseminating and shading mutilation are two crucial issues of corruption for lowered imagery. Spreading has been brought about through far-reaching suspended particles. Shading mutilation thinks about the changeable degrees of debilitating faced by light moving in the water through different frequencies, delivering encompassing lowered conditions administered by a to some degree blue tone [31, 32].

Mingming Sun *et al.* [36] utilized an order strategy for learning and assessing the proposed technique. Highlights are eliminated from the picture. Creators have picked profound learning techniques, and it gives better outcomes. Creators have presented another learning technique with the name RDFM, and the execution of RDFM is amazingly better contrasted with existing strategies. Maria Pia *et al.* [6] utilized an ERP strategy to acknowledge the face and distinguished the cerebrum exercises. For recognizing a face and recognizable proof of mind exercises, creators have used direction choice and profound learning methods. For execution, recognizable proof of calculation, acknowledgment time, and response time were picked as boundaries. The exhibition of the profound learning technique for acknowledging the face is better than the condition of craftsmanship strategy as per the discoveries.

Giovanni Poggi *et al.* [37] utilized a nearby component-based strategy for biometric framework [3], and [4] utilized DCNN for the arrangement of sexual orientation and age. This new technology improved the presentation of the performance of gender and age. The proposed strategy is likewise tried on small size images [4]. Wang Guoyu *et al.* [5] utilized a conventional profound learning technique for applications identified with PC vision. Profound learning strategy can manage multi-dimensional information, and future creators may apply this idea for division reason, which may improve the exactness of the calculation [6].

Harry *et al.* [39] utilized CNN and a profound learning technique for acknowledgment of the face. The proposed method is hearty due to the appropriate component extraction strategy. This strategy is age invariant, and achievement of this usage likewise relies upon qualities of highlights [5]. Alahi *et al.* [7] utilized a profound learning technique for the investigation of the human body. Timofe *et al.* [42] introduced a profound learning strategy with CNN for acknowledging face in the picture. Creators have utilized the VGG-16 design and used the Image Net dataset for preparing and grouping reason [8].

Nandakumar *et al.* [43] suggested interdisciplinary techniques for biometric-based security applications, which may improve the framework's power [9]. Francisco *et al.* [44] utilized nonrepetitive DNN to acknowledge walk investigation, and execution of the proposed strategy was 9% better than existing methods [10]. Sharma *et al.* [11] have applied CNN for the grouping of MRI pictures. The order was superior to the current strategies. Acknowledgment exactness was additionally improved due to 2D-CNN. Palazzo *et al.* [46] utilized RNN for usage reasons. Creators have being used the Image-Net and Cal-Tech dataset for preparing and order.

16.3   Proposed Methodology

In this methodology, consider a contribution as a submerged or satellite images. From that point onward, change the element of an info picture with MxN size. White Balance acquires the yield picture's mean power, which is equivalent to the information picture pixels, therefore keep up. Figure 16.1 shows a flow chart of the proposed technique. An RGB picture has been taken for further process and applied color correction technique. This procedure decides the combined image from the input submerged picture capably. It beats the submerged circumstances' restrictions, takes out the shading projects, and conveys a submerged picture's trademark appearance. To improve the IE, CLAHE performed on the YCbCr model, which shows hues regarding Luma (Y), Cb speaks to the blue distinction of Chrominance, and Cr speaks to a Red contrast of Chrominance. CLAHE is employed to Y parts, and Cb and Cr stay unaltered. Later this procedure, intertwining the separated shading, remedied the picture and improved the image utilizing the multiscale combination strategy trail both low and high recurrence for acquiring new low and increased reproduction. Reconsideration computation on the RGB picture has been done from that point onward, changing over RGB to YCbCr shading space and apply CLAHE on the Y part. Wire the two images utilizing the multiscale combination strategy. Let the info shading picture speaks to as a contributing with A 512×512 measurement, where M and N show the line and a segment of information.

16.3.1   Color Correction

Submerged imagination is affected by the non-uniform concealing cast on account of the digestion of the induced light. Concealing cast thinks about the moving degrees of slight choking [18–20]. In our preliminaries, an essential and compelling white change task is utilized to redesign the image presence by discarding concealing tosses. This white change technique construes the mixed strategy's vital commitment from a one of a kind lowered picture capably [21–24]. It beats the obstructions of submerged

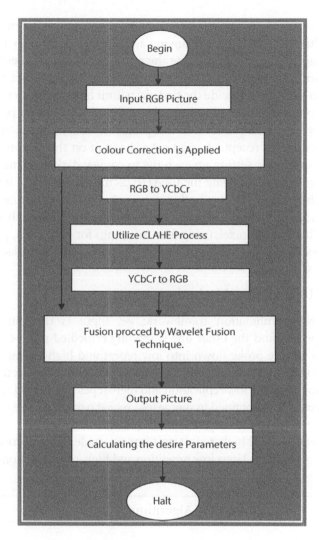

Figure 16.1 Proposed approach block diagram.

circumstances, ousts the concealing tosses, and makes a trademark appearance of the fallen image [9–11]. Regardless, the white alter method is not satisfactory for the difference in penetrability [25 27].

16.3.2 Contrast Enhancement

CLAHE has been recognizable in retaining up a fundamental division after the around-increment of an uproar than that in adaptive histogram equalization (AHE) [3, 28–30]. It finished by constraining the multifaceted nature to alter AHE. The accompanying advance of this strategy is a. Think about an information picture, locate the number of lines and section titles, set histogram containers by making picture change work, and set clasp to go from zero to 1 for IE. b. Decide the first clasp limit by standardized an incentive in the preprocessing step. Consolidate the picture before partitioning the image, whenever required. c. In this progression: split one picture locale, making a histogram receptacle, and get a diagram on the reason of the tile through clasp run for setting up each tile to convey dark level mappings. d. The last stage is to consolidate the CLAHE picture utilizing the interjection dark level planning technique. In this step, emit a bunch of four neighboring layout boundaries, treat the location of the picture covering each tile somewhere, confine a single pixel, using four mappings for each pixel, set up tests to get the pixel, replicate the entire image [3, 7]. It should take place.

16.3.3   Multi-Fusion Method

The proposed combination framework: get input is the differentiation upgraded picture, and the other one is shading remedied picture [31]. Each information picture broke down into low repeat and high-repeat fragments utilizing the wavelet change to three scales. By then, particular mix theories are developed to merge the low replication and high-repeat elements [32–35]. The weighted typical is maintained to merge low-repeat parts, while nearby change is used in the blend of high-repeat sections [36–40]. After the blend technique, the new low repeat and high-repeat portions are made. The improved picture is gotten by redoing the latest low repetition and high-repeat sections [41–47].

Algorithm

Step 1: [M, N] = size (input$_{img}$)   (16.1)

Step 2: The color-corrected image WB is estimated using this equation:

$$WB = input_{img}/\mu \qquad (16.2)$$

$$\mu = \gamma 1(\mu_{inputimg}/\mu_{ref}) + \gamma 2 \qquad (16.3)$$

Where $\mu_{input} = (\mu_R, \mu_G, \mu_B)$ represented the sum of RGB channels of the input image to the grey of shades, $\gamma_2 = (\gamma_R, \gamma_G, \gamma_B)$ represents the gain factor which is calculated using the maximum value of RGB channels, the value of

γ_2 = [0, 0.5] in this range is MurkowskinormConvertinput$_{img}$ from RGB into YCbCr format using MATLAB function.

Step 3: CLAHE is employed to the Y element, Cb, and C remain unaffected. Y_{max} and Y_{min} represent the maximum and minimum value of the luminance model Y channel, the cumulative probability distribution P(f) is uniform. The tiles' size is 8 × 8 to be fixed, and the clip limit is 0.01 to be set. In the end, the improved image is back from YCbCr to RGB space.

Step 4: The fusion of two images with the help of the DWT technique. The average of weights on low-frequency components $K_{W,N}(i,j)$ and $K_{CLAHE,N}(i,j)$ is represented color corrected by WB and contrast-enhanced the image. The fused low-frequency components $K_{F,N}(i,j)$ can be evaluated using this equation:

$$K_{F,N}(i,j) = m_1 K_{W,B,N}(i,j) + m_2 K_{CLANE,N} \qquad (16.4)$$

where m_1 and m_2 = 0.5 denote weighted coefficients, N represents the three scales in DWT decomposition Z(N = 1, 2, 3).

16.4   Investigational Findings and Evaluation

This methodology achieved enhanced images of submerged and satellite imagery. The outcome was acquired by MATLAB14 programming concerning Toolbox (Image Processing). Herein, low differentiation submerged and satellite pictures for estimation are taken for findings [48–53]. This appearance can be assessed PSNR, reproduction time, and Entropy by underneath recipes. The contribution has contrasted, and various strategies appeared in tabular form.

16.4.1   Mean Square Error

It is characterized such as the normal squared contrast among reference signs to the mutilated sign. It very well has been evaluated by involving the squared difference pixel-by-pixel and confining through the total pixel count. Assume M × N is an info picture and is characterized as the upgraded picture. MSE can be determined through this condition.

$$MSE = \frac{\sum_{i=1}^{M}\sum_{j=1}^{N}\left[\text{input}_{img}(i,j) - K_{F,N}(i,j)\right]^2}{M*N} \qquad (16.1)$$

16.4.2   Peak Signal–to-Noise Ratio

This is the estimation requirement of the improved picture condition and is the highly needed component. It very well may be determined in decibels (dB), and it is provided by

$$PSNR = \frac{10\,Xlog_{10}(l_{max} - l_{min})^2}{MSE} \qquad (16.2)$$

16.4.3   Entropy

Entropy is a statistic of weakness, an inquiry in this situation underneath the dissimilar images brought between the improved and the information picture. Entropy determined through this condition: Where Ent speaks to Entropy; M signifies the most elevated estimation of dark level, the possibility of the pace of xi.

A comparison between the existing and proposed methods in terms of PSNR is shown in Figure 16.2. According to our evaluation, the proposed approach achieved an improved value than the current techniques and proposed algorithm to reach up to 80.295 dB value.

The value of entropy measured by utilizing the proposed approach is presented in Figure 16.3 and the maximum value attained by the proposed method is 0.9. A comparison between the existing and proposed methods in terms of PSNR is shown in Table 16.1 and Figure 16.2. The value of entropy measured by utilizing the proposed approach is presented in Table 16.2 and Figure 16.3.

Table 16.1 Comparative analysis of submerged images.

Tag	DCP [1] PSNR	CA PSNR	DWT-DCLAHE [2] PSNR	Proposed PSNR
a	19.102	11.6896	48.290	61.104
b	22.998	5.8530	26.863	52.515
c	19.072	14.7270	45.733	70.234
d	32.946	21.580	60.513	67.675
e	30.641	15.381	29.623	63.259
f	23.856	12.749	54.112	69.128
g	16.305	16.806	32.220	81.295
h	15.009	11.828	31.844	80.666
i	18.651	10.934	27.040	80.324

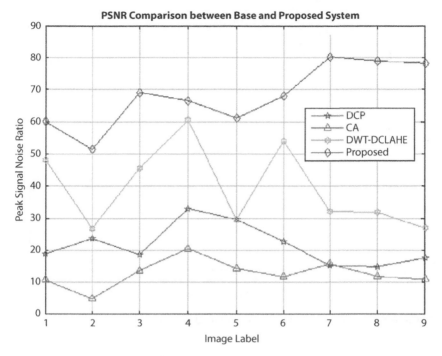

Figure 16.2 Similarity among proposed and existing techniques.

Table 16.2 Proposed method time and entropy measured value.

Tag	Entropy	Time
A	0.756	2.967
B	0.754	1.450
C	0.993	1.289
D	0.570	1.310
E	0.685	1.378
F	0.490	1.388
G	0.996	1.393
H	0.987	1.326
I	0.994	1.359

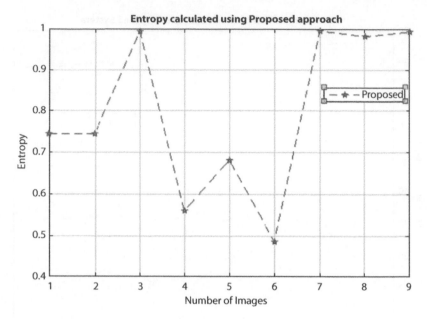

Figure 16.3 Entropy measured using the proposed method.

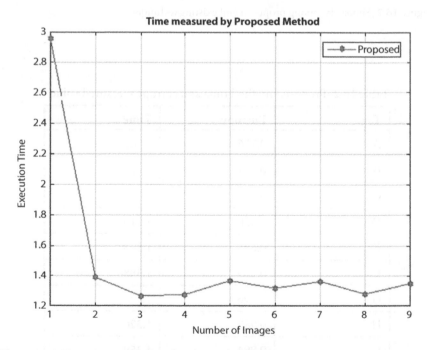

Figure 16.4 Time measured using the proposed method.

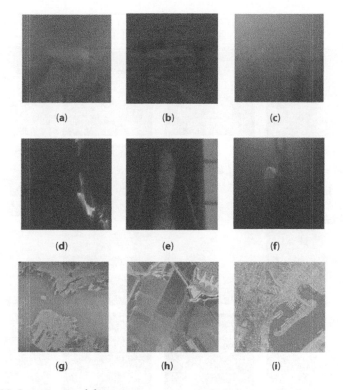

Figure 16.5 Investigational datasets.

The value of time measured by utilizing the proposed approach is presented in Figure 16.4, and the maximum value attained by the proposed method is 1.277. For experimental purposes, six submerged pictures and three satellite pictures are taken in mostly used format jpeg, jpg, png, and tiff as shown in Figure 16.5. For evaluation and experimental purposes we used investigational datasets. Sample of few images of this datasets i.e. six submerged pictures and three satellite pictures are taken in mostly used format jpeg, jpg, png, and tiff as shown in Figure 16.5. Its very clear from Figure 16.6 proposed work is showing better results as compared to other methods and few of the sample output images shown in Figure 16.6. The overall GUI of our proposed work of few enhanced images are shown in Figure 16.7–16.10.

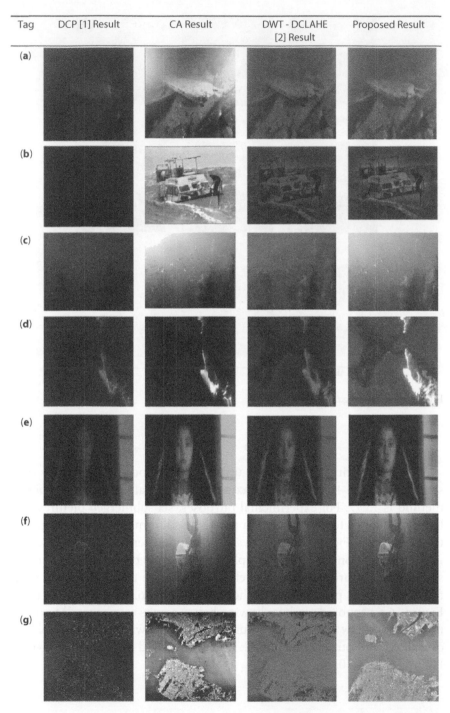

| Tag | DCP [1] Result | CA Result | DWT - DCLAHE [2] Result | Proposed Result |

Figure 16.6 Comparison of outcome between proposed and existing techniques.   (*Continued*)

(h)

(i)

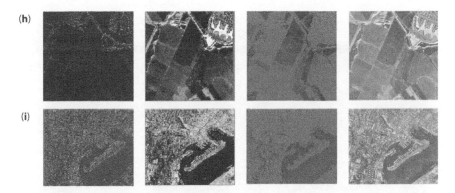

Figure 16.6 (Continued) Comparison of outcome between proposed and existing techniques.

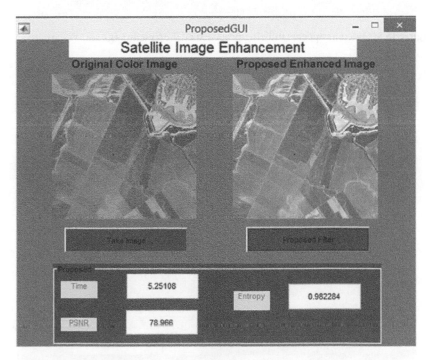

Figure 16.7 The outcome appears utilizing proposed GUI on picture (h).

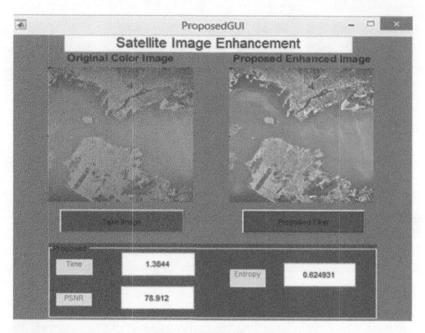

Figure 16.8 Outcome appears utilizing proposed GUI on picture (g).

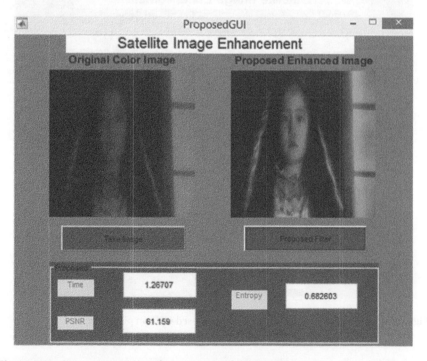

Figure 16.9 Outcome appears utilizing proposed GUI on picture (e).

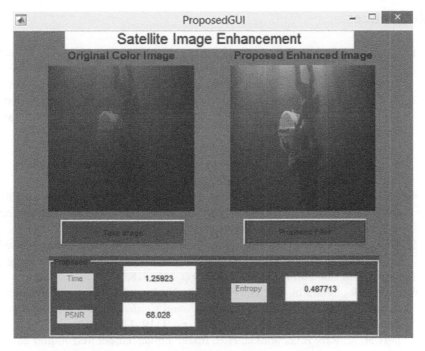

Figure 16.10 Outcome appears utilizing proposed GUI on picture (f).

16.5   Conclusion

This examination represents a submerged and satellite IE utilizing shading adjustment and CLAHE with a multiscale combination strategy. This strategy is better than different procedures and results dependent on PSNR for satellite and submerged pictures that have the principle issue of low complexity and low enlightenment. The fundamental thought process is to get the improved pictures above uproarious, hazy, brilliance, and complexity by consuming the low pixel extend. This estimation can get an extraordinary separated picture that raises the quality of the low differentiated images through brief utilization. This technique has been performed on a few kinds of images like submerged and satellite. Moreover, this work will be reached out to improve calculations for enhancing the outcomes and take additional imagery like clinical, face pictures, and others.

References

1. Chaubey, A. and Atre, A., A hybrid DWT-DCLAHE method for enhancement of low contrast underwater images, in: *International Conference of Electronics, Communication and Aerospace Technology (ICECA)*, vol. 1, pp. 196–201, 2017.
2. Li, Y., Lu, H., Serikawa, S., Underwater Image Devignetting and Colour Correction, in: *International Conference on Image and Graphics*, Springer, Cham, pp. 510–521, 2015.
3. Puniani, S. and Arora, S., Improved Fuzzy Image Enhancement Using L* a* b* Color Space and Edge Preservation, in: *Intelligent Systems Technologies and Applications*, pp. 459–469, Springer, Cham, 2016.
4. Qiao, X., Bao, J., Zhang, H., Zeng, L., Li, D., Underwater image quality enhancement of sea cucumbers based on improved histogram equalization and wavelet transform. *Inf. Process. Agric.*, 4, 3, 206–213, 2017.
5. Wang, R. and Wang, G., Medical X-ray image enhancement method based on TV-homomorphic filter, in: *2nd International Conference on Image, Vision, and Computing (ICIVC)*, IEEE, pp. 315–318, 2017.
6. Sathya, R., Bharathi, M., Dhivyasri, G., Underwater image enhancement by dark channel prior, in: *2nd International Conference on Electronics and Communication Systems (ICECS)*, IEEE, pp. 1119–1123, 2015.
7. Jaiswal, R., Rao, A.G., Shukla, H.P., Image Enhancement Techniques Based on Histogram Equalization. *Int. J. Electr. Electron. Eng.*, 1, 69–78, 2010.
8. Wang, Y., Ding, X., Wang, R., Zhang, J., Fu, X., Fusion-based underwater image enhancement by wavelet decomposition, in: *IEEE International Conference on Industrial Technology (ICIT)*, pp. 1013–1018, 2017.
9. Wang, R., Wang, Y., Zhang, J., Fu, X., Review on underwater image restoration and enhancement algorithms, in: *Proceedings of the 7th International Conference on Internet Multimedia Computing and Service*, p. 56, 2015.
10. Zhang, S., Wang, T., Dong, J., Yu, H., Underwater image enhancement via extended multiscale Retinex. *Neurocomputing*, 245, 1–9, 2017.
11. Kumar, M., Kumar, S., Singh, Y., Gupta, S., A Novel Method For Video Watermarking Using 2LWT in YCbCr Color Space. *Int. J. Electron. Commun. Technol. (IJECT)*, 8, 4, 19–24, October-December 2017.
12. Ghani, A.S.A. and Isa, N.A.M., Enhancement of low-quality underwater image through integrated global and local contrast correction. *Appl. Soft Comput.*, 37, 332–344, 2015.
13. Banerjee, J., Ray, R., Vadali, S.R.K., Shome, S.N., Nandy, S., Real-time underwater image enhancement: An improved approach for imaging with AUV-150. *Sadhana*, 41, 2, 225–238, 2016.
14. Quevedo, E., Delory, E., Callicó, G.M., Tobajas, F., Sarmiento, R., Underwater video enhancement using multi-camera super-resolution. *Opt. Commun.*, 404, 94–102, 2017.

15. Kaur, J. and Sohi, N., Performance improvement of enhancement methods for underwater images, in: *2017 2nd International Conference on Communication and Electronics Systems (ICCES)*, pp. 320–326, 2017.

16. Dubey, N., Tiwari, S.K., Sharma, P., A hybrid DCT-DHE approach for enhancement of low contrast underwater images, in: *2017 International Conference on Recent Innovations in Signal Processing and Embedded Systems (RISE)*, pp. 304–309, 2017.

17. Anwar, S., Li, C., Porikli, F., Deep underwater image enhancement. *Comput. Vis. Pattern Recognit.*, 1, 1–12, 2018.

18. Chernov, V., Koljonen, J., Alander, J., Bochko, V., Video Enhancement Methods for Monitoring Submersible Biological Resources. *IFAC Proc.*, 46, 18, 293–298, 2013.

19. Singhai, J. and Rawat, P., Image enhancement method for underwater, ground and satellite images using brightness preserving histogram equalization with maximum entropy. *International Conference on Computational Intelligence and Multimedia Applications (ICCIMA 2007)*, Sivakasi, Tamil Nadu, pp. 507–512, 2007.

20. Mishra, A., Chaudhuri, D., Bhattacharya, C., Rao, Y.S., Ocean disturbance feature detection from SAR images — An adaptive statistical approach. *3rd International Asia-Pacific Conference on Synthetic Aperture Radar (APSAR)*, pp. 1–4, 2011.

21. Tao, Z., Li, Z., Qin, B., Ocean sand ridges in the Yellow Sea observed by Satellite Remote Sensing measurements. *2011 International Conference on Remote Sensing, Environment and Transportation Engineering*, Nanjing, pp. 528–531, 2011.

22. Mineart, G.M. and Furgerson, J.A., Ocean water-leaving radiance measurements by the Joint Polar Satellite System. *2012 Oceans*, Hampton Roads, VA, pp. 1–8, 2012.

23. Stalin, S.E., Milburn, H.B., Meinig, C., NeMONet: a near real-time deep ocean observatory. *OCEANS 2000 MTS/IEEE Conference and Exhibition. Conference Proceedings (Cat. No.00CH37158)*, Providence, RI, USA, vol. 1, pp. 583–587, 2000.

24. Mittal, A. and Jindal, H., Novelty in Image Reconstruction using DWT and CLAHE. *Int. J. Image Graph. Signal Process.*, 9, 5, 28–33, 2018.

25. Rauschkolb, J., Using GIS and satellite imagery to locate hydrocarbons, in: *ESRI Int. User Conference*, pp. 7–10, 2003.

26. Pacheco-Ruiz, R., Adams, J., Pedrotti, F., 4D modeling of low visibility Underwater Archaeological excavations using multi-source photogrammetry in the Bulgarian Black Sea. *J. Archaeol. Sci.*, 100, 120–129, 2018.

27. Neves, G., Ruiz, M., Fontinele, J., Oliveira, L., Rotated object detection with forward-looking sonar in underwater applications. *Expert Syst. Appl.*, 140, 1–18, 2020.

28. Han, S., Noh, Y., Lee, U., Gerla, M., Optical-acoustic hybrid network toward real-time video streaming for mobile underwater sensors. *Ad Hoc Networks*, 83, 1–7, 2019.

29. Wu, Y., Ta, X., Xiao, R., Wei, Y., An, D., Li, D., Survey of underwater robot positioning navigation. *Appl. Ocean Res.*, 90, 101845, 2019.

30. Ding, W., Cao, H., Guo, H., Ma, Y., Mao, Z., Investigation on optimal path for submarine search by an unmanned underwater vehicle. *Comput. Electr. Eng.*, 79, 106468, 2019.

31. Shariati, S.K. and Hossein Mousavizadegan, S., Identification of underwater vehicles using surface wave pattern. *Appl. Ocean Res.*, 78, 281–289, 2018.

32. Kato, N., Choyekh, M., Dewantara, R., Senga, H., Chiba, H., Kobayashi, E., Yoshie, M., Tanaka, T., Short, T., An autonomous underwater robot for tracking and monitoring of subsea plumes after oil spills and gas leaks from the seafloor. *J. Loss Prev. Process Ind.*, 50, 386–396, 2017.

33. Caballero, I. and Stumpf, R.P., Retrieval of nearshore bathymetry from Sentinel-2A and 2B satellites in South Florida coastal waters. *Estuar. Coast. Shelf Sci.*, 226, 106277, 2019.

34. Poursanidis, D., Traganos, D., Reinartz, P., Chrysoulakis, N., On the use of Sentinel-2 for coastal habitat mapping and satellite-derived bathymetry estimation using the downscaled coastal aerosol band. *Int. J. Appl. Earth Obs. Geoinf.*, 80, 58–70, 2019.

35. Raja, R., Sinha, T.S., Patra, R.K., Tiwari, S., Physiological Trait Based Biometrical Authentication of Human-Face Using LGXP and ANN Techniques. *Int. J. Inf. Comput. Secur.*, 10, 2/3, 303–320, 2018.

36. Wong, W.K. and Sun, M., Deep Learning Regularized Fisher Mappings. *IEEE Trans. Neural Networks*, 22, 10, 1668–1675, 2011.

37. Gragnaniello, D., Poggi, G., Sansone, C., Verdoliva, L., An Investigation of Local Descriptors for Biometric Spoofing Detection. *IEEE Trans. Inf. Forensics Secur.*, 10, 04, 849–863, 2015.

38. Levi, G. and Hassner, T., Age and gender classification using convolutional neural networks. In *Proceedings of the IEEE Conference on Computer Vision and Pattern Recognition Workshops*, pp. 34–42, 2015.

39. El Khiyari, H. and Wechsler, H., Face Recognition across Time-Lapse Using Convolution Neural Networks. *J. Inf. Secur.*, 7, 141–51, 2016.

40. Wang, X., Deep Learning in Object Recognition, Detection and Segmentation. *Found. Trends Signal Process.*, 8, 4, 217–228, 2014.

41. Haque, A., Alahi, A., and Fei-Fei, L., Recurrent attention models for depth-based person identification. In *Proceedings of the IEEE Conference on Computer Vision and Pattern Recognition*, pp. 1229–1238, 2016.

42. Rothe, R., Timofte, R., Van Gool, L., Deep expectation of real and apparent age from a single image without facial landmarks. *Int. J. Comput. Vis.*, 126, 144–157, 2016.

43. Jain, A.K., Nandakumar, K., Ross, A., 50 years of biometric research: Accomplishments, challenges, and opportunities. *Pattern Recognit. Lett.*, 79, 80–105, 2016.

44. Ordóñez, F.J. and Roggen, D., Deep Convolutional and LSTM Recurrent Neural Networks for Multimodal Wearable Activity Recognition. *Sensors*, 16, 115, 1–25, 2016.

45. Nathawani, D. and Sharma, T., Neuroscience meets deep learning. *CMU*, 1, 1–8, 2016.

46. Spampinato, C., Palazzo, S., Kavasidis, I., Giordano, D., Shah, M., Soulyk, N., Deep Learning Human Mind for Automated Visual Classification. In *Proceedings of the IEEE Conference on Computer Vision and Pattern Recognition*, pp. 6809–6817, 2017.

47. Kumar, S., Singh, S., Kumar, J., Face Spoofing Detection Using Improved SegNet Architecture with Blur Estimation Technique. *Int. J. Biom., Inderscience Publ.*, 13, 131–149, 2021.

48. Raja, R., Kumar, S., Rashid, Md, Color Object Detection Based Image Retrieval using ROI Segmentation with Multi-Feature Method. *Wirel. Pers. Commun. Springer J.*, 112, 169–192, 2020.

49. Kumar, S., Singh, S., Kumar, J., Live Detection of Face Using Machine Learning with Multi-feature Method. *Wirel. Pers. Commun.*, 103, 3, 2353–2375, 2018.

50. Kumar, S., Singh, S., Kumar, J., Automatic Live Facial Expression Detection Using Genetic Algorithm with Haar Wavelet Features and SVM. *Wirel. Pers. Commun.*, 103, 3, 2435–2453, 2018.

51. Kumar, S., Singh, S., Kumar, J., Multiple Face Detection Using Hybrid Features with SVM Classifier, in: *Data and Communication Networks*, pp. 253–265, Springer, Singapore, 2019.

52. Kumar, S., Singh, S., Kumar, J., A Study on Face Recognition Techniques with Age and Gender Classification, in: *IEEE International Conference on Computing, Communication and Automation (ICCCA)*, May 2017, pp. 1001–1006.

53. Kumar, S., Singh, S., Kumar, J., Automatic Face Detection Using Genetic Algorithm for Various Challenges. *Int. J. Sci. Res. Mod. Educ.*, 2, 1, 197–203, 2017.

54. Raja, R., Sinha, T.S., Dubey, R.P., Recognition of human-face from side-view using progressive switching pattern and soft-computing technique. *Assoc. Adv. Modell. Simul. Tech. Enterp., Adv. B*, 58, 1, 14–34, 2015.

55. Choudhary, S., Lakhwani, K., Agrwal, S., An efficient hybrid technique of feature extraction for facial expression recognition using AdaBoost Classifier. *Int. J. Eng. Res. Technol.*, 8, 1, 1–9, 2012.

Index

Printed and bound by CPI Group (UK) Ltd, Croydon, CR0 4YY